SAVING THE STATE

FINE GAEL FROM COLLINS TO VARADKAR

STEPHEN COLLINS
AND
CIARA MEEHAN

GILL BOOKS

Gill Books
Hume Avenue
Park West
Dublin 12
www.gillbooks.ie

Gill Books is an imprint of M.H. Gill and Co.

© Stephen Collins and Ciara Meehan 2020
978 07171 89731

Edited by Ruairí Ó Brógáin
Proofread by Neil Burkey
Indexed by Adam Pozner
Printed by CPI Group (UK) Ltd, Croydon, CRO 4YY

This book is typeset in 11 on 16pt, Minion.
The paper used in this book comes from the wood pulp of managed
forests. For every tree felled, at least one tree is planted, thereby
renewing natural resources.

A CIP catalogue record for this book is available from the British
Library.

5 4 3 2 1

For Kathleen, with thanks, and in memory of Andrew Bushe.

ACKNOWLEDGEMENTS

This book is one that both of us have wanted to write for quite some time, and happily the opportunity presented itself towards the middle of 2019. We're extremely grateful to Conor Nagle, who commissioned the project. Although he left Gill Books shortly afterwards, we found ourselves in the very capable hands of Sarah Liddy and her team: Avril Cannon, Teresa Daly, Laura King, Aoibheann Molumby, and copyeditor Ruairí Ó Brógáin. It's been an absolute pleasure working with them. Their patience as we waited – and waited! – for a government to be formed so that we could finish the final chapter is much appreciated.

The book benefits, we believe, from the access that both of us have had over the years to various key figures in the political world. The following chapters draw on a range of interviews conducted specifically for this book, as well as some of our earlier interviews for other projects. We're grateful to the extensive list of people who took the time to speak to us, both on and off the record.

We're also thankful to everyone who responded to our call for images. We received far more than we could include, but we're pleased with the final selection and express our thanks for the permission granted to reproduce them.

We weren't alone in finding that some of our plans for research and interviews were interrupted by the restrictions introduced because of Covid-19. We also fully acknowledge that there is so much more of Fine Gael's history that could be explored. The grassroots and the constituencies are fascinating elements that could be the subject of a book in their own right. But as we began sketching out the project, it grew in size; new chapters were added and others had to be split because of their length. Difficult decisions had to be made about our scope and content!

We've benefited from chats with various people as we were writing, but we owe a debt of gratitude to one person in particular. David McCullagh was unfailingly generous with his time and advice, reading drafts closely, spotting mistakes and offering helpful feedback. Naturally, any errors or omissions are entirely ours.

Thanks must also go to both sets of family and friends for their support and encouragement.

STEPHEN COLLINS AND CIARA MEEHAN,
DUBLIN, JULY 2020.

CONTENTS

INTRODUCTION

'Fine Gael, my party, is the party that founded the state, its institutions. The party that founded the Republic'.

— LEO VARADKAR, SPEAKING AFTER THE 2020 GENERAL ELECTION.

This book tells the story of a party that was all about government, but spent most of its life in opposition; a party that was at different times – and occasionally at the same time – both the most conservative and the most liberal in Irish politics; a party which spent the best part of a century aiming to overtake Fianna Fáil, and then blew its lead over its traditional enemy in less than a decade; a party that eventually entered government with that enemy.

Officially created in 1933, Fine Gael traces its roots back to the Cumann na nGaedheal era of the 1920s and, for some, to the traditions of the old Irish Party. Its history is explored through the lens of its successive leaders in this personality-driven study, and we examine also the ways that members perceive their own history. We have chosen to frame the book as 'Collins to Varadkar', despite the fact that Michael Collins was dead before Cumann na nGaedheal was ever created. This timeline is irrelevant to the Fine Gael faithful. For them, Collins is something of a father figure and he occupies a special place in the party's pantheon of heroes. It is accepted without question by them that he would have been a member if he had lived past 1922. While we have not explored his life, he appears at various points in the following chapters, on those occasions when his name was invoked by subsequent generations to create connections with a glorious past or to add legitimacy to current actions. As we will see in Chapter 14, Collins's memory was a close companion of Enda Kenny's time in government. The Taoiseach cast his role in dealing with the challenges facing the state's sovereignty after the bailout in the same context as Collins's work to secure Irish independence in 1921–22.

We conclude with Leo Varadkar. The election of the openly gay son of an Indian immigrant (though of course there is more to his identity than this alone) showed how far Fine Gael, and the country, had come. Varadkar's later liberal social policies, together with the marriage and abortion referendums, further diluted a waning perception that Fine Gael is a conservative party. For much of its history Fine Gael was a party that was staunchly Catholic and socially conservative. Garret FitzGerald had tried to challenge that in the 1980s, but the hostile reception that his constitutional crusade received, both within and outside the party, did little to convince observers of Fine Gael's commitment to change at the time.

Fine Gael has always been proud of the role that its forefathers in Cumann na nGaedheal played in the founding and development of the Irish Free State. Born amidst the bloodshed of the Civil War, it was a government before it was a party. Kevin O'Higgins famously summed up the reality of the situation when he described himself and his cabinet colleagues as 'simply eight young men in City Hall standing amidst the ruins of one administration, with the foundations of another not yet laid, with wild men screaming through the keyhole.'[1] Over a period of ten years, under the direction of W.T. Cosgrave, party leader and president of the Executive Council, the Cumann na nGaedheal government dealt with challenges to the state. When Fianna Fáil won the 1932 election there was a smooth transition of power from the winners to the losers of the Civil War – a remarkable achievement for a new state created only ten years earlier.

That first decade of independence gave rise to what has become a well-worn narrative in Fine Gael circles. As the title of our book highlights and the following chapters show, politicians and supporters have since invoked the party's role as the founders of the state to demonstrate a long-standing commitment to defending the state – a concept used interchangeably with the notion of saving the state. In the days after the 2020 general election Varadkar told RTÉ News, 'We're the ones who founded the state. We're the ones who established the institutions. We're the ones who made this country a republic. And we'll stand by the state and the republic.'[2]

From that comes another defining characteristic. Fine Gael prides itself on being the party of law and order. 'Not for the first time has this party stood between the people of this country and anarchy,' Liam Cosgrave reminded the party faithful at an ard-fheis in 1977. But this element of Fine Gael's identity has a somewhat murky point of origin. In its efforts to stabilise the nascent state, the Provisional Government stepped outside the rule of law in 1922 when it authorised the execution of four republican prisoners as a message to those who refused to accept the legitimacy of the Free State – a dark episode explored more fully in Chapter 1.

One of the reasons why Fine Gael has been so insistent on the Collins and Cumann na nGaedheal narrative is the problematic reality of the alternative. When the party was created, in 1933, it was not simply a rebranded Cumann na nGaedheal. Rather, Cosgrave's party joined with the National Centre Party and the Blueshirts, and it was Eoin O'Duffy, the leader of the latter, who was chosen as the first president. But he has no place on the roll call of Fine Gael heroes, and instead a wall of silence surrounds his name. Both he and his shirted movement have been a considerable embarrassment to Fine Gael and a source of derision for its opponents. When Varadkar criticised Sinn Féin's plan to hold nationwide rallies after the 2020 election, branding the gatherings a 'campaign of intimidation and bullying', Twitter users gleefully reminded Fine Gael of its Blueshirt history.[3] We address the thorny question of O'Duffy, the Blueshirts and their relationship to the fascism of the inter-war years, and what that means for the party of law and order, in Chapter 2.

Whilst the idea of Fine Gael as the defenders of the state has a long tradition in the party, as we will see at various points in the following chapters, two other elements of its history are now mentioned with increased frequency. Trumpeting Fine Gael's role in making Ireland a republic seems a natural continuation of emphasising the state-building legacy, yet the party has been traditionally quiet on this subject. Under Varadkar's leadership, that has changed considerably and in Chapter 15 we explore Fine Gael's mixed relationship with this key moment in its history.

As discussed in Chapter 5, Declan Costello formulated his Just Society proposals in the 1960s to create a new Ireland and to redefine Fine Gael. The details of the document were specific to that decade, and by the 1970s, as one party activist put it, 'we were the party of the Just Society … but it was a long way behind us by then'.[4] The title, however, has become a useful slogan for subsequent politicians – most recently during the 2017 leadership contest – as shorthand for progress.

After ten years of continuous government as Cumann na nGaedheal, Fine Gael spent the majority of its political life in the shadow of Fianna Fáil, trailing in second place behind its rival in election after election. It managed to scramble into office from time to time in coalition with other parties, but the opposition benches were an all-too-familiar place. Having languished in second place for so long, Fine Gael under Enda Kenny emerged as the biggest party in the state after the financial crisis of 2008–10 had shattered the confidence of the public in the ability of Fianna Fáil to govern. Like his party predecessors, Kenny enhanced his reputation in the Taoiseach's office, and he led the country out of the mire of the EU-IMF bailout. By the time he left office Ireland had the fastest-growing economy in the European Union.

Kenny achieved his goal of being the first leader of the party since the 1920s to retain power in an election after a period in government, but Fine Gael lost 26 seats after a poor campaign in 2016, and some of his TDs began to conspire against him. Seeing the writing on the wall, he stepped down in June 2017 and was replaced by Varadkar. The results of the 2020 election were a major disappointment to Fine Gael. The spread of seats among the parties in the Dáil created uncertainty about the shape of the government, giving rise to speculation, albeit in hushed tones initially, that Fine Gael and Fianna Fáil might do a deal.

Back in 1927 speculation had circulated in some regional newspapers that Cumann na nGaedheal and Fianna Fáil might reunite under the old Sinn Féin banner. But nothing ever amounted from such suggestions. An attempt to fuse Sinn Féin with a pact election in 1922 had already failed. When other countries formed national governments during the Second World War, Fianna Fáil and Fine Gael did not do the same, though Fine Gael did try. The Treaty split continued to define the political children of Sinn Féin long after the 1920s. Charlie Flanagan once recalled, 'Being in a Fine Gael household, one not only had a liking for Fine Gael politics, but a hatred of Fianna Fáil and everything it stood for.'[5] The idea of the two parties working together in tandem was unthinkable for a long time.

What became known as the Tallaght Strategy in 1987 marked a major departure in Irish politics. However, Alan Dukes, leader from 1987 until 1990, was widely criticised in the party for offering support from the opposition benches to the minority Fianna Fáil government. The experiment was not repeated for some time. But political expediency focuses minds, and in 2016 Fianna Fáil entered a confidence and supply deal with the Fine Gael government. This was a clear indication that the main cleavage in the Irish political system, when it came to two of its oldest members, had changed for ever.

Such arrangements opened the door to the prospect of closer collaboration, but when we began discussing this book, we had not anticipated that the final chapter would make such a neat ending. The aftermath of the 2020 general election brought to an end, as Varadkar pointed out, Civil War politics in the Irish parliament.[6] An agreement that would have been unthinkable to the party's forefathers almost a century earlier saw Fine Gael vote for Fianna Fáil's Micheál Martin to become the fifteenth Taoiseach. In the following chapters, we explore how Fine Gael came to be the party it is today and how a coalition with its traditional rival was seen as an option in what was the most extraordinary of circumstances.

1

THE W.T. COSGRAVE YEARS

'It would be hard to imagine anybody who is less true to what we used to consider the Sinn Féin type than Mr. Cosgrave. It is not only that he does not dress in the regulation way – trench coat, leggings and slouch hat and the rest of it; but he has a thoroughly Conservative face.'

— *IRISH TIMES*, 9 SEPTEMBER 1922.

A t Dublin Castle on 16 January 1922, the British handed over control of an independent Ireland to a provisional government led by Michael Collins. The first test of the new state came with a general election on 25 June 1922.[1] In an effort to avert civil war Collins and de Valera signed a pact that would allow the pro- and anti-Treaty factions to return to the Dáil in their existing strength. Neither man appears to have understood the workings of proportional representation, because such a pact was simply not feasible in multi-seat constituencies, with other parties and independents also entitled to enter the fray. Collins repudiated the pact just two days before the general election. Despite widespread intimidation by anti-Treaty forces, who came to be known as the Irregulars, the pro-Treaty panel of candidates polled nearly twice as many votes as its opponents. If the votes of Labour, Farmers' Party and independent candidates are added to the pro-Treaty total the result was even more decisive, with less than 22 per cent of the electorate voting for candidates who opposed the settlement. After the election the Provisional Government issued an ultimatum to the Irregulars to leave the Four Courts and release a hostage they were holding there. The republicans refused, and the Civil War began with an attack on the Four Courts by the Free State army on 28 June. Collins had come under enormous pressure from Churchill to take action after the assassination of Sir Henry Wilson, and the British provided the artillery for the Free State forces to launch a bombardment of the Irregular positions.

The garrison surrendered after three days, but in the course of the fighting the Public Record Office, and much of its invaluable collection of historic documents, was destroyed. Street fighting took place in Dublin, and O'Connell Street was again left in ruins, only six years after 1916. In a major military offensive, the Free State forces drove the Irregulars out of all the major towns by the end of August, with successful seaborne landings in Cork and Tralee. After that the Irregulars took to guerrilla war. Collins took temporary leave from his position as chairman of the Provisional Government to concentrate on winning the war and W.T. Cosgrave was elected by his colleagues as cabinet chairman in his place, while Arthur Griffith continued on as president of Dáil Éireann.

Although circumstances had taken Griffith down a political route, he was more comfortable with the life of a journalist. Born in Dublin in 1871, he later followed his father into the printing trade, which served as his first introduction to journalism. Over the course of his career he developed an impressive résumé of newspaper titles, which included the *United Irishman, Sinn Féin, Éire, Scissors and Paste* and *Nationality.* A skilled polemicist, his writings helped shape a generation of young separatists. In *The Resurrection of Hungary,* published first as a series of articles and then in pamphlet form in 1904, he wrote of how the Austro-Hungarian model of dual monarchy could be applied to the Anglo-Irish relationship. In particular, he proposed that the policy of passive resistance followed by Hungary in the middle of the nineteenth century be adopted in Ireland. His economic thinking was shaped by Friedrich List and Henry Carey, both of whom advocated protectionism. Not only was this the cornerstone of Sinn Féin's economic policies but it would also influence, and divide, thinking in Cumann na nGaedheal throughout the 1920s.

Although 1916 and the subsequent independence struggle were at odds with his policy of non-violence, Griffith remained active in Sinn Féin, which became a very different party to that which he had founded with Bulmer Hobson. He ultimately led the delegation to Britain that signed the Treaty on 6 December 1921. Defending the settlement in the Dáil, he argued, 'We have brought back to Ireland equality with England.'[2] Griffith remained a journalist at heart, and his final involvement with a publication came only a year before his sudden death. *An Saorstát* – the organ of the pro-Treatyites – first appeared in February 1922, reflecting Griffith's belief in the value of a newspaper for advancing a cause. Though Griffith features in the Fine Gael pantheon of great leaders, his legacy, Colum Kenny suggests in a new biography, belongs to no single political party today.[3]

In contrast to Griffith, Michael Collins was seen to be at the forefront of the physical struggle after 1919. Born in Co. Cork in 1890, he emigrated to London in 1906, where he became involved with the Irish Republican Brotherhood through the GAA. The organisational abilities he displayed within the association would later prove invaluable. Like many of his contemporaries, he came to prominence in republican circles through this connection. Later, countless people involved in the campaign for independence would claim to have met or soldiered alongside him. But, as his recent biographers Anne Dolan and William Murphy have observed, 'the image we have of him comes filtered through a sensational lens, exaggerated out of all proportion.' Collins himself knew the power of persona, capitalising on it where he could.[4] The image that endures long after his death is the powerful figure he cut in his commander-in-chief uniform. Had he lived and chosen to become a full-time politician, his personality was such that he might have provided Cumann na nGaedheal with a charismatic rival to de Valera, while his exceptional organisational abilities might have resulted in the creation of a more defined branch structure. Or would his great military reputation have withered, like Richard Mulcahy's? And would his authoritarian streak have been reconciled with the practice of democratic politics? These are the great 'what ifs' of Irish history.

But let us return to the months before his death. On the instructions of Collins, the first meeting of the third Dáil was postponed on a number of occasions during the summer, pending the stabilisation of the military situation. Following the outbreak of hostilities at the end of June, Griffith and the members of the Provisional Government, whose lives were now in constant danger, were compelled to live together under military guard in the newly acquired Government Buildings in Upper Merrion Street, which is now the Department of the Taoiseach. As the war intensified, some ministers brought their families there for safety.

On 22 August, just ten days after the death of Griffith, came the news of Collins's death at Bealnablath. The cabinet met that night in Cosgrave's office and the immediate concern was to ensure that there were no military reprisals. Collins's body was brought back from Cork to Dublin by boat and lay in state in City Hall. He was buried in Glasnevin alongside Griffith, Parnell and O'Connell. Richard Mulcahy delivered the graveside oration.

Although he was acting chairman of the Provisional Government, Cosgrave was not the only name considered by the leaders of the pro-Treaty party. While he had been a founder-member of Sinn Féin and a highly regarded member of Dublin Corporation, Cosgrave did not have the romance associated with the leaders of the armed wing of the independence movement. Richard Mulcahy and Eoin MacNeill were asked by supporters to put their names forward. The dynamic and abrasive Kevin O'Higgins, who never had an easy relationship with Cosgrave, pressed Richard Mulcahy to contest the position. 'O'Higgins' idea was that I should be the head of the Government,' wrote Mulcahy, 'but there was no move to discuss that and as far as I was concerned the position with regard to the army was that I didn't believe that the army could be handled by anyone except myself after Collins' death. Therefore, the question of my taking over the Government would be an utter impossibility at that time.'[5]

The writer Terence de Vere White, who knew many of the leading figures, recalled that, while O'Higgins favoured Mulcahy, support for Cosgrave was so strong that he withdrew his opposition. O'Higgins, though, is reputed to have sneered that 'a Dublin corporator would make Ireland a nation once again.' On the republican side there was a misguided view that Cosgrave and his colleagues would not be able for the task facing them. Writing at the end of August, Liam Lynch suggested, 'Collins' loss is one which they cannot fill. The enemy's position from the point of view of military and political leadership is very bad. We are at present in a much better position.'

Despite the reservations of some colleagues, Cosgrave was confirmed in his position as chairman of the Provisional Government. The first thing he did was to abandon the policy instigated by Collins of deferring the meeting of the third Dáil until the Civil War was over, and he summoned the newly elected TDs to meet on 9 September. At that meeting he was proposed and elected as president of the Dáil, in succession to Griffith, combining that position with his role as chairman of the Provisional Government. In a typically short and pithy speech he set out his priorities.

It is my intention to implement the Treaty as sanctioned by the vote of the Dáil and the electorate, insofar as it was free to express an opinion, to enact a constitution, to assert the authority and supremacy of parliament, to support and assist the national army in asserting the people's rights, to ask parliament, if necessary, for such powers as are deemed essential for the purpose of restoring order to suppress all crimes, to expedite as far as lies in the power of the Government the return of normal conditions throughout the country, and having established Saorstát on a constitutional basis, to speed the work of reconstruction and reparation.

Cosgrave continued to maintain an outward reluctance to accept the leadership, and at his first meeting with the Northern Ireland prime minister, James Craig, he protested: 'You know, I've been pushed into this. I'm not a leader of men.' This self-effacing judgement should not be taken too seriously. Winston Churchill, who knew something about the qualities needed in a leader of men, wrote:

The void left by the deaths of Griffith and Collins was not unfilled. A quiet potent figure stood in the background sharing, like Griffith, the dangers of the rebel leaders without taking part in all that they had done. In Cosgrave the Irish people found a chief of higher quality than any who had yet appeared. To the courage of Collins he added the matter of fact fidelity of Griffith and a knowledge of practical administration and state policy all his own.

Cosgrave typically laughed off Churchill's assessment and told friends with a twinkle in his eye that the only reason he had been described as 'a chief of higher quality' than any of the others was that he had taken the trouble to ask after Churchill's health after a fall from a pony during the tense negotiations of May 1922.[6] The historian Joseph Curran got it about right:

> Cosgrave's self-assessment was too modest, for in his quite commonsensical way he made an effective leader. He delegated authority wisely, handled ministerial disputes even-handedly and was, on the whole, an ideal chairman. His colleagues valued his advice and steadiness and long before he left office his competence and wit had made him personally very popular with voters.[7]

On the day the third Dáil met for the first time the *Irish Times* published a perceptive profile of Cosgrave, pointing out that he 'dresses generally in sombre hues, wears a bowler hat and looks rather like the general manager of a railway company'. It went on to say:

> He is undoubtedly the most capable man in the new Irish Parliament and that may be said without the slightest contradiction of any of his colleagues. As Premier of the Free State he has a formidable task before him but in one way he is almost the ideal choice because he has no violently extremist past to live down and with him the problem of saving face does not arise.[8]

The poet Padraic Colum, a long-time friend and political ally, provides the following pen-picture of W.T. as he took over the leading role in the Dáil in the autumn of 1922:

> He speaks leaning forward, his hands on the barrier before him; his delivery becomes like a series of pistol shots, each word shot out, each word reaching its mark. He is sociable as becomes a Dublin man and abundantly witty. His wit is a Dublin wit. It is founded on a very exact estimate of character. He can reveal character in a mordant phrase. Before his humour, before the phrase that springs up in his speech pretentiousness of all kinds falls away.[9]

During September 1922 the Civil War intensified and Mulcahy proposed that the army be given the power to try and punish a wide range of offences. After long discussion at cabinet the details of an Emergency Powers Bill were agreed. This provided for the establishment of military tribunals, which were empowered to impose the death penalty for serious offences, including the possession of weapons. When the bill was introduced in the Dáil, Cosgrave told deputies that 'those who persist in those murderous attacks must learn that they have got to pay the penalty for them.' In response to suggestions from the Labour leader Tom Johnson, Cosgrave announced an amnesty on 3 October to give republicans a chance to surrender before the new provisions came into effect. Few availed of the option, and the special powers came into effect on 15 October, the day after the amnesty expired.

The first executions took place a month later when four young men, found guilty of carrying unauthorised arms in Dublin, were shot by a firing squad. A week later an execution took place that elevated the Civil War into a new phase. The leading anti-Treaty figure Erskine Childers was captured at his cousin's home in Co. Wicklow and had in his possession a pistol given to him by Michael Collins. He was tried and convicted by a military court and executed the following morning. Cosgrave vigorously defended the execution of Childers in the Dáil on 28 November and he outlined the basis of his government's policy.

What do we want? We want simply order restored to this country. We want all arms under the control of the people who elected us and who can throw us out tomorrow if they so desire. We want that the people of this country only shall have the right to say who are to be armed and who are not; and we are going to get the arms if we have to search every house in the country.

Maintaining that the same law had to apply to the 'intellectual' Childers as applied to the four 'poor men's sons' who had been executed a week earlier, Cosgrave went on:

People who rob with arms are going to be brought before military courts and found guilty. Persons robbing at the point of the gun will be executed without discrimination. This is going to be a fair law, fairly administered and administered in the best interests of the country for the preservation of the fabric of society ... We are going to see that the rule of democracy will be maintained no matter what the cost and no matter who the intellectuals that may fall by reason of the assertion of that right.

The response of the Irregulars to the emergency powers came on 30 November when the IRA chief of staff, Liam Lynch, sent instructions to all battalion commanders to conduct operations against the enemy. No less than fourteen categories of people were directed to be 'shot at sight', including all members of the Provisional Dáil who had voted in favour of the Emergency Powers Act. As well as that, republicans were ordered to kill members of the Senate, High Court judges, journalists and pro-prietors of hostile newspapers and even 'aggressive Free State supporters'. The homes and offices of all these people were also to be destroyed, as were the homes of 'imperialist deputy lieutenant of the county types'. There followed a series of outrages by republicans against politicians, journalists and ordinary citizens.[10]

As the Civil War escalated the government faced other problems. A constitution had to be drafted and enacted to put the operations of the government and the Dáil on a legal basis. A police force was hurriedly established, and in a courageous and an imaginative move the new Civic Guard, later called An Garda Síochána, was established as an unarmed force, in contrast to its predecessor, the RIC. This was one of the most important decisions the government made to legitimise the institutions of the new state. On 6 December 1922, the first anniversary of the Treaty, the new constitution approved by the Dáil in October came into force. The Irish Free State formally came into being and the Provisional Government ceased to exist. Cosgrave was formally re-elected by the Dáil to the position of president.

The republican response to the new constitution was swift. The day after it was enacted two Dáil deputies were gunned down on their way from their Dublin hotel to Leinster House. Seán Hales was killed and Pádraic Ó Máille, the Leas-Cheann Comhairle, was wounded in an outrage that shocked the nation. Cosgrave and Mulcahy were both visibly shaken and angry when they heard the news, according to newspapers. The murders threatened to strangle Irish democracy, because some Dáil deputies fled Dublin for their lives after the shooting. Cosgrave ordered the secret service to go after the fleeing deputies and bring them back to Dublin. He then met each of the worried TDs individually and appealed to them not to be deterred from their patriotic duty.

By this stage Cosgrave had already stamped his authority on the Dáil and was known by his own supporters as 'the Boss'. Seán Mac Eoin, who initially feared that W.T. would not be strong enough to conduct the war after Collins's death, conceded years later that after a couple of months the military was convinced that 'Cosgrave had the punch that was needed'. On the night of 7 December all his authority was required to calm his panicking deputies. A story was told of one TD from Cork who resisted threats of execution by the secret service if he left Dublin and only agreed to stay because he feared Cosgrave's wrath.

Having met his wobbling TDs, Cosgrave then chaired a critical cabinet meeting to consider the government's next move. Mulcahy submitted a proposal from the Army Council for the immediate execution of four imprisoned IRA leaders: Rory O'Connor, Liam Mellows, Richard Barrett and Joe McKelvey. After a discussion Cosgrave went around the cabinet table to ask each minister individually if he approved of the executions. Of the ministers present, Blythe, MacNeill and FitzGerald backed Mulcahy. McGrath questioned the policy, but only O'Higgins initially baulked. Rory O'Connor had been best man at his wedding only a year before and he felt terrible anguish at having to agree to the executions, but he finally did. He was swayed by the argument that if the cabinet did not act ruthlessly there would be more assassinations and TDs would start to resign, turning the Executive Council into a dictatorship.[11]

The next morning the four IRA leaders, one from each province, were executed at Mountjoy Jail. There was outrage among opposition TDs, who accused the cabinet of personal vindictiveness when the decision was announced to the Dáil later that day. 'Personal spite, great heavens, vindictiveness, one of these men was a friend of mine,' said O'Higgins before he broke down in tears, unable to continue. Cosgrave was calmer, telling deputies that it had been impossible for the cabinet to consult the Dáil before acting and he defended the action.

> There is an elementary law in this case. The people who have challenged the very existence of society have put themselves outside the Constitution and only at the last moment, not thinking there was such infamy in this country, we safeguarded this Dáil and the government and the people of Ireland from being at the mercy of these people … There is only one way to meet it and that is to crush it and show them that terror will be struck into them.

The government's decision was supported by 39 votes to 14.

Donal O'Sullivan, the clerk of the Senate, later wrote: 'However this action of the Executive may be regarded from the ethical standpoint it proved to be an effective deterrent, for no other member of the legislature was assassinated during the progress of the Irregular campaign.'[12] However, a host of outrages followed rapidly. On 10 December the house of Deputy McGarry in Dublin was burned down and his young son, aged seven, died from smoke inhalation. An inquest jury later returned a verdict of 'wilful murder'. On 28 December a landmine destroyed the music warehouse of Deputy Denis McCullough, blowing the whole front of the house into the street. In early January the home of a pro-Treaty deputy, William Sears, was attacked. On the night of 13 January Cosgrave's own home, 'Beechpark', at Templeogue, was burned to the ground by republicans. Though young Liam Cosgrave was only three at the time, the bitter, acrid smell of burning timber that night is his earliest childhood memory. Liam went to live with his relatives in James's Street, while Louisa and young Michael went to stay at her father's house. W.T. mostly lived in Government Buildings but also spent some time at the Curragh Camp where he was safe from attack. A few weeks later Dr T.F. O'Higgins, father of Kevin O'Higgins, was brutally murdered at his home in Stradbally, Co. Laois. His body was riddled with bullets in the presence of his wife and seventeen-year-old daughter. Cosgrave's uncle, Patrick, was murdered by republicans at the family home in James's Street.[13]

There was also an orgy of burning and destruction of some of the country's finest houses, which sent some truly patriotic Irish people into exile in despair. Examples of this senseless campaign were the destruction of Kilteragh House in Foxrock, Co. Dublin, owned by Horace Plunkett, the burning of the historic Moore Hall in Carnacon, Co. Mayo, the destruction of one of the finest libraries in the country at the ancestral home of Senator John Bagwell in Clonmel, and the burning of Desart Court, near Callan, Co. Kilkenny. The homes of all these people were attacked because of their connections with the Senate. The Catholic Church came out unequivocally on a number of occasions during the Civil War. In October 1922, Cardinal Logue issued a joint pastoral – not the first of its kind – denouncing the republican campaign in very trenchant terms.

> A section of the community, refusing to acknowledge the government set up by the nation, have chosen to attack their own country as if she were a foreign power … They have wrecked Ireland from end to end. All those who in contravention of this teaching participate in such crimes are guilty of grievous sins

and may not be absolved on Confession nor admitted to Holy Communion if they persist in such evil courses.

In the early months of 1923 the government continued its executions policy in response to republican killings. A refinement of the policy was to sentence republicans to death but to suspend the sentence as long as there were no further outrages in the area concerned. As well as state-sanctioned violence, there were also brutal unauthorised reprisals, some carried out by the army and others by the special police based in Oriel House in Westland Row, Dublin. The most notorious reprisal was at Ballyseedy in Co. Kerry, where Free State soldiers tied nine republicans to a landmine and detonated it. The episode only became known because one of the republicans survived the incident. Another shocking episode was the kidnapping and murder by Oriel House police of Noel Lemass, brother of the future Fianna Fáil leader. There were mass arrests of republican sympathisers, and by April 1923, 13,000 prisoners were being held in jails and internment camps throughout the country. Liam Lynch was killed by the army that month in what was the final serious engagement of the Civil War. Then, on 24 May 1923, Frank Aiken ordered the IRA to stop fighting and to dump arms. De Valera issued a stirring message to the IRA, hailing them as the 'Legion of the Rearguard' who had saved the nation's honour. The Civil War was over.[14]

Cosgrave and his ministers then faced the cold reality of trying to build a viable state. The physical damage to the infrastructure of the country was immense and it took enormous sacrifices and a huge effort of national will to establish the country's institutions and rebuild its infrastructure. The financial burden of repairing the destruction undermined the prospects of realising the lofty aspirations that had inspired the independence movement. Reflecting on this in 1924, Liam de Róiste observed: 'We are paying for the "night out" of our fratricidal strife; the sickness of the "morning after" is still there; heartache, headache, depressing and empty pockets.'[15]

In the absence of republicans, who refused to recognise the legitimacy of the Dáil, Cosgrave had a strong majority in parliament, with the major opposition being provided by the Labour Party. While no formal party structure existed among his supporters, a whip was appointed to co-ordinate their voting strength, and they acted to all intents and purposes like a political party. They were known as the 'Government Party', the 'Ministry Party' or the 'Treaty Party'. Moves to establish a proper political party began on 7 December 1922, with a convention of pro-Treaty supporters in Dublin. They considered a proposal to continue using the Sinn Féin title but this was rejected. Instead the name Cumann na nGaedheal was proposed by Philip Monaghan, the mayor of Drogheda. It suggested a link with an organisation of the same name founded by Arthur Griffith. In the words of the historian Mel Farrell, 'Treatyites therefore reconciled a break with the revolutionary movement while maintaining a link with their separatist past.'[16]

It was not until 27 April 1923 that Cumann na nGaedheal was formally launched at a meeting in the Mansion House in Dublin. Meeting his ministers in advance, Cosgrave had deemed the Boundary Commission and its associated financial implications to be of paramount importance, while Mulcahy wanted to deal with unemployment and education.[17] Cosgrave delivered an opening address outlining the party's policy, which included the playing down of differences, denominational, social and class, as the basis on which the Free State might develop. The cost of joining the party was set at a shilling a year, while branches were asked to pay a minimum affiliation fee of £2. Membership was open to every citizen over eighteen who accepted the party constitution and the principle of majority rule, another way of saying the Treaty. The broad qualification for membership was designed to attract former Irish Party and unionist supporters. This attempt at inclusiveness led over time to charges from more nationalist opponents that the party had turned its back on Irish Ireland and was becoming West British.[18]

With the Civil War over and the bones of a party organisation in place, Cosgrave decided to call a general election. It was held in September, and Cumann na nGaedheal emerged as the largest party, with 39 per cent of the vote and 63 seats out of 153. It was not an absolute majority but as republicans, who won 44 seats, decided to continue their boycott of the

Dáil, it gave Cosgrave a comfortable working majority. However, the total vote for parties that accepted the Treaty, at less than 70 per cent, showed a significant slippage since the pact election of a little more than a year earlier. It was a harbinger of things to come.

In the Dáil, Cosgrave was an effective speaker, as he had demonstrated during the Treaty debates, but he was not an orator and had little time for wordy speeches. His cabinet colleague Ernest Blythe recalled his style:

> Mr Cosgrave was a ready and effective speaker in the Dáil or on a public platform but he was not much inclined to prepare elaborate formal addresses. When such was necessary he resorted to team work and showed himself in advance of other politicians here by having orations prepared by ghost writers who, however, were given his detailed personal instructions.

Another cabinet colleague, Eoin MacNeill, who was one of Cosgrave's speech-writers, recalled in a memoir how he drafted Cosgrave's address to the League of Nations in 1923. 'I had the gratification of seeing it printed afterwards in an American book as an example of Mr Cosgrave's oratory,' MacNeill wrote.[19]

Cosgrave generally behaved in cabinet as first among equals rather than as a charismatic leader. Brian Farrell, in his perceptive *Chairman or Chief?* put W.T. into the chairman category, and on the face of it that would appear a fair categorisation. In a cabinet of brilliant intellectuals like O'Higgins, Paddy Hogan and Eoin MacNeill, Cosgrave did not give the impression of being a forceful leader of men, but that was deceptive. The army mutiny of 1924 (discussed later in this chapter) showed Cosgrave's strength as a leader. Much has been made of his temporary absence through illness, with suggestions that he took to his bed to avoid dealing with the crisis. Whatever the nature of the illness, it was severe enough only to prevent him from attending five cabinet meetings. But although not there in person, there is a strong sense in the minutes that his presence could be felt; memos and letters from him were read aloud. Moreover, all decisions had to be approved by him before any announcements or final judgements were made. On more than one occasion he received visits to his home from ministers. During this period O'Higgins attempted to assert himself, and his ambition to be leader is beyond doubt. But Cosgrave never relinquished control of his cabinet.

In its determination to prove that Ireland was capable of self-government, the Cosgrave government ran a tight fiscal policy as it rebuilt the country. Ernest Blythe, as Minister for Finance, went into Irish folklore for his decision to cut a shilling off the old-age pension in 1924 and to cut the salaries of teachers and other public servants by 10 per cent. The nature of the cuts became a millstone around the government's neck and, ironically, the very people whose Civil War activities made the austere measures necessary were the ultimate political beneficiaries. Repairing the damage caused by the Civil War cost the state £50 million, which came to a quarter of GNP (over €80 billion in 2019 terms).[20]

In spite of the austerity, the Cosgrave government had a number of achievements to its credit during the early 1920s. While W.T. was initially sceptical about the need to develop a pampered diplomatic service, Ireland joined the League of Nations, and Cosgrave led the government delegation to Geneva in September 1923. Joining the League was a vital assertion of sovereignty, and it was on the government's agenda even before the constitutional foundation of the new state was fully in place. Membership was seen as one of the tests of self-government, and failure to join would have implied that there was something wrong with the Free State's constitutional status. The official request was made on 17 April 1923, the first formal diplomatic act taken by an Irish representative abroad. When the Free State was granted membership in September 1923, it was official confirmation that the international community recognised Ireland's sovereign status. Liam de Róiste recorded the moment in his diary: 'Four years ago it would have seemed a mighty thing to have Ireland recognised among the nations as a separate nation. Today it is in the natural course as flowing from the Treaty.' In describing Ireland as 'one of the oldest and yet one of the youngest nations' when addressing the assembly for the first time, Cosgrave used language that would be replicated by Jack Lynch half a century later when Ireland joined the European Economic Community.[21]

There were also notable economic achievements. The Shannon hydro-electric scheme was built at Ardnacrusha, in defiance of economic orthodoxy. The scheme absorbed an enormous proportion of government expenditure and was widely criticised, but it was a vital step in the economic development of the state. The sugar beet industry was also developed as a state project, with factories at Carlow and Thurles. Paddy Hogan, as a dynamic Minister for Agriculture, began improvement in livestock breeding and expanded the trade. His famous slogan was 'You should keep one more cow, one more sow and one more acre under the plough.' Hogan introduced the Land Act of 1923 which marked the final transfer of the land of Ireland from the landlords to the tenant farmers.[22]

A notable feature of the early years in office was a decided shift by the government towards fostering a Catholic ethos in the Free State. When the Attorney General, Hugh Kennedy, sought clarification as to whether divorce would continue to be allowed on the British model, W.T. consulted Dr Byrne, the Archbishop of Dublin, and he asked him to get the views of the hierarchy on the matter. Not surprisingly, the hierarchy expressed its opposition to divorce, and Cosgrave had no hesitation in introducing a bill in the Dáil banning divorce. 'I consider that the whole fabric of our social organisation is based upon the sanctity of the marriage bond and that anything that tends to weaken the binding efficacy of that bond to that extent strikes at the root of our social life,' he told the Dáil.

Despite the end of the Civil War, intermittent violence from republicans occurred throughout the 1920s but it was not the only problem which faced Cosgrave. Towards the end of 1923 and early in 1924 he had to deal with mounting discontent in the army and battles for supremacy among his own cabinet ministers, particularly O'Higgins and Mulcahy, whose differences crystallised around the army issue. The immediate cause of the problem was that the army, which had grown to a massive 57,000 men during the Civil War, was to be reduced in size. There were competing claims for survival between the former IRA men in the army and the professional ex-British soldiers, most of them Irishmen who had served in the Great War, who had been drafted in during the conflict. Far more important, though, was a conflict between two groups who claimed allegiance to the legacy of Michael Collins. One was led by the remnants of the IRB, who formed the leadership of the army and numbered among their group the chief of staff, Seán McMahon, and other senior officers. This group had strong links with the Minister for Defence, Richard Mulcahy. The other group, called the IRA Organisation, was led by Liam Tobin and Charlie Dalton. They had been Collins's apostles and had carried out assassinations on his orders during the War of Independence. During the Civil War they became the nub of the Criminal Investigation Branch of the army, the so-called Oriel House Gang, who played a decisive role in the counter-terror. They had a protector in Joe McGrath, who, although he was Minister for Industry and Commerce, was responsible for their activities.

O'Higgins, as Minister for Justice, became increasingly impatient at the softly-softly approach of Mulcahy to difficulties in the army and with McGrath's support for the Oriel House group. He was determined to get to grips with both factions, sack their senior members and impose on them the authority of the civil power. There were bitter rows at cabinet between O'Higgins and Mulcahy on the one hand and between O'Higgins and McGrath on the other. The issue came to a head at the end of February 1924 when the cabinet decided to demobilise or demote senior officers at Oriel House, including Tobin and Dalton. On hearing the news they responded by issuing an ultimatum to Cosgrave and demanding a meeting. McGrath lent support to their case by resigning from the cabinet in protest at the cuts in army spending. The government responded by ordering the arrest of Tobin and Dalton, and, on the insistence of O'Higgins, the Garda commissioner, Eoin O'Duffy, was given control of the army.[23]

By the end of the episode two ministers, Mulcahy and McGrath, had departed from the government and McGrath and another eight TDs actually left Cumann na nGaedheal. Cosgrave eventually recovered sufficient ground to bring Mulcahy back into the cabinet as Minister for Local Government, following the general election of June 1927, and thus provide himself with some balance once more against O'Higgins. In

October 1924 McGrath and the eight other disillusioned backbenchers resigned from the Dáil in protest at the affair. Cosgrave refused to be panicked and called all nine by-elections for 13 March 1925. Cumann na nGaedheal won seven of them, and that was the last of the army crisis.

The government, though, was dogged by crises in security and Anglo-Irish relations. One embarrassing setback was the report of the Boundary Commission provided for in article 12 of the Treaty. The expectation of the Treaty signatories had been that the Boundary Commission would hand large portions of the North where there were Catholic majorities over to the Free State. Eoin MacNeill was appointed as the government representative on the Commission, which was chaired by an English-born South African, Mr Justice Feetham, and the editor of the *Northern Whig,* J.R. Fisher. MacNeill found himself in a minority position but mysteriously failed to keep Cosgrave informed of what was happening. In November 1925 the *Morning Post* revealed that the commission was about to recommend the transfer of Catholic south Armagh to the Free State and Protestant east Donegal to the North. Cosgrave rushed to London, where he quickly did a deal with the British Prime Minister, Stanley Baldwin, and James Craig to suppress the report. The status quo on the border was retained, with the South preferring to keep east Donegal rather than gain south Armagh. A hugely important part of the settlement as far as Cosgrave was concerned was that the liability of the Free State for the British national debt was cancelled. This was a boost for the cash-strapped government although the agreement that payment of the land annuities would continue took some of the gloss off the deal.[24]

The Boundary Commission debacle was a setback for Cosgrave and his government, and it was followed in May 1926 by a political challenge at home. Éamon de Valera broke away from Sinn Féin and established Fianna Fáil in anticipation of a general election the following year. That election came in June 1927, and it was a stern rebuff for Cosgrave. Cumann na nGaedheal lost 16 seats and ended up with 47 TDs. Fianna Fáil performed impressively, winning 44 seats, but as the party was still committed to an abstentionist policy Cosgrave was able to hold on to the reins of government.

The murder of Kevin O'Higgins on his way to Mass in Booterstown, Co. Dublin, on 10 July changed the political scene fundamentally. The murder was a shocking reminder that Civil War divisions could resurface at any time. The government responded with the introduction of a harsh Public Safety Bill and, more significantly, the Electoral Amendment Bill. The Electoral Bill required that in future all Dáil candidates would have to take the controversial oath, otherwise they would be ineligible to become candidates. This confronted de Valera with a critical dilemma. Either Fianna Fáil now agreed to take the oath or they would not be in a position to contest the next election. De Valera responded by leading his party into the Dáil in August and taking the oath, for the rejection of which he had justified the Civil War, describing it as an 'empty political formula'. In his autobiography the writer Sean O'Casey penned this wonderful description of the event:

> De Valera, pinched and worn and threadbare, studied the question of the oath. He seemed to turn the spiritual side of the question into a mathematical one. His party determined, after tremendous argument, that the taking of the oath could be done without taking the oath, provided they made it plain they didn't recognise the oath when they were taking the oath; that an oath taken under duress wasn't really an oath at all, but just the appearance of one; a deceptive thing, an illusion, a shadow, a ghost-oath. If you believed it was there, it would be there; if you didn't believe it was there, it couldn't be there. Just shut your eyes, close your ears, dispel your thoughts, and speak away, and the thing was done, yet not done.[25]

Accepted wisdom has it that Cosgrave's intention was to force Fianna Fáil into democratic politics through the Electoral Bill; but R.M. (Bertie) Smylie, later editor of the *Irish Times,* recalled years later that Cosgrave reacted with shock when he told him 'Dev is going in.'[26]

Fianna Fáil's entry to the Dáil left Cumann na nGaedheal in a minority. De Valera did a deal with the Labour Party whereby he agreed to support a Labour minority government led by Tom Johnson once

Cosgrave was defeated in a vote of confidence. Fianna Fáil and Labour were so sure of forcing Cosgrave out of office in August 1926 that they didn't even muster their full quota of TDs on the day of the confidence motion. One Labour TD, T.J. O'Connell, was at a teachers' conference in Canada and didn't bother to come home, with the newspapers speculating that Cosgrave would lose by 73 votes to 69.

On the day of the debate the figures began to change as some Redmondite and independent TDs began to have second thoughts about backing what they considered to be the unholy alliance of Fianna Fáil and Labour. The key to the vote turned out to be Alderman John Jinks, TD for Sligo, who has gone into folklore because of what happened. Jinks, a member of the National League led by Willie Redmond, was known to be unhappy at his leader's decision to bring down Cosgrave. One story was that Major Bryan Cooper, a former Unionist who now supported W.T., brought Jinks to a bar and plied the Sligo man with drink. Jinks then disappeared from the precincts of Leinster House and mysteriously ended up on the Sligo train when the division was called in the Dáil. The vote was tied at 71–71 and the Ceann Comhairle gave his casting vote in favour of the government. Cosgrave had survived by the skin of his teeth thanks to the disappearance of Jinks.[27]

Cosgrave won two by-elections at the end of August and, with Fianna Fáil and Labour still licking their wounds from the failed attempt to oust him, he dissolved the Dáil and called a general election for September. The result was that Cumann na nGaedheal increased its strength from 47 to 62 seats, but Fianna Fáil also increased, from 44 to 57. Labour and the other smaller parties took a hammering, and the two big parties were left to confront each other in the Dáil.

Despite its electoral success, important changes had taken place in the composition of the Cumann na nGaedheal leadership, and its Irish-Ireland complexion was not nearly as strong as it had been a few years earlier. The army mutiny had resulted in the departure of Joe McGrath, while Eoin MacNeill lost his seat in June 1927. There had also been some tension in the government over its commitment to free trade. The Minister for Posts and Telegraphs, J.J. Walsh, who favoured the policy of protection that stretched back to Arthur Griffith's Sinn Féin, publicly questioned government policy and, without giving notice to his colleagues, quit politics on the eve of the September 1927 election.

The drift was compounded by the arrival in the party of more conservative former Redmondite and Farmers' Party members along with well-off and educated independents like Bryan Cooper, John Daly and Myles Keogh. W.T. also offered to appoint the last leader of the Irish Parliamentary Party, John Dillon, to the Senate but the offer was spurned. 'I will not serve with people who have blood on their hands,' Dillon is said to have replied. Liam de Róiste captured the changing complexion of the party when he observed in his diary that Cumann na nGaedheal was a composite party, with one section favouring 'moneyed and big farmer interests' and another section closer to Fianna Fáil in an Irish-Ireland policy.[28]

After 1927 Cosgrave was now under increasing pressure in the Dáil and outside, but he didn't lose his nerve. The government worked away doggedly at home and with great success in international affairs, particularly at the Imperial Conference of 1931, where McGilligan broadened the scope of Irish independence and proved that the Treaty could indeed be used as a stepping-stone to complete freedom.[29] As the decade wore on the government's early achievements were taken for granted and it was increasingly portrayed as being out of touch with the concerns of ordinary people. Even the style of dress adopted by ministers served to alienate them from the voters. Formal morning suits, wing collars and top hats were the normal dress code for people of their position at the time, but it gave the government a distant air. W.T. was often portrayed by republican propaganda as a 'West Brit', which was ironic given his strong nationalist sentiments, but his dress code served to reinforce the image.

Meanwhile Fianna Fáil had begun to build up its support after entering the Dáil. Its economic programme was based on the principle of protectionism, and the party concentrated its attacks on the Minister for Agriculture, Paddy Hogan, for his reforms aimed at making Irish agriculture competitive in a free-trade environment. One of the issues Fianna Fáil focused on in particular was the land annuities – payments made to the British exchequer by Irish farmers in return for the loans to buy out their land under the various Land Acts. The issue represented a combination of nationalist rhetoric and economic self-interest as far as farmers were concerned. Cosgrave didn't get a great hearing for his argument that to repudiate the annuities would be 'dishonest and calamitous to the credit of the Saorstát'.

A sardonic London *Times* reporter noted at the end of 1927 how Fianna Fáil was ruthlessly going after the farmers' vote.

> A protected paradise is not the wildest or most dangerous of Fianna Fáil's promises to an electorate which is a curious mixture of shrewdness and credulity. When Mr Hogan, unfolding his admirable programme of benefits for farmers, says "O fortunatos nimium sua si bona norint" [O fortunate are those who know how well off they are], Mr de Valera and his friends send back from a hundred platforms the sinister echo "No rint". They tell the people that Fianna Fáil's accession to power will mean the end of land purchase annuities and already the effect of this reckless promise on a community of struggling small farmers has been very mischievous.[30]

Fianna Fáil also managed to outflank the government by unashamedly playing on old religious divisions. Despite his piety, Cosgrave resisted the prevailing sectarian impulses of the day. He faithfully stood by the agreement of 1922 to appoint representatives of southern unionism to the Senate, despite severe criticism from Fianna Fáil throughout the 1920s who claimed he was involved in a Masonic plot with Protestant senators.

The infamous Dunbar-Harrison case provides an interesting example of the pressures Cosgrave was under. In 1930 the Local Appointments Commission appointed a Protestant, Letitia Dunbar-Harrison, to the vacant position of Mayo County Librarian. The County Council refused to ratify the appointment, on the alleged grounds that Miss Dunbar-Harrison did not speak Irish, but nobody was in any doubt that the reason was that she was a Protestant. The government responded by dissolving the County Council and appointing a commissioner in its place who duly appointed Miss Dunbar-Harrison to the post. The political reaction from Fianna Fáil was one of outrage at the appointment. De Valera maintained that if the functions of the appointee were merely those of an attendant handing out books then religious affiliation would not matter. 'On the other hand, if the whole idea behind the scheme was that the librarian should go into the homes of people, and into the schools, and push the scheme, if instead of her duties being passive they were active, the position was an entirely different one.'[31]

With his political opponents playing a sectarian tune, Cosgrave also came under pressure from Archbishop Gilmartin of Tuam, but he wrote to the prelate as follows: 'As I explained to Your Grace at our interview, to discriminate against any citizen – or exercise a preference for a citizen – on account of religious belief would be to conflict with some of the fundamental principles on which this state is founded.' With pressure mounting on all sides, though, Cosgrave eventually opted for a political fudge, and in December 1931 Miss Dunbar-Harrison was transferred from Castlebar to the Department of Defence library in Dublin. This incident shows some weakness on Cosgrave's part but not sectarianism. Critics of his piety would also do well to note that Fianna Fáil in the late 1920s hounded him for allowing 'immoral publications' to circulate in Ireland and demanded even more rigorous censorship than that in operation.

With Fianna Fáil concentrating on economic issues the government appeared obsessed with security concerns as the IRA continued to engage in sporadic outrage and murder. The Public Safety Acts of 1927 and 1931 and the Jurors' Protection Act gave the government drastic powers and allowed military tribunals to try terrorist offences. Cosgrave and his ministers vigorously defended the need for such measures, but the electorate grew increasingly weary of the security emphasis.

Fianna Fáil cleverly expanded its republican appeal by adding to its policy practical promises based on voters' self-interest. For farmers it was the abolition of the land annuities and for the urban working class it was the promise of jobs through a protectionist policy. Cosgrave called a general election for February 1932 and went to the country promising stability and continuity.

With Fianna Fáil and the IRA hand in glove during the election campaign Cosgrave's tactics became essentially negative. 'The Shadow of a Gunman – Keep it from your door,' read one Cumann na nGaedheal poster. Another had a red flag superimposed on a Tricolour with the message 'We want no reds, keep their colour off your flag.' A newspaper advertisement read, 'The gunmen are voting Fianna Fáil, the Communists are voting Fianna Fáil'. The most famous poster of all read:

> Devvy's Circus, absolutely the greatest road show in Ireland today – Senor de Valera, world famous illusionist, oath swallower and escapologist. See his renowned act: Escaping from the strait-jacket of the republic. Frank F. Aiken, fearsome fire eater. Shaunty O'Kelly, the man in dress clothes. Monsieur Lemass, famous tight rope performer, see him cross from the Treaty to the republic every night, Performing frogs, champion croakers, marvelous trained sheep.

On platforms around the country Cumann na nGaedheal speakers had difficulty getting a hearing as the campaign became increasingly disruptive and the IRA put its muscle behind the Fianna Fáil campaign. Government speakers were shouted down, with opponents demanding, 'Who started the Civil War?' and 'Who ordered the execution of Rory O'Connor?' A standard Cumann na nGaedheal reply to such hecklers was 'And how many banks did you rob?'[32]

While both Fianna Fáil and Cumann na nGaedheal were staunchly Catholic, the hierarchy and the parish priests tended to support the government, with many curates backing de Valera. On his tour of the country W.T. lunched with the Bishop of Kerry on 1 February; he visited the Catholic and Church of Ireland Bishops of Limerick the following day; the next day he had tea with his old friend Bishop Fogarty of Killaloe and then went to meet Bishop Harty of Cashel. Micheál Ó hAodha recalled that as a child he heard Bishop Fogarty preaching at Mass in Ennis during the 1932 campaign when Cosgrave was a member of the congregation. 'So we can only pray that all the saints in heaven, the cherubim, seraphim and choirs, shall join with Saint Flannan to plead before the golden throne that God may look down on all the Dalcassians gathered here in this ancient see of Killaloe to ask before God's altar for divine protection and guidance for our great president W.T. Cosgrave, to whom we extend a céad míle fáilte to Ennis.'

At Cosgrave's final election rally at College Green, Dublin, on 14 February passions boiled over as rival supporters fought each other on the streets and the gardaí had difficulty in quelling the riot. 'There were cheers and counter cheers, scuffles took place among the crowds, free fights developed and batons were drawn,' the *Irish Independent* reported. When the election took place on 16 February the voters opted for change rather than continuity. Fianna Fáil increased its share of the vote from 35 per cent to over 45 per cent while Cumann na nGaedheal dropped from 39 to 35 per cent. In terms of seats, de Valera had 72, while Cosgrave won 57. It was a shattering blow to Cosgrave and Cumann na nGaedheal to lose an election to the forces they had defeated in the Civil War ten years earlier, but a younger electorate was looking to the future, not the past.

The new Dáil assembled at 2:30 p.m. on Tuesday 9 March 1932. De Valera entered Leinster House accompanied by his son Vivion, who had a revolver in his pocket. A number of other senior Fianna Fáil TDs were armed as they entered the Dáil chamber. Frank Aiken had earlier handed out revolvers to some of his colleagues and rumour has it that even heavier weapons were on hand in case of an army coup. James Dillon always claimed in later years that he saw a senior Fianna Fáil politician assembling a machine gun in a telephone booth at the back of the chamber. The belief in Fianna Fáil that a coup was possible demonstrated how severely they still misjudged Cosgrave. True enough, some wild men on the government side had talked about a coup, particularly the Garda commissioner, Eoin O'Duffy. Ernest Blythe was also rumoured to be in favour of such action, but there was no widespread sympathy for such a move in Cumann na nGaedheal and Cosgrave was not prepared to countenance it. He asked colleagues where the rumours were coming from and was told about O'Duffy, whom he had never liked or trusted in the first place.

Tim Pat Coogan recalls that Cosgrave was always wary of O'Duffy. 'In fact, Cosgrave had only persuaded my father [Eamonn Coogan] to act as deputy commissioner in the first instance because he convinced him that a counterbalance was needed to someone whom he regarded as a wild man.' Cosgrave himself took the opening of the sixth Dáil calmly. 'Before the vote, far from being engaged in any frantic plotting, Cosgrave was upstairs playing pontoon with the former Education Minister, John Marcus O'Sullivan.'[33] Handing over power to the forces they had defeated in the Civil War was naturally regarded as a bitter defeat by the leaders of Cumann na nGaedheal, but over time it came to be recognised as a great victory for Irish democracy and one that was every bit as important as the outcome of the Civil War. It was well summed up by the historian Joe Lee, who said that Cosgrave was essentially a moderate, who had to learn that moderates must be prepared, in the last resort, to kill in defence of moderation.

It was due in large measure to him that things did not fall apart, that the centre did hold, that not so many but so few of the rough beasts slouching through the Ireland of the twenties would reach their blood-soaked Bethlehems. And Cosgrave would do the ship of state one final service, by the manner in which he quietly left the bridge and handed over the wheel to the rival captain. Bitter though it was in party terms – indeed precisely because it was so bitter in party terms – it was his finest hour.[34]

The journalist and 1916 veteran Desmond Ryan made a similar point when he wrote in the 1930s that perhaps Cosgrave 'felt like comparing himself to Brian Boru, who had fallen but saved his kingdom'.[35] After losing power the big question that confronted Cosgrave was whether he could save his party.

EOIN O'DUFFY, THE BLUESHIRTS AND THE CREATION OF FINE GAEL

'The government is back to the heady days of the Blueshirts again.'

– MATTIE MCGRATH, INDEPENDENT TD FOR TIPPERARY,
19 FEBRUARY 2019.

E oin O'Duffy had an unremarkable childhood. Born Owen Duffy, he was the son of an impoverished farmer. His self-serving unpublished autobiography paints a picture of a relatively happy childhood in Co. Monaghan, one that was framed by the Catholic religion and tradition and a happiness derived from time spent outdoors, in communion with the land. This wholesome, mostly idyllic childhood would later become the standard against which he would judge independent Ireland.[1]

Unlike some of his contemporaries, O'Duffy did not come from a political family. But he made his name in nationalist circles through his involvement with the GAA. He therefore had more in common with Michael Collins than the likes of Kevin O'Higgins, the Cumann na nGaedheal Minister for Justice whose extended family was steeped in the Irish Parliamentary Party tradition. But while Collins is revered in

Fine Gael circles, any mention of O'Duffy – the party's first president – is studiously avoided. This stems from his leadership of the Blueshirts, an organisation popularly viewed in the same category as the fascist movements that swept swathes of inter-war Europe. Consequently, the role that O'Duffy played, and the involvement of his organisation, in the creation of the party is one that is regularly and purposely overlooked by Fine Gael. A further consequence of the party's general unwillingness to engage with its birth story is that the other elements that contributed to or informed the formation of Fine Gael have also been somewhat neglected. The National Centre Party, which represented the farming interest, and the influence of the old Irish Party – despite the efforts of John Bruton to highlight this element – are virtually forgotten.

Fine Gael was created in 1933 to challenge Fianna Fáil at a time when the opposition, independently, seemed incapable of doing so. By the time of the 1932 election, when Fianna Fáil first took power, Cumann na nGaedheal had every appearance of a party that was worn out after a decade of continuous governance. When the snap election the following year returned Fianna Fáil for a second term, Cosgrave's party was forced to accept that its new role in opposition was more than a temporary arrangement. Members had bought their own propaganda that Fianna Fáil was incapable of governing and that voters would quickly realise that they had made a mistake supporting de Valera's party. A revealing letter to the party's head office in the aftermath of the 1932 election succinctly captured the Cumann na nGaedheal attitude. Any achievements enjoyed by the new government, it was suggested, would simply be a consequence of building on the previous government's legacy, while failures would be due to the 'stupidity and ignorance' of Fianna Fáil.[2]

Two successive defeats disabused Cumann na nGaedheal deputies of such notions. It was in this climate that Fianna Fáil's opponents began to consider how that party might be challenged.

Cumann na nGaedheal was clearly not capable of doing so on its own and none of the other opposition parties in the Dáil were large enough to offer a credible single-party alternative. Talk of the need for a new national party grew, instigated by Senators Arthur Vincent and Alfie

Byrne, who were both concerned by elements of Fianna Fáil policy. The two senators had envisaged the National Centre Party and Cumann na nGaedheal joining together in a reconfigured political landscape before the 1933 election, at which they would win ninety seats, displacing Fianna Fáil.

Frank MacDermot's National Centre Party is a relatively unknown entity in Irish political history. The party's roots lay in the National Farmers' and Ratepayers' Association, established in 1932 in the context of the Economic War and the strain felt by farmers, and following the demise of Denis Gorey's Farmers' Party. As a loose federation of local groups, the NFRA did not have the type of national organisation necessary to lead a campaign, and so, on 16 September 1932, the decision was taken to form a new political organisation that would represent the farming interest. Although not originally described as a political party, that organisation would become the National Centre Party. Patrick Belton, a former Fianna Fáil TD, had been the driving force behind the politicisation of the NFRA. A controversial figure, he was bypassed in favour of MacDermot for the leadership.[3] MacDermot had served in the British army in the First World War, advancing to the rank of major. He emigrated to America after the war, returning to Ireland in 1927. Having unsuccessfully contested the West Belfast constituency in the 1929 British general election, he was subsequently elected in Roscommon on behalf of the NFRA at the 1932 election. Beyond representing the farming community, the Centre Party he now led also sought to 'get rid of bitter memories' of the Civil War and to 'promote good feeling between all classes'.[4] Despite considering itself above Civil War politics, the party was essentially pro-Treaty in its outlook.

However, there was no reconfiguration of the political system before the snap 1933 election. MacDermot was not willing to countenance one, and understandably so. Gorey's Farmers' Party had given the Cumann na nGaedheal government support from the opposition benches after the June and September 1927 general elections, and was rewarded with a parliamentary secretaryship, the forerunner of today's junior minister post. This did not entitle Michael Heffernan to a seat at the cabinet table, where decisions were made, yet because of their support for the government the farmers become closely associated in the public mind with its often-unpopular decisions. Furthermore, while contemporary observers tended to depict the farmers as auxiliaries of Cumann na nGaedheal, in reality, the Farmers' Party was often critical of the government before 1927. It claimed that high taxes and wasteful spending, combined with an urban emphasis, was ruining Irish agriculture.[5] If the Centre Party sought to disperse the 'bitter memories' of the Civil War, joining with the pro-Treaty side flew in the face of its stated purpose. A merger was never inevitable.

Both Cumann na nGaedheal and the National Centre Party ran independent campaigns for the 1933 election, although they did invite supporters to continue their preferences for the other party. Cumann na nGaedheal did so more rigorously than the candidates standing on the farmers' ticket. Although MacDermot's party did not have the budget to match the spending of the two main parties, the nascent organisation showed greater signs of professionalism than the Farmers' Party had and employed clever vote-management strategies in the constituencies it contested. The *Westmeath Examiner* was among those that lauded MacDermot for his organisational abilities.[6]

The results did nothing to convince MacDermot that merging with a larger organisation would be beneficial. Not only did his party hold its own but it also attracted support away from Cumann na nGaedheal. Eleven of the party's twenty-six candidates were elected. While eleven seats were not sufficient to make any material difference to the formation of the government, the election did demonstrate a somewhat consistent performance by candidates representing the farming interest. There was no incentive for MacDermot to compromise his party's identity. Some talks were held with Cumann na nGaedheal, but they did not achieve anything. It appeared that Vincent's and Byrne's dream of a national party would remain just that.

Fianna Fáil unwittingly provided the impetus for the formation of a new party – and it was in this context that the Blueshirts were significant. The Blueshirts came into existence as the Army Comrades' Association. The organisation declared itself to be non-political, formed to offer support to ex-servicemen. It counted among its ranks the leading Cumann na nGaedheal politicians Ernest Blythe, Patrick McGilligan and Desmond FitzGerald. Despite having TDs who sought re-election among its membership, the organisation reiterated that it was non-political at both the 1932 and 1933 general elections. However, its independence was called into question when the ACA became closely associated with Cumann na nGaedheal, and the Centre Party, during the 1933 campaign. That campaign was punctuated by attacks and clashes, and Cumann na nGaedheal candidates, as well as those from MacDermot's party, were routinely targeted. The ACA extended its services to protect the meetings in a climate where W.T. Cosgrave felt that the government had failed to take control. Invoking its roots as the party of law and order, Cumann na nGaedheal politicians were critical of Fianna Fáil for, in their view, allowing lawlessness to prevail.

The ACA thus acted as a defender of free speech, upholding democracy. How then can this be reconciled with the accusation that it was a fascist movement? The uniform with blue shirt was adopted at a meeting three months after the election, in April 1933. This could be read as a declaration of intent. Indeed, with no history of shirted movements in Ireland, it seems that the ACA, despite the leadership claiming otherwise, was influenced by Continental developments.[7] Connections were immediately drawn with Hitler's Brownshirts and Mussolini's Blackshirts.

The extent to which the Blueshirts were really cast in the same fascist mould is explored later in this chapter, but it is important to note here that de Valera interpreted the Blueshirts as Cosgrave had the IRA. The not-so-distant memory of the Civil War coloured judgements and amplified perceived threats. The Fianna Fáil government moved to circumvent any risk. On the weekend of 29 and 30 July, Patrick McGilligan, Ernest Blythe and J.M. O'Sullivan had their licences to possess firearms revoked. Blythe had carried his state-owned revolver only since 1927, acquiring it for protection after O'Higgins's assassination. Not only were all three men prominent members of the National Guard, as the Blueshirts were now called, but they had also been key members of the Cumann na nGaedheal government. While others had their licences withdrawn too, the targeting of former government members appeared calculated. From 1 August the operation to disarm other members of the National Guard moved quickly.

Tensions mounted, and the Garda presence at Government Buildings was stepped up. The threat of violence hung in the air. Despite the increasingly acrimonious atmosphere, O'Duffy persevered with a plan for the annual commemoration of Arthur Griffith, Michael Collins and Kevin O'Higgins. Though scaled back compared with previous years, such a gathering had the potential to descend into violence. It was perceived as a 'march on Dublin', a reference to Mussolini's march on Rome. On 22 August 1933 de Valera's government invoked article 2A of the constitution, banned the parade, and proclaimed the National Guard illegal. This decision ultimately proved to be a turning-point in the development of the party-political system.

The use of article 2A was controversial. It had been inserted in the constitution as a consequence of the Public Safety Act (1931), introduced by the Cumann na nGaedheal government in response to the growing strength of the IRA. A report sent to the Department of Justice by Eoin O'Duffy in his role as Garda commissioner on 27 July 1931 had reported illegal drilling in various parts of the country and communicated that his men were in a 'hopeless position'.[8] The legislation allowed the government to declare a state of emergency, and Cosgrave had used the powers granted under it to move against the IRA. Saor Éire, a communist organisation, Cumann na mBan and Fianna Éireann were prohibited at the same time. Fianna Fáil had been resolutely opposed to the legislation and the manner in which it was rushed through the Dáil in October 1931; the party ended the state of emergency on entering government in 1932 but did not repeal the legislation. That de Valera's government then turned to it so quickly in 1933 to deal with the National Guard concerned MacDermot, who became more open to the idea of strengthening the opposition.

At this point O'Duffy was invited into the discussions. Like MacDermot, he had previously resisted any idea of a formal arrangement for his organisation's non-political stance. But the application of article 2A had focused his mind. An isolated and illegal organisation, with little hope of a future, the National Guard needed respectable allies. The organisation's executive approved the motion to join with Cumann na nGaedheal and the Centre Party on 8 September. The National Guard was later reconstituted as a new organisation within Fine Gael, named the Young Ireland Association.

Subsequent talks resulted in the creation of the United Ireland Party – Fine Gael, to be simply known as the United Ireland Party. This was at the insistence of Frank MacDermot, who was reported to have floated 'United Ireland' at the outset of the discussions and had stood firm thereafter.[9] For MacDermot, this name was an important signifier to voters about the new party's priorities, reflected also in the first point of the Fine Gael manifesto, which spoke of the need for national reunification. Michael Tierney suggested 'Fine Gael'. The choice of an Irish name was important symbolically, and it also represented continuity with Cumann na nGaedheal. The 'organisation of the Irish' was thus to become the 'family of the Irish'. The succinct name was also snappier than MacDermot's wordier title, and it tripped off the tongue more easily. It's hardly surprising that 'United Ireland' was virtually dropped within months and that 'Fine Gael' was more commonly used. Given that MacDermot was so wedded to the name, it is perhaps surprising that it was replaced so quickly. In truth, though, it reflected the fact that, while the Centre Party may have merged as equals, Cumann na nGaedheal was the bigger party. The disappearance of MacDermot's preference coincided, not uncoincidentally, with his own decision to withdraw from the party.

If Fine Gael was to be constructed and accepted as a new party, it also needed a new leader – one who was free of political baggage. That ruled out both Cosgrave and MacDermot, even though Cosgrave was, by far, the most experienced candidate. He had proved himself a safe pair of hands as Minister for Local Government in the revolutionary Dáil, and his department was considered one of the most successful of that period. As President of the Executive Council he held together a government that was essentially a disparate coalition of interests, represented by such strong and forceful personalities as Kevin O'Higgins and J.J. Walsh. Supporters showed their allegiance by referring to Cumann na nGaedheal as 'the Cosgrave party'. But he was also the face of a government that had stagnated, and if he had become leader of Fine Gael it would have immediately established continuity with Cumann na nGaedheal, undoing the purpose of creating a new party. While that was unacceptable to MacDermot, there were elements even within Cumann na nGaedheal who were unsure about his suitability. When Cosgrave did eventually return to the helm after O'Duffy's departure, Tierney lamented that the development 'quite blasts all chances of beating Dev in any measurable time'.[10]

Who was Eoin O'Duffy? And why was the man described by his biographer as one of the most egregious figures of modern Ireland chosen to lead Fine Gael? It is important to remember that, if it had not been for the final phase of his public life, when O'Duffy openly embraced fascism, he would have been remembered as a patriot and state-builder.[11] It was precisely that reputation in 1933 that allowed him to claim the presidency of Fine Gael.

O'Duffy had emerged as one of the leaders of the republican movement through his association with the GAA. This was a typical route, best illustrated by Michael Collins, the most famous of the revolutionary figures to have come up this way. Collins joined the committee of Geraldines GAA club in London in January 1908, becoming club secretary by July 1909 – a role that afforded him great opportunities for networking.[12] Similarly, J.J. Walsh was a prominent separatist who went on to become Minister for Posts and Telegraphs in the Cumann na nGaedheal government and director of organisation for the 1924 Tailteann Games. He earned these roles because of the drive, ambition and organisational abilities he had displayed as Cork county chairman. Under his direction the Cork GAA organisation was rebuilt in 1907. O'Duffy and Walsh had crossed paths through their activism, illustrating the network of contacts to which membership provided access. Involvement with the GAA created opportunities to build and cement relationships, and to prove leadership abilities. The cross-over in membership of the GAA and the republican movement bred familiarity.

O'Duffy joined Harps GAA club in his native Co. Monaghan in 1910, motivated more by the social and cultural aspects than any real love of playing the sport. His talent for organisation made him a valuable member, and it was not long before he was travelling throughout Ulster to promote and help build the association. Between 1912 and 1922 he served as secretary and subsequently vice-chairman of the Ulster Council, before becoming a member of the central executive of the GAA until 1934. Along with Patrick Whelan, he did much to rebuild the GAA in Co. Monaghan, which had gone into decline in the 1890s.[13] His contributions were acknowledged by the contemporary press, which attributed Monaghan's advancement to him.[14]

Similarities between his drive and organisation work in the GAA and later with the IRA have been observed, the former providing the training ground for the latter. O'Duffy attributed his decision to join the Irish Volunteers to his involvement with the GAA and the encouragement he received from Collins, who – O'Duffy's claim went – had approached him because of the strength of Monaghan GAA. In fact O'Duffy's membership predates his meeting with Collins, and this invented timeline illustrates O'Duffy's propensity to revise his personal history. His advancement within the Volunteers owed much to his role in the GAA, providing him with a rich recruitment pool. The energy and commitment he had shown in promoting the association was replicated in his drive for the Volunteers, earning him a reputation as the leading republican in Co. Monaghan. By 1918 he had become a driving force behind the IRA nationally, touring the country, organising and reorganising.

His arrest that year confirmed his credentials in republican circles. On his release he played a key role in the independence struggle, marking himself out as one of the most effective IRA leaders in Ulster. When the IRA was reorganised in 1921, O'Duffy was appointed to GHQ as director of organisation, an influential post previously held by Collins. This placed him at the nerve centre of IRA operations. Such prominence later helped facilitate O'Duffy's work managing the expectations of rank-and-file members in the aftermath of the Truce and subsequently convincing them to support the Treaty settlement. He shared Collins's view that the Treaty would be a stepping-stone towards a republic.[15]

Following Collins's assassination in August 1922, Kevin O'Higgins – in his role as Minister for Home Affairs – sought to appoint O'Duffy as commissioner of the Civic Guard. With a record of organisation in the GAA and subsequently the IRA, along with his republican credentials, O'Duffy was considered a safe pair of hands at a time when the stability of the new state was threatened by Collins's death. Taking up the post in September 1922, he was tasked with building the force that would later become the Garda Síochána, tackling discipline and ensuring an ethos in line with the aims of the new state. He held the post until 1933, when he was controversially dismissed by the de Valera government – before he was ever connected with the Blueshirts.

Before his descent into fascism O'Duffy had moved in the right circles, had proved his abilities, and was both respected and trusted by many of his peers – although W.T. Cosgrave was a notable exception. While he inevitably upset some people along the way, the decision to appoint him first president of Fine Gael was not a problematic one at the time. He was seen by contemporaries as an energetic and somewhat charismatic figure, a man with an 'unimpeachable character and an unassailable record', according to an editorial in the *Kilkenny People*.[16] He seemed to have the promise of being another Michael Collins type: someone who could excite the party in a way that Cosgrave could not. Had Cosgrave demanded it he probably could have retained the leadership.

But while he had shown himself capable of taking charge – even from his sick bed, as seen during the army crisis in 1924 – and making tough decisions, it had never been his style to assert himself in that type of way. In keeping with the attitude that he had displayed towards the state over the previous ten years, he put the needs of both the party and state above personal interest and made unity a central theme in his public speeches on the formation of Fine Gael. Although he declared to the press, 'I have the maximum of confidence in the leader', the reality was that he was unsure of O'Duffy, a man he had not recommended for the leadership.[17] But he was enough of a pragmatist to realise that stepping aside for a leader who was not a TD meant that he would be de facto leader of the parliamentary party in the Dáil anyway.

O'Duffy was to have six vice-presidents, the identities of whom reveal another important element of Fine Gael's birth story. Cosgrave, Michael

Tierney and James Hogan represented continuity with Cumann na nGaedheal, while Tierney and Hogan were also prominent members of the Blueshirts. The National Centre Party was represented by MacDermot.

The inclusion of Peter Nugent and James Dillon is an interesting one. They acted as a bridge to the Irish Party tradition. When the party was virtually wiped out by Sinn Féin at the 1918 general election, several of its members re-emerged in political life as supporters of the Treaty and joined Cumann na nGaedheal. Others found a new political home in the mid-1920s when John Redmond's son William founded the National League, considered the natural heir to the Irish Party. The party disappeared as quickly as it arrived and many of its members, including William Redmond, took the Cumann na nGaedheal whip. Reflecting on his party's roots at an ard-fheis in May 1930, Ernest Blythe spoke not only of revolutionary Sinn Féin but also of the nationalist movements and its supporters who were subsequently attracted into his party.[18]

While Peter Nugent had no personal experience as a politician, his father was John Dillon Nugent, national secretary of the Ancient Order of Hibernians, a secretive Catholic fraternity whose resources he is believed to have used to intimidate opponents of the Irish Party.[19] Son of John Dillon, the last leader of the Irish Parliamentary Party, James was the embodiment of that party's tradition. It was this element of Fine Gael's creation that inspired the future Taoiseach John Bruton. There is a tradition that each Taoiseach hangs a portrait of a significant political leader in their office; that person is typically a key figure from the relevant party's history or from the revolutionary period. When he took office in 1994, Bruton opted for John Redmond, rather than Michael Collins. He has always been keen to emphasise the constitutional nationalist element of Fine Gael's longer history, considering it an important facet that has been too much overlooked.[20]

Fine Gael issued a six-point statement to the press on 8 September 1933, followed by a more detailed 25-point programme on 11 November, before the 1934 ard-fheis. Although the influence of Frank MacDermot can clearly be seen in both documents, their content ultimately – and not surprisingly – represented continuity with much of Cumann na nGaedheal's previous policies. The position on Northern Ireland remained unchanged; plans for tackling unemployment were similar; and reform of the voting system also featured. The most obvious difference was the proposal for the establishment of industrial and agricultural corporations.

Despite MacDermot's protestations that Fine Gael was a new entity, opponents and commentators were quick to claim that Fine Gael was simply a rebranded Cumann na nGaedheal. As the Labour leader William Norton colourfully put it, 'the new move was an attempt to put old wine in new bottles.'[21] MacDermot quickly grew tired of such barbed comments, snapping in the Dáil that he declined to spend his time 'reading up old files for the purpose of defending every past action of the Cumann na nGaedheal party'.[22] He never got over his unease with the merger, though, and he resigned from the party in October in 1935; he later joined Fianna Fáil and served in the Seanad.

In the decades since 1933, as a search of the digitised Oireachtas debates will confirm, this notion of continuity has been perpetuated, with politicians such as Seán MacEntee, Fianna Fáil Minister for Health, claiming that 'the sins of the Cumann na nGaedheal are the sins of Fine Gael.'[23] There have been references in the Dáil and Seanad to Cumann na nGaedheal's reduction of teachers' salaries, alleged patronage, perceived responsibility for partition, unemployment, and neglect of social services, as well as numerous mentions of Ernest Blythe's notorious pension cut, among other political sins – all reintroduced into political debate for the purpose of point-scoring against the Fine Gael party of the day.

By far, though, the quickest and easiest way to antagonise a Fine Gael politician or supporter is to invoke the Blueshirts. In recent years there has been something of an attempt by party members to reclaim the term, self-labelling themselves in a playful, light-hearted way. Nonetheless it remains a useful slur to be employed by critics. Were the Blueshirts Ireland's fascists? The nature of the movement has been the subject of much debate. The very name immediately evokes thoughts of Mussolini's Blackshirts in Italy and Hitler's Brownshirts in Germany. Plenty of photographic evidence exists of blueshirt-wearing members raising an arm in the style of the Nazi salute. But drawing comparisons with European fascist movements – and their shirted uniform in particular – both helps and hinders our understanding of the Irish movement.[24]

The liturgical element of the Blueshirts – a defining component of fascist movements – was highly developed. The choice of colour for the uniform, adopted at the suggestion of Ernest Blythe, was deliberate. Blue is attributed to Ireland's patron saint, and its use connected the movement to the country's historical mythology. The mobilisation of past heroes is central to fascist rhetoric: in France, for example, the Parti Populaire Français invoked Joan of Arc. A connection with St Patrick was created through the incorporation of the so-called St Patrick's cross in the movement's emblems, badges and flags.

Wherever branches existed, in the fashion of the German and Italian experience there were weekly parades and marches after Sunday Mass. Members attending public meetings were required to wear the uniform, a blue shirt with black buttons and a black beret; such gatherings were a show of strength, projecting the image of a disciplined and dynamic mass movement. O'Duffy claimed that at its height the movement had 100,000 members; the actual figure is more likely to have been half that.[25] Styling himself the 'third most important man in Europe', O'Duffy provided the scope for the cult of the leader that is central to fascism. He encouraged calls of 'Hoch O'Duffy', deliberately imitating the German greeting *Heil Hitler*.

Clearly, then, the Blueshirts possessed certain fascist traits, influenced by developments on the Continent. This was certainly how the organisation was perceived by opponents at the time. As P.J. Ruttledge, the Fianna Fáil Minister for Justice, suggested in the Dáil,

> the uniform, and indeed the objects of the organisation which dons the uniform, seem to have been copied, without practically a comma being changed, from similar organisations in continental countries.[26]

Responses such as that by John A. Costello helped compound such views. He declared that

> the Blackshirts were victorious in Italy and … the Hitler Shirts were victorious in Germany, as assuredly … the Blueshirts will be victorious in the Irish Free State.[27]

Prominent members, such as Tierney, Hogan, Blythe and Desmond FitzGerald, also all expressed undisguised admiration for Mussolini. But, as the historian Mike Cronin has emphasised, it is important to acknowledge that the Dáil and the Senate featured in the Blueshirt vision for a restructured Irish state. It was never intended that parliamentary democracy be disestablished (although some members – in the minority – did imply this). It is on this point that the Blueshirt ideology diverged from its Continental counterparts, making it a para-fascist organisation.

There was another side to the Blueshirts: the sports and social gatherings. While these were common to authoritarian movements of both the left and right, there was already a well-established pattern of Irish movements using recreation and entertainment to boost engagement and membership. Meetings of Daniel O'Connell's repeal movement were purposely held on fair days to encourage a spirit of revelry; Father Mathew's temperance movement offered a variety of recreational activities as an alternative to alcohol; and the IRB used sports gatherings as a cover for their political meetings. There was also another uniquely Irish aspect of such an agenda in the 1930s. In the context of rural Ireland at that time, social gatherings offered a release from an otherwise mundane life.[28]

Cinema and imported newspapers and magazines proved extremely popular at this time, and it was for that reason that they were so loudly denounced by the Catholic Church.[29] The excitement that something out of the ordinary could elicit is perfectly captured in Ken Loach's film *Jimmy's Hall* (2014). Based on the true story of Jimmy Gralton and set in Co. Leitrim in the early 1930s, the film shows a small rural community of all ages enthusiastically embracing Gralton's hall – in defiance of the local priest – as a venue for social, cultural and sports opportunities. There was an obvious market for social stimulation. Under O'Duffy's direction, dances, cycling excursions, picnics, sports days, Gaelic football, hurling and boxing matches were organised throughout the country. The appeal was obvious, particularly for younger residents of rural communities. As one former member, Dennis Reynolds from Co. Cavan, recalled,

> Locally when they organised the social stuff, the whole of the young Blueshirts went. It was a great attraction because the other side didn't do anything like that. I suppose if you weren't a Blueshirts you wouldn't normally be getting to a social at that age, but we got to them, and there was great support for them.[30]

Such gatherings were largely intended to boost membership and cement unity in the movement, but they were also influenced by O'Duffy's belief in the power of sport to create a fit and disciplined society. The motivation of those who attended sports or social gatherings is complex, and it is impossible to establish the extent to which they were influenced by political ideology or were simply capitalising on an opportunity to socialise. If the latter was the case for many of the rank and file, it does not negate the fact that the organisation itself exhibited many of the traits of the Continental fascist movements.

If the Blueshirts are best understood as para-fascists, what of Eoin O'Duffy? His leadership of Fine Gael had a promising start. Meetings were held around the country and greater attention was paid to the branch structure than had been the case during the Cumann na nGaedheal era. By March 1934 an energetic O'Duffy had spoken at meetings in twenty-three of the twenty-six counties; increasingly these became Blueshirt rallies, with the right-arm salute a growing feature.[31] Any early promise O'Duffy showed of being the next Michael Collins was not borne out. On reflection, this promise was really the product of his own invention – an example of his predilection for self-aggrandisement. Of his contemporaries, Mussolini and Franco offer more useful parallels in terms of personality and politics. Flawed figures, plagued by insecurity and a hunger for adulation, they wrote and rewrote their personas.[32]

A detailed examination of the activities of the Blueshirts in the aftermath of the formation of Fine Gael is beyond the scope of this book. Curious readers can find greater detail expertly outlined in histories of the movement written by Maurice Manning and Mike Cronin, and in Fearghal McGarry's biography of O'Duffy. Briefly put, the Young Ireland Association was banned, although it quickly reformed as the League of Youth, and the Wearing of Uniforms (Restriction) Bill was introduced by the Minister for Justice, Patrick Ruttledge, in 1934 to outlaw the Blueshirt uniform after some Fine Gael politicians began wearing it in the chamber. Badges, banners and military titles that were considered at odds with public peace would also be prohibited. But the bill never became an act. After an acrimonious debate in the Dáil, the Senate rejected the proposal by 30 votes to 18. The bill was suspended for a period of eighteen months, but by then the perceived Blueshirt threat had receded.

O'Duffy faced his first electoral test as Fine Gael president at the 1934 local elections. It was an opportunity to show that the new party had attracted strong support and that the government's efforts to ban the Blueshirts were unpopular. Contesting the elections also made a break with Cumann na nGaedheal tradition; Cosgrave's party had not attached importance to contesting such elections. The results revealed O'Duffy's political naïveté. Having forecast that the party would take control of twenty out of the twenty-three councils, Fine Gael won control of only six.[33] Thereafter, a new note of extremism crept into O'Duffy's speeches. In particular, his call for farmers to withhold payment of land annuities sat uneasily with Fine Gael colleagues. Such an open call of defiance was difficult to reconcile with the image of Fine Gael as a constitutional party, and leading members were resistant to O'Duffy's proposition that non-payment should be adopted as official Fine Gael policy. James Hogan resigned from the National Executive in protest against what he considered to be O'Duffy's 'generally destructive and hysterical leadership'.[34] In a letter to Tierney, Hogan further claimed that O'Duffy had made 'every conceivable blunder'.[35] Other Blueshirt leaders, including Commandant Ned Cronin and Captain Dennis Quish, were also becoming reckless. Elements of some of their more notorious speeches have been preserved, after Ruttledge entered them in the Dáil record by reading out extracts in the chamber.[36]

As O'Duffy's extremism grew, it was those members of the Blueshirts who were dedicated to democracy – most notably Blythe, Tierney and FitzGerald – who worked to remove him from the Fine Gael leadership. With his growing embrace of fascist ideology, O'Duffy was a leader that a democratic political party, one that prided itself on commitment to law and order, could not afford. This ran counter to the Continental fascist movements, differentiating the Blueshirts from otherwise comparable organisations in Italy and Germany. Talks took place between O'Duffy, Cosgrave, Dillon and Cronin, all of which were held in secret, breeding speculation, rumours and counter-claims about what occurred. Ultimately O'Duffy resigned at a meeting of the party on 21 September. Members had not been forewarned, though the announcement can hardly have come as a surprise. O'Duffy had essentially been stage-managed out of the presidency. He succumbed to cultural extremism long before fascism, seeing his role while Garda commissioner not just as law enforcement but also as a defender of morality. Although his fascist views were evident then, it was only after he departed from Fine Gael that he gave full expression to them.[37]

The whole matter of O'Duffy's resignation from the presidency, according to James Dillon, 'shattered' the party's morale, although he did not 'count the cost of his departure excessive'.[38] His departure left a vacancy that Fine Gael was not quick to fill. Cosgrave, as the de facto leader of the party in the Dáil and the most experienced politician in the parliamentary party, was an obvious choice. That a conscious decision was taken to delay appointing a successor until the ard-fheis, scheduled for March 1935, implied a lack of enthusiasm about Cosgrave resuming duties. When the party gathered on that occasion, Cosgrave was unanimously selected as O'Duffy's replacement. Either the concerns about his abilities had abated or the party lacked credible alternatives. The truth probably lies somewhere in between.

The Blueshirts may have dominated the political scene for about two years, and they had been a critical part of the merger that created Fine Gael, temporarily overshadowing the party, but once O'Duffy was removed from the presidency and the principles of fascism were rejected, the movement petered out, collapsing in on itself.

The organisation's legacy to Fine Gael, however, is disproportionate to its involvement with the party. Opposition TDs – such as Mattie McGrath, quoted at the opening of this chapter – continue to gleefully use the Blueshirts to taunt Fine Gael deputies. As noted in our introduction, when Leo Varadkar criticised Sinn Féin for holding rallies after the 2020 election, some people took to Twitter to share pictures of Blueshirt rallies. It is hardly surprising then that Fine Gael chooses to play down this element of its history, opting instead to highlight the heroic Michael Collins. A membership drive by Young Fine Gael captioned the iconic image of Collins in his commander-in-chief uniform at the funeral of Arthur Griffith in August 1922, 'From leaders of the past to the leaders of the future, join Young Fine Gael.' Focusing on Collins – the 'lost leader' – provides Fine Gael with a marketable, romantic figure, who was appealing long before Warner Brothers decided to make him the subject of the biopic released in 1996.

Collins is inextricably associated with the glory of the revolutionary period, and even before his death he drew attention. He was offered £10,000 from a London agent and $20,000 from the *New York World* for his memoirs.[39] No matter how dubious his reputation was to his opponents, for his supporters and the subsequent party faithful Collins's assassination at the age of thirty-one sealed his fate as a patriot and an icon. He subsequently took his place in the Fine Gael pantheon of great leaders.

This is a problematic, selective interpretation of the party's history. Collins was dead almost eight months before Cumann na nGaedheal was founded and more than a decade before Fine Gael was created. But O'Duffy is too problematic to ever feature in any form of official commemoration. Although he was a complex figure – someone who had all the makings of a patriot – the ease with which 'Blueshirt' can be used as a term of abuse has left party members shy about engaging with their first president.

In 2008 members, supporters and other invited guests of Fine Gael assembled in the Green Isle hotel, Dublin. The leaflet produced for the occasion featured a picture of W.T. Cosgrave on the front. The cover announced the purpose of the gathering as 'The 75th Anniversary of the Founding of the Fine Gael Party'. Addressing the audience, the UCD historian Michael Laffan pondered whether the event was celebrating the right birthday. He was referring, of course, to the fact that W.T. Cosgrave's image was reproduced on the cover of the event's programme, accompanied by the caption 'First President of the Executive Council of the Irish Free State'. Fine Gael did not exist at that time, and Cosgrave was not the party's first leader. It is not surprising that O'Duffy's portrait was not used on that occasion, and it is unlikely to ever be used to represent the party. A message from Enda Kenny, then party leader, inside the leaflet affirmed how he felt 'privileged to follow the noble tradition set down by Collins, Griffith and Cosgrave and our many distinguished leaders since'. Claiming continuity with Collins or Cumann na nGaedheal is a convenient way for Fine Gael to sidestep any need to confront the reality that Eoin O'Duffy – the man indelibly linked with the Blueshirts – was the party's first president. Without the Blueshirts, however, there might not have been a Fine Gael.

JOHN A. COSTELLO AND THE FIRST INTER-PARTY GOVERNMENT

'We are leaving you this country in good shape … Make sure you hand it back that way.'

— Seán Lemass (Fianna Fáil), 1948.

T he nature of the Irish political system changed on 18 February 1948. For the first time in the history of the state, a coalition, describing itself as an inter-party government, was formed. Composed of Fine Gael, the Labour Party, the National Labour Party, Clann na Talmhan, Clann na Poblachta and six independents, it was a disparate grouping, brought together to end sixteen years of Fianna Fáil government. Its existence proved there was an alternative to the dominance of Éamon de Valera's party. John A. Costello of Fine Gael was elected Taoiseach by 75 votes to 68.

Though much repeated, no account of the government's formation would be complete without Patrick Lindsay's recollection of hearing the news. His reported exchange with a garda in Galway illustrates how a sense of change hung in the air.

I drove into Tuam and I saw there the large physique of a man, a civic guard, who was standing on the footpath. I pulled in diagonally and lowered my window.

'Guard, is there any news from Dublin?'

'At ten past five this afternoon, Mr John Aloysius Costello was elected Taoiseach of this country.'

I knew by the way he said it, that this really meant something to him and I said: 'Guard, would you like a drink?'

'We'll have two.'

'Will you want a minute, until I park this car?'

'Leave it where it is. We have freedom for the first time in sixteen years.'

We had more than one drink that day.[1]

The garda's pleasure was mirrored in the Dáil, where Oliver J. Flanagan, then an independent, proclaimed, 'Thanks be to God that I have lived to see this day.' The inter-party government's term in office – best remembered for the declaration of the republic and the failure of the Mother and Child scheme – was industrious, at times fractious, and, above all, lively.

Not since Cumann na nGaedheal left office in 1932 had Fine Gael politicians experienced government. In the sixteen years since then, Eoin O'Duffy had resigned the presidency and W.T. Cosgrave had returned to the helm, remaining in the post until his retirement in 1944. He was succeeded by Richard Mulcahy, another key figure from the Cumann na nGaedheal era. By the time he became leader, the party was in disarray, with politicians acting more like independents, some of whom were busying themselves with their other careers. Fine Gael was also beset by financial difficulty. The party's image was not helped by the fact that its president was now a member of the Seanad, rather than the Dáil; Mulcahy had lost his seat the previous year. Its fortunes were further undermined by the emergence of Clann na Talmhan. Created in Galway in June 1939 to represent the interests of small farmers, the party attracted votes away from Fine Gael, as well as from Fianna Fáil.

Coming out of the 1948 election with thirty-one seats, Fine Gael was the largest party that made up the inter-party government. As leader, Mulcahy should have become Taoiseach. Indeed, he had written to the leaders of the other four parties after the results, inviting them to enter discussions about forming a government. But he was too closely connected to the Civil War to be acceptable to the republican Clann na Poblachta. Founded only two years earlier and led by the former IRA chief of staff Seán MacBride, the party had its roots in protest against the Fianna Fáil government's handling of republican prisoners, and it became home for those republicans disillusioned with the party.[2]

Having been IRA chief of staff during the War of Independence, Mulcahy then served as chief of staff of the army during the Civil War, becoming commander in chief after Collins was killed. As Minister for Defence in the Cumann na nGaedheal government he had been an outspoken critic of the republican movement. His connection with the execution of seventy-seven republican prisoners during the Civil War earned him the reputation with his opponents of a murderer. This label spread in the republican community, and on a visit to Boston in October 1925 he encountered protesters carrying signs that read, 'Mulcahy executioner of Erskine Childers', 'Mulcahy the King's butcher' and 'Mulcahy Irish Benedict Arnold'.[3]

Free from such baggage, John A. Costello was the compromise Taoiseach. MacBride had earlier suggested Sir John Esmonde, the Fine Gael TD for Wexford who had previously served as an Irish Party MP, but he readily agreed to Costello, whom he described as 'businesslike and capable'.[4] Costello's political ideology, like Esmonde's, was shaped by the constitutional nationalist tradition, and he identified with the Redmondite strand. Unlike W.T. Cosgrave and Éamon de Valera, Costello had no role in the fighting during the Easter Rising and the independence campaign that followed, or the subsequent Civil War. Although never having held ministerial office, he was an experienced politician. He served as Attorney General in the Cumann na nGaedheal government from 1926 until 1932, representing the Free State at Imperial Conferences and meetings of the League of Nations, giving him an insight into the workings of international politics. He was first elected to the Dáil for the Dublin County constituency in 1933. Although he lost his seat in 1943, he won it back the following year and would hold it each subsequent election until his retirement in 1969.

Like many politicians of his era, Costello attended Mass most days. His faith became particularly pertinent in commentaries on the Mother and Child controversy in the 1950s and led to an enduring myth that he described himself as a Catholic above all else (see below). Double-jobbing was a feature of Irish political life at this time, and Costello was no exception. He had a stellar legal career, which often distracted his attention from his service as a TD. His passion for the law was such that, in opposition, he was essentially a part-time politician. This would later prevent him from becoming the sole leader of Fine Gael in 1959.

For many years, he was a neglected figure in Fine Gael. The major survey of party members undertaken by Michael Gallagher and Michael Marsh in 1999 found that he was the least popular of the past Fine Gael Taoisigh. Gallagher and Marsh could offer no explanation, but they suggested that his relatively low score may simply reflect the fact that many Fine Gael members had little knowledge of him and his record. This has been addressed in recent years. The publication of David McCullagh's extensive biography in 2010, the annual Costello Commemoration in Dean's Grange Cemetery, inaugurated in 2016, and events to mark the seventieth anniversary of the declaration of the republic have made his name more prominent.

Costello did not seek the office of Taoiseach. In a letter to his son Declan he revealed his anxieties, admitting to a 'fear amounting almost to terror that I would be a flop as Taoiseach and bring discredit on the new administration if it was formed.'[5] He was, to use Brian Farrell's classification, a chairman rather than a chief, and at cabinet meetings he sat at the side, not the head, of the table. One of his greatest achievements was holding together such a disparate coalition.

Costello did not select his own cabinet. Rather, the departments were divided up among the government members, and party leaders nominated their respective choices. Only two TDs in the new cabinet had previous ministerial experience. Both of these were from Fine Gael, which as the largest party got the greatest number of ministries. Costello filled them with well-known names, some of whom stretched back to the Cumann na nGaedheal era. The highly experienced Patrick McGilligan took the important portfolio of Finance. Given the clashes he had with Finance civil servants as Minister for Industry and Commerce when he was planning the Shannon Scheme in the 1920s, and the fact that he bypassed the department entirely to announce that he had funds for the project, there was a certain irony in his appointment. With the Shannon Scheme he had proved himself capable of big thinking, though he would have presented a challenge to the conservative-minded department.

Richard Mulcahy's appointment as Minister for Education further emphasised continuity with the Cumann na nGaedheal era; as already noted, Mulcahy had then served as Minister for Defence and later of Local Government and Public Health. If he could not be Taoiseach, Mulcahy might have expected a more prominent portfolio, although Education suited him. He showed restraint at cabinet meetings, and he confined himself to his brief. McGilligan and Mulcahy were joined at the cabinet table by his party colleagues Seán Mac Eoin in Justice, T.F. O'Higgins in Defence, and Daniel Morrissey in Industry and Commerce.

In contrast to Costello's appointment of long-serving politicians, Dr Noël Browne of Clann na Poblachta was made Minister for Health on his first day in the Dáil. Completely inexperienced in politics, it has been suggested that his nomination was intended to allay concerns by Fine Gael about a strong republican presence at the cabinet table.[6] He cut a lonely figure in the cabinet. Seán MacBride, the Clann leader and son of the revolutionaries Major John MacBride and Maud Gonne, took the External Affairs portfolio. Because of his responsibility for Ireland's participation in the European Recovery Programme, he regularly wandered into matters under the purview of Finance and had far greater influence over economic policy than any of his predecessors.

The Labour leader William Norton became Minister for Social Welfare and Tánaiste; he was a close confidant of Costello during their term. His party colleague T.J. Murphy was made Minister for Local Government, and, following his death in April 1949, Michael Keyes was elevated to minister.

James Everett of National Labour took Posts and Telegraphs and caused a scandal (discussed below), while Joseph Blowick of Clann na Talmhan went to Lands and Fisheries and made little impact. Blowick could reasonably have expected Agriculture, but that post was filled by James Dillon, who represented the independents in the cabinet. Dillon had left Fine Gael over its continued endorsement of neutrality during the Second World War, and he refused invitations to rejoin when the government was being formed. By becoming Minister for Agriculture, he achieved one of his political ambitions, and he would be far happier in that post than his later role as party leader when he eventually returned to Fine Gael (see Chapter 5). With Dillon holding that portfolio, Blowick lost the opportunity to make a mark in the area of greatest relevance to Clann na Talmhan supporters.

The inter-party government featured strong personalities, differences of opinion in policy and sometimes conflicting ideologies. As government chief whip, Liam Cosgrave had a hard task. Seán Lemass's response to his party's defeat, quoted at the opening of this chapter, indicates that he fully expected the government to be a temporary arrangement and that Fianna Fáil would soon pick up the reins of power once more. With a relatively strong opposition and a proliferation of often contradictory views among the parties in power, the inter-party government could have been very unstable. This was not helped by the fact that the principle of collective responsibility that had operated at cabinet level since the birth of the state was virtually abandoned. That the government lasted for almost three-and-a-half years is remarkable. This was due in large part to Costello's leadership. Cosgrave later reminisced that, as different as they were, the cabinet members were 'united in their dedication to John Costello as a man of the very highest integrity'.[7]

The so-called 'Battle of Baltinglass' shone a spotlight on Costello's efforts to present a united public face. In his capacity as Minister for Post and Telegraphs, Everett, a National Labour TD for Wicklow, took the decision to transfer a postmaster's job in a post office in his constituency in 1950. The Baltinglass branch had been passed down through generations of the Cooke family since 1880. But when Katie Cooke tried to pass the postmistress role to her niece, Helen, she was informed that only direct relatives were eligible for succession. As upsetting as this news was, the family was further incensed to learn that Everett had awarded the branch to Michael Farrell, son of a local Labour councillor who was known to be a close friend of the Minister. The whole affair smacked of corruption and jobbery, and it made a mockery of the anti-corruption platform that members of the government had assumed during the 1948 election campaign. In the face of fervent opposition from local people in Baltinglass and criticism from Fianna Fáil TDs, Everett maintained that the decision was fair. The embattled minister refused to consider his position amidst calls for his resignation. Costello backed Everett, refusing to give time for a private member's motion calling for an inquiry.[8] As Taoiseach, he was attempting to preserve the unity of his government, but the whole debacle led to resignations from Clann na Poblachta and Fine Gael. The government's reputation was tarnished.

Because of the existence of a variety of views on economic policy, Costello was also more active in directing budgetary policy than either Cosgrave or de Valera had been as head of their governments. He was aided by Patrick Lynch, an economist in the Department of Finance who was transferred to the Taoiseach's office following the recommendation of Alexis Fitzgerald, Costello's trusted son-in-law. The first capital budget was introduced in 1950. Although within the remit of Patrick McGilligan's Department of Finance, the genesis of this innovation lay in a speech, written by Fitzgerald and Lynch, that Costello delivered to the Institute of Bankers in November 1949. By separating capital investment from other spending, the potential for borrowing for capital projects would not be constrained by the need to balance the budget.[9] McGilligan strongly supported the direction in which Costello and his advisers took economic policy. His own Shannon Scheme in the 1920s was testament to what could be achieved through state involvement. T.K. Whitaker is often popularly thought of as having ushered in a new era of economic planning in Ireland after 1958; but to qualify for Marshall Aid, governments had had to devise a plan for spending.[10]

While seeking to maintain financial stability, Costello found capacity for investment in the arts. His government introduced the first Arts Bill – one of his passion projects – that led to the establishment of the Arts Council, albeit after he had left government in 1951. Costello had shown his commitment to the arts through his long-standing efforts to recover thirty-nine Impressionist paintings bequeathed by Hugh Lane to Ireland. As Attorney General in the 1920s, Costello had been involved in attempts to secure the return of the paintings from the National Gallery in London. As Taoiseach he once more took up the case. During trade talks in 1948 he informally raised the issue with the British Prime Minister, Clement Attlee, although to no avail. He did, however, introduce the possibility of the two countries sharing the pictures, which would later become the case.

A campaign to persuade emigrants to return to Ireland was organised in 1949 and 1950. The brochure *Ireland is Building*, published in 1949, promised jobs, good pay and a secure future. Irish workers were invited to return home to participate in the 'rebuilding of Ireland for our children's children'. The strategy was underpinned by a consensus among political leaders that housing was a priority.[11] This area was one of the big success stories for the inter-party government in general and for Labour, which controlled the Department of Local Government, in particular. The construction of local authority housing jumped massively from 744 units in 1947 to 8,117 by 1950. A fall in unemployment was a natural corollary of this boom in the building industry.[12]

The Department of Agriculture was also a success story during this period. Although James Dillon was officially an independent, he was associated with Fine Gael in the eyes of many and his achievements may well have reflected positively on the party. Dillon was in the fortunate position of becoming minister at the time when loans and grant aid came through from the Marshall Plan; the money received was largely earmarked for agriculture, in the belief that Ireland's future lay in farming. Dillon was also a minister in a government that favoured greater capital investment. One of the main beneficiaries of this extra funding and economic thinking was a land rehabilitation scheme, launched by Dillon's department in 1949 and formalised in the Land Reclamation Act (1949).

The project sought to rejuvenate four-and-a-half million acres of land made derelict because of the quality of the soil and damaged by the policy of compulsory tillage that operated between 1940 and 1948. Farmers who wished to participate in the scheme would have two-thirds of the cost covered by the state. For Dillon personally, this project represented a continuation of his father's work; John Dillon had been heavily involved with the Irish National Land League in the late nineteenth century. As he admitted to the Dáil, 'I do not deny that it gives me a certain satisfaction to have been appointed by my own people to repair the land in 1949 which the Land League recovered for our people in 1879.'[13]

Irish governments have since been criticised for concentrating funds from the Marshall aid programme on agriculture, with Mary E. Daly observing that other European countries made better use of the opportunities and resources offered.[14] But, as Brian Maye has suggested in the context of Dillon's land reclamation scheme, whatever the economic impact, the psychological impact of bringing hope to very poor districts, especially in the west of Ireland, was great.[15] The project was a big success for the farmers who participated, marking Dillon out as a minister who could deliver. Department of Finance officials were less enamoured, however, and, as Dillon's biographer notes, there was an extraordinary exchange of letters between the minister and the secretary of the Department, J.J. McElligott, in which Dillon asserted his power and admonished the secretary.[16]

The removal of a large statue of Queen Victoria from the Kildare Street entrance of Leinster House shortly after the inter-party government took office was an early indication of the government's attitude towards the symbols of the Anglo-Irish relationship. The departure of the 'famine queen' prompted much comment; but by far the most dramatic development in Anglo-Irish relations occurred while Costello was in Canada in September 1948. There he declared his intention to withdraw Ireland from the Commonwealth, making it a republic. Doing so would finally settle the question of Ireland's constitutional status. Although de Valera's 1937 constitution, by his own admission, had made Ireland a republic in everything but name, the precise nature of the country's status was ambiguous. Although it was Clann na Poblachta that first introduced the prospect of repealing the External Relations Act on the day that the inter-party government took power, it was an objective shared throughout the government. De Valera also offered reassurances that his party would not oppose any moves to repeal the act.

The External Relations (Executive Authority) Act had been a return to 'document number 2', the unsuccessful alternative to the 1921 Treaty that de Valera had produced during the debates. Removing the Crown from Irish affairs as he systematically dismantled the Treaty once in power after 1932, his External Relations Act retained an external link with Britain. As he explained, 'we are an independent republic associated for foreign policy with the states of the British commonwealth.' Consequently, the British monarch still authorised the credentials carried by Irish diplomats. Costello described the bill as a 'constitutional monstrosity'.[17] By 1947, it was evident that the Act had not had the desired effect of settling the question of Ireland's status; any link with Britain served to undermine the claim that Ireland was in effect a republic. De Valera sent instructions to the secretary of the Department of External Affairs, Frederick Boland, to begin preparations to repeal the act, although it ultimately fell to the inter-party government to do so.

Several explanations have been advanced for why Costello announced Ireland's intentions when and where he did. One of the more interesting ones relates to a dinner hosted by the Governor General of Canada, Lord Alexander, on 4 September. It was an event that was punctuated by two, rather big, slights. These occurred only days after Costello complained that he had been cold-shouldered by Alexander at a tea party at McGill University and after there had been a toast only to the King at the meeting of the Canadian Bar Association that Costello addressed. At the dinner, a replica of the cannon known as Roaring Meg sat on the dining table, otherwise decorated with a green, white and orange flower arrangement. This was a politically sensitive, or in this case insensitive, symbol. The

Apprentice Boys had used Roaring Meg in the Siege of Derry in 1689, and the cannon serves as a hallowed symbol of unionist triumph, or, as Costello saw it, the 'gun used against our people'. The replica had been presented to the Governor General when he was made a Freeman of the city of Derry six months earlier. It seems that it did not occur to anyone that it would be in bad taste to use it as a table decoration.

To add insult to injury, it was understood by the Irish guests that a toast would be made to both the King and the President of Ireland, but the latter did not happen. The myth formed that Costello declared the republic in a fit of pique because he had been insulted. Through the retelling of details of the evening to multiple people on his return to Dublin, he perpetuated this interpretation.[18]

Costello's announcement may have been dramatic, but it was not sudden. The External Relations Act had been discussed at a meeting of the cabinet on 19 August, the last before Costello departed for Canada. It seems likely that repealing it had been agreed then. What had not been agreed was how and when the announcement would be made. But, as one commentator put it shortly afterwards, Costello was 'almost like a child with a secret, could not hold it'. In a letter to the Tánaiste, William Norton, Costello explained that 'it was really the article in the *Sunday Independent* that decided me.' He was referring to the front-page story published by the newspaper on 5 September, the day after the dinner, under the headline 'External Relations Act to go'. That evening, pressed for a comment from a Canadian journalist, he declined to say anything further. Before the story ever broke, though, he was already scheduled to give a press conference on 7 September, and it was at that event that he confirmed that the External Relations Act would be repealed and Ireland would leave the Commonwealth.

Costello returned to Dublin to a gathering of several thousand at the Mansion House, where he declared that the removal of the External Relations Act would end bitterness and remove all strife between every section of the people. James Dillon was not in attendance, and his absence was interpreted by some as a silent protest against Ireland's withdrawal from the Commonwealth. Dillon, however, was firmly opposed to the

External Relations Act, and his absence was presumably due to other reasons. Publicly, at least, Costello's ministers showed their support for their Taoiseach's actions.

Removing Ireland from the Commonwealth had the potential to cause an identity crisis for Fine Gael. Speaking at the party's ard-fheis only four years before Costello's announcement, Richard Mulcahy had told his audience: 'We stand unequivocally for membership of the British commonwealth.'[19] This was a policy that stretched back to the party's roots in Cumann na nGaedheal. Throughout the 1920s and into the early 1930s, W.T. Cosgrave's government had worked within the framework of Commonwealth membership to push the boundaries of Irish independence. Garret FitzGerald, a supporter but not yet a member of Fine Gael, recorded in his autobiography that the decision to sever the connection had added to his unhappiness with the party. During the 1944 election, he had canvassed for Costello and had reassured residents of Waterloo Road that Fine Gael supported membership of the Commonwealth.[20] Others claimed that it would cost Fine Gael votes from the Protestant community, which typically supported the party. Addressing such criticisms, Costello spoke warmly, in almost fawning tones, of the 'Protestant minority'. He told members of the Dáil, 'They have their part to play here and when this bill has become law they will find that the position, so far from being in any way impaired, will be very considerably improved.'[21]

Costello piloted the Republic of Ireland Bill through the Dáil, and not, as would have reasonably been expected, the Minister for External Affairs. The Taoiseach was taking ownership of the process and also using it as an opportunity to further explain his position, addressing some of the concerns held within his party and by its supporters. In a marathon three-hour speech during the second stage of the bill, he very cleverly played to Fine Gael's longer history to justify the declaration of the republic. He pointed out that Cumann na nGaedheal had defended and honoured the letter of the Anglo-Irish Treaty of 1921, and, as he saw it, it was the British government that first tampered with the terms. They did so, he argued, by allowing Éamon de Valera to slowly dismantle the Treaty after he took office in 1932. Consequently, Costello's interpretation went, the British government had released those who defended and protected the Treaty from any obligation to continue upholding it.

He also positioned the decision in the longer republican tradition. While the birth of the republic could be seen as a vindication of the 'stepping-stones' theory that Michael Collins had presented during the Treaty debates, Costello went even further. Drawing on the challenge that Robert Emmet had issued in the nineteenth century to future generations, the Taoiseach conceded that the existence of partition meant that Emmet's epitaph could not yet be written. But, he explained, 'under this bill, the establishment of the Irish Republic constitutes the most important step yet taken to enable Ireland to take its place among the nations of the earth.'[22]

Symbolically, the republic came into existence on Easter Monday, April 1949, the thirty-third anniversary of the rising. In Cork, Tom Barry, commander of the old IRA, read the 1916 Proclamation from the steps of City Hall. Blazing tar barrels on the Dublin Mountains, which could be seen from the city centre, framed the scene on O'Connell Bridge, where the birth of the republic was to be marked in the capital. Crowds thronged the space, and the Tricolour flew from surrounding buildings. Just after midnight, a twenty-one-gun salute ushered in Ireland's official status as a republic. Chants of 'Up the Republic' rippled through the crowds of thousands. At one minute after midnight, Radio Éireann broadcast the historic words:

> These are the first moments of Easter Monday, April 18th, 1949. Since midnight, for the first time in history, international recognition has been accorded to the Republic of Ireland. Our listeners will join us in asking God's blessing on the Republic, and in praying that it will not be long until the sovereignty of the Republic extends over the whole of our national territory.[23]

Though not intending to dampen spirits, the broadcast served as a reminder that the question of Northern Ireland could not be escaped.

Amidst the joyous celebrations to mark the birth of the republic, the spectre of Northern Ireland loomed. While projects such as the drainage of the Erne were the product of cross-border co-operation, the Republic of Ireland Act added figurative distance between the two parts of Ireland. Files relating to the Erne Scheme show that the Department of External Affairs did not mention any potential effect that repeal might have on Dublin–Belfast relations.[24] But in response to Ireland leaving the Commonwealth, the British government enacted the Ireland Act. Speaking in the House of Commons in May 1949, the Prime Minister, Clement Attlee, reassured unionists of their position and, for the first time, a guarantee was given that any change in the status of Northern Ireland would only occur with the consent of its parliament (which was dominated by Unionists).

Aside from easing unionist fears, naval concerns must also have featured in the British decision-making process; without a base in Northern Ireland the task of keeping shipping lanes open would have been virtually impossible.[25] Whatever the motivation, partition was further entrenched. In his efforts to take the gun out of politics, Costello actually helped plant the seeds of what became the border campaign in the 1950s.

From the viewpoint of the new 26-county republic, the Republic of Ireland Act changed political debate in a number of ways. Fianna Fáil, the Republican Party, had played the green card since its creation in 1926, repeatedly painting Cumann na nGaedheal and later Fine Gael as west-British and pro-Commonwealth, implying a lack of commitment to a republic. The declaration of the republic challenged that narrative. It also facilitated a change in the language of politics. Despite the problems of the 1950s, Irish policy-makers were beginning to look to the future. By the end of that decade the debate about the symbols of independence had been replaced with a discussion about joining the European Community and about how best to build a modern economy. Seán Lemass's rising tide and economic recovery is popularly pointed to as a crucial factor in the modernisation of Ireland, but it is important to remember that the declaration of the republic also allowed the language of politics to modernise and move forward.

The declaration of the republic is Costello's most obvious claim to the old Sinn Féin tradition, but his commitment to the Cenotaph at Leinster House is also telling. Unveiled in 1923 by the Cumann na nGaedheal government, the monument commemorated Arthur Griffith and Michael Collins and, after 1927, Kevin O'Higgins. The wooden structure fell into a state of disrepair and was dismantled under Fianna Fáil in 1939. Its restoration became one of Costello's pet projects while he was in office, raising questions about the extent to which he really was neutral when it came to Civil War politics. Cabinet minutes from 7 May 1948 show agreement, on the Taoiseach's recommendation, that a permanent monument be erected at the 'earliest possible date'. The structure that now sits on Leinster Lawn is Costello's legacy, linking his name with some of the greats of Fine Gael history.

As the defining moment in the government's foreign policy, the declaration of the republic overshadows the other measures that the inter-party government, under the direction of Seán MacBride, busied itself with between 1948 and 1949. A somewhat muted issue previously, partition had made its way onto the political agenda in 1939–40 after a number of IRA incursions from independent Ireland into the North during the Second World War. Pressure from Northern nationalists for an anti-partition campaign grew during the 1940s. Although the change of government did not bring about a change of policy in the Department of External Affairs on the subject of partition, with Seán MacBride as Minister for External Affairs it was inevitable that the republican goal of ending partition would colour policy formulation. Concerned that Clann na Poblachta was stealing Fianna Fáil's clothes, de Valera embarked on a worldwide anti-partition campaign between 1948 and 1951; apart from reminding the Irish community abroad that Fianna Fáil was still the Republican Party, his tour has otherwise been described as a 'policy of futility'.[26]

Costello's government also used the international stage to pursue an active, though ultimately unsuccessful, campaign to end partition. When Ireland became a founder-member of the Council of Europe in May 1949, Irish delegates saw the forum as an opportunity to remind international colleagues about the problem of partition. But they spoke so frequently and extensively on the subject that they were regarded as boring and small-minded. An invitation to join NATO the same year was also considered an opportunity to highlight the issue of partition. Despite a shared opposition to communism, the cabinet-approved reply explained that the government could not countenance joining an organisation that included a member responsible for the 'unnatural division' of the country. It was hoped that America would put pressure on Britain to withdraw from Northern Ireland, but it was a foolish, unrealistic expectation. It showed that MacBride seriously overestimated the country's importance on the international stage. America and Britain were bonded as allies in a war in which Ireland, even though it had shown favouritism on occasion behind the scenes, had officially remained neutral. Besides, both countries already had bases in Northern Ireland, rendering the rest of the country irrelevant from a military viewpoint. This strategy was very much driven by MacBride, and it was at odds with the views of colleagues such as James Dillon, whose preference for joining was consonant with his attitude towards neutrality.[27] In response to Ireland's claim that it could not join NATO unless partition ended, the message came back that Ireland need not join NATO.

With the country also blocked from joining the United Nations by the Soviet Union – eventually admitted during a brief thaw in the Cold War in the mid-1950s – and with few embassies around the world, Ireland was virtually sidelined from international politics. This was a considerable contrast with the last time that some Fine Gael politicians had been in power. Those who had served as Cumann na nGaedheal TDs in the 1920s had been part of a government that was committed to playing an active role on the international stage, considering it crucial for cementing the Free State's status as a sovereign state. Significantly, Desmond FitzGerald, Kevin O'Higgins and Patrick McGilligan, the successive Ministers for External Affairs during the first decade of independence, diversified foreign policy beyond Anglo-Irish relations, making it truly international. With Ireland having also been a well-respected member of the League of Nations under the de Valera government, the country now became more insular as a result of the foreign policy pursued by MacBride. His remark to the Dáil in the summer of 1948 that 'the continuance of partition precludes us from taking our rightful place in the affairs of Europe' made it clear that, as long as the country remained divided, Ireland would not play a more active role internationally during his tenure.[28] The contrast in strategy and activity can be read in the pages of *Documents on Irish Foreign Policy*, the excellent multi-volume publication that reproduces material primarily from the National Archives.

On the home front, the inter-party government became mired in the Mother and Child controversy near the end of its time in power. As Minister for Health, Noël Browne wanted, in his own words, to 'revolutionise the quality of the health services'. Tuberculosis had claimed the lives of thousands of Irish people. It especially thrived in the crowded conditions of the Dublin tenements, and the fictionalised reality of James Plunkett's *Strumpet City* brilliantly captured how devastating it could be. Though the novel was set in the 1910s, and things had moved on, TB was still a very real problem when Browne became minister. A strategy for tackling the disease had been on the previous government's agenda, and the Tuberculosis (Establishment of Sanatoria) Bill was passed into law in March 1945. However, the credit for the virtual eradication of the disease rests with Browne. A medical doctor and himself a survivor of TB, Browne had lost multiple family members to the illness. As Minister for Health he introduced a free screening programme, and his department allocated considerable resources, diverted from the Hospitals Trust Fund, for a large-scale building programme to provide more hospitals and sanatoria for recovering TB patients.

As he recalled in his autobiography, the results were dramatic and immediate. There were 2,000 extra beds by July 1950 and the death rate had dropped from 123 per 100,000 in 1947 to 73 per 100,000 in 1951.[29] The availability of new drugs also contributed to this decline. Though remembered mostly by an older generation, Browne is perhaps most commonly associated now with the Mother and Child controversy, but the virtual eradication of TB is his real legacy.

A scheme providing for free medical services for mothers and their children under the age of sixteen would be the undoing of Browne's ministerial career. He was building on initiatives undertaken by the previous Fianna Fáil government. In 1945, Dr F.C. Ward, parliamentary secretary to the Minister for Local Government and Public Health, proposed a new scheme for mothers and children up to the age of sixteen. Fine Gael was opposed, and, foreshadowing the criticisms that the Catholic Church would make of Browne's proposals, Patrick McGilligan explained that he was defending the 'Christian tradition that there are individual rights which no State can take away and which no State can destroy'.[30] The Church did not comment publicly, although Archbishop John Charles McQuaid had contacted de Valera three months earlier, in January 1946, and the Taoiseach despatched Ward to meet him.

Given what transpired later, the Irish Medical Association's approval of the bill at this stage is peculiar. When Ward resigned after a tribunal of inquiry into allegations of corruption, another Health Bill was introduced in 1947 by Dr James Ryan. By then Health had become a separate department, and Ryan was the country's first Minister for Health.

Fine Gael continued its opposition, and during the Dáil debates Dr T.F. O'Higgins spoke in support of private medical practitioners and their potential loss of earnings. Citing also the pending National Insurance Bill, O'Higgins put it to Ryan: 'Are you not wiping that man financially out of existence?' A subsequent remark reaffirmed O'Higgins's belief that the minister would be 'robbing him [the private practitioner] of his livelihood'.[31]

Ryan's bill was substantially unchanged from Ward's, but it included a section, introduced by James Deeny, the department's chief medical officer, relating to health education that proved problematic, drawing criticism from the Church. The hierarchy wrote to de Valera in October 1947 expressing concern about this element of the legislation, which had been signed into law on 13 August. The means test, which would later dominate the dispute, was never mentioned. De Valera did not reply until two days before the change of government in 1948, citing James Dillon's High Court challenge testing the constitutionality of the Act – which Dillon later dropped – as a deterrent from commenting.

With Fianna Fáil's departure from the government benches, the new inter-party government inherited the Health Act, and part III, which dealt with the Mother and Child service, entered its most controversial phase. The hierarchy of the Catholic Church denounced the scheme, arguing that the provisions went against Catholic teaching and contradicted a father's right and privilege to provide for his family, otherwise known as the principle of subsidiarity. Criticism was also made of the family planning element, which was considered to be something within the purview of the church, not the state.

But the most contentious issue was the absence of a means test, a concern shared by the medical profession, which, represented by the IMA, relentlessly pursued its opposition to the provision. The Mother and Child controversy is popularly remembered as a church-state clash, held up as an example of the inability of Irish governments to resist the influence of the Catholic Church. But the powerful Irish Medical Association, which stood to lose from the scheme's implementation, played an important role in defeating the proposal.

The Health Act was on the agenda for a meeting of the cabinet on 25 June 1948. All ministers were present when possible changes to the legislation were discussed. The most significant of those related to the provision of a free service. Browne was given cabinet approval to proceed with drafting an amendment that would empower the Minister for Health to require payment, but without preventing the provision of a free service. Browne interpreted this as meaning that the cabinet had endorsed a free service that was not subject to a means test. Costello subsequently claimed that the cabinet had only discussed the issue of payment and not the question of a means test. This divergence of opinion would later allow the cabinet to distance itself from Browne. When Browne attempted to write to the IMA in March 1951 claiming that free service was a government policy, Costello blocked the letter.[32]

Following his resignation on 11 April 1951, Browne took the decision to publish his correspondence with Costello, his party leader and the bishops. It had the effect of creating the impression that the Catholic Church alone had been the obstacle to government-sponsored social change. This obscured the role played by the vested interests of the medical profession.[33] In November 1948 Browne had assured the IMA that consultation would take place, but it looked as if this promise was being jettisoned when the *Irish Times* reported the following March that the minister was intending to extend a free service to a 'large section of the community'.[34]

The relationship between Browne and the IMA became increasingly bitter. There were genuine concerns in the medical profession that moves towards 'socialised medicine', which would result in a loss of earnings, were afoot, while Browne was suspicious of elements in the IMA that he considered to be stirring ill feeling, and he took a hard-line approach in his dealings with the association. The complexities of the relationship that eventually led to Browne's resignation are beyond the scope of this chapter, but essentially the IMA balloted its members, who overwhelmingly rejected the scheme, and the association continued its campaign of opposition, assisted by the Catholic Church.

The story of the Church's involvement is well known and has been thoroughly documented, making it unnecessary to cover well-worn ground here. Briefly put, the Church shared the IMA's concerns about 'socialised medicine'. Support in the cabinet for the embattled Browne evaporated. Costello had been wary of the Mother and Child scheme to begin with, and by March 1951 he was utterly opposed. A daily attender of Mass, the strength of his religious conviction is beyond doubt and he generally displayed a deferential attitude towards the Church. The remark that is most often attributed to him is connected with this period. He is reputed to have declared to the Dáil: 'I am an Irishman second; I am a Catholic first … and I accept without qualification in all respects the teaching of the hierarchy and the church to which I belong.' This quotation is frequently cited as proof that Costello's religion underpinned his opposition to Browne's proposals; but in fact it was Brendan Corish of the Labour Party who uttered these words on 29 April 1953 during a Dáil debate on external affairs matters.

On Friday 5 April 1951 the cabinet voted to drop the scheme. The plan was to replace it with one that would satisfy the demands of both the Church and the IMA. The alternative would better reflect Catholic social teaching and would confine free services to those who could not afford to pay. In other words, a means test would be included.

Notice of Browne's resignation came five days later, coming into effect from midnight on 11 April. The consequences of the whole debacle echoed over the decades that followed when it came to policy formulation, and timidity underlined plans to introduce radical social change.[35]

The Mother and Child controversy was in effect resolved in favour of the IMA and the Church. But while the medical association was largely shielded from criticism because of the release of the Browne correspondence, there were longer-term implications for the Catholic Church. Religious practice was widespread in Ireland in the 1940s and 1950s, although this was born more out of social conformity than devout religious belief. The social aspect was also influential: church-going involved access to an array of social activities and offered the prospect of international travel through pilgrimage to Lourdes in south-western France. But the 1950s marked the final flourishing of the Irish 'devotional revolution'. Browne recorded in his autobiography that his growing disillusion with Catholicism was accelerated by the Mother and Child controversy, which evidenced to him that the welfare and care of the Irish people was of only a secondary concern to the Church.[36]

This is not simply the record of a former Minister for Health, soured by his exit from political office. The failure of the Mother and Child scheme did profound damage to the Church's standing with the emerging Catholic middle class. More particularly, the controversy altered many people's perception of the Church and the role it played in politics; it was seen as acting on the 'unpopular side'.[37]

The collapse of the first inter-party government is often associated with the fallout from the Mother and Child scheme. It certainly shook the government, and the possibility that Clann na Poblachta, as a result of internal divisions and Browne's threats to pull out, could have brought the government down cannot be dismissed. But it was actually the withdrawal of support by two independents over a more pedestrian issue – increases in milk prices – that prompted the Taoiseach to request that the Dáil be dissolved. The subsequent election returned a minority Fianna Fáil government. John A. Costello remained on as leader of the opposition, but he was back in the law library soon after leaving office.

Although the resumption of his legal career emphasised the part-time nature of Fine Gael, the party was in a better position than it had been for a long time.

After sixteen years on the opposition benches, a spell in office, overseen by a Fine Gael Taoiseach, confirmed that the party was capable of governing. It was an important message not just for voters but also for the party itself; its confidence had been eroded as each year in opposition passed. For the first time in its existence, the party increased its share of the vote and its seats. Those TDs who had been elected after 1932 had only ever known the opposition benches. The inter-party government changed that. Moreover, the formation of a coalition proved that there was a workable alternative to single-party government. In 1933, 1938 and again in 1944, Fianna Fáil had called snap elections to consolidate its hold on power. De Valera did not risk the same strategy after taking power in 1951. In contrast to 1932, Fine Gael only had to wait three years to return to power. This massively reduced interval lessened the scope for despondency to undermine the confidence that serving in government had brought.

4

COSTELLO RETURNS WITH A SECOND INTER-PARTY GOVERNMENT

'We should make the economy attractive ground for the employment of capital no matter who subscribes it.'

– JOHN A. COSTELLO, BLUEPRINT FOR PROSPERITY, 1953.

Ireland was in dire straits when Fine Gael returned to government in the summer of 1954.[1] Living standards were half those of neighbouring Britain, the economy was stagnant and emigration had risen to a flood. Things were so bad that some influential people were coming to the conclusion that the country was nothing less than a failed state. A sociological study entitled *The Vanishing Irish* summed up the sense of failure.[2] Confronted with that grim reality the second Costello government faced up to painful decisions, which made it deeply unpopular, but it created the foundations for the transformation of Ireland from a poor rural backwater on the edge of Europe to one of the wealthiest countries in the world in the first decades of the twenty-first century. It is an achievement for which the party received little or no credit then or later, even from its own supporters.

John A. Costello became Taoiseach for the second time on 2 June 1954. Incredibly, he made his way to the Four Courts that very morning to conclude a legal case. Having changed out of his robes he bumped into his fellow-barrister Tom O'Higgins on his way out of the Four Courts and offered him the important post of Minister for Health in the cabinet he would be announcing that evening. The two of them then set off for Leinster House. It all seems so amateurish by today's standards and probably even by those of the 1950s, but it fitted with the image of Fine Gael as a party of part-time politicians who turned up in the Dáil after doing a day's work in the courts or family business.[3]

Yet that amateurish stereotype, widely propagated by Fine Gael's political opponents, disguised the fact that Costello was acutely aware of the country's problems and he had assembled a team of expert advisers, the most important of whom was his son-in-law Alexis Fitzgerald, a leading Dublin solicitor and deep thinker, who helped to shape his government's approach.

The first signs of new thinking emerged in an address by Costello to the Fine Gael ard-fheis of 1953 when the party was still in opposition and published later as a pamphlet called *Blueprint for Prosperity*. In it Costello did not simply rely on criticising the deflationary policies of the Fianna Fáil government but went on to outline a specific set of solutions designed to ease austerity and promote economic expansion. Among his key proposals were changes to the rigid protectionism enshrined in the Control of Manufactures Act in order to attract foreign capital into the country, a central savings office and a Capital Investment Board to direct exchequer spending to productive projects.[4]

Early the following year a surprise general election was sprung on the country by de Valera in response to two Fine Gael by-election victories in the spring of 1954. Most Fianna Fáil TDs were as taken aback as the opposition by the move, as the government still had a working majority, but de Valera trusted his legendary instinct for election timing. The campaign was dominated by two issues, the economy and the respective merits of single-party government and coalition.

Fine Gael had a difficult balancing act to perform. On the one hand it had to stake out a distinctive position for itself as the main opposition party but it also had to deal with the imperative of not closing the door to prospective coalition partners, particularly the Labour Party. One of Labour's key election policies was the restoration of food subsidies which had been abolished by Fianna Fáil in 1952. Costello neatly sidestepped the problem by telling the voters that Fine Gael would not dishonour them by idle election promises. 'We do not believe that the Irish people are to be bought,' he said, refusing to give a commitment to restore food subsidies. In line with the *Blueprint for Prosperity* he expressed a preference for encouraging industry through tax relief rather than further protectionist measures which he said 'tend to raise prices and thereby put up the cost of living'. He also hinted that there could be some relaxation of the restrictions on foreign capital being invested in the country. This was immediately seized on by Fianna Fáil, which accused Fine Gael of being unpatriotic. Costello felt obliged to backtrack and promised that protection would continue as one of the permanent features of the economy.[5]

The election result saw a decisive shift away from the government, with Fine Gael gaining ten seats, compared with 1951, to end up with a total of 50. Labour gained three, taking them to 19, while Clann na Talmhan won five and Clann na Poblachta had three. Fianna Fáil dropped two to 67 in the 147-member Dáil. There was a clear majority for a new inter-party government if the opposition could agree on a programme.

There was never much doubt that Costello would lead the new government as Fianna Fáil simply did not have the numbers to govern on its own and de Valera was utterly opposed to coalition. Negotiating the formation of a government, however, was more than a formality. Clear differences of policy and emphasis had developed between Fine Gael and Labour since their first experiment in inter-party government. One potentially big difference was in health, with Fine Gael having strongly opposed the Health Act of 1953 devised by Fianna Fáil. Labour and all the other Dáil parties had supported the plan to provide a framework for a universal health service.

There were even bigger differences on the approach to the economy with Fine Gael moving tentatively towards free trade and a market-driven approach, while Labour remained wedded to state control, protectionism and food subsidies. These conflicting attitudes were a key feature of negotiations and Fine Gael was forced to make major concessions to ensure the participation of the smaller party in government.

Fine Gael's first draft programme offered an examination of the facts and an early announcement of government measures to reduce the cost of living. This was not nearly enough for Labour, which proposed a significant cut in the price of butter from 1 July followed by another cut in the price of butter and flour in October. Costello in effect conceded Labour's demands by offering an immediate reduction in the price of butter and an examination of the price of other commodities with a view to reducing them as soon as possible. Fine Gael also accepted a number of other Labour demands, including the establishment of an Agricultural Wages Tribunal and a specific commitment to continue the protection of Irish industry.

Agreement on these issues paved the way for the second inter-party government, but this time Clann na Poblachta declined to become involved directly, although MacBride offered to play a supporting role from the outside. Fine Gael had eight cabinet posts, Labour four and Clann na Talmhan one, with the Labour leader, William Norton, again serving as Tánaiste.

Fine Gael had been forced to backtrack in the programme for government on its plans to liberalise the economy but there was one powerful minister in the government who was determined to fight with everything he had to drag the country out of its protectionist bubble. That individual was the Minister for Finance, Gerard Sweetman, 'a dapper, abrasive and conservative lawyer with a philosophy of self-reliance and individualism,' whose crucial role in the creation of the successful modern Irish economy has never been properly acknowledged.[6]

Sweetman became Minister for Finance only because Costello's first choice, Patrick McGilligan, who had served in the position in the first inter-party government, didn't want the job. Pleading age and ill-health, he opted instead to become Attorney General. Costello then offered the job to James Dillon, who had only rejoined Fine Gael having been a minister in the first inter-party government as leader of the independent group. Dillon also declined Finance, preferring to return to Agriculture, and at that stage Costello offered the job to Sweetman.

Aged forty-five, Sweetman was bright, abrasive and hard-working. He came from a prominent and well-off family who had been involved in politics for more than a century. An uncle, Roger Sweetman, was elected as a Sinn Féin MP to the first Dáil in 1918 but resigned in protest at the campaign of violence that ensued. Sweetman's plummy accent and privileged background distanced him from many of his Fine Gael colleagues, but especially from the Labour TDs who regarded him with deep suspicion. Educated at Beaumont, a leading Catholic public school in England, he later studied politics and law in Trinity College, Dublin, before joining a solicitor's practice established by his maternal grandfather, Sir George Fottrell.[7]

A supporter of Cumann na nGaedheal from an early age, he was active in the Blueshirts and was elected to the National Council of the League of Youth in 1935. He first ran for the Dáil in the Carlow-Kildare constituency in 1937 but failed to be elected. Two years later he not only supported the Allied cause on the outbreak of the Second World War but attempted to enlist in the British army. His brothers Seamus, George and Denis all fought in the war and Denis was killed at Boulogne on 23 May 1940.

After a second failed attempt to win a Dáil seat he was elected to the Seanad in 1943 and finally made it to the Dáil in 1948 at the age of forty. He was appointed Fine Gael chief whip from 1951 to 1954 and proved himself energetic and efficient. In his drive to impose discipline on an amateurish parliamentary party he rubbed up lots of TDs the wrong way. One acerbic journalist wrote that many of them came 'to regard him as heifers must regard the man who is driving them to market'.[8]

Costello managed to offend Sweetman, even as he promoted him to the most powerful post in cabinet, by telling him he could always rely on advice from McGilligan and John O'Donovan, a young UCD economist who had been appointed parliamentary secretary to the government.

According to Tom O'Higgins, Sweetman was extremely annoyed, as he was determined to be his own man and did not feel the need for help from anyone else.[9] To make matters worse, the story was widely told in Leinster House and repeated in the Dáil by his predecessor as Minister for Finance, Seán MacEntee of Fianna Fáil, who congratulated Sweetman for 'having shaken himself free not only of the Attorney General but also of the Parliamentary Secretary to the government'. He went on to describe Sweetman as one of the ablest ministers in the cabinet as well as one of the most tenacious and courageous.

Ken Whitaker, then a very young assistant secretary in the Department of Finance, struck up an immediate rapport with Sweetman. 'We spoke the same language even if not always agreeing,' Whitaker recalled years later.

> Sweetman was devoted to public service, not from any interest in personal promotion but out of a sense of genuine nationalism. He was a man of honesty, directness and great analytical ability, animated by a sense of concern for the national well being, of great acuteness of mind, of boundless energy taking the steps three at a time with a boyish ebullience and a liking for mischief.

For all his ability, Sweetman remained something of an outsider to Fine Gael colleagues, as well as TDs of the other coalition parties, because of his background, accent and personality.

Sweetman was also a flamboyant character in private life. He dined in the top restaurants, liked fine wine, drove fast cars and liked the company of women. He lived in a big house near Kill, Co. Kildare, and had a number of business interests. A story, almost certainly apocryphal, that did the rounds in Fine Gael was that a group of party activists called to his home one evening and his wife opened the door and called up the stairs: 'Gerard. Some peasants here to see you.'[10] The fact that it was widely believed indicates the image he had with the party faithful.

With O'Higgins in Health and Dillon in Agriculture, the other Fine Gael ministers were Mulcahy in Education again, Mac Eoin in Defence, the young Liam Cosgrave in External Affairs and Pa O'Donnell from Co. Donegal in Local Government. Norton took the important ministry of Industry and Commerce and for the next three years was locked in a battle with Sweetman based on bitter inter-departmental rivalry as well as ideology.

Norton was a shrewd and formidable Labour leader who was determined to defend the interests of his working-class voters. He was cruelly and unfairly caricatured in Noël Browne's memoir *Against the Tide.* The Fine Gael TD Patrick Lindsay who joined the government in 1956 thought Norton was the best speaker in the Dáil, even better than Dillon and Costello. He described him as being 'incisive, sharp and devastating in debate'.[11] Apart from food subsidies he had succeeded in getting most of Labour's key policies, such as pension increases, improved payments under the Workmen's Compensation Act and retirement for men at 65 and women at 60 included in the programme for government. He fought Sweetman tooth and nail throughout the lifetime of the government but paradoxically the outcome of that conflict was a fundamental change of direction for the country.

The promotion of young men like Cosgrave and O'Donnell meant that this was a relatively youthful government. It enjoyed a solid majority in the Dáil and was more workmanlike than its inter-party predecessor. Many years later Liam Cosgrave attributed this to the fact that there was 'less nonsense talked with MacBride and Browne missing'.

Nonetheless, the strains that would ultimately lead to its downfall were evident from early on. In one of his first memorandums to government, Sweetman was blunt about his priorities. 'Current outgoings should be met from current revenue; exchequer borrowing requirements are excessive and there is an urgent need for swingeing cuts in public expenditure … the overall objective should be to secure a substantial easement of the tax burden.' It was a message that was to remain at the core of Sweetman's policy for the duration of the government and it caused strain not only with Labour ministers but the Taoiseach and most Fine Gael ministers as well.

In the early months, though, it seemed that the new government was working well. Whatever his misgivings about talking high office again,

Costello was initially pleased with the way things were going. 'I believe the new government has got off to a good start,' he wrote to a friend. 'I felt it was vital to secure from the start public confidence in the new administration and to make it clear there was no longer any political instability. I believe both objectives have been obtained.'[12]

Dealing with the first major issue to confront his government it looked as if Costello's optimistic assessment was the correct one. On the morning he offered O'Higgins a cabinet post Costello said to his surprised colleague in the Four Courts, 'I want you to become Minister for Health in my government and furthermore I want you to take health out of politics.'[13] It was a tall order considering the damage that the health controversy had done to the first inter-party government and which remained the stuff of political legend for decades.

Appointed to the cabinet at the age of thirty-seven, after only six years in the Dáil, O'Higgins may not have had a great deal of political experience but he came from a family steeped in Irish politics. His father, Thomas Francis, was a founder of the Blueshirts and was a minister in the first inter-party government, while his uncle Kevin played an important role in establishing the state and was assassinated in 1927. His grandfather, also Thomas, was murdered by the IRA during the Civil War. Through his grandmother he was connected with the 'Bantry Band', whose most notable member was Tim Healy, which had been a big influence on the Irish Party for more than half a century.

Tom O'Higgins had to find a way of healing the divisions that had opened up between Fine Gael and Labour over the Health Act (1953). At the core of the problem was Labour's support for a move in the direction of a state-run health service, even if the resources to provide it were not being provided, and Fine Gael's defence of private medicine. Fine Gael was the only party to oppose the Health Act in the Dáil, taking the side of an outraged medical profession. Defusing a ticking time bomb was how O'Higgins described his challenge.

Immediately after taking office O'Higgins had to confront a tricky problem that had the capacity to strangle the new government at birth. The outgoing Minister for Health, Jim Ryan, had signed a regulation requiring the local and national health authorities to provide a range of services from 1 August but O'Higgins was advised that the resources were simply not there to provide the services. If the regulation remained in force it would mean that the existing limited right to hospital admission for less well-off patients and insured workers would in effect be abolished.

O'Higgins had the good political sense to realise that his Labour cabinet colleagues who had supported the legislation in its passage through the Dáil would not take kindly to its postponement at the behest of a Fine Gael minister. He briefed the Taoiseach and the Tánaiste about the dilemma and was then invited to address a meeting of the parliamentary Labour Party, to explain the position. In a persuasive address he told Labour TDs that the legislation as it stood would deprive poor people and insured workers of their priority rights to hospital care. He proposed instead a gradual expansion of the service as resources permitted. Labour TDs were won over, and Jim Larkin Junior, widely regarded as the socialist conscience of the party, proposed a vote of confidence in O'Higgins's handling of the issue. Legislation postponing the implementation of the act was passed by the Dáil before the summer recess and the new Seanad was summoned for an exceptionally early meeting on 22 July to ensure that it became law before the deadline of 1 August.[14]

Having defused the time bomb, O'Higgins went on to implement a fundamental change in health policy which is still at the core of the system in 2020 and it remains the subject of debate and controversy as it was in the 1950s. He moved decisively to establish an insurance-based approach to health for people who could afford it, in tandem with the provision of free state services for the less well off. This was a decisive shift from the model of a state-funded service for all envisaged by Noël Browne and Jim Ryan.

Legislation establishing the Voluntary Health Insurance Board was passed in 1956 and the new model was accepted by subsequent Fianna Fáil governments. It was a move that put paid to aspirations by those on the left for the adoption of a free medical service for all, along the lines of the National Health Service in the United Kingdom. Any such move would have met with determined opposition from the medical profession.

In any case O'Higgins persuaded his colleagues that the country simply did not have the resources for such an approach but instead he argued that the health service could be improved for everybody through his approach. When he brought the legislation into the Dáil in the dying days of the government it was welcomed by many members of the opposition, including a future Fianna Fáil Minister for Health, Seán Flanagan, and future President, Dr Patrick Hillery.

The outcome was a clear victory for Fine Gael and it was in line with the position championed by the party against all others during its period in opposition. In his handling of the complex Health brief, which had destroyed the first inter-party government, O'Higgins demonstrated an impressive range of political skills which led Costello's biographer David McCullagh to describe him as one of the real stars of the second inter-party government.

While the potentially tricky problem of health proved amenable to agreement between the parties in government, the economy emerged as the main battleground in the cabinet. It was not a simple battle between Fine Gael and Labour but often a battle between Sweetman and the rest. It had profound consequences for good and ill in the years to follow and it soured relations between the parties for almost two decades.

Sweetman was consciously at odds with the prevailing political and economic consensus in the Ireland of the 1950s. He was mocked by the news magazine *Hibernia* as having 'one of the keenest minds of the 19th century', but in fact it would be fairer to describe him as a visionary who was determined to drag the country out of its stagnant protectionist backwater and create the conditions for economic development as a free-market economy.

Sweetman ran into trouble from the beginning on what would today be regarded as a non-issue: the price of butter. Fianna Fáil had abolished food subsidies in 1952 and it was a big election issue in 1954. While Costello had refused to give a commitment to restoring the subsidies during the campaign it was a priority for Labour, which insisted as the price of entering government that the price of butter, flour and tea should be subsidised by the state. Costello agreed to a reduction in the price of butter within a fortnight of taking office, with a review of the prices of other commodities to follow.

Sweetman pointed out that the butter subsidy alone would cost £1.25 million a year. To put this in context, the increase in public service pay sanctioned by the government about the same time was £900,000 a year. Sweetman demanded immediate cuts in other areas to cover these two spending commitments. 'No time should be lost in pruning services and personnel regardless of the criticism which any worthwhile economies will inevitably provoke,' he wrote in a memo to colleagues. In response the cabinet agreed that each minister would negotiate his departmental estimate with Sweetman to reach agreement on economies. Disagreements were to be submitted to a newly established Estimates Sub-Committee of the cabinet, composed of Costello, Norton, Sweetman and Dillon. As a result of this committee's work the estimates for the following year were cut by £2.75 million. When the butter subsidy is factored in, the actual cut in spending programmes compared with the previous government was close to £5 million.[15]

Sweetman had to live with the butter subsidy as the price of putting the government together, but he was determined to assert his independence and the primacy of the Department of Finance. On Christmas Eve 1954 he wrote a letter of thanks to the Taoiseach for 'your kindness and understanding … over all the past six months. At times I fear I must have sorely tried your patience.' He concluded by describing himself as 'the most explosive member of your cabinet'.

Early in the new year he had ample cause to explode. Although he had assured the Dáil the previous autumn that the butter subsidy would be the last concession during the financial year 1954/55 (which ended on 5 April at the time), the government decided in early January 1955 to subsidise the price of tea, at an estimated cost of £1.2 million, in order to avert a rise in the price of the nation's favourite tipple. The decision was taken at a special four-hour cabinet meeting called to discuss the exchequer position. The cost of living had been one of the main issues in the election campaign the previous May, prompting commitments by the Labour Party to restore food subsidies. Labour ministers were wedded to food subsidies, and they got their way over the price of tea. The *Leader,* an influential news magazine, commented: 'Mr Norton will at least be able to reassure Mr Larkin that the Labour tail is wagging the dog. No more unfortunate method could have been chosen.' The British ambassador, Walter Hankison, described the tussle over the price of tea as 'pathetic'. The *Leader* asked pertinently whether food subsidies were really the best way that limited public funds should be spent to help the less well off. It claimed that the resources involved could have increased social welfare benefits by a massive 60 per cent.[16]

Costello told the Fine Gael ard-fheis in February 1955 that the party had no illusions about the magnitude of the effort that would be required to repair the ravages of three wasted years under Fianna Fáil. 'I think I am entitled to say that we have not done too badly ... the economic barometer is now steady with at least a tendency to rise.' It was hardly an inspiring ard-fheis speech and made no reference to the *Blueprint for Prosperity* and the promise of new thinking about capital investment and the attraction of foreign capital.

The rapport Sweetman struck up with Whitaker was hugely important. In November 1954, on Whitaker's recommendation, the minister received government approval for the establishment of an inter-departmental committee to review the state's capital programme, something that the Department of Finance had resisted for years. The committee's brief was to examine the programme and establish 'if this large expenditure is contributing to national wealth and productive employment.' After deliberating for more than a year the committee concluded that 'works of social benefit and works of inferior productivity which entail a redistribution rather than an increase in incomes should ... be kept within bounds and a better balance struck in the State capital programme as between economic and social objectives.' It was a conclusion which arrived too late in the government's life to have a serious influence on its fortunes.

The government also proceeded slowly with the tentative election commitment to open up the Irish economy to more foreign investment. Back in 1948 Costello had described the Control of Manufactures Act as 'outmoded and outdated' but did little during his first term as Taoiseach to confront the issue. The second time around he asked the Department of Industry and Commerce to examine possible changes in the act, which enforced a regime whereby industries had to be Irish-owned and financed. He asked if the legislation could be amended 'so as to permit, subject to any necessary safeguards, a greater inflow of external capital into Irish industry'.

The Department of Finance, the Central Bank and the state-owned Industrial Credit Corporation all called for a relaxation of the ban on foreign capital, but the powerful Department of Industry and Commerce, headed by Norton, fought it tooth and nail. In September 1954 Norton said his department did not believe changes in the act were necessary, while repeal would be 'a breach of faith towards those who have set up factories here on the basis of the existence of the Acts'. His memorandum warned that allowing an uncontrolled inflow of foreign capital would create 'the danger of exploitation for selfish purposes which would constitute a grave threat to existing and future industrial development'. When some months later the Taoiseach's private secretary mentioned to Costello that nothing had been done about lifting restrictions on foreign capital, Costello pointed to the reluctance of the Department of Industry and Commerce to amend the act and added that 'in these circumstances no further action was called for'. His biographer David McCullagh describes this as 'an extraordinary admission of helplessness by the Taoiseach'.[17]

Yet while Norton put up a dogged defence of protection, he did bring forward a proposal from his department which was initially designed to protect Irish-owned businesses but was turned on its head to transform Ireland as a magnet for foreign investment in later decades. This was export tax relief, which would eventually morph into the 12½ per cent corporation tax rate that underpinned the development of the Celtic Tiger economy in the 1990s. That proposal for export tax relief was accepted by Costello but met fierce resistance from the Department of Finance and the Revenue Commissioners.[18]

Before that major policy change was implemented the country had endured yet another balance of payments crisis and deflationary budgets.

Things began to go wrong in February 1955 when the government decided not to increase interest rates in line with the UK. It was the first time an Irish government had taken this line since independence. The idea was to keep the cost of living in check and the move was popular with the voters. The problem was an immediate outflow of capital, and the government was forced to backtrack and allow interest rates to rise in early 1956. By that stage the damage had been done and the balance of payments deteriorated. Sweetman's response was to introduce new taxes on goods and to impose import levies to suppress consumer demand. The net effect was another dreary cycle of increased unemployment and emigration. The depressed state of the economy led to wage demands, which were only averted by a government commitment not to tamper with food subsidies.

In May 1956 T.K. Whitaker made a ground-breaking speech, all the more astonishing given that he was a civil servant, in which he outlined the dire state of the Irish economy. He pointed out that living standards were half those of the UK, resulting in massive emigration, low output from industry and agriculture, savings not being put to best use, inflated wage levels out of line with the cost of production and state funding being wasted on non-productive schemes. He pointed out that the remedy would involve reductions in consumption and welfare in the interests of a long-term improvement in living standards.

It was a message that resonated with Sweetman, and on his recommendation the paper was later published in the journal *Administration*.[19] However, it was not a message that many government TDs or the wider public wanted to hear. The Labour TD Jim Larkin made a speech severely criticising the coalition in September 1956, saying it was contrary to Labour's whole tradition to pursue and support negative measures like the curtailment of capital investment, reduced house building and economies that led to unemployment.

However, as the balance of payments worsened again, Sweetman's response was another dose of austerity. 'Let us behave like adults and not like children,' he warned the public in a speech. 'We must keep our heads. We have no cause or excuse for relaxing our efforts until we have closed the fatal gap in our balance of payments.' In a private letter he warned cabinet colleagues of the need to keep spending under control. 'To ignore that need must make for a disastrous worsening of an already serious financial and economic situation.'[20]

By this stage it was not only Labour TDs who were aghast at Sweetman's approach. There was a revolt by younger Fine Gael TDs, led by the Taoiseach's son Declan, who openly challenged Sweetman's policies at a meeting of TDs from all the parties in government. Costello was applauded by many of the Labour TDs present, to the deep annoyance of the Minister for Finance. He told Costello privately that his speech was 'shocking and unfair' and a breach of his responsibilities as a Fine Gael TD.

The unremitting austerity took its toll on ministers. Patrick Lindsay recalled feeling 'thoroughly dejected' and Brendan Corish tried to cheer him up by telling him it wasn't always like that in government. 'Well I'm afraid it's going to be like that for my time anyway, because we are going out the next time,' responded Lindsay.[21] It was against this increasingly gloomy background that senior Fine Gael ministers such as Tom O'Higgins began to agitate for a fresh approach. Alexis Fitzgerald, who acted in a voluntary capacity as an unofficial adviser all through his time in government, suggested that Costello should devise an Irish version of the Queen's speech to set out his programme for the remainder of the government's life. 'A spirit of siege warfare and urgency should be encouraged in the Government and party,' he wrote. Incidentally, he also recommended that a clever young person such as 'that young genius' Garret FitzGerald should be enlisted to improve the party's public relations expertise.[22]

Many of Alexis Fitzgerald's ideas, which chimed with those of the Taoiseach's economic adviser Patrick Lynch, were taken up in a memorandum drafted by Costello which emphasised the economic and political necessity for a major new initiative. 'Positive steps must be taken without delay to bring about a radical cure,' said the memo, which specifically identified a need to promote exports. 'Such a policy would give hope, show that the Government is alert and alive to the necessity not merely of restriction but of expansion which they appreciate is the real and only remedy for present difficulties.' He wanted the new policy initiative ready for announcement in September 1956 to dominate Dáil business and the two by-election campaigns scheduled for the autumn. In particular he wanted one striking piece of legislation which should have a title like 'the Expansion of Exports and Productivity Bill'. This was the germ of an idea which would find its full expression in the First Programme for Economic Expansion produced by the subsequent Fianna Fáil government.

Costello's memo was endorsed with enthusiasm by his ministers, who were growing increasingly desperate to find a way out of the vicious circle of austerity budgets. On 5 October 1956 he outlined his vision in a speech to government TDs and senators. Saying it was time to develop a programme for economic expansion, he announced that companies would be entitled to a 50 per cent remission of tax on new exports, and there would be grants for new factory buildings and hotels. A Capital Investment Committee would be established, and Ireland would welcome foreign investment. 'Faint hearts will contribute nothing either to the solution of our immediate problems or to planning the measures required to ensure future prosperity.' His speech was greeted with enthusiasm by the assembled politicians. A vote of confidence in the government was proposed by a Labour TD, Tom Kyne, and seconded by the Fine Gael deputy Dan Morrissey.[23]

The *Irish Times* summed up the public mood in an editorial. 'The plan Mr Costello announced yesterday is the one that ought to have been put before the country 30 years ago. The pity is that we have had to wait for it until a moment of crisis.' Of course it was precisely because the country was in such a deep crisis that the plan was agreed between the warring ministers and departments. Finance had previously resisted any attempt to establish a Capital Investment Committee and opposed export tax relief while Industry and Commerce had fought off any reform of the Control of Manufacturers Act.

The proposed tax break for new exports was introduced in December 1956. According to Patrick Lynch, it was the first significant departure from the system of company tax introduced in 1842. The potential scope of the measure to attract foreign investment was disguised initially, as the focus was placed on its potential to encourage Irish firms to find export markets. Costello and Sweetman were keenly aware of its potential but were happy to go along with the fiction as a way of undermining protectionism by the back door. Norton did his bit by starting a campaign to attract foreign companies to Ireland and he told Costello the Industrial Development Authority had been instructed to follow up American industrial contacts vigorously and without delay.

The Capital Investment Advisory Committee got down to work immediately. Chaired by a former secretary of Industry and Commerce, John Leydon, it included the economists Patrick Lynch and Louden Ryan, Kevin McCourt of the IDA, Major-General M.J. Costello of Irish Sugar and Ruairí Roberts of the Irish Congress of Trade Unions. Sweetman set it the task of dealing with an expected deficit of £12 million in the capital budget for 1957.

Its first report, published in January of that year, was music to Sweetman's ears but something of a shock for Costello and Norton, as the committee ruled out a cut in capital spending, as that would cause an unacceptable rise in unemployment. Borrowing was not a feasible option so it recommended cuts in current expenditure. In particular it proposed the abolition of the subsidies on butter and flour and the ending of grants to local authorities for agricultural rate relief. 'The elimination of these subsidies would establish an indispensable condition of economic expansion by bringing prices and costs into a more realistic relationship.'

While Sweetman was delighted at this dose of orthodox economic sense, most members of the cabinet were horrified at the prospect of the political storm such measures would unleash, particularly as a general election was looming. Labour ministers were adamantly opposed, and years later John O'Donovan, then a Fine Gael junior minister, claimed that when Sweetman told his Fine Gael colleagues on 25 January 1957 of his plan to abolish food subsidies four of them – O'Higgins, McGilligan, Cosgrave and O'Donovan himself – threatened to resign.[24]

In the event it never came to that as a general election intervened, but most of the proposals were gradually implemented by the subsequent Fianna Fáil government. A vital link between the Costello government's efforts to find a new direction and its subsequent adoption by

Seán Lemass was provided by the decision of Sweetman to promote the 39-year-old Ken Whitaker to the post of secretary of the Department of Finance in May 1956. The promotion of such a young individual to such an important position would have been remarkable in any era but in the hidebound Ireland of the 1950s it was revolutionary. That it happened is, of course, a tribute to Whitaker's extraordinary abilities, but it only came about because there was a minister in charge who was prepared to abandon the 'hitherto sacrosanct principle of seniority'.

Sean Cromien, then a junior civil servant in the department who rose to be its secretary in 1987, recorded the excitement of the event in his diary for Tuesday 28 May.

> Mr Redmond's last day as Secretary. Speculation about his successor during the day. Then about 4.30 news leaked around: the unbelievable had happened. Mr Whitaker had been appointed. Great excitement and a very popular choice ... he has been promoted out of his place in seniority, purely on merit at every turn. It's like the beginning of a new reign. We all wonder what it will mean. We feel it will bring changes. Home, feeling very excited about the news.[25]

In terms of seniority, the civil servant in line to succeed was Sarsfield Hogan. He accepted the decision with remarkable fortitude. Years later Cosgrave told Brendan Halligan that Hogan's patriotic response to what must have been a severe personal blow was crucial to Whitaker's success. Whitaker's appointment, like the struggle to escape from the straitjacket of protectionism, was prompted by desperation at the state of the country. As Tom Garvin has pointed out, 'the rhetoric of the Republic as a failed state was quite noticeable at the time'.[26]

A more positive development that reflected the government's desire to engage with the wider world was the admission of Ireland to the United Nations. The Soviet Union had vetoed Ireland's first application in 1946 but the country was included in a Cold War package deal approved at the end of 1955. After a decade of growing isolation Ireland had now taken its place in the world forum which would define the state's foreign policy for the rest of the twentieth century. A year later the young Minister for External Affairs, Liam Cosgrave, addressed the UN General Assembly and set out a vision of an independent foreign policy. The speech took a strong independent line with internationalist tone. Cosgrave condemned the Soviet invasion of Hungary that year and also the Anglo-French and Israeli invasion of Egypt. The speech, drafted by Conor Cruise O'Brien, then a senior diplomat, and amended by Cosgrave, was widely praised for its strong, coherent tone

A supposed gaffe by Cosgrave in that address generated one of the most enduring anecdotes of Irish political history. According to political folklore, Cosgrave embarrassed himself and his country by calling on Muslims and Jews in the Middle East to settle their differences like Christians. What Cosgrave actually said was that Ireland, as a western country which had undergone foreign rule, had a claim to understand the psychology of the two sides in the Middle East. He concluded by suggesting that the Anglo-French intervention should incite UN member-states not to vain recriminations but 'to renewed efforts under Divine Providence to adjust our differences – the differences that divide the free world – by rational negotiation in a spirit of Christian charity'.

That final paragraph was inserted into the speech by Cosgrave himself. Some years later O'Brien gave a funny but wildly exaggerated version of it in which the minister called on the Arabs and Jews to settle their differences in a Christian manner. In fact the speech was widely praised and did not attract any negative comment at the time. In his report back to Dublin the Irish ambassador to the UN, Frederick Boland, wrote, 'No speech during the debate received anything like the reception accorded to the Minister's. The volume of applause at its conclusion was really remarkable and delegates crowded around the Minister from all sides to congratulate him and express approval of his speech.' Even the British, who were criticised in the speech, described it as a 'magnificent performance'.[27]

Repeating the pattern that had become familiar to Cumann na nGaedheal deputies in the 1920s, success abroad could not disguise the fact that on the domestic front the tide was turning against the government, as by-election defeats in Dublin South-West and Carlow-Kilkenny illustrated. The end came about from an unexpected source: the resumption of IRA violence in the shape of the border campaign launched in November 1956. On the night of 11 November six customs posts were attacked and a BBC transmission station in Derry was destroyed. The raids were launched from the Southern side of the border, and more quickly followed with attacks on police barracks.[28]

The government decided to crack down on the IRA by deploying the army to assist the Gardaí on the border. It issued a trenchant statement on 14 December pledging to crack down on activities that would, if continued, inevitably lead to loss of life and even threaten civil war. Immediately afterwards thirteen men were arrested in Co. Monaghan but they were quickly released because no arms or incriminating documents were found.

The Unionists and the British were unimpressed, particularly as Costello continued to insist that partition was the root cause of the problem and refused to take more robust action to deal with the IRA. However, as far as republican-minded TDs, such as Jack McQuillan, were concerned, the government's approach was too robust. Over the New Year the violence increased. On 30 December a young RUC man was shot dead by the IRA in a raid on Derrylin barracks in Co. Fermanagh. On New Year's Day two IRA men, Seán South from Limerick and Fergal O'Hanlon from Co. Monaghan, were killed in another raid on the police barracks in Brookeborough, Co. Fermanagh. The funerals of the two dead IRA men attracted enormous crowds and were a huge propaganda victory for the republican movement. Ballads composed in honour of the dead IRA men, particularly 'Seán South of Garryowen', fuelled an outpouring of public sympathy for the IRA.

The government decided to deal with the problem by using the ordinary criminal law rather than introducing internment or establishing courts with special powers. This was partly because Costello as a barrister had a strong preference, shared by Labour ministers, for avoiding special measures. Even the use of the criminal code upset some members of

Clann na Poblachta, on which the government depended for survival. On 28 January 1957 the Clann announced that it could no longer support the government and went one step further and put down a motion of no confidence. MacBride tried to claim that the motion was due to disagreement over economic policy, but a statement from the party's Ard-Chomhairle was more honest. It accused Costello and his ministers of 'acting as Britain's policeman against a section of the Irish people'. Fianna Fáil jumped on the bandwagon by putting down its own motion of no confidence, despite its support for the crackdown on the IRA.

Costello felt he had no option but to call a general election before he was defeated in the Dáil, and on 4 February he advised President O'Kelly that he would be seeking a dissolution on 12 February, the day the Dáil was due to return after the Christmas break. There was a great deal of public surprise at the decision and even some Fine Gael TDs felt that Costello should have attempted to fight the no-confidence motion. At this stage, though, with a number of by-elections pending and independent TDs turning against it, the government had lost its majority and had little prospect of survival. It was an appalling economic backdrop against which to fight an election, but Costello saw no other option.

An insight into the reaction of the government was provided by the British ambassador, Alexander Clutterbuck, who reported to London:

> To say the Government is angered and disgusted at MacBride's behaviour is to put it mildly. Another six months would, it felt, have made all the difference ... both on the political and economic fronts a new chapter might have been opened. To be compelled to go to the country at this moment, before they have had time to complete their work on either front, is hard enough; but to be forced to do so through the sheer opportunism of MacBride and his two followers is, they feel, the last word.[29]

Costello launched the Fine Gael election campaign at the party's ard-fheis on 6 February, accepting that the timing was 'gravely damaging to the national interest' but insisting that he had no alternative. He was scathing about MacBride and his party, accusing them of 'criminal and miserable acts of sabotage', adopted because of the government's efforts to act against the IRA.

The main thrust of the government's election campaign was a vain attempt to convince the electorate it had a plan to get the country out of the economic morass. Plans for more spending on capital projects were announced while official figures showed a dramatic increase in exports over the previous year. It also engaged in some blatant electioneering to woo the voters, including a cut in the price of tea. The problem was that after so many years of austerity people simply did not believe the evidence that the economic tide was on the turn, while the vote-buying gimmicks undermined the government's credibility.

Fianna Fáil launched an all-out assault, saying the performance of the inter-party government had demonstrated that coalitions simply did not work. The necessity of single-party rule to get the country out of the economic morass resonated with the electorate and became the dominant issue of the campaign.[30]

The outcome was a dismal result for Fine Gael, which lost ten seats and was back to where it was in 1951. Labour suffered a bigger proportionate loss and was down to 12 seats, while Clann na Talmhan was reduced to three and Clann na Poblachta to one. Fianna Fáil coasted back to power, winning 78 of the 147 available seats.

One episode that has entered political folklore is a story told by Patrick Lindsay of a conversation among a group of ministers as they were being driven to Áras an Uachtaráin to hand in their seals of office. As they passed a well-known pub, the Irish House at Wood Quay, Dillon remarked, 'You know I was never in a public house in my life except in my own in Ballaghaderreen, which I sold because when I saw people home having spent so much money on drink, I decided they were depriving their families of essentials.' Costello then piped up to say that he was in a public house only once in his life, in Terenure, and nearly choked on a bottle of orange. An appalled Lindsay remarked, 'F***. I now know why we are going in this direction today and why we are out of touch with the people.'[31]

That story, amusing though it is, gives a misleading impression of Fine Gael's time in office. In the face of massive obstacles, and bitter internal arguments about the best way to proceed, the government had introduced a number of important initiatives, particularly export tax relief and the provision of industrial grants that would in time transform the country's fortunes. Whitaker was of the opinion that Sweetman, if he had remained in office, would have had the energy and the capacity to make those policies work.[32] Fine Gael's problem was that all the credit ultimately went to the Fianna Fáil government that implemented the policies initiated by Costello's government. Far from reaping any political credit for laying the foundations of prosperity, the perceived failures of the second inter-party government and the bitterness generated between the coalition parties condemned Fine Gael to spending another sixteen years in the political wilderness.

JAMES DILLON, OPPOSITION AND THE JUST SOCIETY

'The Just Society was like milk and apple pie. Who could possibly be against it?'

— JIM O'KEEFFE, FINE GAEL TD FOR CORK SOUTH-WEST,

1977–2011.

F ine Gael was demoralised and directionless in the aftermath of its crushing defeat in the 1957 general election, yet during the wilderness years an idea germinated in the party ranks that would eventually flower into a ringing new call to arms: the Just Society. The title of the policy devised by Declan Costello had more resonance than the detailed content of the document, but it served to attract a whole new generation into a party that was in serious danger of becoming moribund.

When Declan Costello died, on 6 June 2011, profiles of him made continuous references to his Just Society document, written in 1964 in an attempt to reinvigorate the party after seven years in opposition and to address problems in society. In his tribute to Costello the then Taoiseach and Fine Gael leader, Enda Kenny, described the policy as 'an initiative that helped to modernise the party and broaden its appeal'.

Various media echoed this assessment. Writing for TheJournal.ie, Hugh O'Connell claimed that the document 'would define the party for some 20 years', while Deaglán de Bréadún described it in the *Irish Times* as Costello's 'monument'.[1]

From these and other tributes it is clear that many perceive the Just Society to be an important document in Irish political history. It has come to be identified by Fine Gael as a key moment in the party's history, one that has been periodically referred to by recent leaders. It was one of the motifs of the leadership contest in the summer of 2017. The praise that surrounded Costello's initiatives in the days and weeks after his death masks the fact, however, that Fine Gael was not united on the proposals in the 1960s, that the policy had faded away as a priority by the 1970s, and that, while it may be remembered by members, it was not a consideration in policy formulation over the two decades that followed its introduction. In reality the Just Society legacy was, at most, an inspiring slogan – a useful shorthand for subsequent Fine Gael politicians to signify progress.

James Dillon was leader of Fine Gael when Declan Costello formulated his policy. His years as leader, Tom O'Higgins reflected in his memoir, 'were years in which a quiet struggle took place' in the party.[2] Costello was part of a new generation of thinkers who re-evaluated the role of the state and government's commitment to society. A traditionalist, Dillon did not welcome Costello's proposals, undermining them publicly when they were unveiled to the press in 1965. It would be disingenuous, however, to present the debate that occurred within Fine Gael as an inter-generational struggle. Patrick McGilligan was instrumental in convincing the party to adopt the proposal. He was seventy-five at the time. At forty-one, Paddy Donegan was only three years older than Costello, while Patrick Belton was the same age as Costello; both opposed any change in the party's direction.

The division in opinion does not cut neatly across age. Nonetheless there was a perception, which stayed with Dillon throughout his leadership, that he had been left behind by change, a man who had little appetite for political modernisation and was more concerned with completing the work his father had begun.[3]

By the time James Dillon was born in Dublin in 1902 his family name was already well established in political circles. His grandfather, John Blake Dillon, was a prominent member of the Young Irelanders. A group of active cultural nationalists, they staged a disastrous small-scale rebellion, in which Dillon participated, in 1848. After spending some time in exile in the United States he returned to Ireland and was elected MP for Tipperary in 1865. As the Young Irelanders, along with the IRB, are seen as important to the emergent home rule movement of the nineteenth century, John Blake Dillon and his son John Dillon represent the dynastic bonds between the two movements.[4]

First elected in 1885, John Dillon would be a leading figure in the Irish Party for more than thirty years. After the death of John Redmond, Dillon took over the leadership in March 1918. By that stage, however, the party was in a state of terminal decline and it was too late for Dillon to make any intervention of significance. The Irish Party was virtually wiped out at the general election of December 1918, and Dillon was to be the last leader.

Coming from a family steeped in the Irish Parliamentary Party tradition, William Redmond's National League seemed the obvious political home when James Dillon began to consider a life in politics. He was unconvinced by Redmond, however, and quickly dismissed the party. He had also considered Cumann na nGaedheal and Fianna Fáil, and received invitations from both. His eventual decision was influenced by an important friendship that would prove to be a lifelong one. While studying for the bar, Dillon had become friends with Peter Nugent. Nugent's father, John D. Nugent, was a prominent member of the Ancient Order of Hibernians who had also been Irish Party MP for the College Green constituency in Dublin between 1915 and 1918. It was Nugent Senior who encouraged Dillon to stand for election in 1932 in Donegal as a candidate, under the patronage of the AOH, representing the nationalist tradition that was still strong in the constituency. A candidate profile of this nature was a comfortable fit for Dillon, who, despite having no connection with Donegal, accepted the invitation.[5]

There were eight seats to be filled in the constituency at the 1932 general election. Of the outgoing TDs, three were Cumann na nGaedheal and two were Fianna Fáil, with the remaining three seats held by Labour, the Farmers' Party and an independent. This was a fairly consistent breakdown. Dillon's intervention as an independent nationalist had the potential to attract votes away from Cumann na nGaedheal. Despite the national trend of seat losses, the party retained its three seats in Donegal, although it did register a drop in its share of the vote. Dillon put in a convincing performance. Though not topping the poll, he was deemed by the returning officer to be elected on the first count, marking the beginning of a long career in Irish politics.

On his becoming leader of Fine Gael in 1959, Dillon had been a serving politician for twenty-seven years. Starting his career as an independent, he subsequently joined the National Centre Party as deputy leader to Frank MacDermot and was then instrumental in the negotiations that led to the creation of Fine Gael (as seen in Chapter 2). When he first considered entering politics, members of his family had discouraged him from joining either of the two main parties. In their previous incarnation as Sinn Féin, they represented what Dillon's father had opposed. A letter from his uncle on the eve of the 1932 election had urged him, 'Remember of what blood thou art and (so far as in you lies) strike Sinn Féinery down.'[6]

Such a view was unsustainable in the long term. In contrast to MacDermot, who never adjusted to being in Fine Gael, Dillon relaxed into his new party. His membership was disrupted, however, by the outbreak of the Second World War. Ireland declared its neutrality – the ultimate assertion of independence. Although Fianna Fáil and Fine Gael did not follow the pattern of other countries by forming a national government, Fine Gael supported the government's stance from the opposition benches. Believing that Ireland had a moral duty to stand against the advancement of Nazi Germany, Dillon resigned from the party in 1942 in protest at the continued policy of neutrality, and he returned to his original status as an independent. Having been a prominent member of Fine Gael, a move to the back benches and the loss of the benefits that come with party membership meant that this was a far less comfortable fit than it had been in 1932. He remained detached from the party, even though he worked closely with it as a minister representing the independents in the first inter-party government.

John A. Costello brought Dillon back into the fold in May 1952. After the collapse of the inter-party government the previous year, Costello had become leader of the opposition in the Dáil, and Richard Mulcahy remained president of Fine Gael. Mulcahy's decision to step down in October 1959 provided the opportunity to review the arrangement that had been in operation since 1948. Costello was a part-time politician, dividing his time, often unevenly, between the law and politics. Although he expressed interest in formally succeeding Mulcahy, there was a consensus that a full-time leader was needed. Beyond Costello, there was no obvious successor. Many considered 39-year-old Liam Cosgrave too young to step into the leadership, although Cosgrave still put his name forward. Dillon, according to his biographer, did not seek out the leadership through ambition but rather saw it as his duty.[7]

At 10:30 p.m. on 20 October members of the parliamentary party gathered to decide their new leader. Mulcahy counted the ballots and declared Dillon the winner. The breakdown of votes, in what became Fine Gael tradition, was not announced. Dillon allegedly approached Mulcahy afterwards to ascertain the extent to which he had been endorsed, and Mulcahy is reported to have revealed that Dillon received 66 votes, compared with only 6 for Cosgrave. Despite not being an official candidate, Costello supposedly received 26. These figures do not tally, however, as there were no more than 57 votes cast.[8]

Dillon's elevation to party leader blurred the line of continuity with Cumann na nGaedheal while emphasising the Centre Party legacy and hinting at the Irish Party tradition within Fine Gael.

Fine Gael was not alone in changing its leadership that year. After more than three decades at the helm, Éamon de Valera finally departed from Fianna Fáil to begin a new stage in his career as President of Ireland. Seán Lemass succeeded him on 22 June 1959. Comparisons were inevitably drawn between the two new leaders. Though Dillon – fifty-nine at the time of his election to the leadership – was slightly younger, Lemass was seen as the more dynamic of the two. This reputation was forged in his role as Minister for Industry and Commerce.

One year before Dillon took up the role the *Fine Gael Digest* reported that there was a lack of knowledge about what the party was doing.[9] Cumann na nGaedheal had at times been accused of being a government first and a party second, a reflection of the fact that its branch system was somewhat underdeveloped and that the grass roots reported feeling ignored. Whatever the merit of that observation, after O'Duffy's departure Fine Gael displayed little interest in organising its branch structure more efficiently. When Dillon became leader in 1959 he discovered that the branches existed largely on paper only. In an unimaginative approach to re-engaging the membership, he imposed a £400 levy on each constituency organisation. It is estimated that somewhere between two hundred and four hundred branches were registered in the 1950s and 1960s, a figure thrown into stark relief when compared with the 1,700 branches that emerged following Garret FitzGerald's membership drive in the late 1970s.[10] This inertia was mirrored in the organisation of the parliamentary party.

Dillon was not the leader to bring about change. Although seeking to hold more regular meetings of the parliamentary party, he failed to impose any real discipline. Mulcahy had previously attempted the same with a missive issued to the front bench in 1957, but to little effect.[11] In contrast, Seán Lemass, blaming a lack of discipline for Fianna Fáil's defeat in 1948, had established a discipline committee within weeks of that election and busied himself as a 'stern father figure'. He also formed a Central Committee, composed of ten members with specific areas of responsibility, which was to function as a shadow cabinet to drive the party.[12] In the aftermath of the party's second defeat in 1954 he again undertook the work of reorganisation, bringing in a team of young activists to assist with the task. He also recognised that organisation could only take the party so far, and he addressed the ard-fheis that year about the need to reassess policy.[13]

The work he did as deputy leader of Fianna Fáil in the late 1940s meant that he took control of a regulated party that was already used to him exercising power for almost a decade, compared with Dillon, who had only returned to the fold less than seven years earlier and had inherited a party with a well-established attitude of indifference.

By the time Dillon became leader the 16th Dáil had already been in session for almost two years. He noted in his memoir, 'I was saddled with a number of gentlemen whom I certainly would not have chosen.'[14] Either Dillon was being sensitive to those already in their post or it did not occur to him that he could reshuffle the front bench to create his own team. His front bench, as his reminiscences imply, was virtually anonymous. Although senior colleagues considered themselves a shadow cabinet, the minutes of a parliamentary party meeting in 1963 reveal a lot about how it functioned. Paddy Harte, the Donegal East TD elected for the first time in 1961, suggested that the front-bench leaders should be associated with particular departments. Dillon responded that it was for the leader of special-interest groups within the party to take responsibility for the better organising of such groups, and also that they should meet more regularly.[15]

While it is necessary for a leader to devolve power to their senior politicians, Dillon virtually relinquished supervision of the party in this matter. The problem was clearly not resolved, and a request for members of the front bench to be identified was recorded at the 1964 ard-fheis. Before the television era of politics, voters were more likely to know their local politicians than those representing other constituencies or sitting on the front bench. But that supporters and, even worse, members of the parliamentary party could not name the front bench was both telling and damning.

The absence of a clearly defined front bench denied Fine Gael the opportunity to present itself as an alternative government composed of future ministers capable of taking on the various ministerial portfolios. Shadow ministers – as much as the leader – drive a party in opposition. They craft responses to their government counterparts, and they help shape alternative policies. Without leadership of that nature it is hardly surprising that Dillon reported in February 1964 that 'performances in the Dáil were not up to standard'.[16] As leader, he had to accept some responsibility for that.

Fine Gael had a policy problem. John A. Costello had previously asserted that a party in opposition should use the time to develop a broad outline of alternative proposals that could be put to the electorate.[17] But Costello himself was known for putting his legal career above his political career when in opposition. Gerard Sweetman had claimed in 1958 that a 'distinctive policy was not so important' outside an election year. He cited changing political and economic circumstances as impediments to producing anything that could be implemented when in power.[18] He was, perhaps, reflecting on the fact that it had been the economy, not Fine Gael policy, that had propelled the party into power in 1948 and again in 1954. While his suggestion had some validity, the absence of any policy statement left the politically curious wondering what Fine Gael actually stood for.

But two terms in office after sixteen years in the political wilderness clearly inspired some members to review the state of Fine Gael with a view to winning power again. Minutes of parliamentary party meetings show that some contributors emphasised the need to formulate policy in July 1958 and again in September 1959. Dillon's first major policy statement after becoming leader was predominantly concerned, not surprisingly, with agriculture. Five of the six major points dealt with the subject. Fine Gael had a strong base in the farming community, and the first point, which spoke of the need to 'complete the job of eradicating bovine TB', would have been especially welcomed, given the threat this disease posed to the livestock industry.

Given his time as Minister for Agriculture, it is not surprising that Dillon felt most comfortable with that brief. As a nod to industry, the statement also included a point about the need to expand opportunities for employment in the sector. His proposed method for doing so – through private enterprise – foreshadowed his difficulties with the approaches proposed in Declan Costello's Just Society document. Dillon issued this statement partly to set out his stall as the new Fine Gael leader but also because of growing rumours that a general election was imminent.

Fielding ninety-six candidates, Fine Gael went into the 1961 election with the stated aim of forming a single-party government. This was partly because Labour, bruised by its experience of inter-party government, had renounced at its annual conference in October 1960 any form of coalition. But it was also symptomatic of a party that was out of touch with its grass roots. Professional political polling was a development of the 1970s in Ireland. In the absence of such professional techniques, parties relied on local sentiment to estimate their popularity. This deeply unscientific approach only worked if the grass roots were active and engaged enough to interpret local sentiment. Fine Gael was not in a position to do that. Moreover, as though they did not want to admit there was a problem, minutes of the parliamentary party show that any criticism of the organisation was poorly received. In private correspondence with Dillon, John A. Costello expressed concern that aiming for an overall majority would 'not be successful, may do damage and cause such disappointment as to break the spirit of Fine Gael supporters'.[19] His concerns were noted, but the strategy remained unchanged.

As the results were declared in each constituency it became apparent that the party would fall short of its target by a considerable amount. Fianna Fáil returned to power. A minority government, its duration defied the expectations of contemporary commentators. Curiously, Dillon did not take the opportunity afforded by a new Dáil to reconfigure his front bench. If he had felt constrained by inheriting a team in 1959, there was no practical reason for him not to choose his own people for the 17th Dáil. Instead he allowed the parliamentary party to nominate ten members from the Dáil and five from the Seanad. He then added a further five deputies of his own choosing.[20] This approach seems bizarre, especially given Dillon's complaints in 1959. By inviting colleagues to shape the front bench, Dillon may have been trying to overcome the lack of energy in Fine Gael by giving colleagues a sense of ownership over the future of the party. Or it may have been that Dillon was simply not comfortable exercising the type of authority needed to stamp his leadership on the party. The truth probably lies somewhere between the two. Whatever the motivation, the strategy proved ineffective, and, as noted earlier in this chapter, there was a request at the 1964 ard-fheis to disclose the identities of the front-bench members.

The by-elections in the years after the 1961 general election delivered Fianna Fáil an extra seat. Fine Gael won three by-elections arising from the deaths of its own TDs, but in each case it was a family member of the deceased who held on to the seat: Patrick Belton in Dublin North-East, Joan Burke in Roscommon and John Donnellan in Galway East. Newspaper analysis of the results revealed the seeming inertia within Fine Gael, homing in on obvious problems surrounding policy. An *Irish Times* editorial went as far as to suggest that the party would 'fade away' if 'something radical' were not done.[21]

Dillon appears not to have been disheartened by the by-election results, but others in the party were not as indifferent. Both Paddy Byrne and Gerard Sweetman felt that a failure to communicate policies, combined with a lacklustre performance in the Dáil, had impeded the party's prospects at the by-elections. Declan Costello pointed to the fact that the electorate had endorsed Fianna Fáil candidates in two different types of constituency, showing the party's versatility and broader appeal to voters. In reality, though, there was a general perception that there was little to separate the two main parties, except for their total length of time in power. Michael Mills, the *Irish Press* political correspondent, suggested that 'if half of the members of any of the parties were transferred across the Dáil to another party they would be there for six months at least before they would recognise any change'.[22] As the party in opposition, Fine Gael needed to develop distinctive policies.

At this point Costello began to formulate what would become his Just Society proposals. They were also conceived against the backdrop of shifting international thinking on the role of the state. Politicians and policy-makers contributed to this discussion, as did the Catholic Church. Change, at the international level and in Ireland, was made possible by economic transformation, technological advances, and a breakthrough – although there were limitations – in the Church's thinking as a result of the Second Vatican Council. The influence on Costello's thinking of Pope Pius XII's encyclical *Mater et Magistra* (1961), which encouraged state intervention for the common good of citizens, was obvious.[23]

Costello's proposals were designed not only to tackle social issues but also to reignite Fine Gael. Put starkly, by the time Costello brought his proposals to the party it had been in government for only six of the previous thirty-two years. Voters had turned away, and the party faithful were dwindling. Photographs of ard-fheiseanna show few delegates, huddled in small groups, in large but sparsely occupied halls.[24] Minutes of the parliamentary party from the 1950s into the early 1960s are rife with accusations of inactivity and pleas for deputies to attend the Dáil and vote in divisions. Predictions of Fine Gael's demise were not without substance. The debate that Costello initiated, forcing an uncomfortable process of self-reflection, ushered in a fascinating phase in the party's history.

Born on 1 August 1926, Declan Costello was the second child of John A. Costello, then Attorney General in the Cumann na nGaedheal government. Like his father, he had a dual career in the law and politics. Having studied at UCD and subsequently King's Inns, he was called to the bar in 1948 and to the inner bar in 1965. But politics was clearly in his blood, and he was elected a TD at his first general election in 1951. Aged twenty-four, he became the youngest member of the 14th Dáil. He was widely tipped for a cabinet position when his father formed a second inter-party government in 1954, but he was not promoted, to ensure that there could be no accusations of nepotism. Although Costello was from a privileged background, his position as a TD for the working-class constituency of Dublin North-West gave him an insight into the effects of poverty, unemployment and emigration. Reflecting on his political career, he reminisced in an RTÉ interview with David McCullagh that it was during these early years that he began to develop 'very strong feelings about what was happening in Irish society' and how that might be improved.[25] He formulated his Just Society proposal in an effort to alleviate society's ills.

Costello had only one opportunity. If the front bench rejected his proposals, he knew they would not be put before the rest of the parliamentary party for discussion. Acutely aware that the majority of the front bench did not support him, in a bold move he breached protocol and circulated his proposals himself to all members of the parliamentary party on 27 April 1964. His memorandum claimed that his policies were the 'right ones for the country'. He also considered them an opportunity to step out from the shadow of Fianna Fáil, a chance for Fine Gael to define itself as something other than its main rival's opposition. If adopted, the policy would allow Fine Gael to firmly stake its place in the party-political system, he claimed.

Influenced by the success of post-war reconstruction in France and by policies espoused by Hugh Gaitskell, leader of the British Labour Party, Costello argued for economic planning, rather than the government's preferred policy of programming. His proposed policies were based on eight principles, including economic planning for the private as well as the public sector, a ministry for economic affairs, government control of the banks' credit policies, investment in industry, and price control. He also proposed reversing the government's policy of reducing social capital investment and a preference for indirect, as against direct, taxation.

These eight points were discussed over the course of four meetings of the parliamentary party. The reaction at the first meeting, on 29 April 1964, was one of cautious wariness. On that occasion Maurice Dockrell – a prominent Dublin businessman who had represented various incarnations of Dublin constituencies since 1943 – was the only clear voice of opposition. Gerard Sweetman was not as resolute, but his minuted contribution, that the country needed 'alternative governments rather than alternative policies,' left few in doubt about his views. Sweetman would prove to be the most ardent opponent of Costello's initiative.

By the time of the next meeting, on 5 May, deputies had had an opportunity to consider and discuss Costello's proposals among themselves. The nature of the contributions varied between those of Seán Collins, deputy for Cork South-West, who favoured new methods, and of Paddy Donegan of Louth, who preferred maintaining Fine Gael's traditional role as a private-enterprise party.

Patrick McGilligan's was the dominant voice at that second meeting, and his intervention proved crucial. McGilligan was a senior, highly respected member of the party. He had entered politics in 1923 as a Cumann na nGaedheal TD for the former National University of Ireland constituency and was invited to join the cabinet only three months later. As Minister for Industry and Commerce, overseeing the Shannon electrification scheme, he proved to be one of the most innovative members of that government. Not only was he deemed to be one of the three most influential people in office during the two inter-party governments but, crucially, he was also considered to have 'the power of persuasion' over Dillon.[26] Indeed the party leader – though not necessarily agreeing with his argument – considered McGilligan's intervention to have been of 'priceless value'.[27]

McGilligan argued in favour of making full employment and an increase in the standard of living the party's objectives, and – echoing Costello's own concerns – he asked his colleagues to consider the policy upon which they would have based their programme had they formed a government after the 1961 election.

Before the parliamentary party reassembled, delegates gathered for the annual ard-fheis, held on the weekend of 19 and 20 May 1964. By then the media were fully aware of the discussions, thanks to an accidental leak by Paddy Harte, a junior member of the party, and close attention was paid for indications of how the debate was unfolding.

The Just Society proposal did not officially feature on the agenda. To have introduced a largely undiscussed document would have been inappropriate, particularly since the parliamentary party had not yet voted on the matter. Despite this, Costello's philosophy was represented in other ways. Of the 76 motions on the agenda, it was observed that 'almost all of them' could be described as 'socially radical'.

The principal participants began to take up their positions. There were indirect references to the behind-the-scenes discussions, particularly evident in unscripted remarks by James Dillon during his leader's address. Although he did not refer directly to Costello's proposal, he spoke of how Fine Gael would always encourage free discussion but then revealed his distrust when he remarked that 'young men could dream dreams and have visions, but there were no short cuts'. He went on to denigrate 'young men in a hurry' while also singling out Gerard Sweetman for praise.[28] The coded message was easy to decipher.

As the battle lines were being drawn, Liam Cosgrave was surprisingly identified as a supporter of Costello. Despite his conservatism, he had taken a pragmatic approach and recognised in the proposal an opportunity to challenge the dominance of Fianna Fáil. As he put it to those assembled, 'if we are content merely to be critics of Fianna Fáil we will accept a negative role which may be a self-satisfying ordinance but is, in fact, frustrating and unrewarding.' Although not making explicit reference to the document, he had also referred to the necessity of keeping 'slightly to the left'.[29] Rather than this being an indication that he favoured the party's new direction, it could be interpreted as a strategic position, influenced by the possibility of collaboration with Labour.

At the next meeting of the parliamentary party, on 20 May, Cosgrave confirmed his belief that the party should 'appear to be progressive and to be moving with the times'. His ard-fheis speech, taken with McGilligan's earlier intervention, is likely to have been a pivotal factor in the policy's acceptance. Thomas O'Higgins, another senior figure, also announced his '100 per cent support'. But despite the admissions of the Fine Gael heavyweights, some lingering doubts remained.[30]

The final discussion took place on 26 May. The minutes make reference to talks over the weekend that had involved Cosgrave, Michael O'Higgins, Costello, Sweetman and Hayes. A compromise document was produced, although it is likely that its terms were reached between Costello and Sweetman alone. Sweetman was seen as one of the old guard, but his opposition to Costello's initiative was not simply because he was unwilling or unable to change. Garret FitzGerald suggested that Sweetman was not an ideological right-wing politician but rather a man motivated by winning power. Commenting on his pursuit of what he perceived to be in the best interests of Fine Gael, FitzGerald described him as 'quite ruthless'.[31]

Sweetman was clearly concerned about the effect the proposed policy and the shift in direction might have on the party's electoral and financial health. Sweetman had been appointed Fine Gael whip in 1948, a position he retained in opposition in 1951. More particularly, he became national director of organisation in 1957, a post that brought him into contact with the party throughout the country. He had a good working knowledge of Fine Gael's supporters and of the profile of the party's financial backers. When it became apparent to him that Costello's proposals were not going to be rejected, he sought to find a compromise.

The outcome was a revised nine-point document, put before the parliamentary party the following day. There were no substantial changes from the first three points outlined in Costello's original document, and the criticism of the government's policy of cuts in social capital investment remained unchanged. In place of the suggestion that the commercial banks be brought under government control it was suggested that 'the credit policies of the commercial banks must, through the medium of the central bank, be in accordance with the government policy as is provided in the other democratic countries.'

'Where desirable in the public interest' was added to the point that dealt with direct government investment in industry, while the taxation policy was modified to address the poorer sections of the community. Price control was omitted. A ninth point – relating to improving the standard of living in the agricultural sector to equate non-agricultural occupations – was introduced. This is most likely to have been at the insistence of Sweetman, with the farming vote in mind. It was an important addition; an earlier article in the *Kerryman* had rightly claimed that Costello 'had no message for agriculture'.[32] This was a bizarre omission, given the party's voter base, but it arguably reflected Costello's upbringing in the Dublin suburbs.

The party's policy committee, which had been set up in March and was chaired by Liam Cosgrave, was to provide the forum for the process of developing the nine-point policy into a comprehensive programme. Cosgrave described his involvement as filling the role of 'chairman until agreement was reached on an agreed document'; he never participated in the actual drafting.[33] The drafting was conducted mostly at Costello's home, and although assistance was available during the process, Costello wrote the majority of what was produced.

Most fascinating about Costello's document are the sections on social reform. In the introduction he summed up society's ills:

> Too many are unemployed and are forced to emigrate; too many are employed at miserably low wages and salaries; too many have only a small income or pension; many survive on a bare subsistence from a small farm; many are kept just above starvation level (but nothing more) by the inadequate social welfare payments they receive; many live in squalor and appallingly overcrowded conditions.

At almost 40,000 words, the document argued that equality of social and economic opportunities did not exist in Ireland. The nurturing of productive investment to stimulate the economy, it was claimed, had taken precedence over social reform. While acknowledging that 'no government can abolish all the hardships and difficulties of life', Costello asserted that 'many avoidable ones exist in present day Ireland'. This could only be rectified by a 'bold and vigorous programme of economic and social reform'.[34]

Although an extensive document, there was a peculiar omission – one that clearly showed that James Dillon had no involvement in the drafting process. There was no clearly identifiable section on agriculture. This was later rectified when the document evolved into *Winning Through to a Just Society* for the 1969 election.

The 1965 general election was one of the last old-style campaigns; political marketing was on the margins, and campaign organisation was still largely decentralised. Although it was the first televised election, coverage extended only to the results and not the campaign. For Fine Gael it was the first real test of the Just Society – an opportunity for the party to step out from Fianna Fáil's shadow and to convince the electorate that it had created a document not only reflective of a changing Ireland but one that also addressed those areas that had not benefited from Seán Lemass's rising tide.

But the document's reception by certain members of the Fine Gael parliamentary party – in particular the leadership – did not bode well for its prospects among the party's traditional supporters. Furthermore, although the parliamentary party had unanimously endorsed sending Costello's proposal to the policy committee, the decision was not comparable to unanimously supporting the policy itself. And even though the document formed the foundation of the 1965 election manifesto, as the campaign clearly showed, Fine Gael was not yet ready to fully embrace change.

Seán Lemass called a snap election, and the document was completed only after the announcement was made. Although there had been unease among certain elements of the party, no alternative policies had emerged during the course of the year. The Just Society, therefore, became official Fine Gael policy for the election by default. As a campaign tool it would prove ineffective. *Towards a Just Society* was a statement of the problems in Ireland at the time. Although Costello offered some solutions, they were not the type of appealing promises that would be seen in the type of documents produced after Fianna Fáil's giveaway manifesto of 1977. Essentially, what Fine Gael published was a policy document, not an election manifesto in the modern sense. It made little impact on the voters. With limited time to publicise the document, hampered also by restricted circulation, voters never had the opportunity to familiarise themselves with the content. The really curious could write to the party's head office to obtain a copy of the document, at a cost of one shilling and three pence; sadly, party records do not disclose how many requests were received. At the national level the impact was further undermined by the leadership's lacklustre endorsement, while at the constituency level candidates opted instead to concentrate on local issues.

Towards a Just Society was officially unveiled on 18 March 1965. The press launch was a disaster. The organisation that went into it was poor, and not enough copies were available to circulate to the journalists in attendance. To the assembled audience the party leader, James Dillon, declared: 'We shall rely on private enterprise. We are a private-enterprise party.'[35] In two short sentences he contradicted the content of a manifesto that advocated greater state involvement.

Dillon and Costello had categorically denied on the eve of the 1964 ard-fheis that there was a serious breach within the party ranks, but the terms 'crisis' and 'rift' had crept into various newspaper headlines. Dillon's speech gave further credence to the widely spread rumours that Fine Gael was divided on the party's new direction. Naturally Fianna Fáil made much of this. A leaflet addressed to the voters of Dublin South-East described Fine Gael as a 'house divided against itself' and asked, 'how then can it aspire to govern the nation?'[36] John Healy, writing under the pen-name 'Backbencher' in the *Irish Times,* caustically wondered how a party seemingly incapable of organising its own press launch could possibly run a country.[37] In a post-election analysis, Fine Gael head office acknowledged that reports of splits militated against the party, but – in a well-established pattern of failing to reflect realistically and meaningfully on the state of the party – dissension was dismissed as 'imaginary' and the creation of political correspondents.[38] Though Fine Gael had always been a coalition of interests, the press was correct to be sceptical. For many politicians, support had been given because of the absence of any alternative.

The Just Society should have offered not only a useful slogan but also a theme around which the campaign could have been built. As Jim O'Keeffe brilliantly put it about the choice of title, 'the Just Society was like milk and apple pie. Who could possibly be against [it]?'[39] But what could have been a very useful slogan did not feature on much of the party's literature or in its advertisements. The electorate was most commonly invited to 'vote Fine Gael for a better and more secure future for Ireland'. Other advertisements listed some of the main strands of the party's policies but never actually used the term 'Just Society'. In one advertisement voters were encouraged to 'read paragraph 3' of the statement on banking and monetary policy for further details on agricultural credit facilities, but no information was provided about how or where the relevant document could be obtained. Although decentralisation was a feature of general election campaigns at this time, the disjointed campaign that Fine Gael ran when it had such an obvious unifying theme at its disposal only served to raise suspicions that the party was not united behind Costello's initiative.

Despite public appearances, Fine Gael did attempt to run a more professional campaign in 1965. A temporary press bureau and information centre operated in Dublin city centre for the duration of the three-week campaign. It was charged with overseeing the distribution of propaganda and press releases for the party. Notable names who worked in the centre include Michael Sweetman and Joe Jennings. Sweetman, a strong supporter of the Just Society, had previously worked in Canada as an advertising executive and would later succeed Declan Costello on the Fine Gael ticket in Dublin North-West in 1969. Joe Jennings went on to become head of the Government Information Service in the 1980s.

During the campaign the Labour leader, Brendan Corish, reaffirmed that his party would not countenance a coalition. It meant that, in order to displace Fianna Fáil, Fine Gael would have needed to make significant gains. The outcome of the election, however, made little difference to the parliamentary arithmetic. Fine Gael increased its share of the vote by a little over 2 per cent, which was not enough to deliver any new seats. With 47 deputies, compared with Fianna Fáil's 72, the party faced another stint in opposition.

But if the breakdown of seats was relatively unchanged, the complexion of the 18th Dáil was significantly different, reflecting the process of change that was happening in Ireland at that time. Former revolutionaries and long-standing TDs, including Robert Briscoe and Dan Breen, had not sought re-election. The defeat of Seán Mac Eoin for Fine Gael – an IRA commandant during the War of Independence and a member of the Dáil since the 1920s – further marked the passing of the revolutionary generation. Patrick McGilligan, one of Fine Gael's most senior politicians, along with James Ryan of Fianna Fáil, who had been a member of the first Dáil, also left political life. The 1965 election resulted in thirty-seven politicians under the age of forty – compared with twenty-eight in 1961 – being elected to the Dáil.[40]

Costello's initiative inspired a new, young generation, bringing people like John Bruton, Jim Mitchell and Alan Dukes into the party. Fine Gael's true commitment to the Just Society would be tested in the aftermath of the general election. The party had adopted the concept in 1965 because the document was already in preparation and there was no alternative on which to fight the campaign. Some of the more conservative elements took the view that adopting the policy was progress enough, that further work was unnecessary.

The party did not completely shelve the concept, however, but instead conducted its campaign for the 1969 general election under the slogan 'Winning through to a Just Society'. However, there was a sense of disillusion among Declan Costello's supporters, a feeling that the party had not done more to develop the ideas laid out in 1965. By the time of the next election, Costello had retired – temporarily, as it turned out – from politics. The extent to which he was admired by the party's youth was reflected in a statement urging him to reconsider; it was signed by many of the new members that he had inspired.

When the new Dáil assembled on 21 April 1965, Liam Cosgrave proposed James Dillon as Taoiseach as a formality. Lemass was elected and formed a Fianna Fáil government. The Fine Gael parliamentary party gathered later that evening, and Dillon resigned the leadership, to the surprise of many, citing his age as a deterrent to continuing. He was sixty-two. The question of who would succeed him was settled at the same meeting.

LIAM COSGRAVE TAKES OVER

'I don't know whether some of you do any hunting or not but some of these commentators and critics are now like mongrel foxes, they are gone to ground and I'll dig them out and the pack will chop them.'

— Liam Cosgrave, Fine Gael ard-fheis, May 1972.

Liam Cosgrave was catapulted into the leadership of Fine Gael after the 1965 general election defeat with a suddenness that stunned almost everybody in the party. While James Dillon's resignation was expected, its timing – on the day the new Dáil met for the first time – was not. The unopposed elevation of Cosgrave led to a widespread belief that the process was a stitch-up, designed to ensure that Declan Costello would not become leader. That suspicion was fuelled by the fact that Cosgrave's proposer was none other than Gerry Sweetman.

Cosgrave and Sweetman had barely been on speaking terms since the end of the second inter-party government in 1957. This was partly due to disagreement over the austerity budget of 1957; but the real reason for the coolness was more personal. Sweetman had snubbed Cosgrave's father, W.T., then chairman of the Racing Board, by refusing to go out to his home at Templeogue to discuss the introduction of a betting tax;

instead he made the former leader come into the Department of Finance in Merrion Street. 'To Liam that was unforgivable,' recalled the influential senator James Dooge.[1]

Like most people at the meeting, he was stunned that Sweetman proposed Cosgrave. Garret FitzGerald also recalled his surprise at how quickly the succession had been arranged and suggested that if there had been a proper interval Costello would have had a good chance of being elected by the parliamentary party. On the other hand, Costello himself maintained in later years that he was not interested in the leadership.

One way or another, at the age of forty-five Cosgrave followed his father's footsteps and became leader of Fine Gael. Although relatively young, the new leader was widely regarded inside the party and out as a symbol of continuity rather than change. His political judgement was shrewd, but he was uncomfortable on television, which was then becoming the dominant medium of communication. Stiff in public, taciturn but humorous in private, he was fiercely loyal to the legacy of the state's founders and worshipped his father, describing his father's government as 'easily the best government of the State'.[2] At times of crisis de Valera looked into his own heart to see what the Irish people felt,' said Dooge. 'I think that in a pinch Liam Cosgrave always asked himself what his father would have done.'

Cosgrave lived in the family home, Beechpark, in Templeogue, and, like his father, he was a devoted Catholic whose life revolved around politics and horses. He was married to Vera Osborne from a well-known family of horse-trainers in Co. Kildare, and the couple had three children.

The new leader moved to stamp his authority on the party by dispensing with the tradition whereby the front bench was elected by the parliamentary party. He made a number of interesting appointments. Sweetman, far from being rewarded for proposing him for the leadership, was demoted from his dominant position in Finance and made spokesman on Agriculture. He was lucky to be included at all, and, according to one story, it took an intervention from Tom O'Higgins to prevent him being dropped altogether.[3] At the age of fifty-six, Sweetman was the oldest and most domineering member of the front bench. He was chastened for a period, but it did not take him long to bounce back, as he had a realistic view of how he was regarded by colleagues. Asked once why he didn't go for the leadership he is said to have remarked, 'What, with my fucking temper and my fucking accent?'[4]

Tom O'Higgins was appointed deputy leader and spokesman on Finance, while Declan Costello was appointed to Health and Social Welfare. Both their fathers had served in W.T.'s governments in the 1920s, and that was something of enormous importance to Cosgrave. Both were also on the liberal wing of the party, although Costello was the more radical, and they represented a new generation in charge of Fine Gael. The view of the *Irish Times* was that 'the new men represent almost a complete takeover by the new generation; the front bench does not contain a single representative of the civil war days or the old conflicts. In fact, Mr Cosgrave has done a Lemass on Fine Gael and even gone one better.'[5]

Cosgrave expanded his front bench in an unorthodox way by inviting three up-and-coming senators to join it as well. The newly elected Garret FitzGerald, another rising star with a solid Fine Gael pedigree, was asked to join, along with James Dooge, who had been elected in 1961, and the party leader in the Seanad, Ben O'Quigley. FitzGerald plunged himself into intense political activity on his election as a senator.[6]

Cosgrave had a practical and expedient attitude to policy development, as his approach to the Just Society document demonstrated. He was quite willing to adopt the plan, but he had a keen nose for the conservative tendencies of the Irish electorate, particularly the Fine Gael voters. 'Liam, himself, was never a conservative. He never really adopted a conservative position,' said Dooge.

Immediately after his election Cosgrave committed himself to the 'Just Society' programme. He told a press conference the day after his election that it was on issues such as social progress and their importance that Fine Gael differed from Fianna Fáil. 'A bird never flew on one wing' was a widely quoted comment of his when questioned about the growing left wing in the party. His central objective was to maintain party unity, and that meant giving both the liberal and the conservative elements something to hold on to.[7]

W.T. Cosgrave died in November 1965, a few months after his son had taken over the Fine Gael leadership. In the Dáil, Lemass paid a moving and generous tribute to the man he had fought to overthrow by force of arms in the Civil War.

Apart from the sadness of his father's death, Liam Cosgrave's first year of leadership went reasonably well, and he kept both wings of the party happy. After that things gradually began to turn sour and he had to endure sustained pressure against his authority. FitzGerald and Costello were the leaders of the opposition to him within the party and they had the support of many young activists who became known as the 'Young Tigers'. In the early summer of 1965 Costello resigned from the front bench because of a combination of health problems and unhappiness with what he perceived to be an inadequate commitment among his colleagues to his Just Society policy.

Dick Burke, a Tipperary-born schoolteacher who joined Fine Gael in 1966, recalled the impact of the Just Society document. 'It had the effect of positing Declan as a modern, articulate thinker on policy issues. That would have been fine but the Seanad elections of 1965 had thrown up an excellent man called Garret FitzGerald. Then there developed an anti-Cosgravite strain in Fine Gael.'[8] In the first flush of leadership, though, Cosgrave and FitzGerald got along well, with the party leader not only supporting the younger man in his Seanad campaign but appointing him to the front bench. FitzGerald later recalled, 'I found the party leader, Liam Cosgrave, open to some of my ideas and before long I was working closely and harmoniously with him and with progressive elements among the senior members of the party.'[9]

The presidential election campaign of 1966 gave a shot in the arm to Fine Gael but conversely it encouraged divisions in the party. An initially reluctant Tom O'Higgins, who, at the age of forty-nine had no desire to contest the presidency, was persuaded to take on the 84-year-old Éamon de Valera who was seeking a second term. He consoled himself that he had no chance of winning, but he also had no desire to be humiliated. In fact he surprised everybody, including himself, by coming to within 10,000 votes of victory. One of the reasons he did so well was the highly professional campaign run by Gerry Sweetman, who had agreed to be his director of elections.[10] His performance also reflected the huge changes that were taking place in Ireland. Instead of being a backwater cut off from developments in the rest of the western world, Ireland in the 1960s suddenly changed gear. The expanding economy generated by foreign investment, Vatican II, the opening of RTÉ television and the youth culture of the 1960s all combined to initiate change in the country. It was a time when Ireland, in the words of the Nobel prize-winning German writer Heinrich Böll, was 'beginning to leap over a century and a half and catch up with another five'.[11]

According to FitzGerald, the presidential election strengthened the progressive wing of the party, but it also marked the beginning of a struggle for the soul of Fine Gael which continued for decades.

From 1966 until he became Taoiseach in 1973 Liam Cosgrave's position as leader was never secure; his opponents used a series of issues to mount challenges to his authority. The good relationship between Cosgrave and FitzGerald deteriorated after the presidential election and, while an open breach was avoided, it became progressively worse in the years that followed. In the face of growing dissent Cosgrave turned to Sweetman, whose role in the presidential election had revived his reputation, and he appointed him to the powerful position of national organiser. FitzGerald later wrote that Sweetman was tough and had little instinctive sympathy with the younger generation, least of all with the liberal youth of the 1960s. 'He had no malice in him and did not bear grudges but in what he conceived to be the interests of the party he could be quite ruthless.'[12] Dooge thought Sweetman's combative personality was a large part of the problem. 'His obsession with control and with combating people led to a bad atmosphere and there was in turn not a little plotting by the anti-Sweetman group and that soured the atmosphere in the party right up to the time of Gerard Sweetman's tragic death. It is sad to say it but the atmosphere changed quite dramatically after that.'[13]

Both the conservatives and the liberals in Fine Gael took the result of the presidential election as a sign that the party was on the verge of power. As John Bruton later explained, 'It is hard to exaggerate the morale-boosting effect of the success of this campaign on Fine Gael.'[14] With Lemass standing down as Taoiseach and being replaced by Jack Lynch in late 1966, they believed the next election would provide the opportunity for Fine Gael's return to government. The question was whether the party should try to go it alone or should woo Labour before the election. Sweetman and the conservatives believed that if the party held its nerve it had a chance of replacing Fianna Fáil on its own. In any case they doubted whether Labour was interested in coalition. The Labour leader, Brendan Corish, had ruled out coalition in 1961 and had not changed his views since.[15]

The liberal wing of FitzGerald, O'Higgins and Costello believed that Fine Gael's only chance of power lay in a coalition with Labour and urged the necessity of a deal. Costello even believed that a Fine Gael government on its own would not be progressive enough and he wanted to coalesce with Labour to counteract the more conservative elements in his own party. FitzGerald shared this view and began to orchestrate a range of contacts and private meetings with Labour. This soured relations within Fine Gael, because Cosgrave rightly sensed that things were going on behind his back. In any case Labour at this time was set on a left-wing, anti-coalition course. According to Brendan Halligan, who became general secretary of the Labour Party in 1967, 'Corish's opposition to coalition with Fine Gael at this time was based on his experience in the 1954–57 coalition and in particular his experience of Sweetman as someone who was extremely hostile.' The Labour view was that the time was ripe to drive Fianna Fáil and Fine Gael together. 'Going into the 1969 election there was simply no question whatsoever, as far as Corish was concerned, that the party was going to go on a coalition line.' Corish made a strong speech to the Labour Party conference in 1969, saying, 'We will not give the kiss of life to Fine Gael.'[16]

FitzGerald didn't endear himself to his leader by telling him there was growing support in Labour for a coalition deal but only if Cosgrave was not the candidate for Taoiseach. Patrick Lindsay, who was a member of the Fine Gael front bench at this period, recalled:

Liam Cosgrave was a quiet man but inside him was a ring of steel that never showed itself fully. At front bench meetings I began to notice a certain linguistic interplay among three or four of its members. It was probably due to my country instinct that I came to the conclusion that a plot of some kind was under way. My doubts centred around Garret FitzGerald, Tom O'Higgins and Declan Costello.[17]

One of the Young Tigers, John Bruton, has a graphic memory of this period:

Liam Cosgrave wasn't a good communicator, although he could be brilliant on the major set-piece occasions at an event like an ard-fheis. He tended to be silent and then speak only when he had something important to say ... There was a huge influx of young people into the party with very high expectations and then there was the advanced social thinking of the Just Society, which people felt wasn't being communicated adequately. All of those combined created an impatience with Liam Cosgrave's leadership which events proved to be unjustified.[18]

In the face of this discontent Cosgrave relied increasingly on Sweetman, whose knowledge of Dáil procedure, intelligence and energy made him the leader's most valued ally. At the 1968 Fine Gael ard-fheis Sweetman as chairman managed to head off an attempt by the liberals to change the name of the party to 'Fine Gael – Social Democratic Party'. Although most of the delegates appeared to favour the change, Sweetman forcefully pushed through a procedural manoeuvre to have the issue referred to a postal ballot of party members. This resulted in an emphatic rejection of the change by 653 votes to 81.

In early 1969 Costello announced his decision to quit politics and made it clear that he would not be a candidate at the next election.[19] The fact that his enemies were so keen on coalition with Labour made it appear at the time as if Cosgrave had something against the idea in principle, but his approach was at all times pragmatic. His judgement – rightly, as it turned out – was that Labour was hell-bent on a go-it-alone policy. Cosgrave resisted Fine Gael being put in the position of going cap in hand to a scornful Labour Party, but he was not opposed to coalition per se. In May 1968 he authorised one of his TDs, Michael O'Higgins, to make a speech calling on Fine Gael and Labour to form a united front, based on the Just Society principles. The following day Corish bluntly rejected the O'Higgins proposal.

This Labour snub came after a period of hectic contacts between the two parties in late 1967, in the face of a common threat when Fianna Fáil again proposed a change in the electoral system to abolish multi-seat proportional representation. Fianna Fáil had gone to the people with this proposal in 1959 and it was narrowly rejected, but the party did not give up on the idea. Cosgrave appointed FitzGerald to an electoral strategy committee in October 1967 along with Dooge, and they began to work out the effects of the Fianna Fáil proposal to change the electoral system. They concluded that Fianna Fáil would get 96 seats out of 144 under a straight-vote system and 80 under single-seat PR. Cosgrave agreed that talks should be opened with Labour on how to confront the threat, and Garret discussed the matter with Brendan Halligan. FitzGerald maintained that these contacts resulted in an abortive plan for a merger of Fine Gael and Labour in the context of a new electoral system.[20]

Relations with Labour were just one of the problems confronting Cosgrave. He was isolated from many of his colleagues on both wings of the party on the question of PR. In 1959 Cosgrave secretly approved Fianna Fáil's efforts to abolish multi-seat PR and he saw no reason to change his mind just because he was leader of the opposition. He was particularly interested in the possibility of single-seat constituencies with a single transferable vote system. He asked FitzGerald to carry out a private sounding of the Fine Gael front bench to see where everybody stood on the issue. Garret found ten people in favour of retaining PR as it was and eight, including Cosgrave, in favour of single-seat PR. Looking back many years later, Cosgrave had no qualms about his position:

We had fought three general elections without success and as the Labour Party had adopted a go-it-alone policy it seemed to me that there was no alternative but to seek a majority for Fine Gael. I think also that single-seat constituencies avoid competition of an unnecessary and undesirable kind between elected representatives.[21]

A critical meeting of the Fine Gael parliamentary party took place in February 1968. Cosgrave threw everything into an impassioned speech in favour of some form of change in multi-seat PR. He clearly expected to carry the party with him, but after a long debate that went on into the early hours of the morning he was solidly defeated by his own TDs and senators. He was shattered by the defeat, which was widely regarded as a vital test of his leadership. Although a motion of confidence in him was immediately passed by the meeting there was no disguising the blow.

Following the decision Cosgrave spoke in the Dáil against the Fianna Fáil bill to change the electoral system. He argued that as the people had expressed their support for the existing system in 1959 there was no point asking them again and there were far more important issues to attend to than changing the method of voting. When the electorate was offered a choice between the straight vote and the existing system of PR Fine Gael and Labour fought a strong campaign and more than 60 per cent voted No. While there were rumblings from the Fine Gael dissidents, Cosgrave's leadership was not seriously threatened.

In the period before the 1969 election the Labour Party went on a firmly anti-coalition line in the belief that 'the Seventies will be Socialist'. Big names such as Conor Cruise O'Brien, David Thornley and Justin Keating joined the party and were nominated as candidates. Labour entered the election campaign in a highly optimistic mood with an undiluted socialist programme believing it would overtake Fine Gael as the second party in the state. Cosgrave made no secret of his irritation with Labour and its go-it-alone socialist policies. 'They are none of them for 1969. The Labour programme is for 1984,' he said describing the party policies as 'far too doctrinaire and unrealistic'.[22]

The media painted Fine Gael as unfashionable and old by comparison with Labour, although the 'Young Tigers' made some impact with their support for the Just Society. Cosgrave campaigned hard but he was up against a formidable opponent in Jack Lynch, who had taken over from Lemass as Taoiseach in 1966. Lynch gave the deceptive appearance of being weak, particularly after the loss of the PR referendum. In reality the placid pipe-smoking Fianna Fáil leader was shrewd and tough, and he was a marvellous campaigner with an instinctive sympathy for the concerns of ordinary people. With the two opposition parties fighting each other as well as Fianna Fáil, the result was predictable. Vote transfers between Fine Gael and Labour were poor and neither party achieved its potential. Fianna Fáil, by contrast, bounced back from the near-miss of the presidential election campaign and the defeat on PR to register a solid 45 per cent of the vote, winning an overall majority.

The outcome was a huge shock for Labour. While the party won a respectable 17 per cent of the vote, this only translated into 18 seats. It amounted to a net loss of four instead of the massive gains it was expecting. Although new big names like O'Brien, Keating and Thornley were all comfortably elected, a number of traditional Labour rural seats vanished as a result of a red scare waged by Fianna Fáil. The crucial factor in the loss of seats was the collapse of Fine Gael transfers because of Labour's anti-coalition attitude. Fine Gael did better, holding on to the 34 per cent of the vote it obtained in 1965 and increasing its number of seats by three, to fifty. This rudely put paid to the notion that Labour was going to replace it as the second party in the state.

The mood on the opposition side was grim after the 1969 defeat and the atmosphere wasn't helped by an outbreak of squabbling on the Fine Gael benches. The tensions between the two wings of the party erupted into open conflict when TDs returned from their summer holidays still licking their wounds. In the election campaign one young liberal candidate, Maurice O'Connell, who had been selected by his constituency convention to run with Richie Ryan in Dublin South-Central, was dropped by the party's Standing Committee and the conservative UCD professor of law John Kelly was imposed in his place. O'Connell then ran as an independent and scuppered Kelly's chances. After the election Sweetman initiated disciplinary action against O'Connell and five of his leading supporters. They included Vincent Browne, then the editor of a Fine Gael youth magazine, and Henry Kelly, who later became a well-known journalist and television presenter in the UK.

FitzGerald recounts his shock at the news that his friends had been expelled from the party. He took legal advice before sending a letter to the Fine Gael trustees calling on them to reject the decision on the grounds of procedural irregularities. The trustees accepted the argument, and before the end of September, Cosgrave proposed to the Standing Committee that the decision be reversed.[23]

The party's two factions were well represented on Cosgrave's new front bench. FitzGerald was given Education, Ryan got Foreign Affairs and Sweetman was back at Finance. Although he was a new TD, FitzGerald quickly made his mark in the Dáil and the media through his frenetic activity in the Dáil. He spoke on a range of issues and wandered far from his own brief. Behind the bumbling academic image FitzGerald had an acute political brain, and from the beginning his ambition was to become leader of Fine Gael so that he could use the party as a vehicle to implement his liberal vision of Irish society.

Richie Ryan had his own ambitions, but he was fiercely loyal to Cosgrave. He resented FitzGerald as a presumptuous newcomer who wanted to take over the party. Ryan, a peppery and combative operator, did not shirk conflict with FitzGerald and the liberal faction. Newer Fine Gael deputies found themselves being sucked into the fray. The Dublin South TD Dick Burke was asked by Cosgrave to be chief whip – a tall order for a newcomer. Burke asked Sweetman how to handle the job. 'Sit tight, keep your mouth shut and listen,' he was told. 'I did that for a month. One of the first things I did was to get helpers and as there was no such position as assistant whip I lit on another new TD, a young fellow called Bruton, and asked him to help out. He became assistant whip, and we had a great time together.'[24]

Apart from internal wrangles, both Fine Gael and Labour found it difficult to come to terms with the fact that they had allowed Fianna Fáil to win power for the fourth time in a row in 1969. At first there was a lot of hostility between the two opposition parties, with recriminations over the result. Immediately after the election Tom O'Higgins made a sarcastic attack on Labour's new intellectual TDs, describing them as 'the horny-handed sons of toil' who had helped Fianna Fáil back to power. This came as a surprise to the moderates in the Labour Party, who regarded O'Higgins as a potential ally with whom they could do business.

The Labour leadership knew immediately after the election that they would have to change tack on coalition if they were ever to have any chance of breaking the Fianna Fáil dominance of Irish public life. 'I certainly changed my mind about coalition,' said Brendan Halligan. 'I changed it in the television studios looking at seats tumbling down all around me.' A few days later Halligan went to Wexford to meet Corish. 'While we didn't reach any decisions, our minds had certainly been profoundly changed by the experience. We had been humbled and humiliated by it and the primary concern became sustaining the party and keeping it going as a meaningful force in politics.' Leaving aside the Boland constituency review, which drew new constituency boundaries in a blatant attempt to favour Fianna Fáil, Fine Gael and Labour strategists could see that both parties had thrown away an opportunity to win extra seats because of the absence of transfers. Halligan admitted, 'We finally realised that if we were in an STV system we might as well accept the logic of it.'[25]

A tragic event that had a profound political impact was the death of Gerry Sweetman in a car crash in January 1970. Halligan vividly recalled ringing his party leader to tell him the news. Corish's laconic response was, 'Well, coalition with Fine Gael is now possible.'[26] Two by-elections, in Kildare and Longford-Westmeath in April 1970, showed that both Fine Gael and Labour had learned the lessons of the 1969 election. The parties asked their supporters to give their number 2s to the other, and the result proved what a good transfer arrangement could achieve. In Kildare, Patrick Malone of Fine Gael was elected, while in Longford-Westmeath, Pat Cooney won easily. In both constituencies more than 64 per cent of Labour transfers went to Fine Gael.

In early May 1970 the political system was plunged into a crisis that appeared at the time to threaten the foundations of the state. The Arms Crisis resulted in the Taoiseach, Jack Lynch, firing his two most powerful ministers, one of them the future Taoiseach Charles Haughey, the resignation of two others and the institution of criminal proceedings because of a plot to import arms into the state. Liam Cosgrave played a central role in the whole affair. He received two tip-offs about the plot to import arms in the days before the news burst on an unsuspecting public. One of the tip-offs came to him on Garda notepaper and the other was a verbal message from a civil servant. The written tip-off read,

> A plot to bring arms from Germany worth £80,000 for the North under the guise of the Department of Defence has been discovered. Those involved are Captain James Kelly, I.O. [intelligence officer], Col Hefferon, Director of Intelligence (both held over the weekend in the Bridewell), Gibbons, Haughey, Blaney and the Jones Brothers of Rathmines Road and Rosapenna Hotel, Donegal. See that the scandal is not hushed up.

Well-placed sources believed the tip-off came from Chief Superintendent Phil McMahon, a retired head of the Special Branch, who, because of his extensive knowledge and contacts, had been retained by the Garda authorities as an adviser on subversion.[27]

Cosgrave was stunned by the note and he showed it to a journalist and trusted friend, Ned Murphy, political correspondent of the *Sunday Independent*. Murphy made a copy and brought it to his editor, Hector Legge. After some consideration a decision was taken not to publish the story, because of the difficulties in confirming the information and because Legge decided it would not be in the national interest.[28]

When the Dáil next met, on Tuesday 5 May, neither Jack Lynch nor the ministers involved had any idea that Cosgrave was in possession of such crucial information. Lynch took TDs by surprise by announcing at the beginning of the day's business that Micheál Moran, the Minister for Justice, who had no connection with the plot, had resigned. Cosgrave was on his feet immediately.

'Can the Taoiseach say if this is the only ministerial resignation we can expect?'

'I do not know what the deputy is referring to,' came the reply.

'Is it only the tip of the iceberg?' asked Cosgrave.

Cosgrave went on to make the cryptic comment that the Taoiseach could deal with the situation, and he added that smiles were very noticeable by their absence on the government benches. Most TDs and journalists had no idea what Cosgrave was talking about, and Lynch still didn't get the message that Cosgrave knew what was going on.

When nothing further had happened by that night Cosgrave began to wonder whether the tip-offs he had received were meant as a trap. He decided to consult a few of his closest colleagues that evening and asked their advice. Those present were Tom O'Higgins, Michael O'Higgins, Mark Clinton, Denis Jones and Jim Dooge.

'Now, these were occasions on which he wouldn't bring Garret into it. He would be nervous about having Garret there,' said Dooge, who remembered Cosgrave telling them there was something important he wanted to share. Dooge recalled him saying to them, 'I want your advice. What should I do? Is this a plant? Is someone trying to plant this on me to make me go over the top?' According to Dooge's recollections of this subsequent conversation, 'we argued first of all as to whether he could take it as being something he could act on, because he feared the danger of just being hoist on a petard. And we came to the conclusion that, yeah, on balance, we had to act.'

Having agreed on this, Cosgrave said he had a second question about the form of action he should take. 'What do I do? Do I bring it up in the Dáil? Do I go to the newspapers? Do I go to the Taoiseach?' Mark Clinton was the first one who spoke. He said the matter was of such national importance the only thing for Cosgrave to do was go to the Taoiseach, and go to him that night. The others present agreed. 'And Liam went off and rang Jack Lynch's office and established that Jack was still in Leinster House,' Dooge recalled. 'The Dáil had risen and Liam went off for a while and we all sat around wondering what was happening, and he came back and – I always remember it – he sort of stood in the door and closed the door behind him and then he looked up and looked at us and said, "It's all true." I will always remember that. And then he called a front bench meeting for the following morning.'[29]

It seems Lynch didn't in fact quite tell Cosgrave it was all true. He confirmed the substance of the letter but said that some of those on the list, namely Jim Gibbons and Colonel Hefferon, were not involved in the plot. Following Cosgrave's visit Lynch spoke personally to Blaney and phoned Haughey. He asked both men to resign, but they refused. He then went home to consult his wife, Máirín, and at 2 a.m. he instructed the head of the Government Information Service, Eoin Neeson, to issue a statement that Haughey and Blaney had been fired.

When the Dáil met at 11:30 a.m. on 6 May the sensational news of the dismissal of the two ministers had convulsed the country. A third, Kevin Boland, resigned in protest, as did the parliamentary secretary, Paudge Brennan. Lynch proposed to a stunned Dáil that the day's sitting be postponed until 10 p.m. to give his parliamentary party an opportunity to discuss the issue. Cosgrave reluctantly agreed while making the point that a Fianna Fáil party meeting should not take precedence over the business of the country. Dáil deputies of all parties were shocked, and few believed that Lynch could survive. There was a widespread view that he couldn't carry the party with him against Haughey, Blaney and Boland.

Brendan Halligan paints a vivid picture of events.

> The atmosphere in Leinster House for those few days was incredible, the most incredible of my life. Nobody went to bed. For the first time RTÉ put an outside broadcast unit at the Dáil and was running a commentary non-stop. What I can remember as being very new were the huge big vans at Leinster Lawn right outside the back door of Leinster House. There were all sorts of rumours sweeping the place and people, as you saw with the fall of the last Government in 1992, were prepared to believe anything. Except in this case the issues were very serious, they were talking about the

Gardaí, they were talking about the army, they were talking about the role of parliament itself.[30]

When the Dáil met at 10 p.m. on the night of 6 May, Lynch confirmed that one of the reasons for his action was that Cosgrave had come to him the previous evening to say he had some information from an anonymous source connecting the two ministers with this alleged attempt at unlawful importation.

Cosgrave then rose to speak.

> Last night at approximately 8 p.m. I considered it my duty in the national interest to inform the Taoiseach of information I had received and which indicates a situation of such gravity for the nation that it is without parallel in this country since the foundation of the State. By approximately 10 p.m. two Ministers had been dismissed and a third had resigned ... Yesterday when I received a copy of a document on official Garda notepaper which supported the information already at my disposal and which also included some additional names, I decided to put the facts in my possession before the Taoiseach.

During the impassioned debates that took place in the following days Cosgrave described the Arms Crisis as the greatest scandal to hit the state since independence.

> For the second time in the past half-century, in our long and chequered history, this country and our people may thank God that they have this party to maintain and defend and assert the people's rights. Only for this party there would be a real danger of civil war, civil war of the worst kind, of a religious character. This Taoiseach and this Government must now resign and dissolve this Dáil and let the people elect a Government in whom they can have confidence and who will guarantee their lives and liberties, their homes and hearths and show to the world that this country, this

State established by Griffith and Collins, is fit to, and will, govern itself.

In the event Lynch and his government survived, but the Arms Crisis put the internal dissension in Fine Gael on the back burner for some time and, even more significantly, it encouraged the central figures in Fine Gael and Labour to edge towards coalition. According to Halligan, 'the events of May, 1970, had a profound effect on Corish. He came to the conclusion that for the sake of Irish democracy there would have to be an alternative to Fianna Fáil and the only alternative was a coalition with Fine Gael. He very reluctantly came to that decision.'

Doubts about the ability of Lynch to survive re-emerged when Charles Haughey was acquitted in late 1970 of conspiracy to import arms. A special Labour Party conference was held in Cork and it voted to abandon its opposition to coalition. It was by no means a sure thing, because of the hostility of the Labour left and the splits and divisions within Fine Gael. 'During the course of 1971,' said Halligan, 'there were unofficial, informal contacts. These would have consisted on the Fine Gael side of Garret, Declan Costello, Alexis Fitzgerald and Tom O'Higgins and on the Labour Party side, Justin Keating, Conor Cruise O'Brien, Mick O'Leary and myself.' He recalled that there were some discussions about the leadership of Fine Gael because there was a feeling that Cosgrave would be unacceptable to the Labour Party, but the idea of making it a precondition was quickly abandoned.

Dick Burke recalled the fevered atmosphere of the time.

> Garret came into my place as chief whip one day and said: 'We must get rid of Liam. We must get rid of Liam, you know. Brendan has asked for it.' I think he was inciting the Labour Party to press for Cosgrave's removal. I said, 'No, Garret, there will be no coalition without Liam in charge.' He couldn't shift us. It was a pity some people in Fine Gael were so hostile to Liam because in later years the relationship between the Labour crowd and Cosgrave was perfect. All through those years there was this heave, heave,

heave. It didn't mean that we slavishly had to agree with everything Cosgrave said, but on the essential question of who was going to lead the party into a coalition I was never going to accept a situation like that of poor old Mulcahy, who was forced to stand aside.[31]

In the meantime, tension continued to build on the Fine Gael front bench. FitzGerald, despite being party spokesman on Finance, took a deep interest in Northern Ireland affairs, to the irritation of Ryan, the party's Foreign Affairs spokesperson. 'From day one Garret wanted to be leader of the party. No matter who was leader he would have wanted to push him aside,' recalled Ryan.[32] He further revealed that he had in his possession

a list made in late 1971 as to how the party would divide if there was a challenge to Liam's leadership. And it is Garret FitzGerald's list. He visualised there would be three candidates, Cosgrave, O'Higgins and FitzGerald. And in that list he saw that on the first count it would be Cosgrave ahead, FitzGerald second and O'Higgins third. O'Higgins would then be eliminated and on the second count FitzGerald would have a majority. And he has amendments made in his own handwriting, changing one or two people. I should say it is a photocopy I have; someone else has the original. What happened was Garret was at a meeting and had a huge big bundle of papers. He left the meeting in his usual hurry and lifted all the papers except this one, which was left on the table. So we knew he was plotting in 1971 to take over the leadership.

One important issue that drove a wedge between Fine Gael and Labour was the referendum on joining the European Community, which took place in April 1972. Fine Gael, even more than Fianna Fáil, was enthusiastically in favour of Ireland joining the EEC, but the Labour Party was opposed. Prominent Fine Gael figures such as FitzGerald and Dooge were leading members of the Irish Council of the European Movement. One of the rising stars of the party, Michael Sweetman, was a driving force behind the Yes campaign. On the liberal Just Society wing of the party, he was a cousin of Gerry Sweetman, but his politics were very different. He was prone to joke that they were 'second cousins once removed, but not nearly far enough'. Tragically, he was to die in the Staines air disaster of June 1972 in which a number of prominent Irish business figures were killed on their way to Brussels to discuss how the country should adapt to EEC membership.

While some senior Labour figures were half-hearted in their opposition, and some were privately in favour, the fact that the parties were on opposite sides in the campaign helped the Labour left to argue that they should stick to their anti-coalition policy and try to drive the two big parties together.

It was not until June 1972, with the issue of Europe settled decisively, that the real breakthrough came. Corish made a carefully considered speech arguing the case for coalition and Halligan made sure that Cosgrave got a copy in advance. Pressed by the media for a response, all Cosgrave would say was, 'Politics is the art of the possible. The possible looks more probable now.' Shortly afterwards Halligan and Fine Gael's general secretary, Jim Sanfey, arranged a meeting between the two leaders at Sanfey's home in Terenure. According to Halligan's recollections, Cosgrave opened the meeting by saying baldly, 'Brendan, you and I are getting old, and there's not much time left.' While nothing immediate came from the meeting, the way had been paved for a deal.

Meanwhile the rumblings in Fine Gael continued. At the party ardfheis in May 1972 Cosgrave's resentment at his opponents in the party exploded in an unscripted remark during his leader's address. 'I don't know whether some of you do any hunting or not but some of these commentators and critics are now like mongrel foxes, they are gone to ground and I'll dig them out and the pack will chop them when they get them.' Much of his audience and the wider public were puzzled by the reference, but its intended targets, sitting beside Cosgrave on the platform in the City Hall in Cork, got the shock of their lives. 'The tone of this unscripted attack was disconcerting, especially for those of us who were seen as its targets; for a moment indeed, I wondered whether I should leave the platform, as I believe several others considered doing but discretion outran valour,' FitzGerald later wrote in his autobiography.[33]

It was quite out of character for Cosgrave to lash his critics in public, but the mongrel foxes did not forgive Cosgrave for his attack. In early November the strained relations between Cosgrave and Tom O'Higgins, his deputy leader, became visible at a party meeting, according to FitzGerald. This led to a very full, and unusually frank, discussion at front bench meetings on 8 and 14 November. Many speakers at these meetings questioned openly for the first time aspects of Cosgrave's leadership, and in particular expressed concern at what his critics perceived as a withdrawal of confidence on his part from some members of the front bench during the immediately preceding years, together with what was seen as undue reliance on a small group of 'loyalists' on the front bench.

> At the end of the front bench meeting of 14 November Cosgrave asked for 24 hours to consider his position. But when the front bench resumed 24 hours later, he ignored the discussion of the previous day and proceeded as if it had never happened. If this was intended to disconcert those who had initiated this discussion it certainly succeeded.[34]

Towards the end of November political tension rose to fever pitch. An IRA leader, Seán Mac Stiofáin, was on hunger strike in Dublin. The government sacked the RTÉ Authority for allowing an interview with Mac Stiofáin to be broadcast in breach of the law. In the middle of it all the Minister for Justice, Des O'Malley, published legislation to tackle the IRA threat more effectively. The Offences Against the State Act (1972) abolished jury trials for terrorist offences and provided that a person could be convicted of IRA membership on the word of a Garda superintendent.

A public controversy immediately developed, with the media, civil liberties groups and the Labour Party denouncing the government's crackdown as a threat to civil liberties. It was Fine Gael, though, that was thrown into most disarray. Liam Cosgrave's initial instinct, in line with his father's legacy, was to support Jack Lynch's government against the forces attempting to undermine the state.

Most of his colleagues in Fine Gael saw things differently. Some supported the civil liberties argument but most thought that the government had not used existing legislation to clamp down on the IRA and was now engaging in a publicity stunt to cover that failure. When the Fine Gael front bench met to consider the issue on Monday 27 November it became clear that differences on the matter ran very deep. Eventually it was decided to refer a decision to the parliamentary party the following day, without a recommendation from the front bench. 'When the parliamentary party met,' FitzGerald recalled, 'Cosgrave favoured the legislation whereas a majority wanted to oppose on the second stage because they took exception to some of its clauses on civil liberties grounds, including the provision regarding a chief superintendent's evidence.'

After a long meeting in which a substantial majority of TDs spoke against the bill, Cosgrave agreed most reluctantly to go along with an amendment to be proposed by the shadow Minister for Justice, Pat Cooney. When the Dáil debate on the bill began, on Wednesday 29 November, Cooney argued that the government had failed to use the powers that were already available, but it was Cosgrave's speech seconding Cooney's amendment that grabbed attention. 'Communists and their fellow-travellers and soft-headed liberals are always talking about repression,' he said, referring to protest marches that 'degenerated into a rabble and were a disgrace to all associated with them'. In the *Irish Times* John Healy wrote:

> When he had finished not only had he shot the reputations of some of his key men; he had left any hopes for a coalition arrangement lying mortally wounded on the floor of the Chamber. Cosgrave was not merely pulling the party back from an untenable political situation, he was also reminding his deputies that it was the ancestors of Fine Gael who had established law and order in the country and they were not now going to give Fianna Fáil the moral position of taking that from them.[35]

The parliamentary party met again that night, after the leader's speech, and there was still a clear majority against the bill, even though there were rumours that if it were defeated Lynch would call a general election and go to the country on the law and order issue. As the debate dragged on it became clear that many Fine Gael supporters backed Cosgrave's approach.

> There was immediate and widespread condemnation of the party's attitude from supporters all over the country. Telephone calls, letters and messages of all kinds were received from people … in short there was a spontaneous expression of indignation and anger from the core of the party support.[36]

The parliamentary party, though, was not for turning, so Tom O'Higgins, who had supported Cosgrave's line, sought to develop a compromise around a reasoned amendment to the bill.

By 1 December, as the debate dragged to a close, an approach was made to Fianna Fáil to try to get agreement on amendments, but the government, scenting blood, rejected any compromise. In response, Cosgrave called another parliamentary party meeting in the hope of persuading his colleagues to back him, but they rejected his plea, by 38 votes to 8. Six of the eight opponents of the bill then joined the majority, leaving Cosgrave with the support of only one TD, Paddy Donegan from Louth. It seemed to all present that his leadership was doomed. As some of the TDs vainly sought to get Cosgrave to change his mind, FitzGerald went down to the Dáil chamber to advise Tom O'Higgins, who was speaking, on what the party line was.

Then, shortly after 9 p.m. on that Friday evening, a loud thud was heard, and the windows of Leinster House vibrated. The first loyalist bombs had gone off in Dublin. They killed two people, and saved Cosgrave's political life. In the Dáil chamber O'Higgins was attacking Fianna Fáil for its arrogance in refusing a compromise on the bill when word spread that bombs had just gone off in Dublin.

John Bruton has a vivid memory of that night when, as a young TD, he sided with the majority of the party against his leader.

I graphically remember the bombs going off. I was actually in the lobby getting ready to vote and if my memory serves me it was decided in the lobby in a series of huddles that we would back the party leader's line after all. It was as late as that, it was within minutes of the vote that the party cohered again around the leader rather than split. It was a very rare parliamentary event.

As Cosgrave had left the party rooms in the belief that his TDs were intent on defying him, O'Higgins, as deputy leader, took control of the situation and convened yet another parliamentary party meeting, at which it was decided without any dissent to withdraw the Fine Gael amendment.

Cooney intervened in the debate at 9:45 p.m. to announce the party decision and the second stage was passed two hours later. The committee stage of the bill began close to midnight and continued until 4 a.m. on Saturday. When the Dáil then adjourned many in Fine Gael, including supporters of Liam Cosgrave, left for home still believing that he would be replaced as leader the following week. But, unknown to most deputies, Cosgrave, who had been quietly dining in the Dáil restaurant as the drama unfolded, had been briefed by O'Higgins about the party's U-turn. He then went on television to great effect to announce the party's decision and by Saturday morning he was widely seen as the hero of the hour: the man who had stood firm and had been proved right.

Dick Burke recalled that he had had to persuade Cosgrave to take part in the live television coverage of the night's events from Leinster House.

I physically had to push him into the studio and into a chair. They kept the programme going for a few minutes past the deadline and there was Liam. Of course everybody in the country could see now that he was right. It was the highest audience of all time. The parliamentary party met on the following Wednesday. All the chappies who had been talking about a new leader had been defeated by the time they came back because the constituency parties and branches had seen Cosgrave on television.

In a rare interview with Ursula Halligan years after he had left office Cosgrave recalled the dramatic events of those days.

> My attitude was constant. The bill was necessary and its passage had to be facilitated. I was always in favour of the bill and determined that it would pass. In a matter of such gravity the nation must come before party. In retrospect even those who were opposed to its terms realised that it was necessary and indeed in certain circumstances hardly strong enough.[37]

In his autobiography FitzGerald admitted that Cosgrave had been proved right. 'Our emotional opposition to this Act was not subsequently justified by the use actually made of it ... Moreover, in political terms Cosgrave was also right: had we opposed the bill we would, I believe, have been severely defeated in a post-Christmas law-and-order election.'[38] Bruton agreed.

> Cosgrave showed tremendous courage, really, and was right and virtually all the rest of us, including myself, were wrong. I have to say I didn't see the issue first and foremost as a question of trying to topple Liam Cosgrave. I think that we considered he wanted to us to take a mistaken line on the bill itself. But I think in retrospect whatever about the legalities of it he certainly had the politics of it right. The rest of the party, apart from the few who supported him, had it wrong.

Cosgrave's strength of character in being prepared to defy virtually his entire parliamentary party and sacrifice his leadership on an issue of vital national importance was a rare act of political courage. Political virtue is not often rewarded, but it this case it was. Cosgrave was Taoiseach three months later.

7

COSGRAVE AND THE
NATIONAL COALITION

*'Not for the first time has this party stood between the people
of this country and anarchy.'*

— LIAM COSGRAVE, FINE GAEL ARD-FHEIS, 21 MAY 1977.

The disarray in Fine Gael prompted Jack Lynch to pounce and dissolve the Dáil on 5 February 1973, the day before TDs were due back in Leinster House after the Christmas recess. At first there was consternation in Fine Gael, but the election scheduled for 28 February concentrated minds wonderfully and jolted Cosgrave and Corish into action. The two men, accompanied by their deputy leaders and general secretaries, met in Cosgrave's office and agreed within minutes to offer the electorate an alternative government by fighting the campaign on a common platform. It was understood that Cosgrave would be Taoiseach and Corish Tánaiste in the event of victory but there was no discussion of the number of cabinet posts for each party.

Peter Barry explained: 'We drew up the 14-point plan with Labour in no time. The plan was agreed without any problem. The smell of power, you see. Power is the aphrodisiac.' Another important factor was that Cosgrave and Corish got on well. As Corish put it, 'When two people are in agreement with each other you don't have to go through tortuous negotiations lasting three or four weeks.' Having agreed on the principle of coalition, Cosgrave and Corish decided to bring others into the discussion on the contents of the election manifesto.[1]

Fine Gael got commitments from Labour on law and order, Europe, a peaceful solution to the Northern problem, the removal of Irish as an obligatory school subject and the abolition of death duties. Labour laid stress on the removal of value-added tax from food, social reform, increasing house building to 25,000 a year and controlling prices. Garret FitzGerald inserted a clause promising a wealth tax to replace death duties. There was also a private agreement, not included in the document, that farmers would be brought into the tax net.

When the main outlines of the programme were agreed after a couple of hours, Cosgrave decided to let the negotiators hammer out the detail and he decided to go home. According to Brendan Halligan's recollection, he reminded them, 'I am leaving it all in your very good hands but remember what I said, you can put anything in as long as you don't give a commitment to get rid of that act [the Offences Against the State Act].' Labour had fought tooth and nail against the legislation only two months earlier but in the light of Cosgrave's views they backed off.

'We met the night when the election was called. Two and a half hours later we had a programme for government,' recalled Dooge. They agreed to call the arrangement a National Coalition, rather than an inter-party government. The statement of intent, as the draft manifesto was now called, was put to the Fine Gael and Labour parties the following day. Richie Ryan read out the manifesto to the party's TDs and senators and it was greeted with loud applause and a standing ovation. A press conference was called for Leinster House on 7 February when it was unveiled to the public. The political scene was transformed because, for the first time since the 1950s, the voters were being offered an alternative government.

The principal policies in the manifesto were economic. An important commitment was to reduce the rates (property tax) on houses through the removal of health charges, which were then levies by local authorities. Other commitments involved the removal of VAT from food, the abolition of death duties, the introduction of price control and a pledge to control wages. Pledges to tackle poverty, to end discrimination against women, to build more houses, to control rents and taxes and reform local democracy and education were all elements of the manifesto. Reflecting Cosgrave's own concerns, there was also a firm commitment to protect the democratic institutions of the state and to work for peace and justice in Northern Ireland.[2] The package was attractive to voters as it combined economic self-interest with the offer of an alternative government after sixteen years of Fianna Fáil.

The coalition campaign got off to a flying start because of the unified approach of the two parties. Both leaders undertook nationwide tours and urged their supporters to give their second-preference votes to the other party. The same message was also carried on election literature and posters. In his speeches Cosgrave gave details about how the election promises would be funded but he also reiterated traditional themes. In Roscommon on 11 February he said that Fine Gael was asking for support 'to provide a government pledged to uphold the democratic institutions of the State. The outgoing government had failed in this primary duty which would be Fine Gael's first concern.'[3]

It was economics, though, that featured as the main issue. Sensing that things were going against them, Fianna Fáil produced a bombshell a week before polling day. Having attacked the coalition plan to reduce domestic rates, Fianna Fáil now proposed to abolish them altogether. Cosgrave's response was to call a press conference for that afternoon in Leinster House, where he said, 'There is obviously a gale blowing in our direction but we are refusing to join the auction.' The *Irish Press* reported him as adding, 'Our proposals had been dismissed by the government as pie in the sky but now in a last minute effort to buy votes from the electorate they are agreeing with them.'[4]

In posters and advertisements during the campaign the Fine Gael slogan was 'Cosgrave puts the nation first', while Fianna Fáil's message was 'Progress with stability'. On the day before the election the Fine Gael newspaper advertisements stated simply, 'Don't blame the Government. Change it Tomorrow – Vote Fine Gael.' Cosgrave tried to reassure traditional Fine Gael supporters by emphasising the reforming, rather than radical, nature of the coalition. 'We must resolutely defend and protect our great Christian heritage and this can only be done if we continue to improve rather than alter the present system,' he said in Tullamore on 20 February.[5]

Polling took place on 28 February and as the results came in the following day it became clear that there had been no landslide. Fianna Fáil actually increased its share of the first-preference vote compared with 1969, but the coalition pact delivered the crucial transfers needed between Fine Gael and Labour. The outcome was Fine Gael 54 seats, a gain of four, Labour 19, an increase of one, while Fianna Fáil dropped six to 69 seats. It was nothing like the landslide some of the leading coalition figures expected and resulted in an overall majority of just two. But it was enough. Fianna Fáil was out of power for the first time in sixteen years.

Cosgrave's first challenge was to pick his cabinet, and the way he went about it cemented the loyalty of the Labour Party for the duration of the government. On a proportional basis Fine Gael was entitled to eleven seats and Labour four, but Corish decided to make a pitch for five and prepared himself for a tough bargaining session. 'I felt like a manager putting a boxer into the ring,' Halligan recalled. 'Off he went and I went away to chew my fingers to the bone and expected to be waiting until five or six o'clock in the evening.' Instead Corish came back half an hour later and told an astonished Halligan that, before he had a chance to say anything, Cosgrave reportedly said, 'Five seats, Brendan, and you can have the Department of Finance, but if you don't take it yourself we will have it.'[6]

It had always been an article of faith with Labour that getting Finance was the ultimate goal of Labour in government but Corish refused to take it, opting instead for Health and Social Welfare, which were combined into one massive spending department. Cosgrave insisted on keeping the security Ministries of Justice and Defence in Fine Gael hands, and he also wanted Agriculture because of the antipathy between Labour and the farmers. He was equally wary of giving Labour Education because of the potential rows with the Catholic Church. As it happened, the Fine Gael and Labour priorities were compatible.

It was clearly understood by both coalition leaders that Cosgrave would pick the Fine Gael ministers and Corish the Labour ones, but the two men went about their task in very different ways. Over a period of days Cosgrave called senior party figures to his room and asked them if they were willing to serve, without specifying which department. When they said yes they were given no further information, and none of them, with the exception of Richie Ryan, knew with certainty what portfolios they were getting until the Taoiseach read out their names and departments in the Dáil.[7]

The big shock was that Ryan, rather than FitzGerald, was given Finance. 'Oh, good lord, I haven't done economics since I was a student and everybody is expecting Garret to get Finance,' Ryan told Cosgrave when he was asked to serve. 'I am doing it because I respect your judgement,' was Cosgrave's reply.[8] It was not until the morning of 14 March, the day the Dáil was due to meet to elect the new Taoiseach, that FitzGerald received the first hint that he was getting Foreign Affairs and not Finance, as he had expected.

> I was on my way to Leinster House when I passed a friend from the Department of Foreign Affairs, who said out of the corner of her mouth, 'Welcome to Iveagh House'. Shortly afterwards in the restaurant at lunchtime Brendan Corish, the Labour leader, called me over and told me not to be too disappointed if I were not appointed to Finance. 'What's the alternative?' I asked him. 'It could be Foreign Affairs', he replied.[9]

Only after Cosgrave's election as Taoiseach by the Dáil did the Fine Gael ministers know for certain that they were in the cabinet. Cosgrave summoned all his team to his office at 5:30 p.m. FitzGerald recorded in his autobiography that he 'waited in the corridor outside, expecting that we would be called in one by one, but at 5:35 p.m. I was asked to join others inside. As I entered, Liam Cosgrave stepped forward, shook my hand and said, "Foreign Affairs. Is that all right?" I assented.' His wife, Joan, burst into tears in the public gallery when the appointment was announced because she was afraid of flying and hated the idea of the travel her husband would have to undertake![10]

Pat Cooney was left in an even more uncertain position than FitzGerald. Cosgrave didn't even tell him he was going to be in the cabinet until the 5:30 p.m. meeting and, according to Halligan, he was in a fraught mood on the day of Cosgrave's election. FitzGerald had a similar recollection.

> Just three months earlier Pat Cooney, together with Tom O'Higgins, Jim Dooge and myself had led the opposition to the Offences Against the State (Amendment) Bill that had almost cost Liam Cosgrave the leadership of the party. Pat Cooney's description of that bill as comparable only to repressive legislation in South Africa, and his stance at that time on liberal issues can scarcely have recommended him to his leader for this portfolio. True, in the years that followed Pat Cooney moved to the right, but that was hardly predictable in March 1973.[11]

What to do with Declan Costello was another problem for Cosgrave. Costello came back into the Dáil in 1973, having opted out of electoral politics in 1969, and he expected a place in the cabinet. Cosgrave was reluctant to appoint him, despite pleas on his behalf from senior party figures. One story at the time was that John A. Costello personally pleaded with Cosgrave to give Declan a cabinet position, but the Taoiseach simply refused. He eventually offered him the position of Attorney General, just as W.T. Cosgrave had done with John A. Costello in the 1920s. This was widely regarded on the liberal wing of Fine Gael as an attempt by Cosgrave to limit his power and influence. Costello admitted later that he would have liked a senior ministry but maintains that he was pleased enough with his appointment. It was only afterwards when he learned in the job how limited his powers were that he became disillusioned. FitzGerald looked to their shared history in the party as a possible explanation for the portfolios eventually offered to himself and Costello.

He could also have been influenced by memories of his father's Cumann na nGaedheal government of the 1920s, in which my father had served as Minister for External Affairs until 1927; in this connection it may be significant that Declan Costello, who had returned to politics in this election after a period of withdrawal for a combination of health and political reasons, was simultaneously appointed to the post of Attorney General, which his father, John A. Costello, held under W.T. Cosgrave in the latter period of that first government.[12]

Cosgrave's other rival in the party, who also held a historic Fine Gael name, was Tom O'Higgins, but the 1973 election had come at the worst possible time for him. Already selected as the Fine Gael presidential candidate, he decided that he could not credibly run for the Dáil in 1973 and, as a result, he forfeited a senior cabinet position and possibly the future leadership of the party as well.

Apart from FitzGerald and Costello, the rest of the Fine Gael team was relatively easy to pick. With Richie Ryan in the crucial post of Finance, other stalwarts, such as Mark Clinton and Paddy Donegan, were slotted into Agriculture and Defence, respectively. Dick Burke got Education, which Cosgrave was adamant should go to Fine Gael. Tom Fitzpatrick was offered Justice but turned it down and eventually settled for Lands, while a relative newcomer, Peter Barry, was the surprise choice, being elevated to Transport and Power. Tom O'Donnell was the final member of the Fine Gael team in the Department of the Gaeltacht. John Kelly was appointed chief whip. Cosgrave reluctantly left Oliver J. Flanagan out because he had lost the whip some months earlier.

On the Labour side Corish took Health and Social Welfare and appointed Conor Cruise O'Brien to Posts and Telegraphs, Justin Keating to Industry and Commerce, Michael O'Leary to Labour and Jimmy Tully to Local Government. O'Brien was given responsibility for the Government Information Service. Cosgrave told Ursula Halligan that a number of factors influenced his selection, with competence and experience playing a large part as well as geographical location.

It was a mixture of all three; you look for a competent person with experience for instance someone like Richie Ryan who was a long time in the Dáil and was a competent performer with a lot of experience at home and abroad. Then you select people whom you know have sound judgement, I'm thinking of a person offhand like Mark Clinton who again had vast experience. Then you have to consider regional distribution because it is important that a region not only is represented but feels itself represented. Again you must make it a mixture of competence, a man like Peter Barry in Cork, a very experienced businessman who also represents Cork and the people from the west like Henry Kenny, who again was an exceptionally able person but wasn't recognised as such until he got the position.[13]

Cosgrave claims that the personal loyalty to himself of those chosen was not a major issue.

Commentators who have written on this matter either did not know or ignored the facts. I worked with the members of the party irrespective of whether they voted for me or not. The records will show that deputies were appointed to the front bench and eventually appointed to ministerial positions on the same basis.[14]

By the morning of 14 March, when the Dáil was due to meet to elect a new Taoiseach, all the ministers, with the exception of Cooney, knew at least that they were in the cabinet, even if they did not know what post they were getting. When the Dáil met that afternoon Corish proposed Cosgrave for Taoiseach and he was elected by 72 votes to 70. Addressing the Dáil after announcing his cabinet, Cosgrave referred to the media description of it as the government of all the talents. 'I need hardly say that I am glad to have got a place on it,' he added drily.

The coalition entered office brightly and got a good press for the first few months. Its first budget was hailed by the *Irish Times* as 'the greatest social welfare budget of all time' and 'the most progressive budget yet'.[15]

As a result of EEC membership, he had an extra £30 million in spending available to him, which facilitated the type of budget he introduced. The money, which had previously gone on agricultural subsidies, was redirected into social improvement. During the lifetime of the government there were a range of social improvements in which there were a variety of actors as agents of change. The EEC, the courts system, the Commission on the Status of Women and various lobby groups all played an important role in effecting change. The government often legislated in response to demands external to the Dáil, sometimes having no choice but to do so because of legal rulings.

By providing for unmarried mothers and deserted wives, Ryan's first budget represented significant changes in the area of family policy, at once recognising wider changes in Irish society and bringing Ireland closer to the norms of European social-democratic welfare states. This had been one of the demands made by the Irish Women's Liberation Movement and the AIM Group, which had lobbied politicians during the 1973 election. Although equal pay is recorded as an achievement of the National Coalition, it was actually required under the terms of an EEC directive and was a prerequisite to membership of the European Community.

The court system also played a vital role in elevating the position of women in society. Legislation dating from the 1920s restricted women from serving on juries. The Irish Women's Liberation Movement listed repeal of that legislation in its document *Chains or Change,* and change was also recommended in the report by the Commission on the Status of Women. It was the ruling in the Supreme Court case *De Búrca and Anderson v. Attorney General* that caused the coalition to act. Similarly, as discussed later in the chapter, the coalition brought in legislation to legalise the sale of contraceptives before the Dáil because of the Supreme Court ruling in the McGee case. Because of health concerns and the potentially fatal risks posed by any further pregnancies, Mary McGee, already a mother of four children, had ordered contraceptive jelly from England. Customs officers seized it. She took her case to the High Court in 1972, and, after it failed, to the Supreme Court in 1973, which ruled in her favour.

Relations between the coalition parties were so good that in April 1973, at the Fine Gael ard-fheis, Oliver Flanagan was able to declare, 'Now the party of Arthur Griffith stands united with the party of James Connolly.' The presidential election in May which pitted Tom O'Higgins against Erskine Childers also helped to bond the parties, with Labour campaigning for the Fine Gael candidate. Despite this support O'Higgins failed to win and did not do nearly as well as he had against de Valera seven years earlier. The election result brought the government down to earth.

An event later in the year brought reality home in an even firmer fashion. The Arab-Israeli war of October 1973 resulted in the first oil crisis. This led to massive inflation and unemployment throughout the developed world, and it threw the Cosgrave government's economic calculations out the window. Even before the oil crisis, inflation was becoming a big problem in Ireland, with wage increases running at 20 per cent by mid-1973. The oil crisis accelerated this trend and the result was a very sharp rise in prices.

In response Ryan increased borrowing from 8 per cent of GNP in 1973 to 11 per cent in 1974 and a massive 16 per cent in 1975. However, in 1976 he hauled it back to 11 per cent and by 1977 it had been brought down to 9 per cent. One of the most difficult tasks the government had was convincing the trade unions to accept pay moderation at a time when inflation, fuelled by wage increases, was proving the biggest problem in the economy. The unions eventually agreed to a deal that resulted in wages temporarily lagging behind inflation in return for food subsidies which protected the worst off. 'I think in retrospect the economic policies of the government were in all the circumstances quite credible. The unprecedented oil rise in 1973 hit this country, as it did most of the rest of the world, like a whirlwind, resulting in plans and assumptions already made having to be drastically and quickly revised,' said Cosgrave.

The moderate wage agreement secured by the government with the cooperation of employers and unions was indeed remarkable. The maintenance to a large extent of employment and the creating of many new jobs by the IDA and others testify to the effectiveness of government policy. At the end of the period inflation was falling at a steady and continuing rate and agriculture and industry were expanding. At the same time, despite all the adverse effects of the oil price rise which permeated the economy, over 100,000 new houses were constructed, an all-time record for the State.[16]

The two coalition parties faced the oil crisis together. There was just one moment of serious tension when Labour threatened to walk out of government over an attempt by the Department of Finance to restrict social welfare increases. In protecting its social welfare constituency, Labour did very well during the Cosgrave coalition. Total welfare spending rose from £91.6 million in 1972/73 to £274.5 million four years later. Welfare expenditure as a percentage of GNP rose from 6½ to 10½ per cent. Most benefits rose by 125 per cent, well over the rate of increase in both wages and prices. The qualifying age for the old-age pension was brought down from 70 to 66, and groups such as single mothers and prisoners' wives received allowances for the first time. Cosgrave went on record after the start of the oil crisis to say that the poor were not going to bear the brunt of the problem, and he was true to his word.[17]

The political return to the coalition for its focus on protecting welfare at a time of crisis was negligible. Ryan recalled the tempestuous arguments he used to have with Frank Cluskey of Labour around the cabinet table over welfare rates. When the two met for the first time after the 1977 election Cluskey remarked, 'Jaysus, Richie, you were right. You always said we'd get no fucking thanks for all the welfare increases.'[18]

Another achievement of the coalition was a substantial increase in the number of new houses being built, which jumped to an average of 25,000 a year. In all, 100,000 houses were built during the coalition's first four years, an increase of 50 per cent in the public and private sectors. The removal of VAT from food in July 1975 was the fulfilment of another election promise.

A move that ended up doing political damage to Fine Gael was the introduction of a wealth tax. The notion of replacing estate and death duties with some form of wealth tax was a pet project of Garret

FitzGerald. He had tried to have it incorporated in the 'Just Society' programme of 1965 and later failed to have it adopted by his Fine Gael front-bench colleagues in 1969. FitzGerald finally managed to get the idea incorporated in the Fine Gael-Labour election manifesto of 1973, and after the election the task of implementing it fell to Richie Ryan.

> I believe the tax was fully justified, but we introduced it in the middle of the oil crisis when there was enough deflation of confidence and there was a lot of fear that it wasn't the time to do it. I feared not only the electoral unpopularity but the economic effect it was going to have. The Central Bank set up a very careful monitoring operation at my request to watch the capital outflows and we were pleasantly surprised there wasn't any identifiable outflow which appeared to indicate that as introduced the business community accepted it. But it certainly created the impression that the government had a philosophy of 'if it moves tax it and if it doesn't move tax it too.'[19]

The labels 'Red Richie' and 'Richie Ruin' were widely touted by Fianna Fáil, which fought so bitterly against the legislation that it had to be guillotined.

Politically and financially the wealth tax was a disaster for the government. Fianna Fáil's vehement opposition to the tax not only impressed the party's wealthy backers but also attracted popular support from an electorate that has repeatedly demonstrated a reluctance to accept new forms of taxation. On the financial front, the tax brought in less revenue than the old estate duties. When Fianna Fáil returned to power after 1977 the wealth tax was abolished but the estate duties were not reimposed. The net effect was to further narrow the tax base and place a bigger burden on ordinary taxpayers.

Ryan suffered politically as a result of the tight economic situation and became a target of Fianna Fáil criticism. When the heat was at its worst Ryan spoke to Cosgrave and suggested a cabinet reshuffle to take him out of Finance. 'I won't do that. It would be unfair to you because you are being proved right,' was the Taoiseach's response. 'Another factor with Cosgrave was that people would have expected FitzGerald to get Finance in any reshuffle and Cosgrave just didn't respect his judgement.'[20]

As well as being attacked by Fianna Fáil, Ryan was pilloried on a satirical RTÉ television programme called *Hall's Pictorial Weekly*. The coalition as a whole took a drubbing on the programme, but Ryan – depicted as Richie Ruin, the Minister for Hardship – was singled out for special treatment. He recalled that a number of ministers regularly spoke at cabinet meetings about how unfair the programme was and demanded that Cruise O'Brien should intervene with RTÉ. 'Cosgrave and Conor would have no truck with that. They had the same view that you just didn't do that kind of thing. If you are in the kitchen you have to put up with the heat.'[21]

If Ryan was the *bête noire* on the Fine Gael side of the government, Conor Cruise O'Brien occupied that role in the Labour half of the coalition. As well as being Minister for Posts and Telegraphs he was also head of the Government Information Service. During the lifetime of the government O'Brien was regularly involved in controversy about the North. He took a strong anti-republican line and tried to bring the electorate around to an understanding of the unionist position, often inspiring a furious reaction not only from Fianna Fáil and the media but from many of his own colleagues in both government parties. Whatever Cosgrave thought of O'Brien's views he never interfered or asked him to desist. As far as Cosgrave was concerned, O'Brien was Labour Party spokesman on Northern Ireland and was entitled to express his views in that capacity.

Liam Cosgrave did many unorthodox things during his political career but the most stunning was the way he voted in the Dáil against his own government's contraceptive legislation in July 1974. It was one of the most remarkable episodes in Irish political history and it left many of his government colleagues dazed for a long time afterwards. Contraception was a serious political issue when the coalition took office. Under a 1935 act the sale and import of contraceptives was illegal but in 1973 the Supreme Court found the ban on importing unconstitutional and there was a widespread demand for reform of the law. The matter was the responsibility of the Minister for Justice, Pat Cooney, and he instructed his officials to draft a piece of legislation entitled the Control of Importation, Sale and Manufacture of Contraception Bill. This would have permitted contraceptives to be imported and sold to married people only, under licence by pharmacists.

FitzGerald recalled that when the issue came before the cabinet in the spring of 1974 Cosgrave stayed silent during the discussion on the terms of the Bill. 'This was not strictly a government bill but one introduced by the Minister for Justice, Pat Cooney, on his own account, a distinction that I am afraid was far too subtle for many people to grasp. Three times at the meeting Conor Cruise O'Brien endeavoured to extract from the Taoiseach a reaction to the proposed bill but each time he failed. We left the meeting no wiser about his attitude.'[22]

O'Brien remembered things a little differently. 'I had an idea that Cosgrave would vote against. And I pressed him on it in cabinet to tell us what way he was going to vote and all he would say was "a free vote, there must be a free vote. We are all free to vote whichever way we want." I was the only one who pressed him on it.'[23]

The drafting of the bill and its introduction in the Dáil took some time and it was not formally introduced for the second-stage debate until July. By this time there were suggestions that a small number of Fine Gael and Labour TDs were unhappy about the legislation and might avail of the opportunity of the free vote to oppose it. On the Fine Gael side Oliver Flanagan and the Fine Gael leader in the Seanad, Michael O'Higgins, were known to be hostile, while Dan Spring of Labour was another who had serious doubts. He would later absent himself from the vote.

Fianna Fáil, sensing an opportunity to embarrass the government, had no hesitation in opposing the bill and imposing a whip to ensure that all the party TDs voted against it, regardless of their personal views. In contrast, the coalition partners had a free vote – the only one during the lifetime of their government.

The bill was introduced in the Dáil by Pat Cooney, Minister for Justice, on 4 July 1974. He pointed out that the Criminal Law Amendment Act (1935), section 17, provided that it was an offence to sell, import or advertise for sale contraceptives. The Supreme Court in the McGee case had decided that the ban on importing was unconstitutional but had made no finding about the issue of sale. 'We now have a rather anomalous situation that there is no restriction whatever on the importation of contraceptives but there is an absolute prohibition on their sale,' Cooney explained, arguing that the ban on sale could be successfully challenged in the courts by a married couple.

Cooney's bill provided for the sale of contraceptives through pharmacies, but only to married people. Fianna Fáil opposed the measure with what in retrospect seems a parody of moral indignation. Desmond O'Malley, Fianna Fáil spokesperson on Justice, thundered,

> I feel that our duty as a legislature is, so far as we can within the confines of our Constitution, as interpreted for us by the Supreme Court, to deter fornication and promiscuity, to promote public morality and to prevent in so far as we can, there are of course clear limitations on the practicability of that, public immorality.

When the Dáil voted on the bill on 16 July it was defeated by 75 votes to 61. The defeat was bad enough for the government, but the astounding thing was that the Taoiseach voted against it. He was joined in the No lobby by the Minister for Education, Dick Burke, and five other Fine Gael TDs. Dan Spring, known to be opposed to the legislation, did not travel to Dublin for the vote.

Before the vote Cosgrave kept his views entirely to himself. He planned to vote last so that no one else would be swayed by his decision. That strategy came unstuck, however, because the government chief whip, John Kelly, only discovered after the vote had been called that his Taoiseach was going to vote against. FitzGerald recalled:

> TDs had already begun passing through the lobbies when John discovered his error. Appalled at having misled some conservatively minded deputies into voting for the bill on a false premise, he immediately urged the Taoiseach to vote without delay – for,

unaware of John Kelly's activities, Liam Cosgrave had loyally intended to wait until the end before casting his vote so as not to influence other members of the party. Once urged by John, he voted immediately against the bill, and some who had not yet passed through then lobbies decided to follow him. By then, having voted, I was back on the front bench and, seeing what was happening, I said to Pat Cooney, 'Wouldn't it be funny if he defeated the government.' Not realising yet that this was what in fact had happened.[24]

Peter Barry recalled:

Blow me pink when I saw him walking up the stairs. You could have knocked me down. First of all I went pale, but then you couldn't help feeling, well, fair dues. He believes in something, he knows the price he may have to pay for doing it. But of course we had been warned on the Offences Against the State Act that he wouldn't go against his own conscience but we never took it on board, you see. That was a warning. There was principle there and he was going to abide by his own conscience.[25]

O'Brien was not in the least surprised by Cosgrave's vote.

Afterwards some of my colleagues, talking without attribution to the press, said we were all stunned. I wasn't stunned, I was expecting it. I respected his decision. I was, of course, on the other side, but I couldn't say that he had led us in any way to believe that he would do anything else other than what he actually did.[26]

Other people in government, though, were stunned. John Bruton remembers being 'quite shocked to see Liam Cosgrave, Tom Enright and Richard Burke voting against the bill. There was a lot of surprise in the party. I don't think it was the right thing for Liam Cosgrave to do. I would be inclined to be favourably disposed towards most of the things he did but it was a mistake for a Taoiseach not to vote with his own government. It was not collective responsibility.'[27]

One issue that dominated politics from the beginning until the end of the Cosgrave government was the violence generated by the conflict in Northern Ireland and the efforts to devise a political solution. Even before they took office Cosgrave and some of his potential ministers flew to London for a meeting with Ted Heath. At that stage the IRA campaign was at its height, internment still in force, and the British desperately searching for a political solution. Just six days before Cosgrave became Taoiseach the British government published a white paper on the North which was to be the signpost on the road to the Sunningdale Agreement.

Within both Fine Gael and Labour attitudes on the North had undergone a transformation since the beginning the Northern conflict. Cruise O'Brien provided the intellectual argument for change within the Labour Party from traditional republican thinking to a recognition of the consent principle, but it was resisted by a significant number of his colleagues. In Fine Gael, which is still subtitled the 'United Ireland Party', old attitudes were also changing. It was not that there was any sympathy for the IRA or its campaign of violence but even in 1970 there was still a broad acceptance of the traditional nationalist view that the central problem was partition and the British presence in the North. That view was changed mainly by Garret FitzGerald and Paddy Harte.

At first Cosgrave was slow to go along with the new thinking on the North. He was very consciously part of the Sinn Féin tradition and was proud of his father's role in 1916. While Cosgrave was decidedly anti-IRA he distrusted the British and held that the misgovernment of the North for fifty years was the root cause of the problem. However, the increasing brutality of IRA violence in the early 1970s shocked the population of the Republic and prompted a reassessment of received nationalist wisdom which had been largely unchallenged since partition in 1922. Before they took office in March 1973 both Fine Gael and Labour were edging towards an analysis of the North which saw a divided community, rather than partition, as the nub of the problem, and which recognised that there could be no change in the constitutional status of the North without the agreement of the majority of the people there. In a speech in Blackrock, Co. Dublin, a few months after taking office Cosgrave said: 'We must be prepared to recognise the right of the two communities in Northern Ireland to set aside their different views of the eventual shape of Irish political institutions and to establish institutions that will provide the North with a system of government designed to reconcile the two communities in peace and harmony.'

Cosgrave's speech was regarded by the Unionist leader, Brian Faulkner, as 'the most important by a Prime Minister of the Republic for years'. It was made against a background of intense political activity in relation to the North by both the British and Irish governments. The British white paper had been published only days after Cosgrave took office and its broad thrust was acceptable to Dublin, stressing as it did the need for a power-sharing government in the North and some form of Council of Ireland to recognise the Irish dimension to the problem. On the Irish side primary responsibility for Northern Ireland policy has always rested with the Taoiseach rather than the Minister for Foreign Affairs, although the two usually work in tandem. Despite their personal dislike of one another, Cosgrave and FitzGerald worked well in government. 'Indeed the tensions that had previously existed between Liam Cosgrave and myself completely evaporated in government and the differences in our attitudes to Northern Ireland that had caused problems in opposition also disappeared,' FitzGerald wrote.[28]

On 17 September 1973 there was a crucial meeting at Baldonnel military airport outside Dublin between Ted Heath and Cosgrave. The Taoiseach recalled:

> The meeting at Baldonnel between Mr Heath and myself arranged the Sunningdale Conference. That was the start of the arrangements for it. Fianna Fáil was not involved in the preparation for it. Fianna Fáil had left office in March 1973 and Corish and I saw Heath before we assumed office. I met him [Heath] again in London before Baldonnel. There were preliminaries but Baldonnel set the scene for Sunningdale. It lasted all day between Mr Heath and myself.[29]

It took a couple of months to iron out all the difficulties but after agreement in principle on a power-sharing arrangement had been worked out an extraordinary delegation set out from Ireland to Sunningdale Park in Berkshire on 5 December. Cosgrave led a team of nearly forty people, virtually the entire cabinet and the top ranks of the civil service, to the conference. In all, 120 politicians and officials from the Republic, the North and Britain attended the conference, which was designed to end the Northern problem once and for all and put Anglo-Irish relations on a proper footing for the first time in history.

Before he went, Cosgrave tried to discourage a belief that was gaining widespread currency in the Irish media that a major step on the road to a united Ireland was about to be agreed with the British. He urged the Irish public not to 'pin exaggerated hopes on what these talks can produce in the immediate future'. Nonetheless the strength of the Irish delegation and the presence of so many cabinet ministers indicated that Cosgrave saw the talks as the most important since the Treaty negotiations of 1921. The fact that the negotiations began on the 52nd anniversary of the signing of the Treaty added to this impression of history-making, although Cosgrave himself dismisses it as a coincidence.

Unlike during the Treaty negotiations, politicians from Northern Ireland were also at the talks. The chairman of the Executive designate, Brian Faulkner, and Gerry Fitt and John Hume of the SDLP were among the delegates. With power-sharing already agreed, Sunningdale was essentially about the structure of a Council of Ireland.

Cosgrave and Faulkner quickly established a rapport which cemented the process. Before his premature death in 1977 Faulkner recalled that he first met Cosgrave in the early 1950s.

My wife and I spent many holidays in the South, often caravanning with the children in Achill or Connemara or Kerry. It was in the early 1950s on a fair day in the village of Claremorris in County Mayo that I first met Mr Cosgrave, later Prime Minister of the Republic. I had gone to hear what he had to say at a political meeting in the square and afterwards I went up to have a word with him and he invited me into the pub for a drink.[30]

The two men also shared a passion for horses and hunting, which was to prove a common bond when they met at Sunningdale. FitzGerald describes how he was having breakfast with Faulkner on the first morning of the talks when they were joined by Cosgrave. 'They had already met on the hunting field, I gathered, and within minutes they were chatting away about mutual acquaintances. They were quickly on good terms, strolling around the grounds together during breaks in the meetings.'[31]

The central issues were the Council of Ireland and the building of mutual confidence between unionists and nationalists. The Irish government accepted for the first time that unity could only come about with the consent of the people of the North. The British, for their part, accepted that if the people of Northern Ireland ever wanted unity they would support this wish. These two principles have since become the basis for all subsequent approaches by the two governments to the Northern problem. Extradition was another thorny subject which was discussed in the talks; but the negotiations centred on the shape and powers of a Council of Ireland.

The agreement on a power-sharing Executive for the North, which had been arrived at months earlier, was ratified at Sunningdale. The eleven-member Executive, with Faulkner at its head, contained six Unionists, four SDLP and one Alliance member. The settlement was designed to isolate the gunmen on both the republican and loyalist side but both sets of extremists continued their violence unabated and Faulkner gradually lost the support of his own party. The Council of Ireland became the focus for unionist hostility.

As the role and functions of the Council of Ireland continued to be a millstone around Faulkner's neck agreement was reached between the Unionists and the SDLP that the wide-ranging powers for the body, as originally proposed, were unrealistic. Faulkner and his team of ministers met Cosgrave and his senior government colleagues at Hillsborough, Co. Down, in February to agree a more limited formula. The watering down of the Council of Ireland came too late to help Faulkner. In February 1974 a British general election was called by Ted Heath, and the Conservatives narrowly lost power to Labour. In Northern Ireland the anti-Faulkner Unionists swept the boards, winning every seat except West Belfast, which was held by Gerry Fitt. The writing was on the wall for the power-sharing Executive.

In May came the Ulster Workers' Council strike and the spineless capitulation of the Wilson government to it. The short-lived experiment in power-sharing was over, killed by unionist intransigence on the one hand and an over-ambitions nationalist agenda on the part of the Irish government and the SDLP. The continuing campaign of IRA violence only hardened attitudes all round. Just as the UWC strike was starting Dublin and Monaghan were bombed by loyalists. The bombs went off on 17 May, killing 28 people instantly and injuring another 137. Some of the injured subsequently died, making the atrocity the worst terrorist outrage in Ireland or Britain during the troubles. The failure to arrest anybody for the atrocity led to claims in subsequent years that the bombings had not been properly investigated.

Cosgrave was impressed with Heath's commitment and believed that if he had remained in government Sunningdale would ultimately have succeeded. 'Sunningdale mainly collapsed because of the weakness of the Labour government. Indeed I think it is true of all British Labour governments … they hadn't the guts to put the thing through and they didn't stand up to the workers strike. Now if they had stood up to it I think Sunningdale might have worked.' He also points to the deal that Callaghan and Michael Foot did with the Unionists later in the 1970s to get their support in the House of Commons. 'The Labour government on all that were very unrealistic and untrustworthy.'[32]

After the collapse of Faulkner's Executive, Cosgrave could do little except try to keep the situation as calm as possible. In this gloomy atmosphere the coalition concentrated on domestic security and particularly the threat posed by the IRA to the Republic itself. In the autumn of 1973 ministers were told that they and their families now faced the threat of kidnapping by extreme republicans. Cosgrave initiated a cabinet discussion of the issue and it was agreed that if any member of their family was kidnapped they would opt out of the discussion on the matter and that, regardless of the threats, no concessions would be made to the kidnappers. The security provided for ministers was stepped up from the normal armed garda driver to an escort car with two armed detectives.

One of the most shocking IRA atrocities in the Republic took place in March 1974, when the IRA murdered Senator Billy Fox, a Fine Gael politician and a Presbyterian from Monaghan. Fox was murdered when he called at his fiancé's house as it was being ransacked by a dozen members of the IRA who threw the family Bible into the fire during the raid. Fox was chased from the house into a field, gunned down and left to die in agony. The IRA tried to cover up this brutal sectarian killing by denying responsibility for the attack, sending a wreath to his funeral and claiming that Fox was sympathetic to their cause. They also blamed the UDA for the murder. However, the Gardaí captured some members of the IRA gang and all were ultimately arrested and given long prison sentences.

Another ominous development as far as Cosgrave was concerned was the increasing contact between the British government and the IRA towards the end of 1974. This resulted in an IRA ceasefire before Christmas which was extended for the best part of nine months although sporadic republican violence continued. British ministers and officials in the North were in constant touch with Sinn Féin activists to monitor the ceasefire.

During Cosgrave's period as Taoiseach there were a number of spectacular jail break-outs by republicans as well as hunger strikes and frequent civil disturbances. In 1974 an IRA prisoner, Michael Gaughan, died in Parkhurst prison in Britain after a sixty-five-day hunger strike. The funeral in Ireland provided the IRA with an opportunity for massive public demonstrations of support. Another hunger-striker, Frank Stagg, died on 12 February 1976 and the IRA again tried to use it as a huge propaganda exercise. The family was deeply divided on the issue, with the dead man's widow and his brother Emmet Stagg in favour of a private funeral and other members of the family backing a public display. Garret FitzGerald recalls that the British did a deal to hand the body over to the

IRA, who proposed to parade the coffin through the streets of Dublin. The government reacted with fury and the British changed their plans, giving the body instead to the Irish authorities at Heathrow Airport. The plane bringing the body back was diverted from Dublin to Shannon to prevent demonstrations in the capital. Stagg was buried in Ballina and his grave cemented over by the authorities, but the IRA later exhumed the coffin and buried it in a republican plot.[33]

In 1975 the feared kidnapping took place, but it was not a minister at the centre of the drama. Rather, a Dutch industrialist, Tiede Herrema, was abducted. His kidnappers demanded the release of three high-profile IRA prisoners, Rose Dugdale, Kevin Mallon and James Hyland, and threatened that Herrema would be killed within forty-eight hours if they were not released. The government refused to negotiate, and the kidnap gang was tracked by gardaí to a house in Monasterevin. A three-week siege ensued which culminated in the Dutch businessman's release, unharmed.

The following year there was an even bigger security crisis for the government. The country was stunned on 21 July 1976 when the British ambassador, Christopher Ewart-Biggs, was murdered by the IRA just outside his official residence at Sandyford, Co. Dublin. The atrocity provoked widespread calls for tough anti-terrorist measures, and the government responded with the Offences Against the State (Amendment) Act, which allowed terrorist suspects to be detained for up to seven days.

However, this legislation was not introduced until the Dáil returned after the summer recess and by that time civil liberties groups and the media queried whether extra powers for the Gardaí were necessary. When the legislation was passed by the Dáil, Fianna Fáil attacked it strongly and President Cearbhall Ó Dálaigh, instead of signing it, decided, as he was entitled to do under the Constitution, to consult the Council of State about referring it to the Supreme Court. As the legislation was passed under the terms of the Emergency Powers Act (1939), coalition ministers were convinced that its constitutionality could not be in doubt and there was considerable resentment at the President's action.

There was already a deep level of distrust between Cosgrave and Ó Dálaigh. As Taoiseach and President their relationship was purely formal, without any personal warmth. Ó Dálaigh by temperament was the polar opposite of Cosgrave. Exuberant, opinionated, strongly republican in his views, a bit of a show-off and quick to stand on his dignity, he had virtually nothing in common with the taciturn Taoiseach. The President was known to believe that Cosgrave was not assiduous enough in observing the Constitutional proprieties by keeping him informed of political developments, but the Taoiseach in his turn felt that too much was being asked of him. The tension between the two men continued as the coalition struggled with the security threat posed by terrorists.

Jim Dooge, who attended the Council of State meeting summoned by the President, had a vivid memory of what transpired.

> To my mind Cearbhall Ó Dálaigh was more intent on proving to everybody that he could refer emergency legislation to the Supreme Court than he was with the contents of the bill itself. Tom O'Higgins was there as Chief Justice and said that since the matter might come to the Supreme Court he wouldn't give any advice to the president. But Tom Finlay was there as president of the High Court and he gave devastating advice that there was no point referring it to the Supreme Court. The legislation was so clearly constitutional that it was a waste of time. Cearbhall kept trying to say there was a suggestion that he could not refer emergency legislation but Finlay was quite clear that as it was emergency legislation there was no doubt about its constitutionality. After that meeting I was of the opinion that Cearbhall was being irresponsible.[34]

Ó Dálaigh referred the bill to the Supreme Court, to the annoyance of most ministers, and the court found that it was indeed constitutional.

However, before that happened the Minister for Defence, Paddy Donegan, made a dramatic intervention which had serious consequences for the government. Attending a ceremony at Columb Barracks in Mullingar on 18 October he made a short speech during which he attacked the decision of the President.

It was amazing that when the President sent the Emergency Powers Bill to the Supreme Court he did not send the powers of the army, he did not send the seven years maximum penalty for membership, he did not send the ten years maximum penalty for inciting people to join the IRA to the Supreme Court. In my opinion he is a thundering disgrace. The fact is that the army must stand behind the state.[35]

A journalist with the *Westmeath Examiner,* Don Lavery, reported Donegan's comments for the national newspapers. In the days following there were persistent rumours that Donegan had used stronger language than 'thundering disgrace', and it was also widely rumoured that he was drunk at the time. Donegan himself always maintained that he wasn't drunk on that occasion but that he was feeling under the weather because he had been involved in a car crash that morning. He was also emotional over the murder by the IRA a few days before of Garda Michael Clerkin. The death of the garda, who was blown up by a bomb, was regarded at the time as the republican movement's response to the emergency legislation. Whatever the motive for the minister's remarks it plunged the coalition into an immediate political crisis.

When Donegan returned to Dublin later in the day and realised the implications of an attack on the President he went to the Taoiseach and offered to resign but Cosgrave refused to accept it. Instead Donegan sought an appointment with the President to apologise. Ó Dálaigh refused to meet the minister even though he drove up to the Phoenix Park hoping to be admitted to Áras an Uachtaráin and waited for a time in the Park as efforts were made to get the President to receive him. Failing to be admitted, the minister returned to Government Buildings and later issued a public statement. 'I regret the remarks which arose out of my deep feelings for the security of our citizens. I intend to offer my apologies to the President as soon as possible,' he said.

The following day Cosgrave summoned his ministers to meet him in his room and read out a letter from the President protesting at the minister's remarks. The letter said that the relationship between the

President and the minister had been irreparably breached and went on to ask whether the remarks could be construed otherwise than as an insinuation that the President did not stand behind the state. Had the minister any conception of his responsibilities as a minister, and in particular as Minister for Defence?

Two days later the issue was raised in the Dáil when the leader of Fianna Fáil, Jack Lynch, moved a motion calling for Donegan to resign. Cosgrave expressed his regret for the incident but also defended Donegan's record as minister. 'The Minister for Defence did not attack our institutions. He made what he and I regard as a serious comment on what the President did in a disrespectful way.'

The following day President Ó Dálaigh resigned. In mid-afternoon Cosgrave was informed that a despatch rider was on his way from the Áras with a message which he immediately knew contained his resignation. The Taoiseach called senior ministers to his office and having discussed the issue he rang Donegan and accepted his resignation. However, it was too late to stop the President's move. 'The damage done to the government was immense. Liam Cosgrave had been fatally betrayed by his own excessive loyalty to one of his ministers,' was FitzGerald's verdict.[36]

The resignation of the President caused a sensation, and Fianna Fáil put down a motion of no confidence in the government, which was debated by the Dáil on 28 October. The government took a pasting during the debate, but the stability of the coalition was not damaged. As Halligan put it, 'Once it was clear that Cosgrave was not going to require the head of Donegan there was no way we were going to look for his head because we didn't think it was an issue on which to bring down a government.'[37]

Cosgrave sailed through the Dáil debate as if it were a matter of routine. His speech was typically pithy, and in response to some Fianna Fáil deputies who claimed his position as Taoiseach had been put in jeopardy by the crisis he replied: 'The opposition are always worrying about me. When I was in opposition they were afraid I would be toppled from one day to the other. When I am in government they are still afraid I will be toppled.' The coalition won the division by 73 votes to 67. From a narrow viewpoint, Cosgrave's Dáil analysis was right; in political terms the row revealed that the coalition parties were ready to stick together through thick and thin and the Fianna Fáil motion was a failure. However, in the matter of public opinion the coalition suffered grievously, if the media coverage is anything to go by. Ó Dálaigh's resignation was a body blow from which the government never recovered from the viewpoint of public esteem.

Conor Cruise O'Brien recalled that the incident caused strains in the government but not between Fine Gael and Labour.

> In a coalition government a lot of the arguments go on off stage inside the two parties and I think there were signs of strain within Fine Gael. I think Liam didn't want to sacrifice him but I think Garret and others did, on grounds of constitutional propriety. I argued on the other hand that as Donegan had gone to the Park – gone to Canossa if you like – it should be allowed to rest there.

Peter Barry feels that Cosgrave should have accepted Donegan's resignation at the beginning of the controversy.

> Loyalty was a very big thing with him, to a fault, and he didn't like Cearbhall Ó Dálaigh. I understand his loyalty but politically Cosgrave should have accepted Donegan's resignation. I think Paddy would have been a lot happier; I am surmising now but I feel Paddy would not have minded doing his penance. It damaged the government and it damaged Liam. He had to choose between a friend and the right thing and he chose a friend. Paddy was a very undisciplined loose cannon on a very wobbly ship.

One liberal Fine Gael politician who was not regarded as a Cosgrave supporter had sympathy with him on this issue. 'I felt Donegan made a fair charge, although his language was very inappropriate. It was so typical of Liam just defending his minister.'[38]

The negative public reaction to the coalition over the resignation of Ó Dálaigh was compounded by a series of reports in the *Irish Times* at about the same time which indicated that terrorist suspects were being ill-treated by the Gardaí. The stories written by Joe Joyce, Don Buckley and Renagh Holohan caused serious public concern about the tactics being used by the so-called 'heavy gang' to extract confessions from republicans suspected of serious crime. The Minister for Justice, Pat Cooney, strenuously rejected the stories, as did Cosgrave. FitzGerald remembers meeting two senior gardaí, who told him of their worry about the way some confessions had been extracted. He tried to raise the issue in the cabinet but got short shrift from Cosgrave and Cooney. He even contemplated resigning from the government over the issue but decided against it.[39]

With security concerns uppermost in his mind Cosgrave delivered an emotional speech to the Fine Gael ard-fheis in the Mansion House in Dublin in May 1977. He curtly dismissed complaints in the media that the rights of some IRA suspects had been violated by asking what civil rights has been possessed by Billy Fox or by the two gardaí murdered in the course of their duty. He called the *Irish Times* investigation into the heavy gang 'a malicious campaign of vilification' against the Gardaí. Then to thunderous applause he declared:

> Not for the first time has this party stood between the people of this country and anarchy. And remember, those people who comment so freely and write so freely, some of them aren't even Irish, no doubt many of you are familiar with an expression in some parts of the country where an outsider is described as a blow-in. Some of these are blow-ins. Now as far as we're concerned they can blow out or blow up.

This speech became as famous as his 'mongrel foxes' declaration five years earlier.[40]

A short time later, on 25 May 1977, Cosgrave made the biggest blunder of his political career. He asked President Hillery to dissolve the 20th Dáil and called a general election for 16 June. There were divided views in the cabinet over whether to hold an election in June or wait until the autumn, when the economic upswing would have had more time to percolate through to the voters, but the decision to go to the country in June was taken by Cosgrave himself. Not alone was the timing wrong, the government had made no preparations of any kind for a June campaign. Incredibly, the coalition parties commissioned an opinion poll to measure the public mood only after the election was called.

There was a similarly casual approach to preparing the policies on which Fine Gael would fight the election and they were cobbled together after the date was announced. This dreadful preparation for the campaign stemmed from disagreement among ministers about the best date for an election. It was allied to complacency about a favourable outcome as a result of the constituency revision overseen by the Minister for Local Government, James Tully, which was widely regarded as making the re-election of the coalition a certainty. The proliferation of three-seat constituencies in Dublin was designed to maximise the number of Fine Gael and Labour seats, at the expense of Fianna Fáil. On top of the Tullymander, as it came to be known, the coalition parties were encouraged by solid performances in the seven by-elections held during the government's lifetime. In particular, the victory of Enda Kenny in Mayo West in November 1975 and Brendan Halligan in Dublin South-West in June 1976, combined with Fianna Fáil's loss of Donegal North-East to Patrick Keaveney of Independent Fianna Fáil, appeared to indicate that the tide was running in the coalition's favour.

From early in 1977 there was considerable media speculation about the date of the general election. One of Cosgrave's central objectives was to prove that coalition governments could work and that they need not fall apart in disarray, as the two inter-party governments had done. This objective had been achieved by the spring of 1977 when the government achieved four years in office, and an election some time that year was inevitable. Fianna Fáil prepared for it well in advance, appointing a new young team to run the party and devising policies and strategies for an all-out effort to win back power. Fine Gael and Labour, preoccupied with the cares of office, hardly focused on the election until it was called.

Richie Ryan recalled that he heard about the election date after being summoned to the Taoiseach's office. 'Richie, we are going to the country,' said Cosgrave. 'Corish came to me earlier in the week and he is wobbling like a jellyfish. He says the Labour Party might not stick together over the summer. Thornley is in a bad way and there are other tensions in the party. And if we don't go now the government could collapse over Labour's internal squabbles.'

'Oh, Liam, it is too soon,' responded Ryan. 'People are still not convinced that the economy is turning around. The autumn would be the time to go.'

'I have already told Brendan, so we have to go, and I want you to be director of elections.'[41]

Jack Jones of MRBI unveiled the results of the opinion poll, commissioned after the election was called, nine days into the campaign, to a meeting of the campaign committee in Government Buildings. The coalition politicians were left reeling by the result, which showed Fianna Fáil at 59 per cent of the vote, Fine Gael 25 per cent, Labour 10 per cent, unspecified coalition 4 per cent, and others 2 per cent. FitzGerald summed up the mood by remarking, 'Can we undissolve the Dáil?' Dooge was given the unenviable task of taking the information to Cosgrave, but there were no histrionics when the bad news was imparted. 'Can you trust these things?' remarked Cosgrave, who had never made a secret of his own doubts about opinion polls. 'Well, you can trust them to within 4 or 5 per cent,' Dooge responded. 'This means we have no real chance,' came the Taoiseach's laconic response. Dooge recalled:

> Cosgrave fought the whole campaign facing that disaster but he never betrayed a hint of it. He typically fought the campaign scrupulously, refusing to use government resources, the same as Garret did afterwards. He wouldn't even use a government Xerox machine. It was really amazing in hindsight, but Liam fought a very good campaign, knowing that he had no chance.[42]

Meanwhile Fianna Fáil launched an infamous giveaway manifesto which was to cost the country dear in the long run but proved very attractive to voters in 1977. Rates on houses were to be abolished, as was car tax. Grants for first-time house-buyers and a huge expansion of the public service to create new jobs were also promised, but it was the straightforward giveaways that proved so attractive.

While senior coalition figures knew they were facing an electoral disaster they didn't inform their junior colleagues or give any public hint of it. The media, in their blissful ignorance, made the government the clear favourites to win the election. On 2 June, before the government got its bad poll news, the *Irish Times* printed its own poll results under the heading 'Survey indicates Fianna Fáil lead over coalition.' Incredibly, no figures for party support were produced in the poll, which looked at how the electorate perceived the government and the opposition in relation to the issues.[43]

Cosgrave in his election speeches stressed the unity of the coalition. 'The government is a cohesive, united one and I believe it is not immodest of me to say that the team I selected are talented and have done their jobs well and thoroughly. They have come through the most testing of times with determination and drive,' and praised individual Fine Gael and Labour ministers by name.

On 5 June, Cosgrave toured North Tipperary. By this time he knew the bad poll results but he didn't let it show. Dick Walsh, who accompanied him, wrote for the following day's *Irish Times*: 'The script tells the official story. Unscripted, Mr Cosgrave was direct and nearly jovial. He emphasised rates and raised a cheer when he derided Fianna Fáil's promise to abolish road tax.' Getting a dig in at the local Fianna Fáil TD Michael O'Kennedy, who had bought a house in Dublin, Cosgrave praised the two coalition TDs for the constituency, saying, 'You haven't to travel 100 miles to find them.' He asked Fine Gael voters to continue their preferences for the Labour TD, John Ryan. 'Lift your pencil and don't waste a vote,' he said.[44]

On Saturday 11 June, Jack Jones presented the results of a second opinion poll to the coalition campaign committee. It showed that Fianna Fáil had dropped eight points to 51 per cent and gave Fine Gael and Labour some hope that the tide was now running in their favour. However, the campaign was entering its final days and there was not enough time to make further inroads into the Fianna Fáil vote. In the last days of the campaign Cosgrave concentrated on law and order, which didn't go down very well with an electorate preoccupied with bread-and-butter politics. Attacking media commentators who had criticised the Gardaí and reported the conditions of republican prisoners in Port Laoise prison, the Taoiseach was in fighting form. He said that the prisoners had been jailed for 'most heinous crimes of murder, shooting and robbery. They aren't there for not having lights on their bikes. Where else should they be but in prison.'

The Taoiseach's emphasis on security was echoed by Cruise O'Brien, who also attacked Charles Haughey in a BBC radio interview. Richie Ryan and Garret FitzGerald felt this attack played straight into Fianna Fáil's hands and tried to rein in the Cruiser. 'The only argument we had in the coalition at that time, and it didn't involve Liam, was between myself and Garret,' O'Brien remembers. 'I was for having a go at Haughey and I started doing this and then I was told, absurdly in retrospect, that the thing to do was concentrate on the economic issues. We would have lost anyway but would have lost by a smaller margin if we had concentrated on "Haughey is not a safe man" type of charge. There was a good case to be made for that and it would at least, have diverted some attention from the promises.'[45]

The media were totally unaware of the problems besetting the coalition from the beginning of the campaign. Even the massive and warm public response to the leader of Fianna Fáil, Jack Lynch, in his nationwide tour didn't shake the assumption that Cosgrave was going to lead the coalition back to power, a feat that had never been achieved by a coalition leader in the history of the state.

On the Sunday before the election the country's leading political correspondents, interviewed on RTÉ radio, confidently predicted that Fine Gael and Labour would win an overall majority. Sean Duignan summed up the prevailing media mood when he said that if Fianna Fáil managed to win it would be 'the greatest comeback since Lazarus'.[46]

When the boxes were opened on 17 June it quickly became apparent that Lazarus had nothing on Fianna Fáil. The party's vote was up to 51 per cent, a feat achieved only once before, by Éamon de Valera in 1938. In terms of seats the Fianna Fáil performance was awesome. The party's strength in the Dáil increased from 69 in 1973 to 84. Fine Gael slumped from 54 to 43, while Labour declined from 19 to 17. The Tullymander, which had been designed to win the election for the coalition, actually made things worse than they need have been for the government. Three senior ministers – O'Brien, Keating and Cooney – lost their seats in the rout, which gave Fianna Fáil a massive twenty-seat majority in the Dáil. Jack Lynch was as stunned as his opponents by the scale of the victory.

'I didn't think it was going to be as bad. I was one of the more optimistic,' O'Brien recalled. Looking back, Brendan Halligan thought the 1977 campaign was a tribute to Cosgrave. 'A final judgement on Cosgrave as Taoiseach and as a party leader in coalition is that we went out united and fought a united campaign.'

Peter Barry remembers the disillusionment that followed. 'When the government changed, we were depressed and demoralised because we thought we had done a good job. We knew we had been psyched out of it.'[47]

A NEW LEADER: GARRET FITZGERALD

'*Garret had enormous appeal. People liked him and responded to his vision. That was the real reason party membership mushroomed.*'

— PETER PRENDERGAST.

Speculation about Cosgrave's intentions began the day after the 1977 election result, but no serious consideration was given to the possibility that he would step down as party leader at the age of fifty-seven. As all the parties assessed the situation over the weekend, the *Irish Times* published an article suggesting that Cosgrave and Corish might not continue on as their party leaders.

Garret FitzGerald was quoted as saying that he would respond to the demands of the party should Liam Cosgrave decide to resign.[1] This was regarded as ominous by some close supporters of Cosgrave, but the majority of Fine Gael TDs did not even consider the possibility that Cosgrave would step down. FitzGerald says in his memoirs that there was speculation about Brendan Corish, but not about Cosgrave. 'Those of us who felt we knew Liam Cosgrave thought it unlikely that he would opt out of political life at such an early age; he was only 57.'[2]

However, one week after the election, at the first party meeting to review the result, Cosgrave announced his resignation. There had been no consultation with anyone, and the announcement caused consternation. In his speech to the parliamentary party he paid tribute to his Fine Gael colleagues in government, but he mentioned only one by name, and that was FitzGerald. Given their fraught relationship, FitzGerald was as nonplussed as Cosgrave's own supporters, but he was immediately installed as the favourite to succeed. He had been a hugely successful Minister for Foreign Affairs, particularly in establishing the reputation of Ireland as an enthusiastic member of the EEC. His globe-trotting role also meant that he was not tarnished by the negative public reaction to the tough economic measures that had been required over the previous four years or by the various security controversies arising from the response to the IRA campaign of violence.

Richie Ryan was in the United States for the announcement, and he rang Peter Barry to arrange a meeting in Cork on his way to a finance ministers' meeting in Luxembourg. 'I got a room at Cork Airport and we had a chat,' Barry recalled. 'He was trying to mount a "stop Garret" campaign and he wanted me as the person who would do that.' Barry gave the matter careful consideration and took soundings among Fine Gael TDs and senators.

FitzGerald and Barry kept in contact with each other and compared notes of their level of support among the 62 people entitled to vote. 'I reckoned that I had the support of something like 43, leaving him with just under 20. He, on the other hand, believed he had 25 supporters, and was slightly upset that our figures did not tally,' FitzGerald wrote. 'I told him that if only half a dozen members of the party – less than 10 per cent – had allowed both of us to believe they were supporters, that showed a very high level of political honesty!' he added. In the event, Barry decided not to contest the leadership and instead he proposed FitzGerald, who was elected by acclamation on 1 July. Barry had no regrets about his decision, remarking years later:

I would have to say that Garret, with all the problems he would present to you on a personal basis and on a party basis, chasing after every little wisp, jumping up and down in the Dáil and not thinking things out, he was a visionary. There was an awful lot wrong with this country and he shook this party and this country into the 1990s.[3]

FitzGerald, who became leader of Fine Gael at the age of fifty-one, was a product of the new elite that took over the running of the country after the British left in 1922. Both his parents had taken part in the 1916 Rising and his father, Desmond, was Minister for External Affairs from 1922 to 1927, representing Ireland at the League of National and Imperial Conferences. His mother, Mabel McConnell, came from a unionist family in Belfast. Despite her background, she supported the Irish-language movement and became a convinced nationalist during her time at UCD. She was opposed to the Treaty, despite her husband's strong support for it.

FitzGerald was always very conscious of this strand of his family history, and it inspired his lifelong political ambition to promote mutual understanding between nationalists and unionists. He was brought up in the comfortable middle-class surroundings of the Dublin southside and was educated by the Jesuits at Belvedere College. It was there that one of his teachers, Father Roland Burke Savage, spotted his talents as a debater and encouraged him to enter politics. FitzGerald alleged that he even forecast that his pupil would one day become Taoiseach.[4] After Belvedere he went on to UCD, where, as a first-year student, he met Joan O'Farrell, who was two years ahead of him. She was initially unimpressed. 'I took a dislike to him. I thought he was very brash,' she recalled in an interview on Channel 4 in August 1991. Her initial impression was soon overcome, and a romance flowered as they got to know each other. They were married in 1947, when he was twenty-one. They were devoted to each other for the rest of their lives. As Olivia O'Leary put it, 'they glowed in one another's company'.[5] Joan was a huge influence on him throughout his political career. After a sparkling undergraduate career he went on to work in Aer Lingus before returning to UCD as a lecturer in economics.

Encouraged by his old teacher Father Burke Savage, who was now editor of the influential quarterly *Studies,* FitzGerald published his personal manifesto, 'Seeking a National Purpose', in that journal in 1964. He proposed a philosophy for social action that would combine the various strands of Irish society (which he identified as peasant, republican, Christian) while also drawing on universal philosophies and wider traditions. He argued for a society that would be 'neither exclusive nor sectional'.

In a book eight years later expanding on his political philosophy, *Towards a New Ireland,* he referred to the *Studies* article in the epilogue, saying, 'I would place more stress on the need to eliminate sectarianism ... I believe that much of what I wrote on the eve of my entry into politics remains valid as an ideal for Irish society.'[6] He set out his definition of pluralism in the preface to the book as 'a society within which people of different religious, cultural or linguistic traditions would be treated as equal citizens, and would be subjected to no disability because they did not share the tradition that happens to be that of a numerical majority of the population.' He held the view that minorities must have found Ireland 'somewhat suffocating' because of legislation influenced by the traditions of the majority.[7]

FitzGerald entered politics because he wanted to change Ireland in line with his vision of a modern, tolerant European democracy. He strongly believed that coming to an accommodation with Northern unionists, rather than sticking to old slogans about a united Ireland, was the way to proceed. His wider interests meant that, in spite of his Fine Gael pedigree, he was never a true party man, and he confessed in his autobiography that he voted for Fianna Fáil in 1961 out of admiration for Seán Lemass. His political instincts in later years were closer to Labour, and he only joined Fine Gael because he believed it gave him a better opportunity to achieve what he wanted in politics.[8]

At his first press conference FitzGerald said a new emphasis was required to improve Irish society but this must be done through a consensus to avoid a polarisation of the generations which he saw as a potential danger. He emphasised the need for a reintroduction of idealism and a sense of the overall national interest as against the dominance of sectoral interests. 'Having thus reasserted the social-democratic principles of the Just Society policies of the 1960s, I went on to stress the importance of not weakening the coalition option with Labour, so that at all times an alternative government would be available.'

He moved quickly to appoint a team of advisers to help him in his task of reviving the party. Probably the most important adviser of all, who did not have any official position, was his wife, Joan. She was not simply a devoted partner but someone who was deeply involved in his political life. Although she suffered from a debilitating illness as she became older, she accompanied him to political events as often as possible. Her vibrant presence was a huge asset to him in his political life and he relied heavily on her advice and her judgement of people. His belief in the importance of giving women a much bigger voice in Irish politics stemmed from his relationship with Joan. On the other hand, when phone calls from Joan frequently interrupted front-bench meetings some of his colleagues found it hard to contain their irritation.

FitzGerald actively sought to encourage women into Fine Gael during his leadership, which coincided with a conversion to party politics by some politicised women. The Women's Political Association, whose founder-members included Gemma Hussey and Nuala Fennell, was beginning to make an impact on public opinion. The slogan 'Why not a woman?' attracted attention during the 1977 general election campaign.

Writing in the *Irish Press* in July 1977, Gemma Hussey, then an independent senator, speculated that women would welcome FitzGerald as the new leader of Fine Gael as an ally 'who would not only be prepared to listen to them, but who has shown in the past his readiness to take up and defend a new idea or a new way of looking at things'. Nuala Fennell said in her memoirs that she joined the party in 1978 because of FitzGerald, 'his liberalism, his enthusiasm for change and the promise of a better Ireland'. Phil Moore of the WPA wrote of the 'excitement and solidarity felt by the women members' at FitzGerald's first ard-fheis as leader in 1978. 'The party had the opportunity to see that there are splendid women ready and willing to run for Fine Gael and can win; an opportunity denied them before.'[9]

FitzGerald also wanted to create a dedicated space in which young people could participate in politics. By the time that he set the wheels in motion to create Young Fine Gael, there had already been an awareness for some time among certain elements of the party that the country's youth needed to be encouraged into politics and that targeted policies needed to be formulated that would appeal to this demographic. It was former Taoiseach John A. Costello who observed in 1961, 'if the Fine Gael party is to survive it can only do so by attracting the younger people in the country'.[10] An organisation called the Fine Gael Youth Group was formed in 1964 to mobilise canvassers for a by-election, but subsequent efforts to transform it into a national organisation with regional and constituency structures did not succeed.[11]

When Young Fine Gael was eventually formed under FitzGerald's guidance the following decade, it spread rapidly, with branches popping up around the country. The first National Conference was held in November 1977 and Roy Dooney was elected the first national chair. In the years since, YFG has worked in harmony with Fine Gael. But it has also never shied away from demonstrating its independence, as evidenced in the statement issued opposing the programme for government in 2020.

To revitalise the party organisation FitzGerald appointed Peter Prendergast as national organiser and the well-known political journalist Ted Nealon as press officer. Prendergast, who had twice run for the Dáil, had at different times been a member of the party's National Council, which represented constituency organisations, and the National Executive, which was responsible for running the organisation. As a result he was widely known through the Fine Gael organisation, where he was liked and hated in almost equal measure for his direct, no-nonsense style and his keen intelligence. 'It is more important for a party organiser to be widely feared than universally liked and the important thing was that he already knew intimately our organisation at local level – and knew whom he could, or could not, trust,' FitzGerald wrote.[12]

Prendergast had no illusions about what he was letting himself in for. 'The organisation was pathetic. That is the only word for it,' he recalled many years later. An anecdote told by Brigid Hogan O'Higgins, who was a Fine Gael TD for East Galway from 1957 to 1977, epitomised the problem for Prendergast. Allegedly, the secretary of a party branch in East Galway who had emigrated to England in the mid-1950s returned to the county twenty-one years later only to find that he was still listed as branch secretary. 'The main problem was that the party organisation was in the control of the local deputy who had no interest in encouraging strong candidates who might pose a threat,' said Prendergast, who, from personal knowledge, knew that the party had not had an effective organiser since Gerry Sweetman: 'He was a rough diamond who got things done but he was widely unpopular.'[13]

The impact Prendergast had on the party was recalled in 2020 by Kieran Calnan, who was chairman of the Cork South-West constituency for three decades. 'Peter changed the whole dynamic in the party. I met him a number of times along with other constituency chairs and he emphasised the role of the party members. He told us not to be intimidated by elected representatives and to make a decision on candidate selection based purely on a strategy of maximising seats. He also told us to come to him if we had any problems with our local TDs and he would back us. Our job was to win two seats in Cork South-West come what may.'[14]

The 1977 election drubbing brought it home to Fine Gael supporters that the party organisation, which had never been able to match Fianna Fáil in its professionalism, was now in a dire condition. What was particularly worrying was that during its long spells in opposition the organisation had declined rather than developed. Prendergast made no secret of his ambition to remedy this defect by hook or by crook. FitzGerald recalled, 'Under his skilful, subtle – some would say Machiavellian – guidance, Fine Gael was to reach and surpass in sheer professionalism its hitherto dominant rival. Such an achievement was not attained without trauma.' Prendergast knew that 'we had to totally change the organisation. Garret simply said to me: "You do it and I'll back you." When I got into trouble with TDs I would tell him and he'd back me up.'

FitzGerald and Prendergast were agreed that one of the basic problems confronting Fine Gael was the fact that in so many constituencies the sole party TD was inclined to do everything possible to discourage a potentially good running-mate. Taking on the 'quota squatters', as they were called, was one of Prendergast's priorities, but it was one that involved him in vicious conflict with a number of prominent party TDs. Extracting the branches in each constituency from under the thumb of their TD was an essential part of the strategy. That required a new approach to decision-making within the party. As he put it,

> a key element of this was to develop a role for party members who were not seeking election. I consciously set out to create an organisation at constituency level in which the members and not the TD were in charge. One decision was to appoint a constituency organisation and a PR person and crucially neither would be eligible to stand for election.

Another problem was the over-representation of rural Ireland in comparison with town branches. The rules were changed so that, instead of all branches having an equal say, votes at selection conventions related to the membership of each branch. A determined effort was made to involve every single party member by giving them a job to do. Each one was given two hundred homes to work on, to try to build up support and establish detailed information about likely voting intentions. There was a particular concentration on finding out who were undecided voters. 'I had a list of 1,300 names in Dublin South-East who were undecided voters. That gave us a clear target audience for our pitch in the elections that followed.'

FitzGerald set off on a constituency tour in the autumn of 1977 to mobilise support for his new approach. Before setting out he appointed Peter Barry as his deputy leader and appointed almost all the former ministers to his front bench, along with two newly elected TDs, Jim Mitchell and Jim O'Keeffe. During his tour the new leader met constituency organisations and encouraged them to think radically. He also held public meetings wherever he went and in the course of question-and-answer sessions set out his vision of Ireland's future. 'Garret had enormous appeal,' says Prendergast. 'People liked him and responded to his vision. That was the real reason party membership mushroomed. I was the harvester, but nobody joined Fine Gael because of Peter Prendergast. They joined it because of Garret FitzGerald.'[15]

A flavour of the impact made by FitzGerald as he travelled the country was captured by Michael Finlan of the *Irish Times*. 'Garret FitzGerald's full-throttle energy shows no sign of running down as it propels him through the length and breadth of the country imparting the kiss of life to his distempered party.'[16] William Hennigan, a young Dublin accountant who had just returned from working in London, was a witness to FitzGerald's impact. His Cork cousins, who were strong Fine Gael supporters, brought him along to a public meeting in Mallow addressed by FitzGerald, and the impact was palpable. 'I went along not knowing what to expect but was immediately swept up in the excitement. There was something about Garret which was so appealing to people of my age.'

On his tour FitzGerald found great enthusiasm among members – if not among TDs – for changes in the way the organisation worked. He devised a new constitution, which he brought for approval to his first ard-fheis in May 1978. The most important change was the method of electing the national executive so that it would represent the members rather than the interests of the sitting TDs. Among other important reforms was a new weighting system for party branches based on population to counteract what he regarded as an excessive rural bias. To encourage new talent a three-year limit was imposed for officership positions, while the new posts of constituency organiser and public relations officer were formally introduced. The ard-fheis also approved a provision that within two months of any general election that did not result in the party taking office the parliamentary party would hold a secret ballot on the leadership. The move was designed to reduce tension in the party by adopting a mechanism whereby TDs or senators could vote secretly against their leader without having to mount an open challenge.

With the new constitution in place Prendergast was able to proceed with sweeping changes to the organisation. He went around the country to give pep talks to members and also to spot talent locally. He encouraged talented people like Finbarr Fitzpatrick, later party general secretary, who were capable of devising plans to win new seats to take up positions as constituency organisers. 'I met these people regularly to discuss their plans and this gave them a real feeling that they owned the organisation. This was a hugely powerful tool in transforming morale within the party.' The mood changed much more quickly than he had anticipated. He recalled going to a party meeting in a Carlow hotel in the early days for a constituency meeting. 'The members arrived in the hotel looking sheepish and almost a bit ashamed to be involved with the party. A year later they were coming in proudly wearing Fine Gael stickers and bringing new members along with them.' Naturally many TDs were suspicious, not to say downright hostile to Prendergast's drive to take control of the organisation from them. At one particularly fraught meeting Richie Ryan threatened to throw him out the second-floor window of Fine Gael's new head office in Mount Street!

As well as revamping the organisation Prendergast also recruited advisers at the national level, who were to prove hugely important in the years to come. 'Ted Nealon, who was brought in by Garret as press officer at the same time as myself, played a hugely important part in the regeneration of the party. He had proved himself as an outstanding political commentator on RTÉ and he had both the knowledge and the contacts to provide seriously important advice.' Prendergast, in conjunction with Nealon, gathered a group of voluntary advisers who in time became known as the 'national handlers'. Among them were Frank Flannery, Bill O'Herlihy, Enda Marren and Shane Molloy. Another important figure was the accountant Sean Murray, who ensured that the party's finances were kept in order. Peter Sutherland, a barrister, was in charge of policy, while an old hand, Jim Dooge, was responsible for strategy. They gave Prendergast a lot of ideas and the confidence to follow through on them.[17]

Prendergast's background was in marketing and he brought some of the essential tools of that trade, such as focus groups and opinion-polling, to Fine Gael. He found the focus groups particularly important, as it provided a way of understanding the concerns of ordinary people.

I learned an awful lot from the focus groups. The differences between Fine Gael and Fianna Fáil are incomprehensible to most people. It was really important to listen to the words people used to describe their feelings about major issues, as those words are very different from those used by politicians and the media. In our advertising we used the words and phrases gleaned from the focus groups.

In an interview in early December 2019 Prendergast had no doubt that Boris Johnson's election-winning catchphrase 'Get Brexit done' had emerged from a focus group. In a detailed account of that campaign in the *Financial Times* in late December it was revealed that the slogan had indeed emerged from a focus group in September 2019.[18]

Another issue was finding a new head office for the party, which had been based for decades in cramped office accommodation in Hume Street, Dublin. Prendergast decided immediately after he took up his appointment that the old poky head office would not do. He had both practical and psychological reasons for moving. To him, Hume Street symbolised Fine Gael's image as a badly run, amateurish organisation and, on a more practical level, the office space was simply far too small. A more suitable address was found in Upper Mount Street – just opposite the Fianna Fáil head office. The building was bought for £250,000, almost twice what the party had spent at the national level on the 1977 general election. To finance the move a 'buy a brick' campaign was launched among the party membership and it raised most of the money required.

FitzGerald and Prendergast took a big gamble with their first ard-fheis. Fianna Fáil had moved the venue from the Round Room of the Mansion House in Dublin, where both parties had traditionally met, so the new Fine Gael team, not to be outdone, decided to follow suit. The great hall of the RDS accommodated four thousand people comfortably, but Fine Gael in the past had never assembled a crowd of more than half that size, so the move had the potential to be a disaster. In reality it was nothing of the kind and the hall was packed for FitzGerald's first leader's address. The enthusiasm was palpable. Fine Gael was back in business.

FitzGerald was a human dynamo who never seemed to stop. As well as traversing the country, performing in the Dáil and making frequent visits to Northern Ireland and London, he drafted a white paper on Northern Ireland which was based firmly on the principle of 'no reunification without consent', but it set out the benefits Northern Ireland might secure through a political association with the Republic. These included the sharing of facilities in such sectors as industry, tourism and expert promotion abroad. It also raised the possibility of an all-Ireland anti-terrorism force and the involvement of the North in the economic dynamism that had been a feature of the Republic since the late 1950s. In the longer term the document went on to propose a confederal arrangement for Ireland on the basis of complete equality between Northern Ireland and the Republic. There was a broad welcome for the document on both sides of the border but in the years ahead the proposal about an all-Ireland anti-terrorism force was to become a contentious political issue.

Not long after the publication of his white paper FitzGerald drafted a long document for internal party consumption setting out his priorities and preoccupations. This document would form the basis for the Fine Gael manifesto at the subsequent election and for many decisions in government during the 1980s. One of his major concerns was how the country could deal with the labour surplus that would develop inevitably from the large proportion of the population aged eighteen and under. He concluded that a reduction in certain types of public spending and an end to some of the circular transfers that took money off people in the form of tax to channel it back to them in a range of state payments would be required. A major change in church-state relations and political reform were also on his mind.

FitzGerald's frenetic energy had one drawback: he thought he knew more about the portfolios of his front-bench colleagues than they did. While this was probably true in many cases, it caused deep irritation among his more experienced colleagues. FitzGerald was prone to indulge in constant interruptions at front-bench meetings and they often ended up in chaos, running for far longer than they need have.[19] Such was the disarray that Senator Alexis FitzGerald was brought in to chair the meetings. It was a weakness that was to mar FitzGerald's time in government.

He had two years to settle in as leader before his first electoral test in the summer of 1979 in the shape of the European and local elections. A move which was to be of huge importance to the party and country was the decision of Fine Gael to become a founding member of the European People's Party (EPP) in 1976. Composed of Christian Democratic parties from across the EEC, it was destined to be the biggest and most influential group in Europe for the next four decades. Just eight years earlier, Gerard Sweetman had prevented a name change to 'Fine Gael – the Social Democratic Party'. There were some in the party who regretted that decision and continued to regard themselves as social democrats, but the involvement with the leading force in European politics was to prove hugely important for Fine Gael. It enabled the party leaders, in or out of office, to attend the regular meetings of the EPP leaders and establish relationships with some of the key figures in European politics. This was to prove of vital importance to Ireland at critical points in the years ahead. It also meant that Fine Gael MEPs were part of the most influential political grouping in the European Parliament while their Fianna Fáil opponents were confined to the margins.

In 1979 the outcome in both European and local elections was a huge shot in the arm for Fine Gael. In the European elections the party's share of the vote was up 3 points compared with the general election, but Fianna Fáil was down more than 15 points, so the gap between the two was cut to a mere 1½ percentage points – a remarkable recovery by comparison with the 20-point gap in 1977. In the local elections the party also narrowed the gap with its rival and won 310 seats nationally, to 347 for Fianna Fáil. Even more important was the quality of the new councillors, with lots of women and young people coming through. Ten of the new councillors were elected to the Dáil two years later, while two of its unsuccessful Euro-candidates, Alan Dukes and Nuala Fennell, were also elected to the Dáil, both becoming major figures in the party. Richie Ryan was one of the successful Euro-candidates for the Dublin constituency, along with Mark Clinton in Leinster, Tom O'Donnell in Munster and Joe McCartin in Connacht-Ulster. FitzGerald attributed the electoral success to 'the remarkable organisation work Peter Prendergast has put in during the previous twenty-one months in every part of the country and in particular his skill at identifying and securing the adoption of suitable candidates'. But Prendergast believes that the success in the local elections was the more important achievement.

> We did well in the European elections but we had big name candidates like Richie Ryan, Mark Clinton and Tom O'Donnell. Our vote was not up by all that much but the important thing was the local elections where a whole lot of ambitious young people I had met on my travels got elected. For instance, I got Ivan Yates to run at the age of eighteen.

Buoyed up by that electoral success, Fine Gael was in a confident mood going into two by-elections in Cork city and county in December 1979. A long-running postal strike and a range of other discontents had damaged the government, and the Fianna Fáil vote in Taoiseach Jack Lynch's home county collapsed. Fine Gael won the two seats: Liam Burke was elected in Cork city and Myra Barry in Cork East. Prendergast explained, 'When Garret took over we reckoned it would take eight years to recover from the 1977 disaster. After those two by-election wins, I saw we could do it in quicker time than that.'[20]

The Cork by-elections triggered an immediate crisis in Fianna Fáil. Lynch resigned and there was a bitter contest for the leadership between George Colley and Charles Haughey. Colley persuaded Lynch to step down a few months earlier than he had intended, on the grounds that the timing would take Haughey off guard. Unfortunately for Colley, it was a serious miscalculation and, much to his shock, Haughey won by 44 votes to 38 when a secret ballot of Fianna Fáil TDs was held on 7 December 1979. The shattered Colley and his supporters didn't know what to do. Such was the depth of distrust of Haughey that over the next few days Colley had long discussions with leading colleagues, such as

Martin O'Donoghue and Des O'Malley, to consider whether he would even vote for his own party's nominee for Taoiseach.

FitzGerald knew Haughey quite well. The two were born within months of each other and were educated together in UCD. 'Although there were deep differences of personality and outlook, our personal relationship had always been friendly, although not close,' FitzGerald wrote in 1991. He even recalled that Haughey had tried to involve him in Fianna Fáil in 1961.[21] Despite their early friendly relations, their contrasting personalities, styles and vision of Ireland's future came to dominate politics in the 1980s. Haughey was a Dublin city man, a Christian Brothers boy, a GAA supporter, who had become rich quickly by dubious means and believed in flaunting that wealth and aping the behaviour of the landed gentry. One of the reasons Haughey aroused such antagonism in FitzGerald and senior people in Fianna Fáil was that they genuinely feared that he would corrupt the standards of public life. His record in the arms trial added to those fears. The fact that Haughey possessed charisma as well as great leadership ability made him all the more dangerous in the eyes of his opponents.

The source of Haughey's apparently vast wealth was a mystery. He led an extravagant life that was clearly far in excess of his income as a public representative, yet there was no visible means of support for that lordly style of life. Shortly before he took over as party leader he bought Innishvickillane, one of the Blasket islands off the coast of Co. Kerry, and was busy building a house on the lovely uninhabited island. There were all sorts of rumours about how Haughey had acquired wealth during the 1960s, and while the truth was known only to a handful of people, the popular perception was that he had obtained it by dubious means.

Haughey's wealth had become a political issue in the 1960s. It featured in the 1969 general election campaign when it was revealed that he had sold his house Grangemore, in Raheny to the well-known property developer and builder Matt Gallagher for over £200,000 and then bought the Abbeville estate and its 250 acres in Kinsealy for £140,000. 'I object to my private affairs being used in this way. It is a private matter between myself and the purchaser,' came Haughey's response.[22] It was a line he was to maintain for the next thirty years when anybody broached the subject of his extraordinary wealth.

Gerry Sweetman tried to make it a political issue by suggesting that Haughey had benefited from legislation he had himself introduced to amend part of the Finance Act (1965) to ensure that he did not have to pay tax on the profit from the sale of Grangemore. Haughey then publicly announced that he would refer the matter to the Revenue Commissioners, who duly reported that 'no liability to income tax or surtax would have arisen' under the 1965 act even if it had not been amended. This appeared to leave Haughey in the clear, but looked at in the light of the privileged treatment accorded to him by the Revenue Commissioners over more than three decades it may simply have been another case of the institutions of the state acting under duress to protect him.[23]

Far from damaging Haughey, his wealth and the whiff of sulphur surrounding his activities and his involvement in the Arms Crisis proved a powerful attraction for many voters. By the time Haughey was elected leader of Fianna Fáil in December 1979 FitzGerald was convinced that his record, particularly in relation to the Arms Crisis, made him unsuitable for the office of Taoiseach. When it came to the vote on Haughey's nomination for Taoiseach on 11 December 1979, FitzGerald delivered an extraordinary speech to the Dáil. 'I must speak not only for the opposition but for many in Fianna Fáil who may not be free to say what they believe or to express their deep fears for the future of this country under the proposed leadership, people who are not free to reveal what they know and what led them to oppose this man with a commitment far beyond the normal,' he said. He went on to refer to Haughey's 'flawed pedigree' and said his motives could ultimately be judged only by God.

> But we cannot ignore the fact that he differs from all his predecessors in that those motives have been and are widely impugned, most notably but by no means exclusively by people within his own party, people close to him who have observed his actions for many years and who have made their human interim judgement on him ... The feet that will go through that lobby to support

his election will include many that will drag; the hearts of many who will climb those stairs before turning left will be heavy. Many of those who may vote for him will be doing so in the belief and hope that they will not have to serve long under a man they do not respect, whom they have fought long and hard, but for the moment in vain, to exclude from the highest office in the land.

The speech generated a political and media storm, particularly the 'flawed pedigree' reference. FitzGerald later described it as an 'oratorical embellishment' that must have owed something to the hour of the night at which he drafted his remarks. In any case the speech generated a deluge of criticism, some of it from his own TDs, who were unnerved by the negative media response. Yet time would prove FitzGerald right and vindicate his courage in raising the unpalatable truth. In December 1979 he not only got to the heart of the matter, he accurately reflected the mood in the defeated faction within Fianna Fáil.

The 'flawed pedigree' speech encouraged murmurings of dissent from TDs unhappy with the pressure they were under from Prendergast to accept serious running-mates and the more liberal thrust of policy being set out by the leader. 'A minority was actively opposed to the new liberal and social democratic thrust; others who had no strong personal views feared that the new policy emphasis would lose the party more support than it would generate.'

By mid-1980, with a general election on the horizon, the strains between the leader and a considerable portion of his parliamentary party had become acute. At a special meeting of the parliamentary party FitzGerald told his colleagues that he was not happy with the situation.

I could not, I said, be an effective leader of the party if I had to be looking over my shoulder, not knowing where I stood. If I knew the party was fully behind me in what I was doing I would get on with the job with renewed vigour; if not, now was the time to face the problem and draw the obvious conclusion. This had the desired effect. While I knew that some remained unenthusiastic, or secretly hostile, the overt grumbling was stilled.[24]

Haughey was a very different kind of political opponent from the courteous Lynch, who had got on quite well with FitzGerald. Far more abrasive and charismatic with the fallout from the Arms Crisis trailing in his wake, Haughey appeared to fit the image of the 'strong man', the political leader who was capable of greats things, whether good or bad. Prendergast decided that he needed expert advice to get a handle on Haughey and he hired two psychologists to conduct an analysis of his personality.

Surprisingly, they concluded that Haughey was a poor decision-maker, easily swayed and afraid to offend the warring factions in his party and important interest groups. 'This analysis was fundamental to our judgement about how to handle Haughey. We knew he would be indecisive and were able to plan accordingly.'[25]

As the election drew closer Fine Gael concentrated on the growing public discontent with the management of the economy. One of Haughey's first actions on becoming Taoiseach was to make a television address warning that the country's finances were spinning out of control. 'The figures which are just now becoming available to us show one thing very clearly. As a community we are living way beyond our means,' he told the country. 'We have been borrowing enormous amounts of money, borrowing at a rate which just cannot continue. We will just have to reorganise government spending so that we can only undertake those things we can afford.'

Given what emerged a decade later about Haughey's personal finances at the time, the speech was a piece of brazen effrontery, but that was not known in 1980.

The diagnosis was correct but, the problem having been identified, Haughey then proceeded to make it worse by increasing spending rather than tackling the underlying problem. He failed to curb government spending and borrowing and conceded large pay increases to the public service. In early 1981 he sanctioned an astonishing pay increase of 34 per cent for teachers, which was considerably more than they had asked for. The message went out loud and clear that he was a soft touch before his first general election. It was a confirmation of the assessment made by the psychologists engaged by Prendergast.

Things deteriorated rapidly in the first half of 1981, but the budget figures were massaged to disguise the fact that borrowing was rising to the unsustainable level of 20 per cent of gross national product. Haughey's spending spree ultimately led to a massive increase in the tax burden on the working population, which had devastating consequences in the decade ahead.

FitzGerald kept up a sustained criticism of Haughey's economic policies, particularly the strategy of tackling unemployment by increasing the number of public servants, regardless of need. This was compounded by massive pay increases for the public service, which saw rates increase by 30 per cent in 1980 alone. Fine Gael prepared its election manifesto against the background of this appalling financial crisis, but the real problem (described in the next chapter) was that they didn't know the true extent of it. In the draft manifesto the party proposed to eliminate the soaring deficit over a period of four or five years, giving preference to cuts in public spending rather than tax increases as a way to achieve it.

There was also a huge gulf between FitzGerald and Haughey in their approach to Northern Ireland, where violence continued to rage. Haughey had always regarded the national issue as the key to his legacy. He reportedly told Margaret Thatcher during their first meeting in 1980 that no political leader would be remembered for reducing the balance of payments or for adjusting the scale of government borrowing, but the one who came up with a solution to the problem of the North would go down in the history books. Given his role in the Arms Crisis of 1970, and his nationalist rhetoric, Haughey, during his early years as leader was regarded within Fianna Fáil as being 'sound' on the national question.[26]

Haughey's emphasis on the traditional goal of a united Ireland con-trasted sharply with FitzGerald's support for a devolved power-sharing arrangement in Northern Ireland itself as the first step towards any solution. Haughey's meeting with Thatcher in 1980 heralded a genuinely important breakthrough in British-Irish relations, but he showed crass political judgement as he proceeded to dissipate the achievement by insisting that it meant the constitutional position of Northern Ireland as part of the United Kingdom was up for discussion. Thatcher was furious, and progress stalled. FitzGerald took a very different line on the North, supporting the strategy of the SDLP leader, John Hume, who argued that unity by consent was the only goal worth pursuing. FitzGerald harried Haughey in the Dáil and outside it on the issue, even though the electorate in the Republic appeared more impressed with Haughey's nationalist rhetoric, no matter how unrealistic it was.

By early 1981 the omens were good for Haughey. Fine Gael was set back on its heels when the Fianna Fáil candidate, Clem Coughlan, won an emphatic victory in a by-election victory in Donegal in November 1980. After its two by-election victories in Cork in 1979 Fine Gael was in a confident mood, but Haughey, facing into his first electoral test, threw everything into the Donegal contest and came away with a decisive victory.

That success emboldened Haughey to begin preparing for a spring election but his plans were thwarted by tragedy, not once but twice. The intention was to call the election shortly after the Fianna Fáil ard-fheis in February, but on the opening night of the conference, St Valentine's Night, a fire in the Stardust nightclub in the Taoiseach's own constituency killed forty-eight young people. The main part of the ard-fheis, including the Taoiseach's address, was postponed until April, as were his election plans.

Then the North intervened in an unexpected way to throw a spanner in the works. One of the British responses to continuing IRA violence was to withdraw 'special category' status from IRA prisoners convicted after March 1976. This provoked first a 'dirty protest' and then a hunger strike, which led to escalating tension. The leader of the hunger strike, Bobby Sands, was elected to the House of Commons in a by-election in Fermanagh-South Tyrone in April, and he died the following month. Haughey's government made furious but unavailing efforts to end the hunger strikes, and the election date was deferred again in the hope of a solution.

With his options narrowing and the spending targets of the 1981 budget running out of control, Haughey dissolved the Dáil on 21 May, with the general election to be held on 11 June. Fine Gael was ready for the fray. Prendergast recalled, 'We had concluded early in 1981 that Haughey's indecision would prevail and that he would opt for a June election so we were ready for it.'[27] An election strategy committee had been appointed well in advance. It included members of the front bench but also a group of advisers from outside the political system with a range of management and public relations skills. Once the election was under way these advisers would become the campaign committee, as FitzGerald was convinced that TDs concentrating on getting themselves elected could not run a national campaign. The campaign committee was carefully chosen and developed a great rapport with Peter Prendergast and Ted Nealon.

The Fine Gael director of elections was the dynamic Cork barrister and businessman Sean O'Leary. His qualities of warmth, vitality, political gut instinct, natural authority and *joie de vivre,* and his excellent relationship with Prendergast, made him ideally suited to the task.[28] Derry Hussey, a businessman and husband of Gemma Hussey, chaired the committee, which also included the experienced old hands Alexis Fitzgerald and Jim Dooge.[29]

By contrast with 1977, Fine Gael's preparations were meticulous this time around. Candidates had been selected well in advance and a raft of new faces joined sitting TDs on the ticket. Prendergast had been helped enormously in this task by the decision of the Fianna Fáil government to establish an independent constituency commission. This was one of the election pledges implemented by Jack Lynch after the 1977 landslide, designed to ensure that no government would in future be able to manipulate the constituencies for party advantage, as had happened with the Tullymander.

The commission recommended two important changes. One was an increase in the number of TDs, from 148 to 166, and the other was a substantial increase in the number of four-seat and five-seat constituencies and a reduction in the number of three-seaters. Those changes meant that most sitting Fine Gael TDs were reasonably relaxed about having strong running-mates. After the publication of the report FitzGerald told his TDs that if they did nothing more than recover the votes they had lost in 1977 the party would gain fourteen seats, so unless they positively neglected their constituencies they had nothing to fear.

When the election was called FitzGerald grabbed the early headlines by setting off with Joan on a countrywide tour by special train. The train visited nine cities and towns in two days, generating a lot of positive publicity in the process. 'The train had a huge impact. We had made the right call on the timing of the election and had booked the train for the start of the campaign,' said Prendergast. 'It generated huge publicity.'[30]

Fine Gael certainly needed the positive publicity, as the first published opinion poll of the campaign, conducted by Irish Marketing Surveys for the *Irish Independent,* showed Fianna Fáil on 52 per cent – a full nine points ahead of the combined Fine Gael and Labour total.[31] It was the first election campaign where polls were taken seriously by the media, and the scale of the task facing Fine Gael was obvious.

The party had managed to attract a lot of publicity with its manifesto promising a range of goodies, including a state payment for mothers working in the home and a reduction in taxes. It also contained a commitment to rein in runaway borrowing and eliminate the soaring current budget deficit over four or five years. These contradictory aspirations were to cause problems for the party in the future, but they generated momentum for the election campaign. Fianna Fáil got sucked into attacking the Fine Gael pledges and in the process giving them even greater publicity.

FitzGerald generated an air of excitement that countered the traditional image of Fine Gael as a staid, conservative party. His appeal to women and young people was evident on the campaign trail, with enthusiastic crowds greeting him as he travelled around the country. This fuelled the commitment of the party workers, many of them new recruits drawn by FitzGerald's liberal outlook, who participated in the most professional election campaign ever waged by Fine Gael. He recalled:

It was indeed a blissful dawn to what turned out to be a most gloomy decade. I could not but be cheered by finding that at least for the moment there was a genuine appetite for social reform and for more liberal pluralist attitudes … When the sun shone, as it did for at least part of the time during what turned out to be a rather showery early summer, there was a mood of gaiety and warmth and an evident belief that politics could be constructive.[32]

Fianna Fáil also fought a strong and confident campaign, with Haughey holding huge rallies around the country. He continued to promise the electorate more spending to rival the attractive, if equally unrealistic, tax-cutting plans being put forward by Fine Gael. 'Charlie's Song', a lively version of a folk song about Bonny Prince Charlie, became the Fianna Fáil campaign anthem and was played at all the party rallies during the campaign, encouraging voters to 'arise and follow Charlie'.[33]

The opinion polls narrowed as the campaign entered its final week, and the mood in Fine Gael was upbeat. FitzGerald took part in a clunky RTÉ television debate that involved the leaders of the three biggest parties being interviewed in turn by a panel of political journalists. It made for poor television and was inconclusive. FitzGerald was adjudged by the media to have been 'hesitant and slightly nervous'.

When the country went to the polls on 11 June for what was to be the first of five general elections during the 1980s Fine Gael had high hopes of victory. While there was no formal electoral pact with Labour it was widely expected that the two parties would form a government if they had the numbers. In the event that is what happened, but it was a very close-run thing.

The Fine Gael vote was up 6 points to 36.5 per cent, with the party winning 65 seats in the 166-member Dáil, a jump of 23 since the previous election. Fianna Fáil dropped five points to 45.3 per cent and won 78 seats, while Labour slipped to just under 10 per cent and won 15 seats. As if that was not disappointing enough for Labour, its leader, Frank Cluskey, lost his seat. IRA hunger-strikers won two seats, with independents and small parties having six between them.

It was a remarkable result for Fine Gael, given the scale of the defeat it had suffered just four years earlier. The party's share of the vote and its number of seats was the highest since the days of Cumann nGaedheal and, almost equally significantly, more than half Fine Gael's TDs were new members of the Dáil.

By any standards it was an amazing achievement by FitzGerald and his election team. But there was a catch. Although Fine Gael and Labour had 80 seats between them, they were three short of an overall majority. Michael O'Leary, who took over as Labour leader, had a long and friendly association with FitzGerald, and the two men had little difficulty agreeing a joint programme for government. They held their first exploratory meeting in FitzGerald's house in Rathmines and more detailed talks in the home of their mutual friend Gabriel Hogan in Sandymount. FitzGerald was accompanied by his trusted friends and political allies Alexis Fitzgerald and Jim Dooge, while O'Leary was advised by the Labour Party's general secretary, Seamus Scally, and a Sugar Company economist, Willie Scally.[34]

In an echo of the 1950s, Labour insisted on food subsidies for bread, butter, flour and margarine and a commitment that no additional taxes would be imposed on food, electricity, coal, clothing or footwear. These measures were designed to protect poorer voters against the impact of increased indirect taxes which were required to finance some of Fine Gael's pledges. FitzGerald was confident that the social-democratic orientation of the Fine Gael programme facilitated the marrying of the two parties' objectives. 'As few in Labour had actually read our programme and as most Labour Party members had been conditioned to assume Fine Gael was a right-wing party, the inclusion of large parts of the Fine Gael document in the joint programme was seen by many in the Labour Party, quite erroneously, to be a victory for Labour over Fine Gael.'[35]

With the joint programme agreed, the two leaders got down to the horse-trading about ministerial positions, and they agreed on four cabinet positions and three junior ministries for Labour. As in 1977, it was more than Labour was entitled to on a strictly proportional basis, but it was the minimum the party could accept. While the joint programme was endorsed with enthusiasm by the Fine Gael parliamentary party, there was a fierce debate at the Labour Party delegate conference, which took place in the Gaiety Theatre. It was adopted by 737 votes to 487, but the strong minority in Labour who were opposed to coalition in principle was a foretaste of battles to come during the decade ahead.[36]

When the new Dáil met on 30 June its first task was to elect a Ceann Comhairle. The position went to John O'Connell, an independent who after more than a decade as a Labour TD had left the party because of a constituency row with his leader, Frank Cluskey. FitzGerald was then elected Taoiseach as head of a new Fine Gael-Labour coalition. His cabinet caused a sensation because of the youth of some ministers, the appointment of a former politician from outside the Dáil, and the fact that some of the most senior party TDs, such as Richie Ryan and Dick Burke, were left on the back benches.

The 34-year-old John Bruton was appointed Minister for Finance. The Minister for Justice, Jim Mitchell, and the new Minister for Education, John Boland, were also thirty-four. The newly elected Alan Dukes, who was two years older, was given Agriculture. The deputy leader, Peter Barry, was offered his choice of portfolio and chose Environment, the former Attorney General John Kelly was given Trade while Paddy O'Toole from Mayo became Minister for the Gaeltacht. Two survivors of the Cosgrave government, Pat Cooney and Tom Fitzpatrick, were given Fisheries and Forestry and Transport and Posts and Telegraphs, respectively.

One of the biggest surprises of all was the appointment of Jim Dooge as Minister for Foreign Affairs. A world-renowned scientist who pioneered research into climate change and a former Cathaoirleach of the Seanad, he had left politics in 1977, and it took a lot of persuasion on FitzGerald's part to entice him back. His appointment was the brainchild of Joan FitzGerald. It was not the first or last time that FitzGerald was influenced in important political decisions by his wife. She was worried that her husband would be tempted to interfere too much in Foreign Affairs and only somebody of serious stature like Dooge would deter him. As Dooge was not a member of the Dáil, FitzGerald invoked the constitutional provision whereby a senator could be appointed to the cabinet. It was only the second time in the history of the state that it had been used. The appointment could not be made until the new Seanad had been elected and FitzGerald was able to use the Taoiseach's constitutional prerogative to appoint Dooge to the second house. Another innovation was the appointment of Senator Alexis Fitzgerald, who had acted as an informal adviser to his father-in-law, John A. Costello, in the 1950s, as special adviser to the government with the right to sit in on cabinet meetings. The Attorney General was Peter Sutherland, another Fine Gael rising star who was in his mid-thirties.[37]

The four Labour ministers were Michael O'Leary as Tánaiste and Minister for Industry and Energy, Liam Kavanagh in Labour, Jimmy Tully in Defence and Eileen Desmond, the only woman in the cabinet, who was given responsibility for Health and Social Welfare. FitzGerald toyed with the idea of appointing Gemma Hussey, then a senator and a personal friend, to the cabinet but was dissuaded by Michael O'Leary on the grounds that it would generate even more resentment on the back benches.[38]

Some of the appointments, particularly the role of Alexis Fitzgerald, raised objections from Fianna Fáil and the media, but there was considerable internal annoyance at the fact that six of the ministers were from Dublin and four from the surrounding counties, leaving most of the country unrepresented. FitzGerald was impatient at this criticism, which he regarded as unduly parochial. There was also considerable resentment on the part of some deputies, such as Ryan and Burke, at their failure to be appointed while Dooge, who was not a TD, had been given such an important portfolio.

There was also some negative publicity at the shambolic way FitzGerald went about appointing his junior ministers, in such an unseemly rush that some of them ended up swapping their portfolios. One surprise appointment was that of a newly elected young Dublin TD, Mary Flaherty, who became the only Fine Gael woman to win ministerial office in that government.[39]

The excitement surrounding the election of FitzGerald as Taoiseach and the controversy around his innovative team of ministers masked one critical fact. He led a minority government, which depended for its existence on the support of three independents. It behaved as if it was there for the long haul, but its hold on power was precarious from the moment it took office.

GARRET IN POWER

'I want to lead a crusade, a republican crusade to make this a genuine republic.'

— GARRET FITZGERALD, SPEAKING TO GERALD BARRY
ON RTÉ RADIO, 27 SEPTEMBER 1981.

The high hopes that Garret FitzGerald's reforming zeal would herald a new chapter in Fine Gael's history came up against cold political reality on his very first day in power. On his way to Áras an Uachtaráin to receive his seal of office the newly elected Taoiseach was accompanied by the cabinet secretary, Dermot Nally, one of the most outstanding public servants in the history of the state. During the journey Nally told FitzGerald that the country's finances were in a shocking state and that remedial action would be required immediately. It was far worse than FitzGerald had imagined, and it meant that all the worthy ambitions contained in the programme for government would have to be reassessed. He realised that he would need to hold an emergency meeting with his Minister for Finance and his senior departmental officials the following morning.[1]

At that meeting the disastrous financial position of the country was outlined in excruciating detail by the secretary of the Department of Finance, Maurice Doyle, who made no secret of his contempt for all politicians. The 1981 budget introduced by Fianna Fáil a few months earlier had purported to cut the already massive exchequer borrowing level from 15 per cent of GNP to 13 per cent. Instead of taking the measures necessary to meet their stated targets, the previous government had gone on a pre-election spending spree, and unless drastic action was taken the deficit was forecast to reach 20 per cent of GNP by the end of the year. To put those figures in context, the European Union guidelines under which the country has been operating in recent decades limits the borrowing requirement to 3 per cent of GDP.

FitzGerald and his ministers were shocked to discover that the spending estimates agreed by the Haughey government amounted to a work of fiction. 'We could hardly believe the state of the public expenditure estimates we inherited from Haughey: 85 per cent of the projected deficit for the year had already been expended by mid-year,' noted Barry Desmond, Minister of State for Finance, who was amazed that the Department of Finance had gone along with the deception. 'My faith in our public service took a hammering at that time.'[2]

The Department of Finance and its overbearing boss, Maurice Doyle, certainly had questions to answer about why they had gone along with spending estimates they knew to be fiction. FitzGerald discovered that the department's draft 'Review and Outlook', drawn up in the dying days of the Haughey government, had painted a much more optimistic view of the national finances than the one presented to him. It created suspicions among Fine Gael and Labour ministers that they were being taken for patsies by Doyle and his senior colleagues, who seemed prepared to indulge Haughey, only painting the real picture now that he was gone.[3]

Two days after the shock briefing about the country's financial position John Bruton circulated a memorandum to ministers proposing an immediate meeting to consider spending cuts and increases in indirect taxes, which would inevitably have an impact on the cost of living. He came into the Dáil with a supplementary budget on 21 July which included a range of stringent measures designed to bring the deteriorating situation under control. There was a massive increase in the standard rate of VAT, from 10 to 15 per cent, along with increases in excise on alcohol, tobacco and petrol. It meant that Fine Gael's tax-cutting plans had gone out the window at the very start of the party's stint in government. The measures did bring the projected borrowing requirement down, from 20 per cent to under 17 per cent, but it was just the first in a depressing series of harsh budgets that characterised the 1980s.[4]

What was truly galling for Fine Gael was that Haughey and Fianna Fáil showed not the slightest shame for having perpetrated a fraudulent budget on the Irish people. Instead they criticised Bruton for imposing unnecessary hardship on the people as he attempted to deal with the mess they had created. Haughey denounced the government as 'monetarist' but attacked it for not doing enough to correct the public finances. 'The Fianna Fáil response was incredible and totally contradictory,' wrote one contemporary commentator.[5]

FitzGerald was distracted from the problems with the public finances by the continuing hunger strikes by IRA prisoners in the North. He had numerous meetings with Irish and British officials and a series of communications with Thatcher in an effort to press the British into resolving the hunger strikes. He also held a series of difficult and distressing meetings with relatives of the hunger-strikers. At one stage he felt a compromise was within reach, thanks to the efforts of the Catholic Church Commission for Justice and Peace, but it slipped away. FitzGerald blamed covert contacts between the British government and the leading Sinn Féin figures Gerry Adams and Danny Morrison for undermining a potential compromise. On Tuesday 7 July a hunger-striker, Joe McDonnell, died and compromise seemed impossible.

Some members of FitzGerald's government felt he was devoting far too much time and attention to the North when the Republic he governed was in the midst of a budgetary crisis. His close friend and adviser Alexis Fitzgerald shared that anxiety and warned the Taoiseach that his obsessive focus on Northern Ireland was getting in the way of his duty to the state. 'Such advice fell on deaf ears at the height of the hunger-strikes and led to some loss of intimacy with the Taoiseach,' a friend of both concluded.[6]

When violence spread to the streets of Dublin such fears were exacerbated. In the wake of McDonnell's death the H Block Committee, controlled by the IRA, organised a demonstration and march to the British embassy in Dublin. There were about five thousand people on the march, many of them bussed in from the North and some clearly prepared for violence. Along the route from the city centre to the embassy in Ballsbridge they repeatedly attacked the gardaí with stones, pickaxe handles and any other weapons that came to hand. In Ballsbridge they came up against five hundred gardaí behind barriers at the embassy and launched an all-out assault. Some of the rioters came equipped with eight-foot poles, while others ripped up garden railings to make improvised weapons with which to attack the gardaí.

As the mayhem intensified and the mood of the crowd turned ever uglier, there was a real danger that the Garda lines would be breached and the rioters would attempt to burn down the embassy, as had happened after Bloody Sunday nine years before. At one stage the Garda line nearly broke, but in spite of the fact that more than a hundred of them were so badly injured that they had to be taken to hospital, the line held. Then, after almost half an hour of attrition, the order was given for a baton charge. The streets were cleared in a little over five minutes as the rioters fled in front of the charging gardaí.

FitzGerald later recorded his relief at the fact that the gardaí managed to hold the line, because if the rioters had broken through they would have faced a unit of the army as the last line of defence. 'That was a confrontation we were most anxious to avoid,' he confessed.[7]

There was a second march a week later but this time the gardaí did not wait for as long before taking on the mob, and they again cleared the streets within minutes. The violence in Dublin checked the mood of public sympathy for the hunger-strikers but it did sour relations between FitzGerald and Thatcher for a period. In his first six weeks in government there were twenty-five exchanges between the two governments about the hunger-strikes, fifteen of them at prime ministerial level. In early August FitzGerald decided there was nothing to be gained by pressing the British any more.

When things had calmed a little FitzGerald held a conference of his senior ministers and closest advisers to try to plot a course on Northern policy that might lead out of the impasse. There was a hard-headed discussion about the constitutional and legal changes that would be required to convince unionists that the Republic was not a sectarian state. The widely shared view at the meeting was that the territorial claim to the North contained in articles 2 and 3 and the constitutional ban on divorce were serious obstacles to progress. Whether it would be possible to do anything about them was the issue. 'What appeared to us to be desirable might not, it was felt, be politically feasible. For if a constitutional initiative were undertaken on articles 2 and 3 and failed the existing situation might be considerably worsened,' was the conclusion, but FitzGerald was convinced that the issues needed to be raised.[8]

While he was mulling over the issues he gave an interview to the *Cork Examiner* in which he argued that articles 2 and 3, and some of the constitutional provisions that seemed to him sectarian in character, were unhelpful. The response from Fianna Fáil was swift. Brian Lenihan was particularly negative, saying in a television interview that he would lead a crusade against the abolition or modification of articles 2 and 3. 'We will get the support from nationally minded people of this country and we will win.' FitzGerald discussed these exchanges with political correspondents at an off-the-record lunch and decided that, as the debate had begun, he needed to give a strong lead.

On 27 September he gave a long radio interview to Gerry Barry, one of the most respected journalists in RTÉ, and informed him in advance that he would be prepared to discuss constitutional change. When asked about the issue he turned Lenihan's language on its head, saying, 'What I want to do, if I may, is to take a phrase from somebody the other night on television: I want to lead a crusade, a republican crusade to make this a genuine republic.' He added that he was not going to rush into a referendum but would try and lead the country towards becoming a pluralist society.[9]

Haughey immediately denounced FitzGerald, saying his remarks had 'caused deep dismay among all those of us in every part of Ireland who cherish the ideal of unity'. FitzGerald, though, was heartened by what he felt was a surge of enthusiasm from a large section of the people 'who found inspiration in a political credo that responded to their deeply felt frustration at the narrow and exclusive rhetoric' propounded by so many politicians.[10] FitzGerald elaborated on his vision in a speech to the Seanad on 9 October in which he invoked the memory of Seán Lemass, who had once complained about the straitjacket of the Constitution in relation to the North in particular. He also quoted Jack Lynch, who had said that the Constitution should try to accommodate the views of people who saw aspects of it as an infringement of their civil rights and their liberty of conscience.[11] He then asked the Attorney General, Peter Sutherland, to undertake a review of the Constitution, but the process was interrupted by his loss of power a few months later and it was never resumed.

After he left office FitzGerald conceded that his constitutional crusade had been stillborn but he believed that it represented a time bomb ticking away at the heart of the narrow and exclusive form of nationalism to which Fianna Fáil traditionally tied its fortunes. 'In the struggle yet to be fought to determine a basic Irish philosophy and identity those who seek to hang on to a divisive form of single ethos nationalism are ultimately on the losing side.' The battle lines were drawn on 27 September 1981, and 'even though the subsequent uneasy truce may prevail for some time to come the vision I propounded is not dead but sleeping,' he wrote in 1991.[12] Time would prove him right.

In the winter of 1981/82 he had other problems to contend with, the main one being how his minority government could get another tough budget through the Dáil. In early January he went for a short break to the Canary Islands with Joan, but while he was away Dublin and the surrounding counties were hit by the worst blizzard since the 1940s, which brought business in the city to a halt. FitzGerald had to abandon his holiday and dash home to try to reassure the public that the government was serious about dealing with the emergency. Worse was to come that January.

The Minister for Finance, John Bruton, faced an enormous challenge in preparing the budget for 1982, having to reconcile the government's commitment to reforming the tax system with the imperative of reducing the budget deficit. He also had to take into account the Labour Party's natural insistence on providing for a substantial increase in social welfare payments. The commitment to reduce the standard rate of tax from 35 to 25 per cent had to be abandoned. Other commitments, such as tax relief for spouses who worked in the home and an income supplement for low-income families, were included, but there were also big increases in indirect taxes.

The issue that came to dominate, in an echo of the tribulations that beset the Fine Gael-led governments of the 1950s, was a plan to cut subsidies on food and to impose VAT on clothing and footwear in order to finance a massive 25 per cent increase in social welfare payments demanded by Labour. After a great deal of haggling in the cabinet, and a threat by Labour ministers to walk out of the government, a decision was taken to substantially retain the subsidy on bread and flour, with some reductions on butter and milk, but the 25 per cent welfare increase was retained. The Labour leader, Michael O'Leary, observed that the compromise was 'greeted with relief as it resolved the government split. At that stage we were at the end of a desperately intensive period of panic and pressure. We were an exhausted government.'[13] And that was after only six months in office.

Ministers failed to grasp that the extension of VAT to clothing and footwear, at the increased standard rate of 18 per cent, was going to be their Achilles heel. An effort to modify the negative impact by exempting children's clothing and footwear was rejected by Revenue officials on the absurd grounds that women with small feet might be able to avail of tax-free children's shoes. FitzGerald accepted this warped logic and used it to defend the budget, to general derision. Despite their minority position, the prevailing view in government was that the budget would get through the Dáil. One of the few sceptics was Peter Prendergast who had moved from being general secretary of Fine Gael to working as an adviser for John Bruton. 'I knew it hadn't a prayer and I told John that well in advance of the budget. We simply didn't have the leeway in the Dáil to do the job that was required.'[14]

FitzGerald thought differently, on the logical grounds that, as the unprecedented increase in social welfare payments meant that the budget was a seriously redistributive one, the two socialist independents, Noël

Browne and Jim Kemmy, would support it. In the event Browne was persuaded but Kemmy voted against, despite last-minute entreaties from the Taoiseach. The government would still have survived, however, had not the Dublin independent Seán Loftus also voted against the budget.

His decision came as a complete surprise. The government had calculated that he could not afford to collapse the Dáil, as he was likely to lose the seat he had won seven months before, after twenty years of trying. There was shock and excitement inside the Dáil and out when the budget was defeated by 82 votes to 81. Government backbenchers were shattered, and most ministers were deeply despondent, but FitzGerald was not. 'I experienced a moment of total exhilaration: this was it. We were going into battle on a budget that we could defend with conviction and enthusiasm both on social and financial grounds.'[15] There was an immediate and hastily convened meeting of the Fine Gael parliamentary party, at which, despite their shock and anxiety, TDs and senators gave FitzGerald and Bruton a standing ovation.

The Taoiseach then set out for Áras an Uachtaráin to ask President Hillery to dissolve the Dáil. His arrival at the Áras was delayed because one of the President's officials had to be hauled out of a play in the Peacock Theatre. In the interval Haughey and a number of his leading frontbenchers tried to contact the President to ask him not to dissolve the Dáil. Haughey issued a statement saying: 'I am available for consultation by the President should he so wish.'[16]

FitzGerald recalled that when he was finally ushered into the Áras he encountered 'a disturbed and indeed quite angry President Hillery', who was furious at the pressure he was coming under from Fianna Fáil not to dissolve the Dáil and instead to allow Haughey the opportunity to form a government. 'He was so upset by what had happened that he kept me there for three-quarters of an hour, thus leading many back in Leinster House to speculate that he might in fact be exercising his prerogative, the inappropriateness of which in current circumstances he was so vigorously propounding to me.'[17] The events of that night were to become the deciding factor in the sensational presidential election of 1990, which was won by Mary Robinson.

By the time he got back to the Dáil after 11 p.m. to announce that the election would be held on 11 February, FitzGerald found that the election strategy committee headed by the newly appointed Finbarr Fitzpatrick had already assembled and was planning the campaign. They decided on an aggressive defence of the budget as being necessary for the country's economic survival. On his way home in the early hours he was heartened to see Fine Gael election posters left over from the previous June already up on lampposts.

When the campaign team met the following day in Fine Gael head office they developed the theme that the country's financial survival was at stake. 'Ireland in debt is Ireland unfree' was one of the agreed advertising slogans. The image of FitzGerald as a man who was prepared to put the country before party and power was at the core of the message. It was to prove remarkably effective in the most adverse of circumstances.[18]

Fianna Fáil expected to coast to victory, but Haughey misread the public mood. A sizeable chunk of the electorate was shocked by the evidence of his economic mismanagement and his refusal to acknowledge that it had only made matters worse. The 'Haughey factor', as it came to be called, was a serious drag on Fianna Fáil's prospects. The first opinion poll of the campaign in the *Irish Times* showed that the Fine Gael vote, at 34 per cent, was holding up well, while Fianna Fáil, on 44 per cent, was not in the commanding position commentators had expected. Even more significantly, the poll found that FitzGerald was far ahead of Haughey as the public choice for Taoiseach, leading by 51 per cent to 31 per cent.[19]

The poll gave Fine Gael the confidence to continue the fight on the issue of fiscal rectitude, although it did abandon the proposed extension of VAT to children's clothing and shoes. The state of the public finances was the dominant issue of the campaign, and FitzGerald and Bruton hammered away at it. Fianna Fáil was forced to accept the government's analysis and produced an alternative budget at a late stage in the campaign. It was a softer alternative based on a sleight of hand that involved bringing forward the payment of existing taxes, particularly VAT.

Although they were defending a hairshirt budget, the Fine Gael campaign was strong and vibrant, in marked contrast to campaigns in similar circumstances in 1957 and 1977. A flavour of the campaign was evident when the Fine Gael battle bus swept into Cork North-West on 13 February. FitzGerald was greeted by banners welcoming him to 'Collins Country', bonfires blazed, and pipe bands led him in torchlight processions through Macroom, Millstreet and Charleville.[20] The more important campaign was waged on television, where Fine Gael ministers argued their case with passion and conviction night after night. FitzGerald didn't do as well in his debate with Haughey, who gave a smooth performance, but it didn't really matter. He was widely trusted, while his opponent was not.

The country went to the polls on 18 February and when the votes were counted the following day Fine Gael had come tantalisingly close to retaining power. In defiance of all the conventional wisdom, the party's vote was up to 37.3 per cent but it dropped two seats to 63. Labour held its 15 seats but Fianna Fáil gained three, giving them 81. It was a far cry from that party's expectations at the beginning of the campaign, but it put them in pole position to form a government. The king-makers this time would be Sinn Féin – the Workers' Party's three TDs and the independent socialist Tony Gregory. Some unseemly manoeuvring followed as Haughey and FitzGerald attempted to woo Tony Gregory. It was never much of a contest, and Haughey was prepared to promise whatever was asked. It ended in what became known as the 'Gregory Deal', which copperfastened his support through a range of spending projects for the inner city. The Workers' Party TDs also opted for Haughey with the objective of keeping Labour out of office, and he was elected Taoiseach.

Having lost office, FitzGerald put himself before the parliamentary party for re-election, as required by the new rule he had introduced. He won the contest by 62 votes to 5, but that overwhelming endorsement was spoiled by a deeply embarrassing episode for Fine Gael. Immediately on assuming office Haughey offered the European commissionership (vacant as a result of the election of Michael O'Kennedy of Fianna Fáil to the Dáil) to Dick Burke. It was clearly a political stroke aimed at strengthening Fianna Fáil's position, but Burke saw it as an opportunity he could not refuse. There was deep anger in Fine Gael, although the party could do nothing about it except sit tight and watch how Haughey coped with the tribulations of office.

What followed was the most extraordinary government in Irish political history. It began with a botched heave against Haughey's leadership following his disappointing election performance and then went from bad to worse as one political crisis followed another in dizzying succession through 1982. As the budgetary position began again to spiral out of control Haughey's stroke in appointing Dick Burke backfired when Fine Gael won the Dublin West by-election in early summer with an unknown candidate, Liam Skelly. Morale in Fine Gael soared. 'The disappointment that had naturally followed our loss of office three months earlier was replaced by a growing conviction that we would be back in government before long,' FitzGerald recalled.[21]

One reason for that conviction was that the Minister for Justice, Seán Doherty, became embroiled in a series of episodes involving interference in the operations of the Gardaí. There were also rumours that he had authorised the tapping of the phones of political opponents. The climax came in the late summer when the country's most wanted man, the double murderer Malcolm McArthur, was found by gardaí living in the apartment of a friend, who turned out to be none other than the Attorney General, Patrick Connolly. Haughey characterised the event as 'grotesque, unbelievable, bizarre and unprecedented', and Conor Cruise O'Brien subsequently coined the acronym GUBU from the expression. It stuck as a description of that ill-fated government as it staggered from one crisis to another.

Fianna Fáil was plunged into another leadership crisis in October when Charlie McCreevy put down a motion of no confidence in Haughey. Des O'Malley and Martin O'Donoghue resigned from the cabinet to oppose him, but Haughey survived. His minority government did not last much longer in office, however, because the Workers' Party TDs withdrew their support, and in early November it lost a vote of confidence by 82 votes to 80.

The mood in Fine Gael was buoyant going into the election campaign. One commitment made by FitzGerald that was to have enormous repercussions was his acceptance of the wording of an amendment to the Constitution proposed by Haughey's government to copper-fasten the right to life of the unborn. The newly installed Labour Party leader, Dick Spring, refused to be steamrolled into backing it, but FitzGerald was panicked by suggestions from Fianna Fáil that he was 'soft' on abortion.

FitzGerald's son Mark says his father made the judgement that he had to commit himself to the amendment in order to win the election and rescue the country from what he believed was a dangerous government. 'He made the gamble on the eighth amendment even though his heart wasn't in it because he knew that if he didn't then between the Church and Haughey they would wipe the floor [with Fine Gael]. Well, they nearly did. It was a very close election.'[22]

In the campaign itself Haughey sought to distract attention from his government's disastrous performance by accusing FitzGerald of being a lackey of Britain – a traditional criticism made by opponents of Fine Gael. Anglo-Irish relations had deteriorated badly in 1982 because of Haughey's anti-British stance during the Falklands War, and he now reverted to full-blooded nationalism, accusing FitzGerald of acting in collusion with British Intelligence. A suggestion made by FitzGerald six months earlier that an all-Ireland court and all-Ireland police force would be the best way to tackle IRA violence was presented as evidence that he was working hand in hand with the British. Jackie Healy-Rae, then an enthusiastic Haughey supporter, erected posters claiming Fine Gael wanted to bring the RUC to Co. Kerry.[23]

It was absurd but was partially effective in slowing a surge to Fine Gael. The party had pulled level with Fianna Fáil in opinion polls early in the campaign, but it slipped back a bit in the final week. Still, when voters went to the polls on 24 November the Fine Gael vote was up to 39 per cent and the party won seven extra seats, to bring its total to 70 as against 44 per cent and 75 seats for Fianna Fáil. It was the best result for Fine Gael since the days of Cumann na nGaedheal in the 1920s and the party's share of the vote has not been surpassed since.

FitzGerald was on his way back to government with the Labour Party, but this time the coalition negotiations were a more fraught affair than they had been in 1981. The Labour Party had elected a young new leader, Dick Spring, following the defection to Fine Gael of Michael O'Leary, whose pro-coalition stance had been rejected by a party conference. Spring showed his mettle during the campaign by refusing to be bounced into supporting the abortion amendment, and he was determined to get a coalition deal he could sell to his truculent party. 'Fine Gael sought to take every advantage possible of his inexperience,' was the view of Fergus Finlay, who became a long-term adviser and confidant of Spring's.

> A politician with no background or training in economic policy was expected to negotiate with Garret FitzGerald and Alan Dukes about how the currency should be stabilised and about how spi-ralling public expenditure could be managed … It was obvious that they were playing him for a patsy.[24]

That was not the way FitzGerald saw it. 'Although Dick Spring and I only knew each other slightly at this stage we soon established a rapport based on our common commitment to social democratic values and to integrity in public life.'[25]

One way or another, the two leaders and their teams hammered out a deal at a convent in Donnybrook, and when the new Dáil met, FitzGerald was elected Taoiseach by 85 votes to 79. Dick Spring became Tánaiste and Minister for the Environment. Peter Barry was given Foreign Affairs, but there was a surprise at Finance, where Alan Dukes replaced John Bruton, who moved to Industry and Energy. Another surprise was the appointment of Michael Noonan to Justice, while Jim Mitchell went to Communications. John Boland moved to Public Service, Pat Cooney to Defence, Paddy O'Toole to Forestry and Fisheries, and Austin Deasy – FitzGerald's harshest critic in the parliamentary party – was given Agriculture. Gemma Hussey was appointed to Education, giving FitzGerald the opportunity to realise his ambition of appointing at least one Fine Gael woman to the cabinet. It still meant there was only one woman cabinet minister, though, as the Labour team was all male. Barry Desmond was given Health and Social Welfare, Liam Kavanagh got Labour and Frank Cluskey was appointed to Trade, Commerce and Tourism. The Attorney General was Peter Sutherland, one of the rising stars of the legal profession, who had been a Fine Gael candidate in the 1973 general election.

As well as appointing Hussey to the cabinet FitzGerald attempted to show his commitment to advancing women's rights by appointing Nuala Fennell a Minister of State with a brief to co-ordinate a drive on issues affecting women in government departments. She was one of only three ministers for women's affairs in the EEC at the time, but she found her efforts frustrated by the territorial response of most departments. FitzGerald commented:

> All in all she had a thankless task and she found it particularly frustrating when some of her former colleagues in the women's movement criticised her for not doing things she would have loved to do, and might have been able to do, had her best efforts been better received in some key departments.[26]

While the government lasted four years, the level of distrust between Fine Gael and Labour from the start meant it was a bumpy ride for both of them. 'Dick Spring was a disaster,' was Peter Prendergast's assessment. 'Quite often things were agreed at cabinet and then Spring would go off and find that he couldn't get his party to agree. He was not prepared to take on his own people.' Not surprisingly, the Labour Party view is the exact opposite. Finlay recalled that Spring offered him the job of assistant government press secretary, saying, 'I need some help, particularly to mark Peter Prendergast who is going to be government press secretary.' Writing after their time in government, Finlay commented: 'Over the four years that I worked with him I learned to like him enormously. But I never learned to fully trust him. His agenda wasn't mine and our relationship was almost entirely partisan. Ultimately, I think it was destructive.'[27]

What kept the two parties in government together was the conviction in both that another Haughey-led government would be dangerous for Irish democracy. One concern was a return to the low standards of the

GUBU period, while another was a fear that the economy might be fatally undermined. There was also FitzGerald's commitment to working to end the cycle of violence in Northern Ireland. He later recorded in his autobiography:

> The combination of these considerations meant that it was vital not alone for our party but also for the national interest that Fine Gael and the Labour Party should maintain their unity in government for the four years or so ahead. Against this background I had not got the option that as Taoiseach I might have had in other circumstances of bringing the government to an end by dissolution in order to resolve differences that might arise between Fine Gael and Labour.[28]

As a result the government operated in an unusual way; FitzGerald was determined to ensure that it rarely boiled down to Fine Gael simply outvoting Labour in the cabinet. The upshot was a threefold system of decision-making. On Northern Ireland FitzGerald acted as chief rather than chairman, but on most aspects of domestic policy government decisions were arrived at by consensus, and only on very rare occasions was it put to a vote. If a vote threatened the stability of the government it was not taken but renewed efforts were made to find a consensus.

Tension between the two parties erupted within weeks of the government taking office in December 1982. On 9 January 1983 the new Minister for Finance, Alan Dukes, went on radio to say that the planned current deficit for the year ahead would have to be reduced from £900 million to £750 million. Spring, who was in hospital for a painful operation on his back, responded immediately with a public statement, saying there was no agreement between the coalition parties on the matter, and he phoned FitzGerald to express his anger. Dukes was forced to back down in double-quick time. The episode went down in political folklore as a Fine Gael capitulation to Labour but it was more complicated than that.

In fact FitzGerald agreed with Spring that officials of the Department of Finance were being too alarmist in the scale of their demands for a deficit reduction. 'Alan Dukes, pitchforked into the Finance portfolio in the most adverse circumstances conceivable, was in no position to challenge this rather apocalyptic view of his officials,' FitzGerald recalled. Resentment at the way Finance had indulged Haughey's phoney budget figures in 1981 coloured his suspicion of their attempt to panic his new government into a move that threatened its survival. FitzGerald went to see Spring in hospital to discuss the issue, and two days later a statement was issued on behalf of the cabinet saying there was concern on the part of the Taoiseach, the Tánaiste and a number of ministers from both parties at the figure mentioned by Dukes, as there had been no government decision on the matter. The Minister for Finance was forced into an ignominious retreat.

The episode was a critical moment in the life of the government. It revealed a policy of containment on the public finances rather than a determination to confront the problem head on. The harsh political reality was that the coalition would not have been able to survive if cuts on the scale required to make serious inroads into the deficit had been implemented. Within weeks of the government being formed two Labour TDs resigned over minor changes in the welfare system. The clear message was that serious spending cuts were out as long as Labour remained in government.[29] Some Fine Gael ministers felt that it would be better to force the issue and risk a fourth election in less than two years in the hope of an overall majority that would allow them to tackle the public finances. Jim Mitchell was one of the ministers who tried to persuade Fine Gael colleagues of this view, but FitzGerald thought the risk to Irish democracy of a return to power by Haughey was too great.

Throughout the final months of 1982 there had been rumours and newspaper stories that raised a number of questions about the way the Gardaí were operating under the direction of the Minister for Justice, Seán Doherty. Doherty, a former Garda detective, was an avid supporter of Haughey, and he had been promoted to one of the most sensitive positions in the government after less than five years in the Dáil. He had neither the experience nor the temperament for the job, but he was a willing stooge of Haughey.

The controversies involving Doherty during the year of GUBU mounted as time went on. There was the Dowra affair, which involved a witness from Northern Ireland being held by the RUC so that he was unable to give evidence against a brother-in-law of the minister. There was also the Tully affair in Co. Roscommon, where Sergeant Tom Tully of Boyle had successfully resisted an attempt, in which Doherty was involved, to have him transferred. The operation of the Gardaí was one of the issues that prompted Fine Gael's motion of no confidence, and it featured as an issue in the election campaign.

When Haughey lost power, the new Minister for Justice, Michael Noonan, launched an investigation into the situation, and his findings were sensational. He confirmed publicly on 20 January 1983 that the phones of two political journalists, Geraldine Kennedy and Bruce Arnold, had been tapped on the instructions of Doherty, and that normal procedures had not been followed. Even more surprising, he disclosed that Ray MacSharry had borrowed Garda equipment to secretly record a conversation with Martin O'Donoghue during the Fianna Fáil leadership heave in October 1982, and a transcript of the tape had been supplied to Doherty. Assistant Commissioner Joe Ainsworth had acted as the minister's agent in the affair, and the government demanded that both he and the commissioner, Thomas McLoughlin, resign. Fianna Fáil was immediately plunged into another crisis; but Haughey once more defied the odds and survived as leader.[30]

It was the economy, though, that continued to be the dominant preoccupation of the government. There were further clashes between Fine Gael and Labour during 1983. There was an incident in April when, in an address to a business gathering, Dukes warned that subsidies on food, housing and agriculture would have to be reviewed and payment considered for some free health and education services. Labour was furious, and Spring had an urgent meeting with FitzGerald to tell him the timing and tone of Dukes's comments were unacceptable. In a public statement, Spring was clear that 'the Labour Party stands for high public expenditure effectively allocated in the interests of equality and employment recovery'.[31]

There was another clash in the autumn when the spending estimates for 1984 were being discussed by ministers. FitzGerald outlined the grim economic situation in a radio interview and suggested that spending cuts of £500 million were on the cards. Spring was so angry he instructed his ministers to boycott the next cabinet meeting. Gemma Hussey noted the incident in her diary for 1 October.

> Garret arrived rather late; apparently there was a big problem about his broadcast last Sunday where he talked about £500 million in cuts, which apparently sent the Labour backbenchers bananas. Anyway Dick and Garret had a good meeting and an agreement was reached that there would be no more statements off the cuff about figures like that. That didn't leave all of us happy. I thought the whole point of such broadcasts was to prepare people for the difficulties ahead.[32]

As if Fine Gael had not enough to contend with on the economy and the phone-tapping scandal in its first weeks in office, it was plunged into a protracted and bitter internal row on abortion, which did serious damage to FitzGerald's image as a modernising political leader. Before taking office he was committed to liberalising the law on contraception and ending the constitutional ban on divorce. However, the commitment he had given during the election campaign to supporting the wording of a constitutional ban on abortion, put forward by the Haughey government, came back to haunt him.

One evening in late January 1983 Peter Sutherland went to FitzGerald's office in Government Buildings with his formal legal opinion on the wording. FitzGerald was stunned by the assessment of his Attorney General, who had concluded that there were serious flaws in the wording of the amendment. Far from taking the issue out of the hands of the courts, it risked a future intervention of the Supreme Court that might actually permit abortion or alternatively put the lives of mothers at risk.[33] Time would prove Sutherland's assessment correct, but in the fraught political atmosphere of January 1983 it meant trouble.

FitzGerald was appalled and concluded immediately that he could no longer support the amendment as worded. He then consulted his Fine Gael cabinet colleagues and was relieved that they unanimously backed his view. As the Labour ministers had only joined the government on the understanding that they would not be obliged to support the amendment, the issue did not affect them. FitzGerald knew that the decision would be damaging to Fine Gael and would give Fianna Fáil ammunition with which to depict him as 'soft on abortion'. Sutherland was instructed to devise alternative wording, although he warned his colleagues that it was going to be difficult. FitzGerald then made private contact with a leading Catholic bishop to alert him to the problem but was rebuffed when he sought to open a channel of communication to discuss the matter.

It was a month and a number of agonising cabinet meetings later before the Fine Gael parliamentary party was informed of the problem. After hearing Sutherland's opinion, they opted by a large majority to back a new wording, which stated that nothing in the Constitution could be invoked to invalidate the law prohibiting abortion. The new wording was rejected by Fianna Fáil and the Catholic Church and it prompted a serious split in Fine Gael. There was complete confusion when the bill with the new wording came before the Dáil. Fine Gael and Labour TDs split three ways. A majority of TDs in both parties supported it, but some voted against, while others abstained. The government's wording was rejected, and the original Fianna Fáil amendment was then put to the Dáil. It was passed with the support of eight Fine Gael and four Labour TDs.

The campaign on the eighth amendment to the Constitution was one of the most bitter in the history of the state. 'It was conducted on emotional lines and almost totally without regard as to the actual issues at stake as set out in Peter Sutherland's opinion,' was FitzGerald's view, with which it is hard to disagree.[34] When the country went to the polls in September the Fianna Fáil amendment was carried by a two-to-one majority. The episode was a disaster for Fine Gael. The split in the parliamentary party meant that a small minority were now deeply suspicious of FitzGerald, and he, by accepting the need for an amendment in the first place, had alienated a significant segment of liberal opinion. Haughey had displayed his usual cynicism, and it paid off politically, even if it con-demned the country to decades of bitter division on the issue of abortion.

The government's attempts to wrestle with the appalling economic situation and the controversy over abortion led to long and energy-sapping cabinet meetings. FitzGerald's eagerness to discuss issues in depth meant that he was an appalling chairman. Cabinet meetings that should have lasted two hours often went on all day and sometimes did not end until late at night. The exhausting nature of those meetings was summed up by Gemma Hussey in her diaries as nights when 'warm gin and cold chips' were presented to weary ministers in the early hours.

After the row over the spending estimates for 1984 the two parties in government moved cautiously and in consultation to prepare the budget. FitzGerald and Spring agreed that food subsidies would have to be cut by about a third, and the measure was included in the draft budget that was approved by the cabinet in January 1984. After the meeting, however, Spring tested how some of his backbenchers might react to the measure and he met with a furious response. Over the weekend before the budget Spring, FitzGerald and Dukes gathered in the Taoiseach's house and rewrote some of its sections. Food subsidies were retained in full and tax increases agreed to make up the shortfall.

By that stage the budget had gone to Cahill's, the printers, and had to be recalled. When the cabinet met on the Tuesday, Fine Gael ministers were stunned to discover the changes made at Labour's behest. 'We should all have resigned then and there,' Jim Mitchell said a few years later. 'I don't blame Spring so much as Garret. After all Spring was only fighting his own corner as best he could but Garret let us down and we should not have stood for it.'[35]

The problem was that Spring was hanging on to the Labour leadership by the skin of this teeth. At his party conference in Dublin in April 1984 he almost lost control when the party chairman, Michael D. Higgins, led a frontal assault on him over the issue of coalition. Higgins denounced coalition with 'the redneck fundamentalists' of Fine Gael and came very close to winning a majority of delegates for a motion that would have destroyed Spring's ability to remain in government.[36]

Michael Collins and W.T. Cosgrave at the funeral of Arthur Griffith, 16 August 1922. (© *Hulton Archive/Getty Images*)

Young Fine Gael recruitment poster featuring Michael Collins as a leader from the past (*c.* 2008). An example of how Collins's name and image have been invoked by subsequent generations.

An early Fine Gael membership card. (*Courtesy of Alan Kinsella*)

Eoin O'Duffy, Blueshirt leader and first president of Fine Gael, addressing a meeting in Bandon, Co. Cork (*c.*1934). (© *Central Press/Getty Images*)

Taoiseach John A. Costello outside 10 Downing Street on 17 June 1948, with Irish High Commissioner to the UK John Dulanty (left) and Minister for Agriculture James Dillon. Costello would announce in September that Ireland was withdrawing from the Commonwealth. (© *Ron Burton/Keystone/Hulton Archive/Getty Images*)

The first inter-party cabinet, 1948. Seated, left to right: Noël Browne (Health); Seán MacBride (External Affairs); Bill Norton (Tánaiste and Social Welfare); John A. Costello (Taoiseach); Richard Mulcahy (Education); Tom O'Higgins (Defence); T.J. Murphy (Local Government). Standing, left to right: Dan Morrissey (Industry and Commerce); Jim Everett (Posts and Telegraphs); Patrick McGilligan (Finance); Joe Blowick (Lands and Fisheries); Sean MacEoin (Justice); James Dillon (Agriculture). (© *Keystone/Getty Images*)

James Dillon addressing a Fine Gael ard fheis flanked by posters of Michael Collins and Arthur Griffith (*c*.1950). (*Courtesy of Fine Gael*)

Richard Mulcahy, Minister for Education in the Irish inter-party government, addressing an election meeting at the GPO in O'Connell Street, Dublin, 31 May 1951. (© *Keystone/Getty Images*)

In 1954
after Three Years of Fianna Fail

In 1951
when the Inter-Party was in power

All these rises in price are due to deliberate action by the present Government

VOTE 1, 2, 3 FOR FINE GAEL CANDIDATES:

CROTTY   FIELDING   HUGHES

IN ORDER OF YOUR CHOICE

AND REDUCE THE COST OF LIVING

Published by the Candidates and Printed by " Kilkenny People " Ltd., James's Street, Kilkenny.

Fine Gael flyer for the 1954 general election. After the election, John A. Costello formed his second inter-party government. (*Courtesy of Alan Kinsella*)

A young Declan Costello at Leinster House in the 1950s. His 'Just Society' document sought to change Fine Gael and Irish society in the 1960s, and has been a source of inspiration for subsequent politicians. (© *Irish Times*)

A delegation from the SDLP meets with Taoiseach Liam Cosgrave and other senior figures in the National Coalition government. Pictured, from left to right: Declan Costello, Garret FitzGerald, Conor Cruise O'Brien, John Hume, Liam Cosgrave, Gerry Fitt, Paddy Devlin and Austin Currie. (© *Independent News and Media*)

Garret FitzGerald addressing the first national conference of Young Fine Gael, November 1977. (*Courtesy of Fine Gael*)

Garret FitzGerald cutting the ribbon at the opening of the new Fine Gael headquarters on Upper Mount Street, Dublin, 1978. Among those gathered in the crowd are a young Enda Kenny, former leader James Dillon, Monica Barnes, Alexis Fitzgerald, Tom Fitzpatrick, Paddy Harte and Jim O'Keeffe. (*Courtesy of Fine Gael*)

Garret FitzGerald and Margaret Thatcher signing the Anglo-Irish Agreement at Hillsborough Castle on 15 November 1985. Standing, from left to right: Peter Barry, Dick Spring, Tom King and Geoffrey Howe. (© *Peter Kemp/AP/Shutterstock*)

Fine Gael leader Alan Dukes and Taoiseach Charles Haughey greeting Australian Prime Minister Bob Hawke in October 1987, along with other party leaders, Dick Spring, Des O'Malley and Tomás MacGiolla. (© *Independent Newspapers Ireland/NLI Collection/Getty Images*)

Taoiseach John Bruton at the start of the 1997 general election campaign with the other rainbow coalition leaders, Proinsias De Rossa and Dick Spring, on Dublin's Grafton Street. (© *Photocall Ireland*)

Four Fine Gael leaders: Alan Dukes, Garret FitzGerald, John Bruton (and his daughter), and Liam Cosgrave. (*Courtesy of Charlie Flanagan*)

A key moment in the 2002 general election campaign. Michael Noonan is hit in the face with a custard pie while campaigning in Roscommon on 30 April, as shocked Fine Gael candidates Denis Naughten and John Connor look on. (© *James Connolly/Picsell8*)

A happier Michael Noonan as Minister for Finance on budget day in October 2013. (© *Mark Stedman/Photocall Ireland*)

Enda Kenny chats with Queen Elizabeth II in the Taoiseach's office under the gaze of Michael Collins during her historic state visit in May 2011. (© *Tim Rooke/Shutterstock*)

Taoiseach Enda Kenny campaigning in Galway during the 2014 local and European elections with Hildegarde Naughten, who won a Dáil seat in 2016. (*Courtesy of Barry Cronin via Fine Gael*)

Enda Kenny with former Taoiseach Liam Cosgrave and Minister for Justice Charlie Flanagan. (*Courtesy of Charlie Flanagan*)

Enda Kenny and Liam Cosgrave gaze at the image of W.T. Cosgrave during a film shown in the GPO as part of the 1916 centenary commemorations. (© *Irish Times*)

Leo Varadkar and his rival Simon Coveney during the contest for the Fine Gael leadership in May 2017. (© *Fergal Phillips/Independent News and Media*)

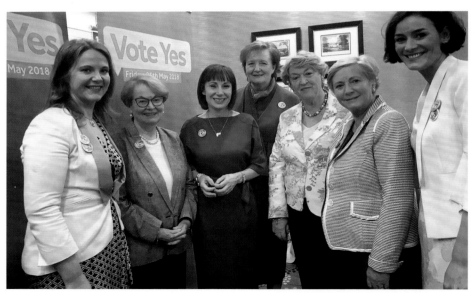

Fine Gael politicians past and present campaign for a Yes vote to repeal the eighth amendment to the Constitution in 2018. From left to right: Catherine Noone, Gemma Hussey, Josepha Madigan, Madeleine Taylor Quinn, Nora Owen, Frances Fitzgerald and Kate O'Connell. (*Courtesy of Josepha Madigan*)

Four Fine Gael MEPs elected to the European Parliament in May 2019. From left to right: Maria Walsh, Seán Kelly, Mairead McGuinness and Frances Fitzgerald. (© *Stavros Tzovaras/ EPP Group in the European Parliament*)

Taoiseach Leo Varadkar and Fine Gael director of elections Paschal Donohoe campaigning in Dublin on 14 January, the first day of the 2020 general election. (*Courtesy of Fine Gael*)

As early as 1927 there were discussions about the possibility of Cumann na nGaedheal and Fianna Fáil coming together, as shown in this *Dublin Opinion* cartoon. It was not until 2020, almost a century later, that Civil War politics finally came to an end. The extraordinary circumstances in which this occurred is summed up in this photograph of the new Fianna Fáil–Fine Gael–Green Party cabinet, socially distancing because of the Covid-19 health crisis, after receiving their seals of office from President Michael D. Higgins in Dublin Castle.

There was a sequel to the budget row in the summer of 1984 when anxiety in the Department of Finance at the worsening state of the public finances prompted renewed pressure to introduce the cuts in food subsidies, and this time the cabinet, including the Labour ministers agreed. However, the announcement on the eve of the August public holiday turned into a public relations disaster. With most ministers away on holidays, Spring was left to defend the decision. 'Appalling flack going on about the food subsidies,' Gemma Hussey noted in her diary. 'The hysteria from Michael D. Higgins, Joe Higgins of the Labour left, John Carroll (trade union leader), the housewives, you name it, as well as Fianna Fáil's Michael O'Kennedy being extremely rude on radio. The media are totally gone off mad.'[37]

There was another stalemate between the coalition partners on the appointment of a new EU commissioner to replace Dick Burke. A former Labour minister, Justin Keating, wanted the job and Spring pressed his case. Although FitzGerald had supported Keating's case almost a decade earlier, he took a different attitude this time around. 'Fine Gael, restive about what it saw – or at times imagined – to be a Labour Party tail persistently wagging the Coalition dog, was in no mood to concede this European appointment to a Labour nominee,' he recalled.[38]

FitzGerald was keen to appoint a serious, heavyweight candidate to the post, but he did not want to lose a senior minister. Peter Prendergast came up with the ideal solution: send Peter Sutherland to Brussels. He was ideally qualified for the post, and the appointment of the Attorney General would avoid the prospect of a by-election. Prendergast suggested the idea to Joan FitzGerald, who responded with enthusiasm and proposed it to Garret during a family Sunday lunch.[39]

Spring agreed to the appointment but on one condition: he insisted on the right to propose the new Attorney General. His choice was a long-standing friend and political supporter, John Rodgers, who was still a junior counsel and had to be elevated to the senior ranks before the appointment could be confirmed. FitzGerald had serious qualms about appointing someone he didn't know who was still a junior counsel, and Haughey denounced the decision in the Dáil.[40] It developed into yet another negative controversy for the government, although in time Rodgers proved to be a great success and Haughey, in a rare admission of fallibility, publicly conceded he had been wrong.

In a more harmonious vein, the government launched its agreed national economic plan, called Building on Reality, with a great deal of fanfare in the ballroom of Iveagh House. The plan was full of pious aspirations for boosting the economy but contained few hard decisions about cutting public spending. Still, for a time it gave the public some confidence that the government was at least attempting to get to grips with the economy.

FitzGerald had more success on an issue that was dear to his heart and had motivated him to go into politics in the first place: Northern Ireland. He devoted a great deal of energy to persuading the British and particularly the Prime Minister, Margaret Thatcher, that a serious initiative was needed to end the violence that was causing so much suffering and death. He began in 1983 by establishing the New Ireland Forum, which aimed to get a consensus in nationalist Ireland about a new approach to the problem. FitzGerald had long felt that the nationalist aspiration for a united Ireland would have to be modified or refined if unionist consent was ever to be forthcoming, and he was supported by the leader of the SDLP, John Hume. Some of his ministers doubted that the Forum would achieve anything, but they were persuaded to give it a try.

There was a tense struggle at the Forum, which pitted Fianna Fáil against all the other nationalist parties, with Haughey sticking rigidly to the old nationalist demand for a unitary state. The final report, published on 2 May 1984, listed three possible options: a unitary state, a federal or confederal arrangement, and joint British-Irish authority. Haughey, true to form, denounced the report for offering alternatives to a unitary state. Thatcher then dismissed the three options one by one at a press conference in December 1984, which followed an Anglo-Irish summit with FitzGerald in London. Asked by a journalist about the Forum options she listed them off, saying 'that is out' to each. The 'out, out, out' response caused a political storm in Dublin, and FitzGerald was pressed by supporters and opponents to respond in kind. He refused to do so and instead initiated an intense round of diplomacy in the first half of 1985 to get Thatcher to modify her position.

His initial forbearance paid off handsomely, as Thatcher was persuaded that radical thinking was required to break the endless cycle of violence. Urged on by her influential cabinet secretary, Robert Armstrong, she concluded the Anglo-Irish Agreement of November 1985, which represented the biggest change in relations between the two countries since the Treaty of 1921. Under the terms of the agreement the Irish government was given a role, through the Anglo-Irish Intergovernmental Conference, in representing the views of the nationalist community in the North. A permanent Irish secretariat was established at Maryfield in Belfast to give concrete expression to the agreement. It was a political and diplomatic triumph for FitzGerald and his Minister for Foreign Affairs, Peter Barry.[41]

Buoyed up by the warm public reaction to the agreement, FitzGerald went back to his constitutional crusade. His government had one important success on that front by liberalising the law on contraception. The tenacity of the Minister for Health, Barry Desmond of the Labour Party, was critical to that endeavour. He swept away a law introduced by Haughey in 1979 and famously described by him as 'an Irish solution to an Irish problem', which only allowed married people to legally buy contraceptives.

Desmond got his measure through the Dáil by 83 votes to 80 but at the cost of losing the support of three Fine Gael TDs: Oliver J. Flanagan, Alice Glenn and Tom O'Donnell. One Labour TD, Seán Treacy, also voted against the bill and was expelled from the party, never to return.

The bill also resulted in the final breach between Des O'Malley and Fianna Fáil. O'Malley made a powerful and emotional speech to the Dáil explaining why he could not vote against the bill and concluding with the republican catch-cry, 'I stand by the Republic.' It started the process that led to the setting up of the Progressive Democrats at the end of 1985.

Emboldened by the success of the legislation, FitzGerald decided to go for broke in 1986 with a referendum to remove the constitutional ban on divorce. He had established an Oireachtas Committee on Marital

Breakdown shortly after he took office for the second time. The committee's work was slowed by obstruction from Fianna Fáil, but it finally issued a majority report recommending the repeal of the constitutional ban. Michael O'Leary, the former Labour leader who was now a Fine Gael TD, proposed a private member's motion on the issue in 1985. While the government voted it down, on the grounds that the timing was not right, FitzGerald decided it was time to tackle the issue, which was one of the central planks in his constitutional crusade.

In theory, Fine Gael had been committed to removing the constitutional ban on divorce since 1978, when a motion on the issue was passed at FitzGerald's first ard-fheis as leader. Although a vocal minority in the party remained opposed to change, it was now or never for FitzGerald, as the government was clearly in its final years in office. One Fine Gael minister, Patrick Cooney, was strongly opposed to divorce and at his insistence the referendum was proposed by the parties in government rather than the government per se.

FitzGerald and Spring held a press conference to announce their decision to put the issue to the people, and at first the omens looked good. The first opinion poll of the campaign in early May showed 57 per cent in favour of repealing the ban, 36 per cent against, and only 7 per cent having no opinion.[42]

After that it was downhill all the way. The Catholic hierarchy, not surprisingly, came out against divorce and called on people to vote No. Although his party was theoretically neutral, Charles Haughey and most of his leading frontbenchers came out strongly against divorce, and in many parts of the country the party organisation was the backbone of the No campaign. What Fine Gael TDs found really galling was that Haughey was widely known in political circles to be carrying on an extramarital affair with the well-known fashion journalist Terry Keane. He even had the gall to travel to France for a romantic tryst with Keane at the height of the campaign after issuing a statement expressing his opposition to divorce in the following terms: 'For my own part, I approach this issue from the point of view of the family. I have an unshakable belief in the importance of having the family as the basic unity of our society.'[43]

The anti-divorce campaign concentrated on the economic hardships it would impose on women and children and its impact on property and pension rights. Although it had published a bill spelling out how divorce would work, the government parties struggled to explain how the system would operate and they were increasingly on the defensive.

The concerted efforts of Fianna Fáil and the anti-divorce campaign proved decisive in undermining support for removing the ban. When the referendum was held in early June the proposed change was rejected by a decisive 63 to 37 per cent. It was a bitter blow for FitzGerald, and it left his constitutional crusade in tatters. It was also a deeply demoralising blow for the coalition, as both parties came to the realisation that they had little chance of winning the next election. As they soldiered on through the second half of 1986 the political and economic pressure mounted.

FitzGerald had conducted a cabinet reshuffle early in 1986, which added to the stresses and strains in the cabinet and gave the impression of a shambolic government that was losing its grip. The big move, which went without a hitch, was the return of Bruton to Finance, with Dukes moving to Justice. The reshuffle was botched when Barry Desmond refused to move from Health and after a night of drama the Taoiseach was forced to change his plan. FitzGerald's intention was to ease the pressure on ministers such as Dukes and Desmond, who had taken the brunt of the criticism levelled at the government, but the last-minute changes simply reinforced the perception that he was losing control. Gemma Hussey was pencilled in for a move from Education to European Affairs, which was to be given cabinet status, but a combination of Desmond's refusal to move from Health and problems about splitting Foreign Affairs scuppered the plan.

Dukes was despatched to tell Hussey about the change of plan. 'Alan obviously felt very awkward about telling me – I presumed he had been sent by Garret and my first reaction was to have a quick weep, to Alan's kind consternation,' she recorded in her diary. Salt was rubbed in the wound when she was summoned to FitzGerald's office to be told of the change, which he said was due to her raising difficulties about the division of responsibilities in Iveagh House.

I stumbled back upstairs, deeply upset, but had dutifully accepted the situation ... It appears that the original restructuring which Garret had intended was that there would be a new Foreign Affairs Ministry, the amalgamation of Public Service and Finance and Barry Desmond moved to Environment with John Boland in Health and Social Welfare. Of course Barry's position of refusing to move wrecked all that and I got shafted.[44]

The autumn of 1986 was a time of attrition for the government. Back in Finance, Bruton was determined to tackle public spending rather than relying on even further tax increases to keep the public finances under control. While the government's strategy was beginning to work, progress was far too slow and public frustration grew as unemployment soared. Emigration had come back to haunt the country once more, with many graduates unable to find jobs at home. The mood of gloom was all too reminiscent of that which beset the second Costello government in its final months in office in 1957.

It became clear in October that Fine Gael and Labour would not be able to agree a budget for 1987. Government spending was seriously off target by September and another overrun in borrowing was inevitable. That prompted a loss of confidence by the financial markets and an increase in borrowing costs. FitzGerald proposed to his cabinet colleagues that to steady the markets the government should announce its intention of reducing borrowing the following year and give a commitment that it would not engage in any further increases in tax. The Labour ministers objected, but FitzGerald did what he had never previously done in government: he insisted on a majority decision in the cabinet regardless of Labour opposition.[45] The coalition was in effect dead but the two parties decided to stay in office until after Christmas to conclude some important outstanding business, particularly the Single European Act and the Extradition Act. Both measures met with fierce resistance within the Labour Party, the objections being led by Michael D. Higgins, but the government managed to stagger to the Christmas break, surviving on the casting vote of the Ceann Comhairle.

The coalition formally came to an end on 20 January when the four Labour ministers officially announced that they were leaving as they could not support the budget being devised by Fine Gael. It was an amicable parting considering the strain they had all been under. Gemma Hussey recorded in her diary:

> Our final cabinet meeting was slightly strained and obviously very hard for Dick. We took a formal vote at noon and then Dick handed over his prepared letter of resignation. There was a session of slightly sad, slightly emotional handshakes (a warm embrace for me from Barry and Ruairí).[46]

Fine Gael was now in government on its own. Some ministers, including Jim Mitchell, felt they should go ahead and present their budget to the Dáil. Although it would face certain defeat it would focus debate on the national finances. Instead, at FitzGerald's urging, the uncompromising budget, which included deep spending cuts, further increases in indirect tax and small welfare increases, was published. He then went to the Áras and asked President Hillery to dissolve the Dáil. The election date was set for 17 February. FitzGerald opted for a four-week campaign, rather than the usual three weeks, to give his party time to explain their position to the electorate.

With Labour gone, some in the party had hopes that an alliance with the PDs would be possible, but approaches were rebuffed. Fine Gael was on its own in arguing for reduced borrowing and deep cuts in public spending as the only way out of recession. It was not a message the voters wanted to hear. The party's election manifesto outlined an aspiration to create a 'virtuous circle' of sustainable public spending, lower taxes and more jobs, in contrast to the 'vicious circle' which had got the country into the mess. It seemed like a pious aspiration, rather than an achievable policy.

The main slogan of the Fianna Fáil campaign was 'Health cuts hurt the old, the poor and the handicapped.' This message was plastered on hoardings all over the country for months before the election campaign even began. While the party did accept the basic arithmetic of the outgoing government's budget, the populist nature of the appeal during the campaign did not seem to indicate that Haughey was about to address it in a serious fashion. His record of fighting the government tooth and nail on every single public spending cut for the previous four years suggested that he would adopt a much more relaxed attitude towards public spending. He had maintained again and again that spending cuts were unnecessary, and he lambasted the government for its 'Thatcherite' and 'monetarist' policies. As almost all professional economists were also preaching the need for stricter control of public spending, Haughey attacked them as well.

The first opinion poll of the campaign in the *Irish Times* gave Fine Gael only 23 per cent of the vote, with Fianna Fáil on 52 per cent and Labour on 5 per cent. The big surprise was that the PDs were on 15 per cent and clearly going to have a decisive influence on the result. As the long campaign wore on, however, Fianna Fáil's commanding lead in the opinion polls began to slip, just as FitzGerald had hoped. However, the Fine Gael vote did not increase by nearly as much as was needed, given the party's isolation. The strength of the PD campaign was a double-edged sword for Fine Gael: on the positive side the party cut into the Fianna Fáil lead, but on the other hand it picked up disillusioned Fine Gael supporters.

By the time the votes were counted on 18 February, Fine Gael had reconciled itself to defeat. The party won 27 per cent of the vote and 51 seats. While it was not as bad as the party top brass had feared at the beginning of the campaign, it meant they were returning to opposition. Haughey was on his way back to the Taoiseach's office, but the silver lining was that he had not achieved the expected overall majority, falling three short with 81 seats. The PDs won 14, Labour 12, the Workers' Party 4 and others 4. It meant that his government would have to find some accommodation with the opposition in order to survive.

One hugely important development in the later stages of the campaign that was barely noticed by the media was a proposal from FitzGerald to establish an all-party economic forum along the lines of the New Ireland Forum. On the day he stepped down as Taoiseach to be replaced by Haughey he made an impassioned plea in the Dáil for unity in dealing with the economic crisis.

> That is going to require, on our part certainly, a degree of good will and constructiveness in opposition greater than any of us in opposition have previously found it possible to accord and, on the part of the government, necessarily a corresponding response in terms of a willingness to be open with the opposition and the House and to seek and rely on our support when things need to be done for the sake of our country.

It was a generous, patriotic response to the loss of office which had a decisive impact on Irish politics in the years ahead.

UNDER PRESSURE: ALAN DUKES

'It was done, I think, to damage me, to make sure the result was as bad as it could be, so that I would be cast in the worst possible light.'

— ALAN DUKES, REFLECTING ON AUSTIN CURRIE'S ABSENCE
FROM THE DECLARATION IN THE 1990 PRESIDENTIAL ELECTION.

At 11:30 a.m. on Wednesday 11 March 1987, in a lengthy and emotional speech, Garret FitzGerald announced to a gathering of the party's TDs, senators and MEPs that he was stepping down as leader of Fine Gael. There was some surprise and a lot of regret at his decision but a general acceptance that it was the right thing to do after a decade in the role. By then Fine Gael was, in his own words, 'a somewhat different party, performing a somewhat different role than what it was when I took over'.[1]

What FitzGerald didn't say at the time was that the party was suffering an identity crisis. The divisions that had emerged in the 1960s over Declan Costello's Just Society became far more pronounced when FitzGerald took the party into government in 1981. Unlike Costello, he actually had the opportunity to implement his policies and, in doing so, worked to recast Fine Gael as a liberal party. As discussed in the previous chapter, he had had to carry out a delicate balancing act as he attempted to keep together a party internally divided on all the major socio-moral issues that faced his government. This was the party that Alan Dukes inherited in March 1987.

Gemma Hussey's diaries record that Dukes had been mentioned as a possible successor to FitzGerald in October 1986.[2] When the time came, succession was settled through a leadership contest that also included Peter Barry, the outgoing Minister for Foreign Affairs, and John Bruton, the outgoing Minister for Finance who had been side-by-side with FitzGerald throughout the general election campaign. Hussey's and Michael Noonan's names were also mentioned, but neither took the plunge. Bruton would later succeed Dukes, and Barry was a formidable politician. Fine Gael is sometimes thought of as a demoralised, and perhaps broken, party by the time that FitzGerald stepped down; but it is worth remembering that the party could offer three strong and viable candidates.

Barry was the favoured choice of most senior ministers, but there was more energy about the Dukes and Bruton campaigns. In contrast to the well-publicised leadership contest of 2017, the ten-day campaign to decide FitzGerald's successor was conducted largely in private. Dukes was fastest out of the blocks with a round of media interviews. His campaign team was composed of young, up-and-coming TDs like Ivan Yates, Gay Mitchell and Alan Shatter and they targeted the younger Fine Gael TDs and senators. Dukes went from being described as the 'dark horse' on 12 March to 'the bookies' favourite' four days later.[3]

Votes were cast on Saturday 21 March 1987 and, in keeping with tradition, the breakdown of the ballots, counted by FitzGerald and Kieran Crotty, chairman of the parliamentary party, was not revealed. When the announcement was made, the party hierarchy was surprised that Dukes had emerged as the winner.[4] An obviously delighted Dukes emerged from Leinster House just after 1:30 p.m. that Saturday and walked hand in hand with his wife, Fionnuala, to the Kildare Street gates. There they were met by cheering grass-roots members, many wearing rosettes to show their support. Some raised Dukes on their shoulders. This triumphant scene of adulation and support would contrast sharply with the general tone of his time at the helm.

Born in Dublin on 20 April 1945, at forty-one Dukes was then Fine Gael's youngest leader. Unlike FitzGerald and Cosgrave before him, his father was not a former TD, minister or Taoiseach. In fact, as a senior civil servant who became head of the Higher Education Authority, Jim Dukes was, outwardly at least, non-political. As Alan Dukes explained, while his mother 'hated' Fianna Fáil and Éamon de Valera, 'we weren't a very political family.' His father decided how to vote at each election according to the candidates' policies, rather than political affiliation.[5]

That Dukes did not come from a strong Fine Gael background is likely to have contributed to the feeling that he wasn't 'typical' Fine Gael. Educated at the Irish-medium Coláiste Mhuire in Dublin, he had a lifelong passion for Irish. Colleagues have suggested that he is at his most relaxed when conversing in Irish. While studying economics at UCD he was taught by Garret FitzGerald, who would later encourage him to contest the 1979 European elections. During his time in college he was captain of the UCD fencing club, something that was frequently commented on in the media in later years. 'When other students were getting drunk and chasing girls, Alan was taking part in debates in Irish or fencing when he was not studying,' one contemporary recalled.

Tall and thin, with a razor-sharp mind, the chain-smoking Dukes cut an unlikely figure in politics. Always courteous, he was quite happy to talk to anyone and engage in vigorous debate, but he always had to have the last word. The fact that he was usually right impressed some people but antagonised others. He had a laconic sense of humour, illustrated in an exchange with John Bruton during a particularly lengthy cabinet meeting near the end of FitzGerald's second government. Bruton, who had replaced Dukes as Minister for Finance, passed him a note that asked, 'Alan – how did you keep your sanity?' 'Did I?' came the deadpan response.[6]

As Minister for Finance, Dukes had developed a reputation for mastery of detail, and his open-door policy with Fine Gael backbenchers ensured that he was highly regarded by TDs, even if few of them knew him well. 'Alan Dukes was a workaholic, a calm Minister for Finance whose command of his brief was astounding,' Gemma Hussey wrote in her diary not long after serving in the cabinet with him.

He like Garret was not 'one of the lads' though never realised it. I found his cool style of argument, particularly about education, quite maddening. Alan, all 6'4" of him, smoked incessantly, smiled most of the time, seemed – as he still does – unmoved by anything I could throw at him.[7]

Her assessment was echoed by the *Evening Herald,* which commented: 'He does not shout, get angry or disturbed. Alan Dukes just mows down his detractors with icy calm and unbeatable logic.'[8]

FitzGerald never named his preferred heir, but the consensus has been that he favoured Dukes. He always strenuously denied this, and he certainly took no part in the campaign, leaving the country the day after he announced his decision to step down and returning only for the count.

Dukes belonged to the socially progressive wing of the party. He had voted in his first general election in 1969 and was impressed by Declan Costello's Just Society, which he considered a 'move away from the kind of stultifying conservatism of Irish society'.[9] During the 1982–7 government, along with FitzGerald and Hussey, he had been closer to the Labour ministers than most of his colleagues. In an interview after his election as leader Dukes established continuity with FitzGerald's general ethos. He told Donal Kelly of RTÉ: 'We want to build a party that is going to contribute to the process of guiding change in Ireland … In Fine Gael we're going to look at all of the issues, at the changes that we can see taking place in Irish society and guide those changes in a way that's going to benefit the people.'[10]

When asked the following day on RTÉ by Caroline Erskine what kind of changes he envisaged he replied, 'All kinds of changes. Changes in the social area. Changes on the economic front. Changes that will come about simply because of the structure of the Irish population, because we have such a young population.'

He went on to talk about the failed divorce referendum, rejecting the proposition that voters had spurned Fine Gael's liberal policies; on the contrary, he claimed, the conversation during the campaign showed that there was a broad consensus on the need for changes in the law in relation to judicial separation and on the status of women and children.[11] For the more conservative elements of the party – already uneasy because of FitzGerald's agenda – the implications of such views were problematic.

Dukes was clearly determined to continue in the direction in which FitzGerald had shifted Fine Gael. This would prove difficult, though, and not just because of the party's internal division. Despite his suggestion that there was an appetite for change, the bruising experience of the eighth amendment and the failure of the divorce referendum made social issues a hard sell for the party. By supporting the economic policies pursued by Haughey's government (discussed below) there was nothing that made Fine Gael distinctive. The party was, as the *Evening Herald* put it, in an 'ideological no man's land'.[12] Not for the first time in its history, Fine Gael was faced with the challenge of how to define itself as something other than Fianna Fáil's opposition. Rather than dealing with that challenge, the party would opt for blaming its new leader.

Dukes also knew the problems facing him from within the party. When asked during the campaign why his colleagues should vote for him he had replied, 'We need somebody who can weld, keep together, all the various elements in the party.'[13] For this reason he appointed John Bruton, seen to be on the party's conservative wing, as his deputy leader, although he moved him from Finance to Industry and Commerce. Michael Noonan became the party's new spokesman on Finance. His front bench, announced on 26 March, represented a degree of continuity, and he retained those who had served as ministers, though he reshuffled some of the portfolios. Bernard Allen was spokesman on Health, Seán Barrett on Justice, Peter Barry on Foreign Affairs, George Birmingham on Labour, John Boland on Environment, Richard Bruton on Energy, Paul Connaughton on Defence, Austin Deasy on Transport and Tourism, Avril Doyle on Marine, Gemma Hussey on Education, Enda Kenny on Gaeltacht Affairs, Jim Mitchell on Social Welfare and Jim O'Keeffe on Agriculture, with Ivan Yates as junior spokesman on Trade and Marketing. Fergus O'Brien replaced Barrett as chief whip.

Dukes did not make room for some of the younger TDs who had been behind his leadership campaign, and they were both surprised and disappointed at the lack of change. As one TD put it at the time, 'The problem is that it looks like the government the people have just rejected.' As his tenure progressed, Dukes would become more and more detached from his front bench.

While Dukes's leadership marked a period of instability as the infighting between the party's two wings continued, for some, resentment dated back to his elevation to the cabinet in 1981. Having unsuccessfully contested the 1979 European elections, Dukes tasted electoral victory in the June 1981 general election, although he took a seat in Kildare only on the last count and without reaching the quota. On his first day in the Dáil as a TD he joined an exclusive, if largely ill-fated, club of first-time deputies who had been appointed to ministerial office straight away. Based on the reputation he had cultivated while working as an agricultural economist in Brussels, FitzGerald made Dukes his Minister for Agriculture. Dukes felt the jealousy that his appointment caused, conscious that some colleagues saw him as a 'Johnny-come-lately'. 'They didn't make life particularly easy for me,' he recalled.[14]

Dukes had a meteoric rise. It has since been suggested that a spell as a back-bench TD could have served as a useful apprenticeship, helping him to navigate and possibly avert some of the difficulties he would encounter as leader.[15] But it is worth remembering that FitzGerald never spent a day on the back benches before his leadership either. Moreover, while Dukes might have been 'green' when it came to parliamentary politics, he began his professional career as an economist with the Irish Farmers' Association, which is known for its robust debates.

When Ireland joined the EEC in 1973 Dukes moved to the IFA's Brussels office. After Dick Burke was appointed a European commissioner in 1977, he asked Dukes to be his chief of staff, and he was working in that capacity when asked by Fine Gael to contest the first elections to the European Parliament in 1979.

Only days after forming a government in 1987, Charlie Haughey had to contend with a bleak forecast on the condition of the public finances. The subsequent budget, unveiled by the new Minister for Finance, Ray MacSharry, on 31 March, was even more severe than the wide-ranging cuts that had been in John Bruton's proposed budget before Fine Gael left office. Massive cutbacks in health and education services and in building grants were announced, while expenditure targets were tightened. Parties on the left attacked the budget, but both Fine Gael and the Progressive Democrats were broadly supportive.[16]

Fine Gael's new Finance spokesman, Michael Noonan, began by saying he had great pleasure in welcoming Fianna Fáil's acceptance of the Fine Gael analysis of the problem.

> This is grand larceny of our policy as put before the electorate …
> If the government were subject to the Trades Description Act they
> would be in the dock tonight for putting before the Irish people a
> product totally different from what they were contracted to deliver.
> I am glad they realised there is a better way.[17]

This extraordinary U-turn by Fianna Fáil, contradicting everything the party had been saying for the past four years, created an immediate dilemma for the new Fine Gael leader. The party abstained on the budget vote, but leading members of the front bench were in two minds about how to proceed from there.

Fine Gael was in competition not only with the Fianna Fáil government but also with the Progressive Democrats on the opposition benches. On the day of his election as leader Dukes had launched a blistering attack on the PDs, saying they were a force for instability in Irish politics and would not last. There was bad blood between the two opposition parties, because Fine Gael believed the PDs had reneged on a vote transfer pact, discussed by officials from both parties before the election. A form of words was agreed with the PDs about how they would respond to an appeal from Garret FitzGerald to give transfers to the PDs.

Following strong pressure from Bobby Molloy and Pearse Wyse, O'Malley's response was actually hostile. Both parties were deeply suspicious of Haughey and not sure how to respond to his conversion to budget prudence. While both parties had argued for the policies that Haughey was following, they were now tempted into competitive outrage about the impact of public spending cuts. This prompted a political mini-crisis just before the Dáil summer recess as cutbacks in the health service began to provoke street protests. On the advice of Fine Gael's Health spokesman, Bernard Allen, the front bench decided to oppose the Health estimate unless some of the planned cuts were modified. Haughey responded aggressively and threatened to call a general election for 15 July if the estimate was voted down by the Dáil.

There was consternation in Fine Gael, as the last thing the party wanted was to provoke a general election in which Haughey might finally win his long-cherished overall majority. Dukes sought a meeting with Haughey, and the two men agreed a formula for broadening the scope of a national review of the health service. In the light of that minimal concession Fine Gael announced that it would abstain on the vote. There was no escaping the fact that it was a fig leaf, and a transparent one at that. The PDs gleefully denounced 'Fine Gael grovelling', claiming that the party had fallen on its face, while Tomás Mac Giolla of the Workers' Party called it 'unconditional surrender'.[18]

Fianna Fáil took delight in rubbing salt into the wound. Haughey's spokesman, P.J. Mara, told political correspondents that it was 'game, set and match to Mr Haughey'. He went on to joke, 'It is the first time in Dáil history that an opposition has been brought down by a government.' Luckily for Fine Gael, the Dáil adjourned for a four-month summer recess that same day, but it was a salutary lesson. The party clearly had to find a way of ensuring that it was not going to be repeatedly in a similarly embarrassing position.

Peter White, the party's young press officer, was determined that lessons had to be learned so that Fine Gael would not stumble into an election at an inopportune time. He had begun working for the party three years earlier, when it was in government, and now found himself in a vital position among the opposition leader's small staff. Before going on holidays in July 1987 he wrote a memo to the leader that began by making an essential point: 'The exact content of one's strategy is less important than actually having a strategy.' He went on to outline the options facing Dukes. He would have to decide whether he wanted an early election or devise a strategy to justify propping up the government until the right time arrived.

> I believe that we should aim for a late election and that we should start to defuse the 1988 budget debate in September. I see no difficulty with capturing the high ground with a more elaborate version of the Fine Gael statement of 6 March 1987. It takes no great leap of the imagination to draft a statesman-like script which would bring the public and the mainstream media behind you.

He went on to advise Dukes that if he accepted the need for such a strategy aimed at making him Taoiseach in 1989 or 1990 he would have to steer the party through very difficult times. It would require an approach aimed at winning public support while coping with the inevitably hostile response from elements of the party membership. 'Your authority must be absolute,' he wrote, advising Dukes to rejig the front bench by appointing some younger people and to put in a chief whip whose loyalty to him was beyond question.[19] The chief whip at the time was Fergus O'Brien, one of the party's old guard who had not supported Dukes for the leadership.

Dukes reacted positively to the suggestions and, after their return from holidays in late August, he began to prepare the ground for an announcement. Meetings were arranged with leading journalists, including the editor of the *Irish Times*, Conor Brady, and the *Irish Independent* leader-writer Seán Cantwell. The scale of the financial crisis was discussed, along with the need for a realistic and patriotic response by all in a position to make it.

A long-standing speaking engagement at the Tallaght Chamber of Commerce on 2 September was chosen as the moment to launch a new style of politics to the Irish public. The speech contained an unambiguous commitment to not bringing down the government as long as it adhered to responsible budgetary policies. 'When the government is moving in the right direction I will not oppose the central thrust of its policy,' Dukes informed his audience. 'If it is going in the right direction, I do not believe that it should be deviated from its course, or tripped up on macro-economic issues.' He went on: 'I will not play the political game which produces the sort of phony economic analysis which has passed for opposition in the past.'

The political correspondents were tipped off about the significance of the relevant passages, and the 'Tallaght strategy' was launched to a fanfare of approval from the media and the public.[20] It was the main front-page story in the *Irish Times* the following day, with the paper's political correspondent, Denis Coughlan, writing that Dukes had 'offered direct and unsolicited support for the Government's budget of 1988 provided it met certain basic requirements on public expenditure, employment and taxation.' He wrote that the move would ensure the stability of the minority government well into 1988 and would also buy Dukes valuable time to reorganise Fine Gael.

The editorial in the same paper hailed the move as a landmark in Irish politics and 'a rare display of political maturity'.[21] In the years since then it has often been overlooked, or simply forgotten, that FitzGerald made a similar offer on results night in 1987.

Dukes later recalled that Haughey was 'rather baffled at the beginning. This wasn't the kind of politics that he was used to.'[22] The reaction from other opposition parties was, not surprisingly, negative, with the PDs' Finance spokesman Michael McDowell denouncing the move, along with Labour and the Workers' Party. However, it had the immediate effect of improving public and investors' confidence in the economy after the downward spiral of the previous decade. In 2016 one of Ireland's leading political scientists, Gary Murphy, described the Tallaght strategy as 'one of the most selfless political acts in modern Irish history'.[23]

Although the public responded well to the Tallaght strategy, there was a considerable amount of grumbling in Fine Gael among TDs and in the wider party organisation. Some members of the front bench – most notably the acerbic John Boland and the perpetually cranky Austin Deasy – made little attempt to disguise their hostility to Dukes and his strategy. Peter White repeated the advice he had given his leader the previous summer, that he needed to undertake a big front-bench reshuffle and sack his main critics, including Deasy and Boland; but the new leader recoiled from such radical action at that stage. He did take White's advice to reach out to the public beyond the Leinster House bubble, though, by doing a number of interviews with feature-writers and television chat shows.[24]

Despite the positive response from the media to the Tallaght strategy, Fine Gael TDs became restive when opinion polls showed no improvement on the party's 1987 election performance. In March 1988 a disgruntled Deasy resigned from the front bench, triggering media speculation about unrest in the party. This was followed by a memorable intervention by the former junior minister John Donnellan, a blunt-spoken popular figure in the party. In an interview with the *Connacht Tribune* in April 1988 he remarked, 'If it was raining soup Alan Dukes would be holding a fork.'[25] The comment entered political folklore and over time came to define the period of Dukes's leadership.

In response, the leader took action to remove the whip from Donnellan. This was hardly surprising, but Dukes made a serious error of judgement by asking John Bruton to second the expulsion motion at the parliamentary party meeting. While Bruton was not opposed, he felt it was wrong of Dukes to involve him, as Donnellan had been a strong supporter of his in the leadership contest. In the event, the motion was seconded by the party's Justice spokesman, Seán Barrett. It was carried by a substantial majority, but only after a long debate and an attempt to water it down had been defeated. The episode showed that there were serious doubts among some TDs about Dukes's leadership.

Dukes did not help himself with an unguarded interview with Deirdre Purcell of the *Sunday Tribune* during the summer of 1988. Reflecting back on a meeting with a leading bishop during the divorce referendum campaign, he remarked that only the circumstances of the meeting had prevented him being 'dug out of that bastard'.[26] The comment caused an immediate furore and helped to alienate Dukes from a swathe of party members who were either offended by the comment or at the very least felt that it put them on the defensive in their communities.

Shortly afterwards he decided that it was time to act on Peter White's advice of a year earlier and reshuffle his front bench. He dropped John

Boland, Bernard Allen, Fergus O'Brien and Enda Kenny. He brought in Ivan Yates, Alan Shatter, Jim Higgins and Madeleine Taylor Quinn, all of whom had been stronger backers in the leadership election. It was a decisive move, which helped to shore up his position with the front bench, but it left some powerful enemies on the party's back benches.

Dukes's first major electoral test came in 1989. As the tough medicine administered by the Haughey government and sustained by the Tallaght strategy began to have a positive impact on the economy, Fianna Fáil's popularity soared. Tempted by high poll ratings, Haughey seized on a Dáil defeat on a non-binding motion calling for financial assistance for haemophiliacs infected with the AIDS virus to call an election. It was a major miscalculation. The move was regarded by Dukes and the Fine Gael front bench as a betrayal of the Tallaght strategy, and they made it clear that there would be no return to the policy after the election.

Fine Gael had plenty of time to prepare for the contest, which was held on the same day as the European elections. White, turning Mara's quip of a year earlier on its head, said it was the first time a government had surprised itself with the timing of an election. In the interval before the election was called Fine Gael made a coalition pact with the PDs. Dukes and his closest allies were unenthusiastic about the move, but he was persuaded by his deputy leader, John Bruton, that it made sense. Bruton had been a loyal deputy and supported the Tallaght strategy uncondi- tionally, so Dukes felt compelled to go with his advice.[27] In a reversal of the position during the 1987 election, this time the PDs were anxious for an election pact, while Fine Gael was reluctant. The pact was agreed on the day Haughey dissolved the Dáil, and the government got a shock when it was announced two days later.[28]

The pact reflected Fine Gael's commitment to budgetary discipline and the PDs' support for tax cuts. There were some inherent contradic- tions, but it did have the advantage of preventing squabbling between the parties during the election campaign. The problem was that the lack of enthusiasm for the deal was palpable, and the pact failed to catch the public imagination. The PDs had been on a downward spiral in the polls, and their hopes that the pact would reverse the trend proved unfounded.

The election campaign was dominated not by the economy or tax cuts but by the health cuts, to the great frustration of Fianna Fáil, which felt the media did not give it the credit it deserved for the economic recovery.

Fianna Fáil's massive pre-election poll ratings declined steadily during the campaign as the party was attacked from all sides for the health cuts. When the votes were counted, on 26 May, Haughey had failed for the fifth time to win an overall majority.[29] But the alliance of Fine Gael and the PDs did not capitalise on his weakness, with gains being made instead by Labour and the hard-left Workers' Party. Fine Gael increased its share of the vote from 27 to 29 per cent, which translated into an additional four seats, giving the party a total of fifty-five. The PDs slumped from fourteen seats to six. Between them the two parties fell far short of the number of seats needed to form a government.

Meanwhile, although Fine Gael's vote had actually increased, albeit marginally, in the 1989 election, Dukes's leadership was under pressure. The party's constitution, amended by FitzGerald, required the leader to submit himself to the parliamentary party for re-election if it was not in government after a general election. When the parliamentary party gathered on 28 June, Austin Deasy spoke critically of Dukes during the three-hour meeting, emphasising, in particular, an inflexibility in his approach both to problems in the Dáil and towards those within the party who disagreed with him. He claimed that senior members of the party were not being consulted. At that stage, however, colleagues were not ready to move against the leader. Given that Haughey was not certain of forming a government, and that the prospect of another general election was very real, Deasy's criticisms were considered ill-timed. John Bruton, seconded by Peter Barry, moved a motion of confidence in Dukes. The secret ballot that followed was counted by Garret FitzGerald and Tom Enright, chairman of the parliamentary party.[30] Dukes was re-elected. But within twenty-four hours his credibility as leader received a serious blow.

When the new Dáil convened the next day, Charlie Haughey's bid to be Taoiseach was defeated by 86 votes to 78. It was the first time in the history of the state that the Dáil failed to elect a Taoiseach. Haughey was constitutionally required to resign, but, describing the situation as 'unprecedented in our history', he told the Dáil he had consulted the Attorney General about what to do and, as he did not want to precipitate another election, he proposed to remain in office while consultation with the other parties about future arrangements continued. Dukes rose to say that, in the circumstances, he agreed with Haughey's proposal.

The Fine Gael front bench had anticipated what Haughey would do, and some members argued for a robust response. Senior Fine Gael lawyers were consulted, and they proffered the same advice to Dukes as the Attorney General had to Haughey, so Dukes opted for a cautious response. FitzGerald later recalled his astonishment.[31]

It was Dick Spring of Labour – showing himself to be a formidable opposition leader – who refused to accept the situation, stating that, as the Taoiseach had failed to retain the support of a majority of TDs, he should resign, in accordance with the Constitution.

There was bedlam in the chamber as Haughey denied that he was acting outside the Constitution. Dukes tried to recover some ground by belatedly calling on Haughey to resign, while Garret FitzGerald backed him up, accusing Haughey of failing to abide by the Constitution.

After an adjournment for a few hours Haughey returned to the Dáil to say that he would go to the President and resign, but that he would continue in office in an acting capacity until a new Taoiseach was elected. Spring was the hero of the hour and was widely acclaimed in the media for having forced Haughey to capitulate. For Dukes it represented a fatal loss of authority. 'What happened to Alan wasn't an accident; it was a choice,' one of his allies remarked later. 'Being correct took precedence over political rhetoric. It was a fatal mistake.' A senior Labour figure summed it up: 'It was the defining moment at which Dick became leader of the opposition.'[32]

Faced with another spell in opposition, and conscious of mounting criticism, Dukes tried to find a way into government by proposing a coalition of Fianna Fáil and Fine Gael, but only if Fine Gael got seven of the fifteen cabinet posts and Haughey agreed to rotate the office of Taoiseach with him. The offer was rejected out of hand. Although Fine Gael and Fianna Fáil finally entered talks about a coalition of equals in

2020, such an arrangement in the 1980s was still unthinkable. While Dukes never seriously thought it would be accepted, he believed he had earned the right to demand a high price in the light of the Tallaght strategy. But although Haughey would not do business with Fine Gael, he did take the historic decision to abandon a core Fianna Fáil value. As Albert Reynolds put it, 'Power. Getting power. Keeping power. That was it and he had to be in government at any price.'[33]

Haughey returned to government as head of a coalition created with the Progressive Democrats. As discussed in Chapter 9, the arrival of the PDs in 1985 proved to be a turning-point in Fine Gael history, offering discontented party members an alternative political home. In the circumstances of 1989, the PDs' move into government brought to an end the 'Fianna Fáil or Fine Gael' pattern of party competition. In 1948, 1954, 1973 and twice in the 1980s Fine Gael had been an essential element in the effort to remove Fianna Fáil from power. But with Fianna Fáil now willing to consider alliances with other parties, it was possible for voters to influence the composition of government without including Fine Gael.[34] Moreover, support from the opposition benches similar to the Tallaght strategy was less pressing. The result was that Fine Gael became far less relevant to the formation of a government. This was to have lasting implications.

There were twenty-seven days after the general election and four meetings of the Dáil before Fianna Fáil and the PDs finally sealed their coalition deal and Haughey was formally elected Taoiseach. He announced a cabinet containing two PD ministers, Des O'Malley and Bobby Molloy, with Mary Harney as a junior minister. When the Dáil adjourned for its summer recess things in Fine Gael appeared calm on the surface, but Dukes never recovered from his disastrous first day of the 26th Dáil.

Without the political discipline provided by the Tallaght strategy, he often appeared at a loss about how to conduct himself as leader of the opposition. While he regularly attempted to bait Haughey in the Dáil chamber, in private he continued to behave as if the Tallaght strategy was still in operation and had regular meetings in the Taoiseach's office. This culminated in a disastrous intervention in a controversy over broadcasting legislation devised by the Fianna Fáil Minister for Communications, Ray Burke.

The nub of the bill was an effort to divert some of the licence-fee money from RTÉ to the commercial radio sector. Legal commercial radio only began in Ireland in 1989, and Century Radio, the first national station, quickly ran into financial difficulties. That prompted the Haughey government, which had close associations with the station's owner, Oliver Barry, to attempt to allocate some of the licence fee to keep it afloat. There were media reports that the PDs were resisting Burke's efforts, and Fine Gael moved to exploit the tensions in the government.

It came to a head in the Dáil at the end of May 1990 when Dukes asked Haughey if the legislation was going to be enacted. He went on to ask, 'Is it the Taoiseach's intention to stand his ground on this bill or does he now find that the ground is going from under him?'

Haughey's response was curious. 'Deputy Dukes is fortunate that I am an honourable man.'[35] This cryptic response sent alarm bells ringing in the heads of some Fine Gael TDs and advisers. The government lost no time in briefing political correspondents that the person lobbying them on behalf of Century Radio was Alan Dukes.

It was a defining moment, and Gerald Barry wrote a full account in the *Sunday Tribune*.[36] The media passed on to other matters, but anyone with a close interest in the affairs of Fine Gael should have been deeply disturbed.

The party's Communications spokesman, Jim Mitchell, and press officer, Peter White, later met Dukes to find out what was going on. They were horrified to hear that he had gone to Haughey to discuss the financial problems being encountered by Century Radio, without telling anybody in Fine Gael. Mitchell was incensed that his leader had gone behind his back and left him in a hugely embarrassing position.

Fianna Fáil sources briefed the media about what had gone on, with the result that Fine Gael's efforts to exploit the government's difficulties backfired.[37] The other opposition parties in the Dáil then turned their fire on Fine Gael. Spring asked the Taoiseach to disclose the content of any secret meetings, while Proinsias de Rossa, the Workers' Party leader, went a step further, asking for a statement from the Taoiseach 'either by himself or jointly by himself and Deputy Dukes on the secret negotiations that have been in progress regarding the emasculation of RTÉ.'[38]

As far as the media and the public were concerned, this was only an aspect of the broadcasting story, but it further undermined the confidence of Fine Gael TDs in their leader. Mitchell seriously considered resigning from the front bench and was only persuaded not to do so by Michael Noonan and Seán Barrett.

The mess typified the way Dukes dealt with a practical problem. Fine Gael supported the development of commercial radio. The national independent radio was having teething problems, so he saw no reason why the state should lend its weight to help it against the RTÉ near-monopoly by scrapping RTÉ 2FM. The problem was that Mitchell had heard rumours about some moves involving 2FM and used that week's private members' time to explore the issue. 'Somehow,' a Dukes supporter explained, 'Alan had not joined the dots between his well-intentioned problem-solving and what his party's private members' time in the Dáil might unearth. So Alan allowed Jim to lead a Dáil debate with an assault on government without informing him of how he had brought concerns about that same issue to Haughey.'

The party's spectacular failure in the 1990 presidential election was used as the excuse to move against Dukes, but his leadership was in trouble long before then. He had been eclipsed by Dick Spring in the Dáil, who many saw as the real leader of the opposition. Even his allies had become frustrated with his style of leadership. But Fine Gael had problems that extended beyond Dukes, to the subject of its identity. Focusing on the leader, however, allowed party members to conveniently sidestep the hard task of self-assessment.

During the summer of 1990 the party began to look increasingly directionless, and leading members of the front bench simply lost faith in Dukes's ability to be a successful leader. His appointment of a new party general secretary added to the sense of unease. Following the 1987 general election Eddie O'Reilly, a teacher and party activist from Wexford, had been appointed to the position. Senior people in the party felt that he was out of his depth, and he was removed from the post in April 1990. Instead of conducting interviews for his successor Dukes simply appointed his political adviser Joe Kenny to the job. It added to a sense that the leader's office was at odds with the rest of the party.

Emily O'Reilly described the relationship between Kenny and Dukes as 'quite extraordinary. They were each other's best friends and confidantes in a relationship that had come to exclude virtually every other Fine Gael activist and Oireachtas member.' She observed that Dukes's relationships with other frontbenchers had been whittled away until only Kenny was left. Dukes had only met Kenny, a committed party activist, for the first time during the 1987 general election, but the two men hit it off immediately. After his election as leader he invited Kenny to be his political adviser. O'Reilly recalled:

> Political colleagues found Dukes intensely difficult to relate to. There was a failure to empathise or click on an emotional level. But, in the ebullient, friendly, intensely likable 'cute hoor operator' Joe Kenny the party leader had found a soul mate.[39]

Tensions were fraught by the time the 1990 ard-fheis rolled around. Dukes had contemplated challenging his opponents in the party, but he had been persuaded not to do so by his allies. Instead he tried to bring his party together by announcing that Fine Gael would contest the forthcoming presidential election. He promised a 'candidate of vigour, stature and substance,' and the audience responded by leaping to their feet and cheering. Garret FitzGerald was part of the platform party and it was immediately and widely presumed that he was the candidate to whom Dukes was referring. FitzGerald had the type of appeal that could attract votes in a presidential election from beyond Fine Gael's traditional support base. But he was not interested, as the *Irish Press* had reported at the beginning of the year.[40] Fitzgerald had observed that Dáil politics was all about policy, which he loved, and kissing babies, which he did not, while the presidency was all about kissing babies.[41]

In truth, Dukes was only signalling his intention that the party would contest the election. The identity of its candidate was yet to be decided, although Dukes had Peter Barry in mind. Though rarely commented on, Austin Currie, who would eventually become the party's candidate, was also present on the platform. On reflection, it was a premature announcement, but it is also understandable that, given his vulnerable position, Dukes wanted to deliver some news that might boost morale. There was also nothing new in Fine Gael making announcements before doing the research, as Liam Cosgrave's decision to call the 1977 election showed.

Having promised a candidate, there was no going back. FitzGerald was resolute, so Peter Barry was pursued. But he also declined. By the autumn of 1990, despite having committed itself to the election, Fine Gael had no candidate. John Kelly, Paddy Cooney and Mark Clinton were among the stalwarts who refused an invitation. The list went on. Dukes's approach to Tom O'Donnell, a prominent figure in the pro-life and anti-divorce campaigns of the 1980s, smacked of desperation. One member of the party likened the frantic search to a 'bizarre game of spin the bottle'.[42]

Dukes would later rationalise the decision to contest the election by citing party morale. 'It would have been very difficult for the party to support a candidate from somewhere else,' he explained more than a decade later.[43] That might have been so, but the mismanagement of the selection process, made public by the newspapers, could hardly have helped the mood. Headlines such as 'FG looks to Barry for Park race', 'Hotheaded John B. [Keane] rules out campaign for the Presidency' and 'Currie now FG hot tip for Park' give a flavour of the reporting on the party's search for a candidate.[44] The *Kerryman* was more blunt in the headline for its round-up of the campaign in July: 'The Presidency: Fine Gael still hunting for a candidate'.[45]

The situation was further exacerbated by the fact that, as early as January, Dick Spring had indicated that Labour would contest the election, and Mary Robinson had launched her campaign in May, while Brian Lenihan had been selected by Fianna Fáil in June.

Finally, in September, Austin Currie was unveiled as the Fine Gael candidate. He too had resisted the nomination, but he eventually relented and visited Dukes in his Leinster House office on 5 September to confirm that he would stand. Dukes is reported to have replied, 'You have made me a very happy man.'[46]

The behind-the-scenes activities that led to this moment have been comprehensively described by Emily O'Reilly in *Candidate,* her account of the presidential campaign. Briefly put, at the same time that Currie was being wooed, renewed attempts were being made by Jim Mitchell to convince Peter Barry to run. By that stage, though, Barry was too disenchanted with Dukes's leadership, and he wasn't for turning. Currie was temporarily out of the picture because of a two-week family holiday in Yugoslavia, although Dukes did phone him during that period. On his return he attended a dinner at Dukes's home in Co. Kildare on 5 August, where he reiterated that he was not interested. Dukes made a further appeal in his Leinster House office on 28 August, and his supporters piled on the pressure in the days that followed. Eventually, Currie relented.

Dukes had good reason to describe himself a 'very happy man'. Rumours had been flying that, unless a candidate could be found, he would have to resign the leadership. The *Irish Press* published a front-page article in mid-September saying that a number of front-bench members – Jim Mitchell, Michael Noonan, Seán Barrett and Maurice Manning – were plotting to move against Dukes. The report said they intended to propose a motion of no confidence in Dukes if he was unable to produce a credible presidential candidate, and if the motion failed they would resign.[47] Although the plotters denied it, the nub of the story was true. Austin Currie gave Dukes a temporary stay.

Born in Coalisland, Co. Tyrone, Currie first entered politics in 1964 as the Nationalist Party MP for East Tyrone and was active in the civil rights movement. He was particularly attuned to the sectarian discrimination underpinning the methods of housing allocation. Frustrated with his party's slowness to modernise, he became a founder-member of the SDLP in August 1970 and he represented that party in the Northern Ireland Assembly from 1973 to 1974 and again from 1982 to 1986, having served in between on the Constitutional Convention. With the closure of the

Assembly in June 1986 and the return of direct rule from London, Currie became politically redundant.

Garret FitzGerald phoned him in May 1989 to ask him to contest the Dáil elections. Currie's wife and children were instrumental in the decision-making process, encouraging him to think of a future in which the family might lead a relatively normal life.[48] They lived in the shadow of police protection, and at one point in December 1986 it was reported that the police were keeping a watch on their home because of intimidating behaviour directed at Currie's wife.[49]

Currie accepted the invitation, moved to Lucan, Co. Dublin, and was elected for Fine Gael in the Dublin West constituency at the 1989 general election.

A confidential opinion poll on potential presidential candidates conducted by MRBI for Fine Gael in July 1990 had found that neither Currie nor Avril Doyle, who was also being considered, 'measured up to an acceptable level on any criterion'. To Dukes's horror, the report concluded that 'neither is given the remotest chance of being elected'.[50] Currie was privy to the disastrous findings, but, with assurances from the anti-Dukes wing of the party that they would back his campaign, he had relented. Jim Mitchell, named in the *Irish Press* article as one of the front-bench members likely to move against the leader, was appointed director of elections by Duke in an effort to tie him in to the campaign. What followed publicly exposed divisions within Fine Gael.

Peter White, the party's press officer, described the campaign as being 'so horrendous' that 'it was like having a tooth extracted over two months'.[51] There was no organised campaign in some of the constituencies. Anger and a sense of betrayal over how the campaign was handled are palpable in the relevant sections of Currie's memoir, *All Hell Will Break Loose,* published a decade after the election. Opinion polls repeatedly placed him third, behind Lenihan and Robinson.

Currie's former status as a prominent politician in Northern Ireland did not translate across the border. If anything, his Northern background militated against him. The MRBI poll found that 70 per cent of those surveyed would not vote for him for that reason.[52] Currie later recorded in his memoirs how partitionist suggestions that he was not a real Irishman because he was from the North angered him.[53] His prospects, of course, were also undermined by the very public knowledge that he had been far from the party's first choice. On the day of the count Claire Grady reported on the strange reality of a party accepting defeat before a single ballot box had been opened.[54]

From the Fianna Fáil viewpoint, as Niamh O'Connor, Lenihan's campaign manager, put it, 'it was probably the worst campaign ever and the whole thing was pretty nasty.'[55] It was a disaster, not least because of the efforts of Garret FitzGerald, who, on RTÉ's *Questions and Answers* programme on 22 October, challenged his fellow-panellist Brian Lenihan about his involvement in the efforts to pressure President Hillery not to dissolve the Dáil after the defeat of the 1982 budget. The subsequent controversy torpedoed Lenihan's campaign and caused a crisis in the Fianna Fáil-PD coalition that forced Haughey to sack his presidential candidate from the cabinet, in which he was Minister for Defence.

Rumours about Dukes's leadership were rife as the campaign neared its end. There were some tempestuous meetings of the campaign team in the party's head office, the most dramatic of which involved Dukes hurling insults at a party frontbencher, Madeleine Taylor Quinn, after she declined to go on a television programme. Many of those present were shocked at this outburst by their characteristically calm leader and wondered if he was buckling under the strain.

As the results came in on 8 and 9 November, Dukes's future was being openly discussed. 'Defiant Dukes facing an early FG heave' was reported on the front page of the *Irish Independent*.[56] While he announced in a television interview on the evening of 8 November that his leadership was not in question, privately Dukes knew this was not the case, although he later recalled that he had not expected the challenge to come until early the following week. But as he made his way to the count centre in the RDS for the declaration he received word that notice of a no-confidence motion had been given by Fergus O'Brien, a senior politician representing the Dublin South-Central constituency and former chief whip. In O'Brien's view, Dukes lacked charisma and was not open to new ideas.

Fine Gael, he believed, needed someone like John Bruton who would invigorate and renew the party's fortunes.[57]

Dukes returned to Leinster House to consider his options. With the party leader otherwise indisposed, the absence of Austin Currie from the declaration further shone a light on Fine Gael feuding. As Mary Robinson gave her impassioned victory speech, in which she delivered the now-famous line about how the women of Ireland 'instead of rocking the cradle, rocked the system', the optics on the stage were a PR disaster for Fine Gael. Brian Lenihan, placed second, stood behind Robinson, flanked by his party leader to his left and the Labour Party leader, Dick Spring, to his right. Fine Gael looked like the sore losers who had not bothered to turn up.

Jim Mitchell had told Currie that it was not necessary for him to attend the declaration – an instruction that Dukes believed was given to 'make sure that the result was as bad as it could be'. Currie shared this view, considering the advice 'clearly motivated by a different agenda, to get rid of Alan Dukes as leader'.[58] He recorded in his memoir that the episode shocked him and diminished his respect for his adopted party.[59]

Dukes was initially determined to fight. His chief whip, Jim Higgins, quickly assessed the mood in the parliamentary party and told him that he was hopelessly outnumbered. Other loyalists, such as Alan Shatter and Jim O'Keeffe, gave Dukes the same advice. Still, he went on the 'This Week' radio programme on Sunday lunchtime and *Questions and Answers* on television on Monday night believing he could sway a majority of parliamentary colleagues to back him. Joe Kenny and the former general secretary Finbarr Fitzpatrick tried to whip up support in the party organisation, but it was a hopeless cause.

Meanwhile predictions reported in the *Evening Herald* from Seán Barrett, Industry and Commerce spokesman and one of Dukes's opponents, suggested that Dukes would receive support from about twenty-five of the party's seventy-three members eligible to vote on the motion.[60] Speculation in the *Sunday Independent* placed such important figures as Gay Mitchell, Nora Owen, Monica Barnes and Jim O'Keeffe in the pro-Dukes camp. But the list of those opposing him was far greater.

Aside from John Bruton and Barrett, it was believed to include the front-bench spokespersons Peter Barry, Michael Noonan, Jim Mitchell, Richard Bruton and Ted Nealon, as well as the junior spokespersons Charlie Flanagan, John Farrelly, Phil Hogan and Michael Lowry, among others. Some people outside the parliamentary party saw it as a battle between the liberal and conservative wings of the party, or opponents and supporters of the Tallaght strategy, but it was fundamentally about the nature of Dukes's leadership.

On 13 November, the eve of the no-confidence motion, Dukes pre-empted his detractors and resigned the leadership. A no-confidence motion was never going to create the space for a conversation about the party's purpose. By averting the vote Dukes saved Fine Gael (and himself) from a potentially bruising experience. On a personal level, doing so left the door open for him to continue on the front bench. After two months and plenty of long walks he claims to have got over the worst. His wife, however, was angrier for longer than he was about how he had been treated.[61]

The efforts by a section of the party to oust him ushered in a new phase in the party. Until then, John Bruton pointed out, Fine Gael had acted like a family.[62] Now, however, the party began to turn on its leaders as frustrations grew. It became, in the words of the journalist Olivia O'Leary, a 'serial leader killer' – a clear sign of a party in free-fall.[63] Dukes was succeeded by John Bruton, who survived no fewer than three no-confidence motions before becoming the first Fine Gael leader to be ousted in this way by the party. Fine Gael had moved into the era of blaming the leader, rather than critically and honestly reflecting on the party itself.

11

OUSTED: JOHN BRUTON

'The government must go about its work without excess or extravagance and as transparently as if it were working behind a pane of glass.'

– JOHN BRUTON, DÁIL ÉIREANN, 15 DECEMBER 1994.

John Bruton was the unanimous choice of the parliamentary party to replace Alan Dukes. Ivan Yates mounted a half-hearted challenge, but he pulled out of the contest twenty-four hours later in the face of scorn from colleagues, who made it clear to him that it was no time for posturing.

At a press conference following the decision of the parliamentary party on 20 November, Bruton announced his ambition of putting Fine Gael at the centre of Irish politics. In pursuit of that objective he proclaimed his commitment to repealing articles 2 and 3 of the Constitution, which contained the territorial claim to Northern Ireland. He also made it clear that he was committed to another attempt to remove the constitutional ban on divorce and to reframing the debate on neutrality. 'If Europe is worth creating it is worth defending. We can stand back and let others outline a scheme of European defence or we can take part and have a real say in it.'[1] It was a typically bold presentation by Bruton, who was a very different character from his predecessor. The new leader's passionate, emotional approach to politics was a complete contrast to the cool, detached air that had characterised Dukes's leadership.

Although he was still only forty-three, Bruton had been in national politics for twenty-one years. He came from a comfortable farming background in Co. Meath and was educated at Clongowes Wood College, the elite Jesuit school, before going on to UCD. Elected in 1969 as a TD for Meath, he was the youngest member of the Dáil and represented an often-overlooked strand in Fine Gael. His family background was in the Centre Party rather than Cumann na nGaedheal, and he was proud of it and its antecedents in the Irish Party. He had been inspired to become involved in politics at a very young age by the Just Society policy of Declan Costello, and he was one of the 'Young Tigers' who helped to revitalise the party in the late 1960s.

While some people in Fine Gael, and many outside it, regarded him as representing the more conservative, rural wing of the party, that was an oversimplification of his political position. A committed Catholic, he certainly had more of an empathy with rural TDs than with some of the middle-class Dublin liberals who had been attracted into the party by Garret FitzGerald, but he was fully committed to the vision of social justice and fairness represented by the Just Society. In her diaries Gemma Hussey described him in the following terms: 'John Bruton, clever, untidy and hardworking, loud-voiced and boyish, frequently an original thinker but difficult in his over-reaction to opposition, and at the same time capable of immense charm when losing an argument – someone whose obvious patriotism is so attractive.'[2]

Shortly after Bruton took over, Joe Kenny departed as general secretary and was replaced by Ivan Doherty, who had begun as western regional organiser in 1985 and moved to head office during the Dukes period. Doherty already had a good relationship with Bruton. 'John was very open,' Doherty recalled. 'He always asked your opinion and listened to advice. He mightn't always take it but he took it seriously.'[3]

The first problem confronting both of them was the financial crisis facing the party. It was already massively in debt before the 1990 presidential election, but the cost of that disastrous campaign had sent the deficit through the roof. The director of elections, Jim Mitchell, spent more than £1 million in a doomed effort to rescue the campaign, and it left the party with a crippling debt that threatened its viability. These were the days before state funding of political parties, and at one stage there was not enough money in the party's bank account to pay the staff and senior officials. Ivan Doherty recalls that he and Peter White had to defer cashing their pay cheques because they knew there was not enough money in the party's Bank of Ireland account to meet them. Some staff members had to be let go and others took pay cuts in the drive to remain solvent. Serious consideration was given to selling the head office in Mount Street, and it was only shelved when a new mortgage on the property was negotiated with Bank of Ireland.

The scale of the financial problems was a serious distraction from politics for a considerable period. The appointment of Michael Lowry as chairman of the trustees was an important step on the road back to solvency. He had been responsible for clearing the debt on Semple Stadium in Thurles for the Tipperary GAA and he played an important role in helping Fine Gael to follow a similar path.

Most Fine Gael TDs had little interest in the party's finances and were more focused on whether Bruton would be any more successful than Dukes in stamping his authority on the Dáil and wresting back leadership of the opposition from Dick Spring. Initial hopes were soon damped as Spring, buoyed up by Robinson's victory in the presidential election, continued to grab the headlines with his uncompromising attacks on Haughey. One instance was the Labour Party's pressure that prompted the government to agree to establish a judicial tribunal into the beef industry following a 'World in Action' report on British television into the operations of the Goodman group.

While opinion polls were reasonably good for Fine Gael and its new leader in early 1991, the party's national convention in May, designed to freshen up its image, turned into a public relations disaster. The format for the convention was designed by Eoghan Harris, a former Workers' Party activist and RTÉ producer who had devised the blueprint for Robinson's election victory. Harris was hired by Bruton to try to inject new thinking into Fine Gael, and he proposed an unorthodox approach to the national conference. Gone were motions from branches and long-winded speeches from members of the front bench; instead the prescription was for short, snappy contributions from leading party figures on the major problem of the day, unemployment.

It was all going swimmingly until the comedian Twink came on stage during the televised segment of the conference to do a short turn. She made fun of an incident in the Dáil bar a few months earlier in which the RTÉ political correspondent Una Claffey had been the victim of inappropriate behaviour by a Fianna Fáil TD, Ned O'Keeffe.

'Following the sketch delegates and members of the parliamentary party expressed dismay at its lewdness,' the *Irish Times* political reporter Maol Mhuire Tynan wrote. 'Many claimed it as crude and insulting and trivialised what had been a serious incident involving Ms Claffey.'[4] To make matters worse, in an RTÉ radio interview the following day Bruton refused to apologise, on the grounds that it was a comedy turn of which he had no prior knowledge.

The *Irish Times* political editor, Dick Walsh, observed that the televised coverage of the conference was meant to show that Fine Gael was ready to shrug off its dowdy image and look the 1990s in the eye.

> But it took less than 90 minutes for the idea to go sour, the issue [unemployment] to be obscured and the outlook to be called into question by a tasteless sketch which set out to make a political point but ended up insulting at least half the population. It was a shame that the first voice from this new Fine Gael was such a cracked one. It was also an amazing political blunder.[5]

The episode put Bruton on the defensive, and poor opinion polls and the party's increasing financial difficulties in the year that followed compounded his problems. Nonetheless he undertook a tour of the constituency organisation, with two basic objectives. One was to explain the financial problems facing the party and attempt to deal with them; the other was to set out a vision of what Fine Gael stood for, summed up by the slogan 'Every person counts'. 'That slogan was designed to encompass my belief in social justice,' he recalled, 'in being pro-life and in being committed to policies that catered for all in society rather than privileged groups or special interests.'[6]

When Haughey was forced to resign at the beginning of 1992 and was replaced as Taoiseach by Albert Reynolds, things became even worse for Fine Gael. Bruton's satisfaction rating dropped below the level achieved by Dukes in his final days, and some people in the party began to wonder if they had made a big mistake.

Following the leadership change in Fianna Fáil, the coalition with the PDs began to fall apart. Shortly before taking over as Taoiseach, Reynolds had referred to the coalition as 'a temporary little arrangement'.[7] This attitude was publicly reflected in a warm-up speech to the Fianna Fáil ard-fheis in March 1992 delivered by the up-and-coming Brian Cowen. 'What about the PDs? When in doubt leave out,' he remarked, to thunderous applause.[8]

Tension between the parties was fuelled by a serious controversy over abortion in 1992. What became known as the X Case involved a decision by the Attorney General, Harry Whelehan, to refuse to allow a minor, who had become pregnant as the result of sexual abuse, to travel to Britain for an abortion. Reynolds proposed an amendment to the constitutional ban on abortion that would affirm the right of an individual to travel and to receive information. The third prong of the amendment was a redefinition of the abortion ban itself, which was attacked by liberals, including the PDs, as being too restrictive and by conservatives for being too broad.

Throughout the autumn, politics was focused on the row between the coalition parties and by Labour's increasingly aggressive attacks on the government. Fine Gael often appeared to be on the sidelines, and the X Case controversy that dominated the headlines throughout the year did not help the main opposition party, which was divided on how to respond.

Relations between the coalition partners came to crisis point in November of 1992 when a motion of no confidence in the government following the conflicting evidence given to the Beef Tribunal by Reynolds and O'Malley came before the Dáil. The PDs refused to vote confidence in the government, and Reynolds called an election for 25 November, the date already set for three referendums designed to deal with the implications of the X Case.

The general election campaign revealed a precipitous decline in support for Fianna Fáil and a substantial rise for Labour. Spring's commanding performances in the Dáil over the previous two years suddenly began to pay off as Labour rose from 17 per cent in the first *Irish Times* poll of the campaign to 22 per cent in the final one. Fine Gael remained static at about 25 per cent. There was intense media speculation in the final week of the campaign about the prospect of Labour replacing Fine Gael as the second party in the state.

Labour managed to set the agenda for the campaign by claiming at the outset that Spring was a credible candidate for Taoiseach, even if only on a rotating basis. This helped to turn the campaign into a personality contest between Spring and Reynolds, and it left Bruton on the sidelines. 'A key element of the Labour campaign was to undermine support for Fine Gael and its leader,' one observer wrote, 'and the notion of Spring for Taoiseach was another way of achieving that purpose.'[9]

There was a naïve belief in the main opposition party that the old rules still applied and that the only alternative to a Fianna Fáil-led government was a Fine Gael-Labour coalition with the Fine Gael leader as Taoiseach. This did not take account of Labour's new ambition of replacing Fine Gael as the second-biggest party, or the fact that Spring had developed a strong antipathy to Bruton during their years in government together in the 1980s.

At the beginning of the campaign the central question was what kind of government could replace Fianna Fáil. Bruton tried to create an alternative in the public mind by floating the idea of a 'rainbow coalition' made up of Fine Gael, Labour and the PDs. He didn't seek the agreement of the other parties before announcing it, and the Labour response was hostile. 'I think it was awful politics, very bad politics,' Spring said in the wake of the campaign. 'One thing we were not going to be was to be taken for granted and that took us for granted. It was Fine Gael at their worst.'[10]

By dint of his attacks on Fianna Fáil and Fine Gael during the campaign, the Labour leader managed to avoid committing himself about what he would do in the aftermath. Spring's hostile attitude to Reynolds implied that he would not even consider coalition with Fianna Fáil, but he carefully managed to avoid committing himself to any course of action, apart from pitching himself as a potential Taoiseach. The strategy paid off, and even if the polls had flattered Labour a little towards the end of the campaign the party ended up with 19 per cent of the vote, compared with 25 per cent for Fine Gael and 39 per cent for Fianna Fáil. In terms of seats Labour had its best election ever, going from 15 to 33, while Fine Gael dropped 10 to end up with 45.

There was no disguising the bitter disappointment in Fine Gael at the failure to capitalise on Fianna Fáil's weakness, but as the campaign developed into a contest between Spring and Reynolds the party was sidelined and could do little about it. The only good thing to emerge from the 1992 election was that the party actually brought in more money than it spent. One vital lesson that had been learned from the 1990 presidential election was that there was no point throwing money at a campaign when it was too late.

Gary Murphy noted that Labour's relative popularity was based primarily on Spring lambasting Fianna Fáil, Haughey and Reynolds while in opposition. A second factor was Labour's go-it-alone political strategy and the view that if there was no overall majority Fianna Fáil and Fine Gael should go into coalition. But once the votes were counted, Dick Spring changed his anti-Fianna Fáil and anti-coalition tune.[11]

That change of tune shocked Fine Gael and exploded the assumption in the party that, despite the poor election result, it would lead the next government. Instead of opening talks on forming a government with Fine Gael, as was widely expected, Labour announced its intention of negotiating a left-wing platform with Democratic Left before entering discussions with other parties. As that process began, a critical recount was taking place in Dublin South-Central to determine whether Eric Byrne of DL or Ben Briscoe of Fianna Fáil would win the last seat. At times there was just one vote in it, but after a series of recounts Briscoe was declared the winner. The loss of the seat was crucial, because if Byrne had been elected, Labour, DL and Fine Gael combined would have had enough seats to form a government. Without it they were a seat short.

As Labour dragged out the talks on a left-wing alliance, Bruton remained adamant that DL could not be included in a coalition and he stuck by his strategy of trying to put together a coalition involving Fine Gael, Labour and the PDs. He had wide support in the party for the position. Peter Barry not only backed it but let it be known that he would resign from the party if it agreed to include DL in government. Fine Gael was even more dismissive of the notion that Spring could be a rotating Taoiseach. Labour took its time about coming to an agreed platform with DL, and Spring did not deign to meet Bruton until 6 December. The mood for that meeting was set the day before the meeting by the Labour MEP Barry Desmond, who said on radio that Spring would use it 'to put manners on John Bruton'.[12]

If the preliminaries were bad, things got even worse on the day of the meeting, which took place in the Shelbourne Hotel. That morning the *Sunday Independent* published the result of an opinion poll that showed that Fine Gael had sunk to 19 per cent since the election, while Labour had climbed to 30 per cent. Ivan Doherty, who drove Bruton to the meeting, recalls that on the way they heard an interview on the car radio with a senior Labour adviser, Pat Magner. 'I remember him saying Labour would not breathe life into the Fine Gael corpse and that set the tone for the meeting.'

During the meeting Spring remained on his feet while Bruton was sitting down, and it gave the impression that Bruton was getting a severe dressing down. In fact Spring stayed standing because of excruciating back pain that had plagued him for a decade, but his stance conveyed the tone of the meeting. 'It was surreal,' Doherty remembered. 'It was almost like a humiliation.' Spring demanded that Bruton acknowledge past mistakes and commit himself to a new kind of partnership arrangement by sharing the Taoiseach's office. It was Doherty's view that 'Spring was being very arrogant and it was obvious at that stage that he had no intention of going into government with us.'[13]

When Bruton emerged from the meeting it was clear to onlookers that he was shattered. The *Irish Times* front-page headline the following day was 'Suitability of Bruton to be the focus of talks,' referring to Labour's determination to pursue the goal of taking the Taoiseach's office. Bertie Ahern of Fianna Fáil remarked on television the following day that Bruton looked as if he had seen a ghost.[14]

Bruton reported back to the Fine Gael front bench, who backed him on rejecting a rotating Taoiseach, but there were some voices in favour of modifying the opposition to the inclusion of DL, although by that stage Eric Byrne's defeat made the issue academic, as it left the Fine Gael-Labour-DL combination one seat short of an overall majority.

There was a further meeting between Spring and Bruton, and on 9 December a Labour negotiating team met Fine Gael and the PDs, but they avoided giving a commitment to opening tripartite discussions. Bruton was hoping to form a government involving Labour and the PDs but Spring's antipathy to the notion of the PDs' involvement was intense. Instead Labour announced that it would discuss a policy platform with any other party.

Fianna Fáil, which had bided its time as the other parties bickered, pounced. Immediately after the election, Martin Mansergh, the experienced adviser to the Taoiseach, had been given the task of devising a policy document that would form the basis of negotiations with Labour if the prospect ever arose. He trawled through every policy statement produced by Labour over the previous decade and put together a document that he felt would be compatible with the positions adopted by both parties during the election campaign.[15] Labour negotiators were stunned at the speed and content of the Fianna Fáil document and quickly got down to serious talks. To the astonishment of Fine Gael, the demands for a rotating Taoiseach and the inclusion of DL in government were dropped. Spring settled for being Tánaiste as well as Minister for Foreign Affairs, with a special office in the Department of the Taoiseach to implement the programme for government.

It took four meetings of the Dáil to elect a Taoiseach, but the die was cast and Labour did the previously unthinkable. One observer commented that the Fianna Fáil-Labour coalition came as a surprise to almost everybody. 'No rational observer of the Irish political scene felt this was likely given the antipathy shown by Spring to Fianna Fáil in the course of the previous Dáil and the widely expressed view that Reynolds could not work within a coalition format.'[16] In the longer term the move damaged Labour, but the immediate result was to inspire another bout of soul-searching in Fine Gael.

Fine Gael was in a deeply demoralised and bitter mood following the formation of the Fianna Fáil-Labour coalition with its massive majority of 101 out of 166 seats. It was well positioned to govern for the rest of the twentieth century, leaving Fine Gael in no man's land. It gradually dawned on people that the Fianna Fáil decision three years earlier to abandon its core principle of not entering coalition had left that party with a capacity to move left or right, depending on circumstances. That meant it had a real prospect of being permanently in government. The corollary for Fine Gael was that it faced permanent opposition. As Gary Murphy has observed, 'a very lonely air descended on Fine Gael and John Bruton who could not quite believe that Labour had decided to embrace Fianna Fáil.'[17]

Bruton's immediate priority was to hold on to the leadership. One of the rules introduced in the FitzGerald era was that after an election if the leader was not Taoiseach he had to put himself before the parliamentary party for a new mandate. Ivan Doherty sensed immediately that Bruton would struggle to retain the leadership, and the same sense gripped many TDs. 'Total despair descended on Fine Gael,' Yates recalled. 'Our traditional alliance party had forsaken us and done the unthinkable. Initially we didn't know whether to attack or befriend Labour knowing that we would never get into government without them.' He met Bruton to warn him that he would inevitably face a challenge to his leadership at some stage. 'I need to know that in all circumstances you will fight to retain your job. There is no point in preparing defences if you fold your tent like Dukes,' said Yates, who coolly demanded a senior front-bench post as a reward for his loyalty.[18]

In the event there was no challenge to Bruton in the immediate aftermath of the election. Dukes made a critical speech, but others, with reservations about the leader, held their fire. Yates was rewarded for his bluntness by being made the party's Finance spokesman in place of Michael Noonan in the new front bench. Nora Owen was appointed deputy leader and spokesperson on Foreign Affairs, Phil Hogan got European Affairs and Regional Development, Gay Mitchell was Justice spokesman and the newly elected Frances Fitzgerald was given Arts and Culture. She had only joined Fine Gael before the election and her rapid elevation caused some resentment in the party. Another important move was the election of the Tipperary TD and businessman Michael Lowry as chairman of the parliamentary party.

A powerful axis involving Lowry, Yates and the up-and-coming Phil Hogan developed in the party. The future held very different prospects for each of them. Lowry rose in the following years to be a crucial member of Bruton's government, only to fall from grace in spectacular fashion. Yates also rose in the political world but ultimately left it for business, and went bankrupt in the crash, subsequently reinventing himself as a 'shock jock' broadcaster.

Hogan's trajectory went in the opposite direction. He came to grief early on and had to resign as a junior minister, but he made it back to government and ended up as an influential figure on the world stage as EU Trade Commissioner in 2020, before he was forced to resign in sensational fashion in August of that year for breaking Covid-19 regulations.

All that was in the future, but the three musketeers proved invaluable allies for Bruton, who was left in a vulnerable position after the 1992 election. As well as the trio of enforcers, Bruton had an inner circle of people he really trusted and relied on, particularly his brother Richard and the chief whip, Enda Kenny.[19]

One of the prescient things Bruton did after 1992 was to build up a relationship with the other opposition leaders. He held lunches with the new PD leader, Mary Harney, and with Proinsias de Rossa of DL. During these lunches the three opposition leaders tried to co-ordinate their Dáil strategy. He later recalled: 'That was very helpful in developing relations between Fine Gael and the DL in the longer term although we had no idea that it would become an important issue for both parties sooner rather than later.'[20]

Peter White, who decided to move on after almost ten years as party press officer, was invited to address the parliamentary party before he left, and he gave them an unvarnished view of their performance.

> As individuals you are grand: many of you have become friends who I respect but collectively the parliamentary party is well-nigh unsellable. Why? Because it consistently had failed over a decade to show the only human quality that matters two damns, the only quality people vote for: courage.

Warming to his theme, White outlined how the party was addicted to soft-option politics on issue after issue. Even the Tallaght strategy, a courageous initiative, drifted into something that could credibly be portrayed as cowardice.

> Outside of the early 1980s Fine Gael has pursued a policy of trying to offend nobody. The screamingly obvious fact is that there is not, and never was and never will be, a market for the broadly sensible but invisible party. Our policies are grand, but it is on issues where blood, mud and swords swirl, that character is defined.

He listed a series of issues, such as the Shannon stopover, public-service pay and the X Case, where the party had backed away from taking a strong, coherent line. 'A party which offends nobody makes no impact. A party without impact slips in the polls.' He warned the TDs and senators against turning on each other.

> It is a lack of courage to attack your own team, your own leader when the going gets tough. It is precisely when your leader is in trouble that the party should rally to the flag. How do you expect to get good coverage when members of the parliamentary party feel the need to demonstrate their wisdom to journalists by dumping on their own side?[21]

As the Fianna Fáil-Labour coalition bedded in there was no disguising the despondent mood among Fine Gael TDs, who struggled to see how they would ever make it back to government. As a tactic designed to buy time and chart a course for the future, Bruton established an independent commission to advise on the party's future strategy, chaired by the businesswoman Gary Joyce. The commission's report was more critical than Bruton had expected. 'There can be little doubt that Fine Gael is in a state of crisis,' it said at the outset. 'The party has become deeply internalised; it relates only to its own membership and, even then, very poorly.' Echoing Peter White's criticisms, it stated: 'The party must communicate what it is and, in order to do that, it must know what it is.' The report had ninety-seven detailed recommendations; but their implementation was soon overtaken by events.

During 1993 the Fianna Fáil-Labour coalition appeared to go from strength to strength. The steady improvement in the economy was accompanied by progress towards peace in Northern Ireland. Reynolds signed the historic Downing Street Declaration in December, in which the Republic formally accepted the consent principle in relation to the future of Northern Ireland and the British declared they had no selfish strategic interest in holding on to the province if a majority of people wanted to leave the United Kingdom. Reynolds and Fianna Fáil soared in the opinion polls and it looked as if the government was set to last for a long time.

As Bruton struggled to make an impact as leader of the opposition, discontent began to grow in the parliamentary party and there was persistent media speculation about a leadership heave. A reflection of the growing discontent was that Jim Mitchell spoke publicly of Bruton suffering from a 'charisma deficit'. Matters came to a head in February 1994 following an *Irish Times* opinion poll that showed Fine Gael at only 16 per cent and Bruton's satisfaction rating at 29 per cent, a massive 33 points behind the Taoiseach, Albert Reynolds.[22]

When the Dáil met the day after the publication of the poll, mutterings in the parliamentary party turned to panic and the so-called Gang of Four front-bench TDs, Jim O'Keeffe, Charlie Flanagan, Alan Shatter and

Jim Higgins, decided it was time to remove the leader. Over the previous few weeks they had taken soundings and came to the conclusion that a majority of TDs agreed with them. The party chief whip, Enda Kenny, became aware of what was going on and alerted Bruton, who had already been tipped off that something was afoot. The two of them waited to see what the plotters would do.

The move came two days later when O'Keeffe approached Bruton before the start of Dáil business at 10:30 a.m. and asked him to meet a delegation of senior deputies later in the day. Bruton asked O'Keeffe what it was all about. 'He shuffled about from one foot to the other,' Bruton told journalists later. Having got the clear signal of what was happening, he agreed to an interview with the Gang of Four at 2:15 p.m.

When the four arrived at Bruton's office at the appointed time they were kept waiting for nearly two hours before they were admitted to his inner sanctum. When they were finally allowed into Bruton's presence they discovered to their shock that he had with him in the room his chief whip, Enda Kenny, his deputy leader, Nora Owen, and the chairman of the National Executive, Donal Carey. They remained present as the plotters nervously asked him to consider his position. Bruton told them in forceful terms that under no circumstances would he consider resigning and that, on the contrary, he would fight them tooth and nail. Before they had a chance to formally resign, Bruton fired them from the front bench.[23]

The confrontation took place on a Thursday, and the motion of confidence in Bruton's leadership was scheduled for the following Tuesday. It was the first time in the history of the party that a motion of confidence in the leader was taken. Despite the fact that the plotters had been carrying out soundings among their colleagues, the move against Bruton came as a surprise to many Fine Gael TDs and senators. But when Alan Dukes and Michael Noonan went on RTÉ radio to join the attack on Bruton it was clear that he had a fight on his hands. The strong backing of Yates, Hogan and Lowry helped to stem the tide as they cajoled and threatened wavering TDs.

Bruton personally called to the homes of a number of TDs and senators in the days before the vote to ask for their support. He received a painful rebuff when Frances Fitzgerald refused to come to the door to speak to him as she was allegedly having a bath. Bruton was particularly hurt by this, as he had promoted Fitzgerald immediately after her election to the Dáil in 1992 ahead of the long-serving Theresa Ahern, with whom he had always been on good terms.

Ivan Doherty recalls that, in spite of the fact that his political life was on the line, Bruton, to his credit, told party officials like him that they should not become involved in the struggle as it was their job to serve Fine Gael and not any particular leader.[24]

The critical party meeting on 15 February went on for nearly eight hours. Noonan and Mitchell were the main speakers against him, along with the Gang of Four. Frances Fitzgerald was another who made a strong speech calling on him to step down. Kenny, Hogan and Yates spoke strongly in defence of Bruton. The long-serving Kildare TD Bernard Durkan rounded on the rebels and reminded them that their disloyalty threatened the future of the party.

Bruton was the last speaker. 'He started off in a low tone, measured but clearly emotional. He spoke about commitments in life and how seriously he took them – to his wife and family and most of all to his party, Fine Gael.'[25] Following his speech a vote was taken by secret ballot, and Bruton emerged triumphant. The tellers, Peter Barry and Michael Lowry, did not disclose the figures but it was widely speculated that Bruton had come out on top by 41 votes to 25. 'Leader in stronger position after win in confidence vote' was the headline in the *Irish Times* the next day.[26]

In the aftermath Bruton undertook a big front-bench reshuffle. Apart from the Gang of Four he dropped two leading figures, Michael Noonan and Alan Dukes, along with Frances Fitzgerald.

Over the following months there was a gradual improvement in Fine Gael's fortunes. There was a reasonable performance in the European elections in June, with the party holding on to its four seats and increasing its share of the vote to 24.5 per cent. More importantly, though, two critical by-elections were held on the same day. In the Mayo contest, triggered by the appointment of Pádraig Flynn as European Commissioner, it was widely expected that his daughter, Beverly Flynn, would retain the seat for Fianna Fáil. However, a barnstorming campaign by the Fine Gael newcomer Michael Ring confounded received wisdom. Campaigning on the slogan 'Give the Dáil a Ring', he demonstrated a vote-getting ability that was to become legendary. Bruton arrived at the count in Castlebar to wallow in the unexpected victory.

'There was pandemonium in the hall,' the party's director of elections, Pádraic McCormack, recalled. 'Ring and his wife Anne were lifted shoulder high, the cheering and the clapping lasted for several minutes, with everyone trying to pat him on the back. John Bruton had a smile from ear to ear.'[27]

Equally important for Bruton's future, even if not widely appreciated at the time, was the election the same day of Eric Byrne in Dublin South-Central. Fianna Fáil's loss of two seats changed the arithmetic in the Dáil and meant that an alternative government made up of Fine Gael, Labour and Democratic Left was feasible. It was regarded as more of a mathematical possibility than a realistic option, but as serious tensions developed in the governing coalition some people in the Labour Party began to wonder if it might not provide an escape route.

When the Fianna Fáil-Labour government fell apart in November 1994 after months of bickering, those by-election results proved crucial. The appointment of the Attorney General, Harry Whelehan, as president of the High Court was the ostensible cause of the breach between the government parties, but it had been looming for a number of months, particularly since the report of the Beef Tribunal and Reynolds's claim that he had been vindicated. Two further by-election results in Cork, which came through as the government was breaking up, meant that Hugh Coveney won a seat on the south side of the city for Fine Gael while Kathleen Lynch of Democratic Left won the vacancy on the north side. It meant that an alternative government now had a secure majority if Labour opted to switch partners.

The long-drawn-out collapse of the government was one of the most sensational episodes in the history of the Dáil, and what made it all the more dramatic was that the principal debates were broadcast live on television. The upshot was that Reynolds, having lost a vote of confidence, was forced to resign. At that stage the general assumption was still that Spring and the new Fianna Fáil leader, Bertie Ahern, would put the coalition back together, and negotiations on a new programme for government began.

With those talks trundling towards a conclusion Bruton went on the offensive and gave a dramatic radio interview on RTÉ's 'This Week' programme on Sunday 4 December in which he made an impassioned plea to Labour not to trust Fianna Fáil again.

> Two weeks ago the Labour Party on principle withdrew from government. They can't, they can't go back in and reward with high office people whom they now know were involved. How can any Labour person face their children and explain to them that what was a principle last week, justifying resignation and a huge political crisis, doesn't matter at all this week? At the end of the day in politics you have got to live with your conscience. I don't think there is any way that any honest and conscientious member of the Labour Party could possibly reward people who conceal the truth.

In the interview Bruton also questioned the advice given to Reynolds by the Attorney General, Eoghan Fitzsimons, and demanded a Dáil debate on his actions.[28]

Seán O'Rourke recalls that Bruton said 'very offensive' things about Fitzsimons, who immediately rang RTÉ to say he had been seriously libelled. There was a frantic scramble of phone calls as the interview continued, and when Bruton emerged from the studio he was met by the ashen-faced head of news, Joe Mulholland, who exclaimed: 'Jesus, John. The next thing we'll have to have is Section 31 for Fine Gael.'[29]

Initially Bruton also met with a hostile reaction from Labour. 'John Bruton gave what seemed to us like an agitated interview on the radio news … It seemed like sore losing,' wrote Fergus Finlay, and that was the general response of the media, which characterised it as the last throw of the dice by a desperate man.[30] This time, however, luck was on Bruton's side, and his interview helped to stop Spring in his tracks. An article by

Geraldine Kennedy in the *Irish Times* the following day casting doubt on the sequence of events being portrayed by Fianna Fáil reinforced the Labour leader's doubts, while an editorial in the same paper questioning his judgement really rattled him.[31] It was now Labour's turn to panic.

At 2 a.m. on Tuesday 6 December, with a little over twenty-four hours to go before the Dáil was due to elect a new government, Spring rang Ahern to say the deal was off. 'For about four minutes I dropped myself back down on the pillow and said "Hell", Ahern recorded.[32] Immediately after ringing Ahern, Spring called Bruton, asking for a meeting later the same day. He didn't spell out what he wanted but Bruton knew something significant had changed. He rang Ivan Doherty to tell him about Spring's call and to tease out what it meant. 'If he's ringing you at two in the morning it means the talks with Bertie have broken down and he is turning to you,' was Doherty's assessment. He in turn rang Nora Owen, who had already had a call from Bruton and shared the assessment that Fine Gael was being handed a make-or-break opportunity.[33]

When the news broke on an unsuspecting public the following morning it was clear that the political landscape had been transformed. 'Bruton's resurrection puts Lazarus in the shade' was the headline in the 'Drapier' column in the *Irish Times* a few days later, and it summed up the extraordinary turnaround in his fortunes. 'Last week John Bruton was dead in the water. As dead as Liam Cosgrave was before the Dublin bombs of December 1972. Next Tuesday or Wednesday John Bruton will be elected Taoiseach.'[34]

Bruton appointed a negotiating team of Michael Lowry and his brother Richard to engage with the other parties. No preconditions of any kind were specified. The proposal for a rotating Taoiseach could be on the table if Labour wanted to talk about it, while the objections to the participation of DL were dropped. Both moves were essential to the formation of a rainbow government. 'By this stage Lowry was Bruton's closest adviser and confidant. He was the main man in the inter-party negotiations,' according to Yates.[35]

Senior Labour figures came to the same conclusion and were impressed by the skilful way Lowry handled the negotiations. He did make one gaffe, by suggesting in a radio interview that Labour's demand for a rotating Taoiseach was out of the question, but Enda Kenny was sent out to do an interview later in the day to smooth Labour's ruffled feathers. This time around Fine Gael accepted that Labour was entitled to ask for the post of rotating Taoiseach but argued that it was not feasible, given the likely three-year lifespan of the government. In return Lowry accepted that Labour should have the Department of Finance, for the first time in the party's history, as well as holding on to Foreign Affairs.

Bruton at first was dismayed at the prospect. Ivan Doherty recalls travelling to Enniskillen for the funeral of Senator Gordon Wilson's son on the day the preliminary negotiations began in the home of the Attorney General, Dermot Gleeson. In those pre-mobile phone days they had to drive around the outskirts of Enniskillen to find a public phone box so that Bruton could speak to Lowry about the progress of the talks. 'They are insisting on Finance,' an agitated Bruton told Doherty when he returned to the car. 'Look, John, do you want to be Taoiseach or do you not?' Doherty recalled saying to his leader. 'Let them have Finance if that's what it takes.'[36]

After that, formal negotiations on a programme for government between Fine Gael, Labour and Democratic Left got under way. Lowry had remained close to Noonan in spite of his involvement in the heave against Bruton and relied on his advice during the negotiations, something he kept secret from his leader. For one crucial meeting in Fine Gael head office Noonan was brought into the building through an alley that led to the back gate, and he took up residence in a room at the top of the building so that Lowry could slip up and consult him about important issues. 'Did you ever think you'd see the day when I had to be smuggled in the back door of Fine Gael headquarters while the Stickies [DL] are welcomed in the front door?' he remarked.[37]

Once Fine Gael conceded that Labour could have Finance the talks went swimmingly. And so it was that on 15 December, a little more than a week after he had been written off as a political failure on the way to oblivion, John Bruton was elected Taoiseach. He made a memorable speech to the Dáil, in which he said, 'Public office is a privilege that must be paid for in hard work and long hours. The government must go about its work without excess or extravagance and as transparently as if it were working behind a pane of glass.' Over the following two-and-a-half years he confounded his critics by the confident and competent way he exercised power; but his 'pane of glass' reference was to come back to haunt him.

Two of the most powerful posts in the cabinet went to Labour politicians. Spring remained as Tánaiste and Minister for Foreign Affairs while Ruairí Quinn took Finance. The Fine Gael ministers were Michael Noonan in Health, Richard Bruton in Enterprise and Employment, Nora Owen in Justice, Enda Kenny in Tourism and Trade, Michael Lowry in Transport and Communications, Ivan Yates in Agriculture and Hugh Coveney in Defence and Marine. The leader of Democratic Left, Proinsias de Rossa, was given Social Welfare. A Bruton loyalist, Seán Barrett, was appointed government chief whip, while another staunch supporter, Bernard Durkan, was a junior minister in de Rossa's department.

Bruton surprised a lot of people with the efficient and open-minded way he ran his three-handed government, which came to be known as the rainbow coalition. His contacts with the DL leader, Proinsias de Rossa, over the previous two years in opposition had established a bond which smoothed their relations in government. They were united in their wariness of Dick Spring, but trust was gradually established between the three. At the outset Labour ministers were suspicious of Bruton and were not sure that the government would even work. Fergus Finlay recorded that he viewed the newly installed Taoiseach with some trepidation, as he remembered him as 'an intellectual bully' during the 1980s and not someone who could pull a set of strong personalities into a coherent team. 'I was wrong – or else he had changed quite a bit,' Finlay recorded. He recounted how Bruton reconstituted the cabinet subcommittee on Northern Ireland and invited a number of officials, including Finlay, to attend every meeting and give their opinions frankly. 'From that moment until I resigned 18 months later I found John Bruton open, honest and always willing to listen. Status didn't matter at meetings with him – if you had an opinion he wanted to hear it.'[38]

During the negotiations on the formation of a government it had taken some persuading for him to let Labour have Finance, but in retrospect he believes that it was a very good development. 'It worked out very well in the short term, as Ruairí Quinn proved a fine Minister for Finance, but it also had a longer-term impact, in that Labour came to appreciate the financial limitations that operate in every government. Labour took ownership of the government's entire approach in a way that had not happened in the 1980s.'[39]

One particularly important challenge that faced Quinn was the future of the corporate tax regime. It had its origins in the export tax relief introduced by Gerry Sweetman in 1956, which had helped to make Ireland an attractive location for foreign direct investment in the 1960s. When Ireland joined the EEC in 1973 it was forced to phase out the zero rate but was given until 1980 to do it. At that stage a 10 per cent rate on manufacturing activity was introduced, with EU approval, and it was extended to financial services in 1987.

However, in 1996 the EU withdrew approval for all special rates, which had to be phased out by 2010. There was intense debate in the government about how to proceed, and a decision was taken to introduce a common rate of corporation tax for all companies, whether in manufacturing or services. At that stage the standard corporation tax rate was 28 per cent, and officials in Finance argued for a new 20 per cent rate across the board, or 15 per cent at the very least.

There was furious lobbying by the IDA in favour of a standard rate of 10 per cent, and eventually the government settled on 12½ per cent. The European Commission agreed, with some reluctance, and Quinn announced the introduction of the 12½ per cent rate, which proved so important in attracting the major American tech companies to Ireland in the years ahead. John Bruton reckons that this decision was one of the most important taken by his government, as it had a huge impact in creating the wealthy pre-Covid Irish economy of 2020.[40]

Dealing with the peace process was a huge challenge for Bruton, who had a natural antipathy to Sinn Féin. He was very conscious that he came from the Centre Party tradition of Fine Gael, which owed more to the Irish Parliamentary Party than to Cumann na nGaedheal. One of his first acts as Taoiseach was to have a picture of the Irish Party leader John Redmond, rather than the usual Fine Gael choice of Michael Collins, installed on his office wall, along with one of Seán Lemass. Finlay observed that Bruton regarded the peace process he had inherited as buying in to the 'Sinn Féin agenda', and every instinct of his body rebelled against it. Still, he was acutely aware of his own bias and did his level best to keep the process on track. He paid careful attention to the views of de Rossa, Nora Owen and the Attorney General, Dermot Gleeson, as they persuaded him to swallow hard in the interests of the process.[41]

An indication of Bruton's approach was that for his first meeting with Gerry Adams he asked a senior official in the Department of the Taoiseach, Paddy Teahon, to accompany him rather than his special adviser, the former secretary of the Department of Foreign Affairs, Seán Donlon. When Teahon, who at that stage headed the economic division in the department, asked why he was being included instead of Donlon, Bruton replied, 'If there is anybody Gerry Adams is likely to distrust more than myself it is Seán Donlon, so I need you to come with me instead.' Teahon, who later became secretary of the department, and a crucial figure in the peace process, said some years later that it was to Bruton's immense credit that he was aware of his own limitations in dealing with republicans.[42]

There were serious difficulties in keeping the peace process on track, as Bruton and the British insisted that IRA decommissioning had to be part of the process, and Sinn Féin resisted. Spring adopted a more conciliatory approach to Sinn Féin to compensate for Bruton's more critical attitude.[43] Bruton found it difficult to contain his impatience with republican foot-dragging on decommissioning, but by contrast unionists regarded Bruton as the first Taoiseach to understand their position. While that did not earn him much credit with his own electorate, it kept the process inching forward and was important in getting agreement with the British on the Framework Document which was an essential step on the road to the Belfast Agreement.

Bruton recalls that he spent 70 to 80 per cent of his time as Taoiseach dealing with Northern Ireland. Much of this involved an endless round of meetings, which often proved unproductive but which were necessary to keep the peace process going. He was also annoyed by constant media questioning about the intricacies of the process. It provoked him to remark to a local radio reporter in Cork, 'I am sick of answering questions about the fucking peace process.' At the time the remark, which was recorded before the interview started, was cited as evidence that he was not committed to the process.

> What prompted that was the endless questions from journalists seeking to detect minor, insignificant differences of emphasis from one day to the next. I had to be careful that in answering the same question for the forty-first time that I didn't give a slightly different answer than I had given to an earlier one, as it would be blown up out of all proportion, with potentially damaging consequences for the peace process. Looking back, I just put the expletive in the wrong place in that sentence.[44]

In 1996 republicans abandoned their ceasefire and bombed London again in order to extract more concessions from John Major's government. The Canary Wharf bomb, which killed two people and caused hundreds of millions of pounds' worth of damage to property, came as a shock to both governments. Even if it soon became clear that it was a bargaining-tool rather than a full-scale return to violence, that was not apparent at the time. Some of Bruton's political opponents tried to suggest that the IRA's return to violence was somehow his fault, but he points out that it had taken months for republicans to prepare and plan the bombing, while all during that period they were supposedly negotiating the peace settlement. He also says that some of his critics had a different view on what the whole process was about. In his words,

> I put a high priority on protecting the institutions of this state and ensuring there was no tolerance for private armies or arms dumps. My first responsibility was to the people of this state. Others had

different views and probably believed that other objectives were more important.[45]

The rainbow government had more success on the economy, where Quinn quickly mastered his brief and established credibility with his cabinet colleagues. The economic recovery gathered pace, with record levels of growth emerging under his competent management. Social partnership, which had developed under Fianna Fáil after 1987 as a central element of the economic recovery, was continued, despite criticism by Fine Gael of the process while in opposition. Partly this was due to Labour's continuation in government, but it also reflected a big change in approach by Fine Gael. According to one political scientist, this 'astonishing volte-face seems to have been a product of Bruton's experience of government and his conviction that the Christian Democratic dimension of Fine Gael should be given precedence over the neoliberal strain.'[46]

Despite its success, the rainbow coalition, like governments of all hues before and after, found itself dragged off course by the march of events. Quinn's first budget, in February 1995, was overshadowed by a political blunder by a member of the staff working for his junior minister, Phil Hogan. Late on the morning of budget day he faxed the main points of the budget to a journalist working for the *Evening Herald*. It went against all the traditions of budget confidentiality, and there was an immediate political uproar. Bruton consulted the Attorney General and asked Hogan to resign. The junior minister was left with no choice but was shattered that his political ambitions appeared to be in ruins. 'Wrong call, I felt, and still do,' Ivan Yates recorded. 'I was devastated for Phil and spent the evening in his office. It was terrible, painful and a waste of political talent, albeit, given his career since then, a temporary waste of talent.'[47] Looking back at it from the viewpoint of 2020, Hogan can recall how shattered he was at the time. 'It was such a big disappointment. I was the first one to break John Bruton's pane of glass. It is rare in politics that someone gets a second opportunity, so I was lucky.'[48]

In fact the resignation probably put Hogan on track for what turned out to be a glittering political career, as everybody in Fine Gael felt he was owed another chance. His rehabilitation began almost immediately, when he was elected chairman of the parliamentary party to replace Michael Lowry, who was now in cabinet.

The pane of glass was broken again later the same year when the Minister for Defence and the Marine, Hugh Coveney, was accused of attempting to use his influence to help his quantity surveying firm to obtain a contract. He insisted that a casual remark had been misinterpreted, but he nonetheless resigned from the cabinet and was replaced by Seán Barrett. Bruton appointed Coveney to the most senior minister of state post available, at the Office of Public Works, and he was in effect a super-junior minister, attending pre-cabinet meetings with the senior Fine Gael ministers.

With the economy going well, the government decided that it was time to revisit Garret FitzGerald's constitutional crusade with a second attempt to remove the constitutional ban on divorce. Pressure for a second referendum had been building steadily since the late 1980s. A critically important development was the tenacious manner in which the Fine Gael TD Alan Shatter managed to get a private members' bill expanding and clarifying the grounds for separation accepted by the Dáil in 1989. It was the first time in thirty-five years that a private members' bill had been passed by the Dáil. The Judicial Separation and Family Law Reform Bill, with its explicit measures on financial settlements for children, 'set the scene for a rerun of the divorce referendum'.[49] A commitment to hold a referendum was part of the rainbow coalition's programme for government, and the issue was put to the people in November 1995.

Just as had happened in 1985, the strong support for constitutional change in the opinion polls began to evaporate during the referendum campaign. The No campaign was well organised and had the support of the Catholic Church. The slogan 'Hello, divorce. Goodbye, Daddy' gained traction during the campaign, and in the final days there were strong indications that it could be defeated for a second time. The government went on a desperate offensive in the final weekend of the campaign, with Bruton taking a strong line in speeches and media appearances.

Bruton was widely regarded as a conservative on social issues, so his impassioned support for removing the ban on divorce had a serious impact. 'The Taoiseach did a brilliant interview on radio on the last Sunday of the campaign and undoubtedly swung some undecided voters our way,' Fergus Finlay recorded in his memoir.[50] Swinging even a few undecided voters was crucial, as the referendum was carried by a minuscule margin of 9,114 votes. It was the closest referendum result in the history of the state, 50.2 per cent voting Yes and 49.8 per cent voting No.

The government suffered a serious blow at the end of 1996 when the Minister for Transport and Communications, Michael Lowry, was forced to resign when details of a tax-evasion deal with Dunne's Stores during his business career were leaked to the *Irish Independent.* He had been locked in dispute with a 'cosy cartel' of Fianna Fáil business interests connected to CIE, but the emergence of the fact that he had broken the law brought his ministerial career, and his influence in Fine Gael, to a sudden end.

It was a serious embarrassment for the government, and Lowry was gone within forty-eight hours of the news appearing. As he posed with the Taoiseach for photographers on the steps of Government Buildings to announce his resignation an emotional Lowry turned to Bruton and said, 'My best friend. Friends for ever.'[51]

In the long run the disclosure, which came from court documents, came to have serious implications for Fianna Fáil too, as the documents revealed massive payments by Ben Dunne to Charles Haughey. The immediate impact was to damage Fine Gael, although the speed with which Lowry left office mitigated it to some extent. The government established a judicial tribunal chaired by Mr Justice Brian McCracken to look into payments made to both Lowry and Haughey.

Probably more damaging to the government's standing with the public was the controversy over compensation for women infected with hepatitis C through receiving blood transfusions. The Minister for Health, Michael Noonan, set up a compensation scheme to provide generous payments to the women affected, but some of the victims took their case to court. One victim, Brigid McCole, who took the legal route, died before her case could be heard. Even though the government ordered that compensation be paid to her family, Noonan was plunged into controversy over his handling of the issue. Particularly damaging were charges of insensitivity to women's lives that were levelled by some of the victims following ill-judged comments in the Dáil after Mrs McCole's death. (The impact of this on Noonan's career is explored more fully in the next chapter.)

Another area in which the government came under pressure was crime. The Minister for Justice, Nora Owen, was targeted by Fianna Fáil and its Justice spokesman, John O'Donoghue. She was subjected to constant grilling in the Dáil as if she was personally responsible for every serious crime that took place. Then, on 25 June 1996, the crime journalist Veronica Guerin was shot dead as she sat in her car at traffic lights near Newlands Cross on the Naas dual carriageway.

It was an outrage that shocked the country to the core and led to a fundamental reassessment of how to tackle organised crime. Owen responded by establishing the Criminal Assets Bureau, which proved very successful in combating serious crime over the subsequent decades and was one of the outstanding achievements of the rainbow government.

Despite the controversies and setbacks, including the BSE crisis of 1996, which led to the slaughter of tens of thousands of animals and the temporary loss of export markets, the standing of the government was high in the early months of 1997. The question facing Bruton and his ministers was whether they should serve out the full term and hold an election in November or go to the country a little earlier when they still had the initiative. Ultimately Bruton went for June.

Political folklore developed around this decision suggesting that Bruton personally favoured November but that Dick Spring insisted on June, supported by the Minister for Agriculture, Ivan Yates, who argued vehemently for June, on the grounds that the farmers would have serious gripes in the autumn. Fergus Finlay disputed this, saying it was Fine Gael strategists who first suggested an early election. A number of senior Fine Gael figures remain adamant that the decision was made to keep Labour on side. Bruton himself is happy to take responsibility for the decision. 'If we left it until November we would have been a sitting target for every interest group. For instance, the public service unions were lining up to make demands. On balance I felt it was better to take control of the agenda, and as Taoiseach it was my responsibility to make the final decision, so I opted for June.'[52]

Fine Gael waged a good campaign, on the back of high poll satisfaction ratings with the government and the Taoiseach. The rainbow parties decided to fight the campaign together on a joint platform. It was the first time this had happened since 1977 and it made for a real contest, as the alternative government was an alliance between Fianna Fáil and the PDs. The two opposition parties committed themselves to reducing tax rates as the centrepiece of their policy agenda. The rainbow parties sought a mandate for a fairer reform of the tax system which favoured lower-income earners, but enough voters were won over by the Fianna Fáil-PD formula to swing the election in their favour.

When the people voted on 6 June, Fine Gael gained ten seats and Democratic Left lost two; but the real weak link was Labour, which dropped from 33 seats in 1992 to 16. Still, it was a close-run thing as to who would form a government. While Fianna Fáil had also gained seats, the outcome was a disaster for the PDs, who dropped from ten to four. In the end Bertie Ahern was elected Taoiseach of a coalition government which depended on a number of independents for its survival.

In August the McCracken Tribunal heard evidence about the vast amounts of money that Charles Haughey had extracted from wealthy people to finance his lifestyle. Former Fine Gael ministers were left kicking themselves in frustration at not having waited until November, when the public would have had time to absorb the findings of the tribunal.

Interviewed about what happened, Bruton says he is not sure if the result would have been any different in November and points to the fact that by gaining ten seats Fine Gael did what it had only ever done once before, back in 1951: the party actually gained seats coming out of government. He believes the rainbow coalition had very substantial and lasting achievements to its credit, among them the overhaul of the criminal justice system to enable it to fight organised crime and the introduction of the 12½ per cent corporation tax rate. 'These two policies have had a serious impact on the country which has lasted to this day,' he said in 2020.[53]

In the immediate aftermath there were high hopes in Fine Gael that the Fianna Fáil-PD coalition, which relied for survival on the support of three independents, might implode. It looked vulnerable in the face of the sensational revelations at the McCracken Tribunal, particularly as Ray Burke was forced to resign as Minister for Foreign Affairs. By the autumn it had steadied; the independents who supported it, led by Jackie Healy-Rae, were rock-solid. For Fine Gael it was back to the all-too-familiar slog of opposition. In Bruton's opinion,

> Being leader of the opposition is by some distance the most diffi-cult job in politics. You are caught between the demands of party activists who want you to be unremitting in attacking the gov-ernment and floating voters who want you to act responsibly in the national interest. Navigating those contradictory pressures is almost impossible.[54]

The mood in Fine Gael darkened as the party and its leader began to slide in the polls the longer opposition lasted. In the autumn of 2000 Fine Gael unveiled what turned out to be one of the most disastrous publicity campaigns in Irish political history. In an effort to point out the short-comings of the 'Celtic Tiger' economy, Fine Gael plastered giant posters all over the country featuring the 'Celtic Snail'. The pricey campaign to eradicate the 'Celtic Snail' backfired in spectacular fashion. Instead of focusing public attention on the government's failure to deal with industrial unrest and growing infrastructural deficiencies it was greeted with derision. Andrew Bushe in the *Irish Echo* summed up the embar-rassment at the time.

> The campaign is already the butt of jokes and there is a danger the Coalition will closely embrace the tiger while the snail will be associated with Fine Gael. It was John Bruton who ended up being slimed.[55]

Austin Deasy, predictable and petulant as ever, put down a motion of no confidence in Bruton in November 2000. Ivan Yates recalled that he was alerted to the motion by Phil Hogan. 'The bould Austin Deasy has tabled a motion of no confidence in Johnny Baby,' Hogan remarked. 'I think he's on a solo run.' A council of war was summoned in Bruton's office, and Yates was despatched to pour scorn on 'this crazy and disloyal venture'. Deasy was dismissed as a serial opponent of three successive party leaders, and the pro-Bruton camp felt he would only get five or six votes. In the event, while the motion was defeated, it received the backing of twenty-four members of the parliamentary party. The writing was on the wall for Bruton.[56]

Three months later there was another heave, and this time it was led openly by Michael Noonan and Jim Mitchell. Bruton was determined not to go without a fight, and Hogan, Yates, Nora Owen and Richard Bruton rallied to the cause once more and were his most vocal defenders at a lengthy parliamentary party meeting. Most of the Munster TDs and senators came out against Bruton but, even though his cause looked hopeless, he made an impassioned forty-minute speech at the end of the meeting telling his colleagues they would be very foolish to depose him on the grounds of a newspaper opinion poll. He also addressed leading liberals in the party, such as Alan Shatter and Monica Barnes, who had called for him to go, pointing out that he had done what they had failed to do by persuading the Irish people to permit divorce. 'John's speech was the best I ever heard,' declared Brian Hayes after the meeting, while his long-time opponent Michael Creed admitted it was a 'tour de force'.

But in the end his fighting speech couldn't avert the inevitable, and Bruton was defeated by 39 votes to 33. An emotional Maurice Manning, who admitted he was personally devastated by the result, summed up the mood. 'I think the party has made the wrong decision but it is done now and we have to move on.'[57]

12

MICHAEL NOONAN AND
THE DEMISE OF FINE GAEL

*'I want to give politics back to the people. I want to give Fine
Gael back to the people.'*

— MICHAEL NOONAN, SPEAKING AFTER HIS ELECTION

AS PARTY LEADER.

By the time Austin Deasy put down his motion of no confidence
in John Bruton, change seemed inevitable. Deasy's motion
failed because Bruton's opponents were not organised, but
Michael Noonan later recalled that many people in the party
had decided that there would be a new leader. 'I either became part of
the change, or they'd change for somebody else', he said.[1]

As seen in the previous chapter, the motion of no confidence that
finally ended Bruton's leadership was proposed by Jim Mitchell and
seconded by Noonan. The strategy had been decided by the two men
at a meeting in the house of Noonan's secretary, Mary Kenny, sister of
Joe, who had been Alan Dukes's right-hand man. They had agreed that
both would contest the subsequent leadership election, with the winner
making the other man his deputy leader.

The leadership contest played out over the course of one week. Apart from Noonan and Mitchell, Enda Kenny and Bernard Allen also put their names before the 72-member parliamentary party, although Mitchell and Allen later withdrew. Noonan emerged victorious over Kenny by 44 votes to 28 on 9 February 2001.

At fifty-seven, Michael Noonan was Fine Gael's oldest leader. He had been a TD for almost twenty years and most of that time had been spent in senior roles. Born in Loghill, Co. Limerick, in May 1943, he followed in his father's footsteps and became a secondary school teacher, studying firstly at St Patrick's College and then at UCD. His interest in politics was influenced by his mother, Anne, who was active in Fine Gael. It was while working in Dublin as a teacher that he joined the Dublin branch of the party. His political career formally began when he took a seat on Limerick County Council in 1974, and he was elected to the 22nd Dáil for Limerick East in 1981. He served as Minister for Justice from 1982 to 1986 and as Minister for Health between 1994 and 1997, and he was briefly Minister for Energy and then Industry and Commerce after Garret FitzGerald's cabinet reshuffle in 1986. In opposition he was an important member of the party's front bench.

Máirtín Mac Cormaic, a vastly experienced Dáil reporter with the *Irish Independent*, marked Noonan's accession to the leadership by observing in the *Limerick Leader* that Noonan stood out for him as one of the best TDs he had encountered over his twenty years in Leinster House.[2] With a distinctive voice, a razor-sharp tongue and a talent for wit, Noonan was not short of intelligence. Dermot Morgan helped to make Noonan a national figure with a wickedly funny impersonation of him as Mornin' Noon an' Night in his 'Scrap Saturday' programme on RTÉ Radio in the early 1990s.

Despite his wit, Noonan conveyed a harsh and uncompromising image, especially in comparison with the wily Bertie Ahern. For those members of the party who believed that Bruton was the problem, Noonan would not be the solution. Faced with a different type of Fianna Fáil leader he might have fared better; but Ahern was an electoral phenomenon, and, as an *Irish Times* headline explained after the 2002 election, 'Ahern was Fianna Fáil trump card in appealing to electorate'.[3]

In his first press conference, held on the same day that he became leader, Noonan said he wanted to reunify the party and to change Irish politics. 'I want to give politics back to the people. I want to give Fine Gael back to the people.'

In a bold move that was clearly meant as a shot across Fianna Fáil's bows, he ordered an immediate ban on all corporate donations to his party. Fine Gael had profited from such donations, relying on them at times when the party coffers were seriously depleted. The businessman Ben Dunne, for example, had donated a total of £202,000 to the party between 1987 and 1994. Noonan himself had received £3,900 from Dunne towards his 1992 election expenses, and his Limerick East constituency was the beneficiary of £3,000 in 1993 and 1994.[4] Now Noonan set a limit of £1,000 on donations from any individual. Future election campaigns would be financed from membership funds and small donations from 'ordinary' supporters.

The new leader was setting his party apart from Fianna Fáil, which would be the only major party still seeking backing from corporate sources. Reflecting on all the revelations that had poured out of the tribunals in recent years, Noonan described such donations as a 'cancer in the body politic'.[5] With the Taoiseach, Bertie Ahern, having only recently defended corporate backing, Fine Gael was taking a stand as the party of honesty. It was not the first to occupy this position, and Noonan's declaration moved his party closer to Labour and others who had called for an end to corporate funding. But, given that Fine Gael itself had previously relied on such financial backing, this was a strong and decisive start to Noonan's leadership. The announcement grabbed the headlines.

Banning corporate donations was an easy win. Beyond that, to borrow the words of the *Irish Examiner,* Noonan was a 'one-chance leader with [a] mountain to climb'.[6] Time was not on his side. At most, if the Fianna Fáil-PD government served a full term he had a little over a year and a half to revitalise a party damaged by leadership heaves. Moreover, the focus on the leadership of Dukes and then Bruton had distracted attention from problems greater than personality failure. Fine Gael was simply drifting.

The same article in the *Examiner* observed that in order to deliver votes Noonan would have to give the party a new beginning. But the relatively quick succession of leaders since FitzGerald's retirement, combined with a low tolerance for less-than-immediate results, meant that there was no space or time for the party to engage meaningfully with the electorate. The party had policies, but the voters were simply not connecting with them.

The unveiling of Noonan's newly constructed front bench did little to steady the party. He stuck with his pact and made Jim Mitchell his deputy, as well as spokesman on Finance. This was in contrast to Alan Dukes, who had appointed John Bruton, one of the other contenders in his leadership contest, as deputy leader. But not only did Noonan not opt for Enda Kenny, his leadership rival, he unceremoniously dropped him from the front bench. Kenny was furious, and he called an impromptu press conference at which he voiced concern that omitting him sent a negative message about participating in democratic leadership contests.[7]

Noonan's decision could be seen as the sidelining of a rival, and some described it as an own goal; others suggested that the new leader was unimpressed by what he perceived as Kenny's failure to capitalise on opportunities that had been given to him.[8] Whatever the motivation, it left those who had supported Bruton and then Kenny feeling sour. As a party veteran said, 'There was a brutality in how the Noonan camp treated John and then there was a vindictiveness towards Enda.'[9]

Leaving aside the controversy that Kenny's demotion caused, the composition of Noonan's front bench was interesting. Gone also were John Bruton and his most loyal supporter, Nora Owen. Bernard Allen, who had at first put his name forward for the leadership contest before withdrawing and giving his support to Kenny, was also dropped. But just enough Bruton supporters were included for Noonan to defend himself against the charge of purging his opponents. Richard Bruton, Jim Higgins, Gay Mitchell and Brian Hayes all held on to their places. Noonan claimed that the necessity for a geographical spread had influenced his choices – offering this as an explanation for dropping Kenny – but his front bench had a clear Dublin bias, in response to the fact that the party was languishing in the polls in Dublin constituencies.

The presence of Deirdre Clune, Frances Fitzgerald and Olivia Mitchell added some gender balance to the line-up amidst concerns that Noonan was not 'women friendly'.[10] Essentially, though, Fine Gael remained dominated by men. Paul Bradford, who had managed Noonan's leadership campaign, was rewarded with the job of chief whip, giving him the right to attend front-bench meetings. In appearance, with only fifteen members, it looked like a slimmed-down team; the new leader, however, had created a system of personal cabinets, whereby each front-bench member would have their own 'cabinet team' consisting of two TDs and one senator. This considerably widened the extent to which members of the parliamentary party had access to policy formulation and the decision-making process.

Noonan never had a chance to find his feet as leader. The first ard-fheis for any new leader is a defining moment in their career, but Noonan lost the opportunity for an early boost to his leadership. Scheduled for the first weekend in March, the gathering had to be cancelled amidst fears that foot-and-mouth disease would spread from Britain to Ireland. The last wave of the disease and the devastation it caused to livestock was fresh enough in living memory for a need for minimising risks. With Noonan describing the bringing together of more than five thousand rural and urban supporters from around the country as 'irresponsible', Fine Gael took the decision to replace the national gathering with a smaller convention of its Dublin members.[11] The leader's address went ahead and was broadcast live by RTÉ, as would normally happen at an ard-fheis, but it was a fairly pedestrian performance. In classic Miriam Lord-style, the colourful sketch-writer suggested that Noonan had 'inexplicably attempted to energise the nation by slipping it a sedative in the form of a speech'.[12]

Having once been a very accessible member of the front bench, Noonan grew withdrawn and his confidence diminished as scandals hit the party. In March, only a month after assuming his new role and declaring Fine Gael closed to corporate donations and when he should have been coming off the high of his first ard-fheis, the party's credibility took a serious blow. Matt Cooper, editor of the *Sunday Tribune,* reported that an uncashed cheque for $50,000 (£33,000) was sitting in a safe in the party's head office. Its existence had not been declared to the Moriarty Tribunal, which had been investigating possible links between donations and government decisions. This particular donation was a dubious legacy of Michael Lowry's time as Minister for Transport, Energy and Communications in the mid-1990s. Lowry, on official advice, had granted the second mobile phone licence in Ireland to Denis O'Brien's Esat Telecom company in 1995. Telenor, a Norwegian communications company with a 40 per cent stake in Esat, later wrote the party the sizeable cheque. The existence of the cheque revitalised claims that had been circulating for several years that Esat had received favourable treatment during the licence-awarding process.

Resurfacing as it did during Noonan's leadership meant that the cheque became the new leader's problem. The undisclosed donation left Fine Gael on ambiguous moral ground. Advice given to the then leader, John Bruton, was that the party was not legally bound to declare it to the Moriarty Tribunal; but morally Fine Gael should have felt obliged to do so. Noonan sought to deflect attention away from his party by distinguishing Fine Gael's standards from those of Fianna Fáil. Speaking on RTÉ Radio, he claimed that the issue was 'much smaller' than the activities of Charlie Haughey, Liam Lawlor or Ray Burke, which were under scrutiny by the tribunal.[13]

No doubt Willie O'Dea of Fianna Fáil relished using his regular *Sunday Independent* column to write a rejoinder in which he suggested, 'rarely has political hypocrisy been so glaringly exposed.'[14] With extensive column-inches dedicated to the controversy in the daily newspapers, Fine Gael's ability to project itself as the party that would maintain standards in government was severely undermined. The saga caused further rifts in the party as efforts were made to distance the new leader from his predecessor. Noonan explained that he took a 'different view' of the legal advice Bruton had received and that he had decided to reverse the decision.[15]

Alan Shatter, the party's Justice spokesperson, was even more direct than Noonan, saying that it was 'wrong' for the party not to have informed the tribunal of the donation. The obvious attempts to create a 'then' and 'now' narrative led to Martin Cullen of Fianna Fáil asking if there were two Fine Gaels.[16]

Noonan's leadership and confidence were further undermined a couple of months later by another financial scandal. Revelations came in May that for nine years up to 1997 the party had been evading tax by making under-the-counter cash payments to its staff. Totalling £120,000, the money was paid in respect of overtime, Christmas bonuses and payments to casual workers. In its handling of the controversy the party again introduced the concept of a new Fine Gael. The chairman, Pádraic McCormack, stated that Noonan had given TDs a firm commitment that the practice would never be repeated.[17]

Noonan is arguably Fine Gael's unluckiest leader. The 'new-leader bounce' never materialised as issues predating his time at the helm resurfaced. He was convinced that people within the party were leaking these stories to damage his leadership.[18]

The Tipperary South by-election in June 2001 delivered a much-needed confidence boost for him. The election was necessitated by the death of Theresa Ahearn, and Senator Tom Hayes comfortably won the vacant seat, increasing Fine Gael's share of the vote by 9 per cent.[19] But Ahearn had held the seat for Fine Gael since 1989, so the victory made no material difference to the party's strength.

Noonan was in an unenviable position. It was a must-win election for him, and he invested a great deal of energy in Hayes's campaign, but victory was not as gratifying as capturing a seat from another party. Nonetheless Noonan capitalised on the positive PR and challenged Bertie Ahern to call the election. But before the Taoiseach finally did that Noonan found himself at the centre of unwanted media attention as the ghosts of his past came back to haunt him.

In January 2002, in an extraordinary move, RTÉ broadcast a drama based on the hepatitis C scandal of the mid-1990s. Michael Noonan was Minister for Health when details of the public-health disaster had begun to emerge. More than a thousand women were infected as a result of being given contaminated anti-D, a blood product, between 1976 and 1994. John Bruton's rainbow coalition announced in 1994 that the contamination had occurred, and the government's subsequent handling of the episode became a political scandal. In particular, the Minister for Health, Michael Noonan, was widely criticised for the aggressive way in which state lawyers dealt with Brigid McCole, who had been infected in 1977 and was eventually diagnosed in 1994. The dying woman sued the state and was sent threatening legal letters on her deathbed to force her into a settlement. She died on 2 October 1996, six days before her test case was due to be heard in the courts. Her husband never recovered from her treatment by the state and her subsequent death, and he took his own life in April 2000.

Noonan repeatedly apologised for how Mrs McCole had been treated, but it was inevitable that the legacy of his time in Health would follow him, and he was asked about his treatment of the woman during his first press conference after becoming leader. Speaking on RTÉ's *Prime Time* days later, Noonan said that her death had been one of the emotional and intellectual watersheds of his personal and political life, an event that had changed him.[20] But the *Irish Times* suggested that he had a 'long way to go in assuaging doubts', while questions were raised in *Fortnight* and other publications about the extent to which the public would have confidence in him at election time.[21]

Though the spectre of Brigid McCole hung over Noonan's every move as leader, a television drama thrust the controversy back into the spotlight. Called *No Tears*, it reminded the public of the details of the scandal and of Noonan's involvement in it in a way that questions at press conferences never could. The implications were summed up by Seán Moncrieff with his usual sharp wit when he wrote that Fine Gael would 'take a pasting' as people voted against 'that baldy actor'.[22]

The four-part serial, heavily promoted by RTÉ, told the story of two women who had been infected as a result of contaminated anti-D injections. Though fictional characters, they were an amalgam of those real women who had been similarly affected. One character was based on Brigid McCole, and the actor, Brenda Fricker, privately met members of the McCole family in preparing for the part, while Mrs McCole's consultant acted as the programme's medical adviser. The first episode was broadcast on 14 January 2002, with a far-from-flattering portrayal of the Minister for Health. The final episode was watched by 555,000 people, and although this was fewer than the number who had tuned in for the previous episodes, *No Tears* was still the most-watched programme on RTÉ television that night by a considerable margin.[23]

No Tears never used his name, but, not surprisingly, Noonan was critical of the production, particularly the timing of its release. Interviewed for an RTÉ documentary broadcast the following year, he complained,

> The portrayal of me was fiction. It wasn't in accordance with the fact. Even the events portrayed, some of them didn't happen at all, and others were twisted, distorted to show me in the worst possible light. I thought it was a very unfair piece of broadcasting. But if I put that to RTÉ, even today, they'll say, 'But, Michael, you understand drama. Drama is different from documentary. Things don't have to be accurate in drama. We do things for dramatic effect which are not necessarily true.'[24]

Fergal Bowers, then editor of IrishHealth.com and author of *Hep C: Niamh's Story* (1997), judged the portrayal to be, on balance, an 'honourable, accurate and sensitive portrayal of the events as they occurred'.[25] But the drama drew criticisms beyond Fine Gael circles. Bruce Arnold commented in the *Irish Independent* that Noonan had been 'grievously wronged'.[26] Significantly, one of the survivors who had taken a case against the state, Mary Quinlan, believed that Noonan had been turned into a 'stage villain'. In her opinion the series was 'not fictional enough to be a drama nor is it real enough to be fact'.[27] Nonetheless it raised a lot of questions about women's rights, and damaged Noonan with female voters.

As the life of the 28th Dáil was nearing its full term, an election was due in the first half of 2002. Michael Noonan finally had his first ard-fheis as leader in February 2002, and he entered it in full election mode. Building on the promises to voters (discussed in detail later in this chapter) that the party had already made, Noonan spoke to all sections of society. Summed up as 'pious aspirations in a plethora of sound bites',[28] his leader's address was, as we will see below, a bizarre departure for Fine Gael.

With Fianna Fáil taking pleasure in mocking the dismal state of the opposition at its own ard-fheis, Fine Gael was facing electoral meltdown. The *Sunday Independent*-IMS poll of 10 March put the party at a mere 21 per cent nationally. Although a two-point increase from the last such poll, published in December 2001, the result did not presage a slow increase in support for Fine Gael. Of particular concern was the 14 per cent share of the vote predicted in Dublin.[29] This signalled disaster. It should be noted, however, that the plethora of opinion polls conducted during the election and the accuracy of their findings raised concerns about the ways in which such polls were being carried out. All the campaign polls, as well as the exit poll, overestimated support for Fianna Fáil while underestimating Fine Gael and the independents.[30]

With speculation mounting that an election was only weeks away, Noonan went to see the leader of the Labour Party, Ruairí Quinn, on 10 April to discuss the possibility of a pre-election pact that would include a ten-point joint policy statement. But Quinn was adamant that his preference was for a coalition with Fine Gael and the Green Party, and that Labour would fight the election on an independent platform.[31] Quinn later spoke of an 'intensity' of 'desperation' in Noonan's approach.[32] It is hardly surprising. Rather than focusing his energies on reigniting the party, Noonan had had to spend the first months of his leadership doing damage control. The embattled leader knew that coalition was the only hope of taking Fine Gael into government – and of saving his own position. But without a pre-election pact he would have a hard time convincing voters that a government led by his party was an option.

Just after 9 p.m. on Wednesday 24 April, as a routine adjournment debate was concluded, the Taoiseach, Bertie Ahern, announced in the Dáil that he would be going to Áras an Uachtaráin the following morning to request that the 28th Dáil be dissolved. The chamber was practically deserted, and the *Irish Independent* reported that many TDs, including some on his own benches, were left 'open-mouthed in amazement' at the timing.[33] Though Ahern had caught many by surprise with the way in which he made the announcement, the campaign had been slowly gathering momentum for months. Ahern opted for the minimum three-week campaign, and polling day was to be 17 May.

Ahern's government – the longest serving in peacetime – had presided over the Celtic Tiger years and faced into the election in a strong position. Under John Bruton, Fine Gael had launched the embarrassing Celtic Snail poster campaign to highlight the other side of the boom. Although the claims were valid, the clumsy messaging could not override the fact that the economy had enjoyed five years of unprecedented growth and had outperformed all others in the OECD.

Nonetheless, as the three-week campaign got under way Fine Gael had an obvious target – more convincing than its failed £160,000 stunt – that could damage the Fianna Fáil-PD government. The coalition had recklessly increased public spending to unsustainable levels. But rather than attacking this, Noonan opted instead for a 'feel-good' campaign, at the centre of which were extravagant promises that had already been made before the election was formally announced. Noonan had made the bizarre pledge in January to compensate those who had lost money on shares after Eircom was floated on the stock market in July 1999. Half a million people had snapped up the shares, at a price of €3.90 each; they first rose in value but by September that year had slid below the floatation price. Shareholders who did not sell early found themselves massively out of pocket.

Noonan proposed allowing small investors to offset their Eircom losses against taxable income. The glaring problem with his plan was that it made no provision for those – the elderly on state pensions only or recipients of social welfare – who were not taxpayers. The pledge smacked of populism. Despite inserting himself into a debate on RTÉ's *Liveline* programme, he had little success in convincing listeners that his proposal was anything more than an election stunt.[34]

Noonan's suggestion further compounded the perception that Fine Gael was turning into a giveaway party. The previous December Jim Mitchell had announced that, if elected, the party would establish a £20 million fund to compensate taxi-drivers affected by deregulation. The Fianna Fáil-PD government had introduced legislation that ended the system of control over the number of taxi licenses that local licensing authorities could issue. Once in operation, the number of taxis on the roads increased substantially, while the cost of a plate dropped from £80,000 to £5,000. It was good news for those seeking to enter the business but a disaster for the resale of plates bought before deregulation. Mitchell had not consulted his leader about this announcement, and Noonan attributed it to the fact that Mitchell was seriously ill. (Few people knew about Mitchell's deteriorating health at the time.) Although a solo run, coming as it did from the deputy leader and spokesman on Finance there was no reason for people to dissociate it from the party.

In characteristic fashion, Bertie Ahern labelled the promises 'mad', while the Labour leader, Ruairí Quinn, recalled, 'If I was amazed at this nonsense, Fine Gael supporters were horrified.' Quinn related in his memoir a conversation with a Fine Gael-turned-Labour voter who is alleged to have remarked that her former party might as well set up a stall outside the Leopardstown races to reimburse disappointed punters.[35] But Fine Gael forged ahead with its misguided approach.

'Vision, with Purpose', the party's manifesto, was awash with other promises, including £2 billion in tax concessions. Leaflets distributed throughout the country informed recipients that the party wanted to reward those who worked hard by keeping taxes low. Fine Gael miscalculated how such proposals would be received. The timing was poor. Public finances were slipping, and although the proposals had been costed by the Department of Finance, they assumed economic growth at levels most people did not believe would be sustained.[36] Clearly disgusted by the turn of events in the party, Garret FitzGerald saw Fine Gael's strategy in the context of Fianna Fáil's tendency for promising 'this, that and the other'.[37]

If Fine Gael had dumped John Bruton to find a more charismatic leader who would connect with the public, Michael Noonan was not it. Such was the momentum behind Bertie Ahern that, by 1 May, Paddy Power was offering odds of 1/16 that he would be the next Taoiseach.[38] Meanwhile Donal McCarthy of Ladbrokes explained, 'No matter what price we give Noonan, people just aren't putting money on him. Even in Limerick nobody is biting.'[39] As Ahern zipped around the country (with commentators raising questions about the speed at which his motor cavalcade was travelling), Fine Gael encountered its lowest point of the campaign on the last day of April. A young woman shoved a custard pie in Michael Noonan's face moments after he began his walkabout in Boyle, Co. Roscommon. A photographer, James Connolly, captured the encounter, and his picture made the front page of newspapers the following day, adding some colour to the press during a campaign that was otherwise pretty dull. The woman was apprehended by Frank Feighan, then a councillor, who released her after she explained that she was five months pregnant. 'She was shivering and I felt pity for her more than anything.'[40]

With the opinion polls in the final stages of the campaign showing Fianna Fáil on course for an overall majority, Michael McDowell engaged in a publicity stunt that produced the most memorable moment of the canvass. He ascended a telephone pole with a poster that read, *One-party government? No, thanks.* McDowell was Attorney General in the Fianna Fáil-PD government and was campaigning to win back his Dáil seat. Alan Dukes criticised the stunt at the time, arguing that the PDs couldn't have it both ways: either they remain loyal to their coalition partners of the previous five years or they explain to the voting public why Fianna Fáil should not be trusted in government.[41]

With the benefit of hindsight, McDowell's intervention is understood to have been a turning-point in the election. It was a shrewd move, designed to capture the attention of those disenchanted with Fianna Fáil. With Fine Gael trailing in opinion polls, those who wanted to influence the formation of an alternative government knew that a vote for the party was virtually a wasted one. The best way to prevent a Fianna Fáil government, McDowell's argument went, was to vote for the Progressive Democrats. Here he was drawing on lessons from the past: by entering government with Fianna Fáil in 1989 the PDs had augmented their place in the party system and had, temporarily, made Fine Gael redundant to the formation of a government. Now, in 2002, the PDs were again catapulted into a pivotal position as McDowell's message struck a chord with voters.

Noonan enjoyed a brief moment of triumph as polling day loomed. The only televised leader's debate of the campaign was hosted by Miriam O'Callaghan of RTÉ, and 1.28 million people tuned in to watch Noonan and Ahern debate the issues. Although both sides claimed victory afterwards, commentators generally agreed that Noonan was the winner. But the debate came only three days before the vote, and Noonan did not land any devastating blows. Like Bruton before him, outperforming his rival would not propel Noonan into the top job.

The story of the 2002 election was the meltdown of Fine Gael. And the human-interest element of that story was the traumatic loss of Nora Owen's seat. Her defeat was an omen of what was to come. The party's one-time deputy leader, former Minister for Justice and grandniece of Michael Collins, had served Dublin North in the Dáil since 1981. Electronic voting was piloted in her constituency, as well as in Dublin West and Meath, in 2002. The government had spent €54 million on machines that were meant to revolutionise the way voting was conducted. Gone were the 'stupid old pencils', as Bertie Ahern called them during Leader's Questions in the Dáil, in these three constituencies: all voters had to do was press a button next to the corresponding picture of a candidate and, having made their selection in order of preference, press another button to cast their vote. Within hours of the polls closing, the outcome would be known.

It sounded simple, but, as Jim Glennon, one of the Fianna Fáil candidates in Dublin North, recalled, people were not as comfortable with technology then and a lot of voters had a fear about pressing the wrong button.[42]

The results for the two Dublin constituencies were declared in Citywest Hotel. The efficiency of the computers that tabulated the votes negated the need for multiple counts and declarations. It meant that the results came faster – though not as fast as promised, and it was the early hours of the morning before any declarations were made. In the absence of tallies, the candidates had no sense of how the vote had gone and no lead-in time to prepare themselves. Nora Owen's sense of frustration was palpable in her colourful description of waiting for the announcement. 'You can see nothing, you can smell nothing, you can hear nothing. It's all happening inside the bowels of some computer.'[43]

Dublin West declared first. Brian Lenihan of Fianna Fáil topped the poll, while the Fine Gael hopeful Sheila Terry was edged out by Joan Burton of Labour. The result for the four-seat Dublin North constituency came shortly afterwards, just before 3 a.m. As the candidates were lined up, Jim Glennon glanced behind him in an attempt to read the names on the sheet of paper carried by the returning officer, John Fitzpatrick. Not seeing his name listed, he ran his right hand across his throat to signal to his people that he had not been successful. Nora Owen was standing next to him and he told her, 'You're all right, Nora.' When she asked how he knew, Glennon explained, 'I've just looked over my shoulder at John's sheet of paper. He has four names, and you're one of them.' 'Oh, thank God for that,' she replied. But when the declaration came it was Trevor Sargent of the Green Party, Seán Ryan of Labour and Jim Glennon and G.V. Wright of Fianna Fáil who were named as the constituency's new TDs. When written in longhand and read upside down, 'N. Owen' bears a resemblance to his own surname, Glennon later explained.[44]

A visibly shaken Owen was comforted by Seán Ryan, her long-time constituency colleague. His sensitive embrace of the defeated politician became the defining photograph of the election. Glennon later rang Owen to apologise to her and her husband for his mistake; the pair remain friendly.

In the end Nora Owen came in seventh, ending a career in national politics that spanned almost two decades. Had the count been conducted in the traditional way she would have known from early on that her seat was lost. 'I'm very, very shattered. It's heart-breaking. I just have an empty feeling. It was like being stabbed very quickly,' she explained in an interview afterwards.[45]

The reliability of the system has since been questioned, and the Commission on Electronic Voting reported in 2004 that it had 'not been able to satisfy itself sufficiently as to the accuracy and secrecy of the chosen system.'[46] The Fine Gael Mayo TD Michael Ring later posed the question in the Dáil, 'Did Nora Owen lose her seat at all?'[47]

In its haste to keep step with technological advancement, the government overlooked the public's love of tallymen and the marathon count. The machines were brought out again in constituencies for the second referendum on the Nice Treaty later that year, but they were then retired into storage, at a cost of €145,000 per year. The failed, pricey experiment was never repeated. The 7,500 machines were occasionally thought of in the years that followed, and Michael Noonan suggested in early 2012 that there might be a market for them in Irish theme pubs around the world.[48] They were eventually sold for €70,000, a small fraction of the original cost, later that year. Deeming them 'a foolish investment', the former minister Nora Owen bade 'good riddance to bad rubbish'.[49]

Nora Owen was the first of a long list of high-profile Fine Gael politicians who lost their seats. As counting got under way in the rest of the constituencies the following day, the list of casualties grew. A defining moment for the party and its supporters came when John Bowman, presenting the RTÉ coverage, held up a sheet of paper in his studio. As the camera zoomed in, viewers saw Xs through the photographs of ten members of the front bench who had been defeated. It was a powerful image, a pictorial representation of the party's meltdown. As Bowman put it, 'It's the elite of Fine Gael.'

Despite the atrocious result nationally, Noonan's own vote held up in Limerick East and he was elected on the first count, behind Fianna Fáil's poll-topper Willie O'Dea. In total, the party lost twenty-three seats. With only thirty-one TDs in the 29th Dáil, it was, Noonan said, a 'devastating blow in terms of numbers, in terms of the quality of the people who have lost their seats'.[50] Only three seats were won in Dublin. In Dún Laoghaire, which had previously returned three TDs, the party failed to have anyone elected; it was one of a number of constituencies that did not elect any Fine Gael TD. Of the thirty-one candidates elected, only two were women. A newcomer, Olwyn Enright, won a seat in Laois-Offaly and Olivia Mitchell held on to hers in Dublin South, while the front-bench members Deirdre Clune and Frances Fitzgerald both lost theirs. The party had consistently resisted implementing positive discrimination, and a review after the election found the small number of women representatives to be a strategic weakness.[51]

As counting continued around the country on 18 May, Noonan spoke to Charlie Bird for the Six One News and announced his intention to resign, 'I took over the party when there was an expectation of very serious seat losses. A lot of people pledged their faith in me to reverse the decline. I didn't reverse the decline, so I accept responsibility.' Watched over by a bronze statue of Michael Collins behind his left shoulder, Noonan expressed his belief that the party would be inspired by Collins and the founding fathers, and that it would rebuild.[52] Far from being a symbol of Fine Gael's great history, the presence of Collins was a reminder that the party was trapped in the past. As we will see in the next chapter, when Enda Kenny undertook the herculean task of rebuilding Fine Gael, Frank Flannery advised that they forget about 'history, traditions, places in history, famous old faces and political records'.

It was a difficult election on many levels for Noonan. His wife, Florence, known to friends and family as Flor, had played an active role in the campaign. As her husband, whom she had married in 1969, toured the country she was out canvassing most nights in his Limerick East constituency. But privately the family were dealing with the reality that Florence, like her mother before her, had Alzheimer's disease, and that it was getting worse. Noonan only opened up about her condition in an emotional interview with Pat Kenny on RTÉ's *Frontline* in May 2010; by then she had been suffering for twelve years and was in the end stages of the debilitating disease.[53]

When Michael Noonan resigned as leader just short of his fifty-ninth birthday it seemed his political career was behind him. Few leaders come back from the type of devastation that Fine Gael suffered in the 2002 election, but Noonan would later enjoy an astonishing revival of fortunes. Appointed Minister for Finance by Enda Kenny in February 2012, he oversaw economic recovery in the aftermath of the IMF bailout. He isn't without his critics, yet he has also been lauded for being the safe pair of hands that steadied the economy. As Juno McEnroe wrote in the *Irish*

Examiner, 'He was the minister in charge when Ireland exited the bailout and history will remember that.'[54] But all that lay in the future. In May 2002, Fine Gael's obituary was being written.

13

ENDA KENNY PICKS
UP THE PIECES

*'His name would not have been the first, or the second or even
the 23rd that would have occurred to me as a future leader
of Fine Gael.'*

VINCENT BROWNE, WRITING ABOUT ENDA KENNY
IN THE *IRISH TIMES*, 7 FEBRUARY 2001.

A depleted and bruised parliamentary party limped back to Leinster House after the 2002 election disaster. As Michael Noonan had announced his resignation on the night of the count, the first task was to elect a new leader. A two-day meeting of the parliamentary party was held in the Citywest Hotel in Saggart, Co. Dublin, at which the surviving TDs and senators debated how they would go about it.

There was a consensus that they should not wait until a proposed new electoral system involving the party membership came into operation. There was some controversy over that decision, and Young Fine Gael issued a statement saying that the election should be put back until after the summer. Two of its leading members, Leo Varadkar and Lucinda Creighton, wrote to the party chairman, Pádraic McCormack, advocating delay; but the majority of TDs and senators were having none of it and they decided that a new leader should be appointed before the first meeting of the 29th Dáil on 6 June.

McCormack and the outgoing party leader in the Seanad, Maurice Manning, oversaw a straw poll to gauge the mood. It showed that Enda Kenny was the frontrunner but it was not decisive, so a date was set for a leadership election. Four candidates put their names forward: Enda Kenny, Richard Bruton, Phil Hogan and Gay Mitchell. On the first count Bruton had 17 votes, Kenny 16, Hogan 9 and Mitchell 7. When Mitchell was eliminated Kenny moved into the lead with 19, as against 18 for Bruton and 12 for Hogan. Then on the final count, when Hogan was eliminated, Kenny moved to 29 as against 20 for Bruton.[1]

Enda Kenny was now leader of Fine Gael after more than a quarter of a century as a TD. He was the third leader in the space of sixteen months, but to most observers the post seemed more like a poisoned chalice than a glittering prize. Fine Gael had been in power for a paltry two-and-a-half years out of the previous fifteen, and that short interval had happened by a fluke. The party had last won an election in November 1982.

Despite all that, Kenny struck an upbeat note as he addressed the media after his election. 'Fine Gael's political mourning is over. This party is getting up off the floor and we are determined to demonstrate all over Ireland that we are a force to be reckoned with in the future,' he said, to cheers from his colleagues and barely suppressed sneers from the media.[2]

Enda Kenny became leader of Fine Gael at the age of fifty-one, although he still looked and sounded very much like the youth who had been first elected to the Dáil as a TD for Mayo in November 1975. He won a by-election caused by the death of his father, Henry Kenny, a junior minister in the Cosgrave government and a hero in Co. Mayo, having played on the county's first all-Ireland winning team of 1936. Enda Kenny was a young national-school teacher when he was plunged into politics after his father's death but he took to it like a duck to water. John Healy in the *Irish Times* described him on his first day in the Dáil as having the joyful demeanour of the captain of a minor all-Ireland winning football team.

As a young man in Dublin, Kenny lived life to the full and enjoyed a night on the town. To some of his serious-minded party elders, including Garret FitzGerald, that gave the impression of frivolousness, and he had to await promotion for longer than some of his young colleagues who were elected in the 1981–82 period. He was appointed a junior minister in Education by FitzGerald in 1986 but did not feature in the party's front bench when Dukes was leader. He backed Bruton in 1987, and when Bruton became leader he was made chief whip. He played a vital role in helping his leader survive the 1993 heave, and when Bruton took over as Taoiseach he was rewarded by appointment to the cabinet as Minister for Trade and Tourism.

Although his experience as minister provided him with important experience in the world trade talks, he generated more publicity from his role at Tourism, where he gave the impression of having a more light-hearted approach to government than some of his colleagues. This disguised a political shrewdness that enabled him to avoid becoming embroiled in serious controversy, as so many of his colleagues did.

In 1992 Kenny's man-about-town life changed when he married Fionnuala O'Kelly. She was an important figure in the Haughey government, serving as head of the Government Information Service after a stint in the Fianna Fáil press office. As well as providing stability in his personal life, her knowledge and appreciation of politics was to prove an invaluable aid.

His initial bid for the leadership in 2001 came as a surprise to many, particularly in the media, and he was widely written off. One of the reasons he was so underestimated was that he was never a great debater and did not shine in Dáil exchanges. He often appeared more comfortable speaking Irish than English, a trait he shared with Alan Dukes. What Kenny lacked in debating skill he more than made up for in political nous and a truly amazing level of energy. That energy, allied to his natural optimism, fortified him for the hard slog of rebuilding the party in spite of all the doubters. The ability to keep going in the face of widespread derision, particularly in his early years as leader, bespoke an inner conviction that his critics were unable to fathom.

The scale of the task ahead of him was illustrated by the simple Dáil arithmetic that showed Fianna Fáil with 81 seats to Fine Gael's 31. It was no surprise that so many commentators gave Kenny no chance of making significant inroads into Fianna Fáil's massive fifty-seat lead. To make matters worse, Fine Gael had only three seats in Dublin.

One intangible factor was that throughout his political career Kenny's inner conviction was accompanied by a healthy dollop of good luck at regular intervals. He was fortunate to survive the 2002 meltdown at all. In seventh place on the first count in the five-seat constituency, he had resigned himself to losing his seat but managed to overhaul his running-mate, Jim Higgins, on the eighth count. It was the narrowest of escapes.

The media tone about Kenny's leadership qualities was set by the journalist and former Fine Gael Young Tiger Vincent Browne, who wrote in the *Irish Times* that 'his name would not have been the first, or the second or even the 23rd that would have occurred to me as a future leader of Fine Gael.'[3] In a radio interview Kenny said that he was going to 'electrify the Fine Gael party,' and Browne took delight over the following years in predicting that Kenny was going to 'electrocute' Fine Gael. Miriam Lord in the *Irish Independent* had a more benign take on Kenny, while his biographer John Downing described her depiction as 'a sort of cheery bumpkin image that persisted and became something of a bugbear for him'.[4]

In defiance of that cheery caricature, there was a hint of steel about his early moves as party leader. His first test was the Seanad election, which takes place a couple of months after every Dáil election. The Seanad is often a staging-post for TDs who have lost their seat but want to make it back to the front line, or for ambitious newcomers who see it as their route to the Dáil. Fine Gael desperately needed to get politicians such as Jim Higgins, Brian Hayes and Deirdre Clune, who had lost their Dáil seats, back into national politics through the Seanad. There were also up-and-coming young politicians, such as Joe McHugh, Frank Feighan and James Bannon, who had excellent prospects of returning to the Dáil if and when the tide turned.

The problem facing Kenny was that a number of outgoing Fine Gael senators with no interest in being elected to the Dáil were also in the race. They had a good relationship with the party councillors who make up the greater part of the electorate and were difficult to dislodge. On Kenny's direction, the party's head office set out to get candidates with Dáil potential elected in place of 'professional senators'. Councillors were told that the party's future depended on the plan being executed, and most of them obeyed the direction from head office. Only two of the 'professional senators' survived the cull. One was Paddy Burke from Mayo, a close friend and ally of Kenny, who was exempt from the purge, and the other was Paul Coghlan, a popular and wily Kerryman who managed to edge out Deirdre Clune by a fraction of a vote. Described by the general secretary, Tom Curran, as 'the one who got away', Coghlan didn't bear a grudge and was to prove a vital ally of Kenny in the years ahead.

One important decision he made immediately after his appointment was to retain Mark Kennelly to run the leader's office. Kennelly had occupied that position under Noonan, having worked for the party in various capacities for the previous decade. From a staunch Fine Gael family in Co. Kerry he began as an assistant to the Munster MEP John Cushnahan and spent four years in Brussels before moving to Dublin to become a ministerial adviser to Michael Lowry and then to Alan Dukes. When the rainbow government left office he worked for Fine Gael in Leinster House, first for Bruton, then for Noonan and finally for Kenny.

One important function performed by Kennelly was to act as a link between Fine Gael and the European People's Party, the powerful political grouping to which Fine Gael belonged. He ensured that from the start Kenny attended the regular meetings of EPP leaders, which took place before European Council meetings. The contacts he established through the EPP were to prove vital to Kenny when he became Taoiseach in the throes of the financial crisis. More to the point, Keneally became the gatekeeper for Kenny and stuck closely to him through thick and thin for the following fifteen years. Another element of continuity was the party general secretary, Tom Curran, who had been in the job since 1999 and had an important role to play in the drive to rebuild the party's electoral base after the 2002 meltdown.

Kenny landed himself in trouble not long after he took over the leadership when an anecdote he told at an event to mark the departure of the party press officer, Niall Ó Muilleoir, was represented as a racist comment by the *Sunday Independent*.[5] Some hours before the event Kenny had been told the shocking news that his good friend and former Tipperary TD David Molony had died suddenly. That prompted him to tell a story about a visit the two of them had made to Portugal many years earlier in the company of Maurice Manning. The punchline of the not very funny story involved a Moroccan barman using the n-word.[6] If anything, the anecdote was designed to show the absurdity of racism, but that is not how it was portrayed, and Kenny was forced to offer an abject and unreserved apology for using the word.

The episode appeared to confirm the doubts of Kenny's critics but in the longer run it did him no harm. For one thing, people outside the media bubble had no difficulty in deciding that an anecdote did not make him a racist. More importantly, it was a valuable lesson to Kenny never again to let his guard down with journalists. One of his well-known traits was to tell funny stories and do impersonations at the drop of a hat. He learned the hard way that in the wrong company that could be fatal for a party leader and while he didn't undergo a personality change he was more careful about his audience in the future.

His natural bonhomie stood Kenny in good stead as he set out on the long slog of touring the party organisation to begin rebuilding shattered morale. Unlike many politicians who have to grit their teeth to deal with the back-slapping side of politics, Kenny genuinely enjoyed meeting people from all walks of life. He loved the banter and the individual stories he encountered as he crisscrossed the country, meeting party members and attempting to rekindle the enthusiasm of the organisation.

Apart from his energy Kenny's great advantage was that he was an authentic representative of the Fine Gael grass roots. When the party's vote collapsed in Dublin in 2002 it was the old rural heartlands that held firm. Some of Fine Gael's more fickle middle-class supporters in

Dublin may not have been impressed with his west of Ireland accent and his open, affable demeanour but it went down a treat with the party members outside the capital. In his first month as leader he addressed eight regional meetings, bringing him into direct contact with more than four thousand party members. It was a punishing schedule, which he was to keep up over the following years. 'Kenny went from town to town, from meeting to meeting, spending endless hours talking and listening,' said one admiring colleague. 'He was brilliant at it. From the moment he was elected leader he became a model of application – a workaholic.'[7]

At those party meetings Kenny belted out night after night what politicians refer to as 'a single transferrable speech'. An early one he made to five hundred party members at the Menlo Park Hotel in Galway on Monday 24 June 2002 was a typical example. He acknowledged the pain and frustration of loyal members who had seen the party perform so badly in the general election, despite all the evidence of low standards in Fianna Fáil over the previous five years. 'I hear you and I promise you change,' he told them. 'We made the fatal mistake of behaving not as an effective opposition but as a government in waiting.' He pledged that as party leader he would take every opportunity to expose 'the crassness and contempt that lies at the heart of the Fianna Fáil-Progressive Democrats coalition'.[8]

He also set a positive tone in the parliamentary party by avoiding the vindictiveness that had become a feature of its recent history and giving prominent positions to those who had contested the leadership election against him. He appointed his leading rival, Richard Bruton, as deputy leader, Gay Mitchell was appointed Foreign Affairs spokesman and Phil Hogan got Enterprise. In the years ahead Hogan was to become his most trusted and valuable ally. His constituency colleague and rival Michael Ring was also appointed to the front bench, as were younger TDs such as Simon Coveney and Denis Naughten, along with the newly elected TDs Olwyn Enright and John Deasy. He also offered to appoint his predecessor, Michael Noonan, to a senior post, but the offer was declined. Given the small size of the parliamentary party, there was a job for almost everyone.

Barnstorming the party membership and establishing a more cordial atmosphere in the parliamentary party set the right tone, but Kenny took the vital extra step of instituting a root-and-branch examination of the party structures. He appointed Frank Flannery, CEO of Rehab, who had played an influential role in the party since the 1980s, to head a committee tasked with examining the party and coming up with concrete proposals for its revival. The outcome was a punchy 42-page report entitled '21st Century Fine Gael' which was presented to a private meeting of the parliamentary party in the Knockranny Hotel in Westport in early September.[9]

The report was a wake-up call for everybody in the party. Its most attention-grabbing section was the introduction, which featured two dramatic graphs. The first illustrated the decline in party support in the six elections over the previous twenty years from 39.2 per cent in November 1982 to 22.5 per cent in 2002. The second extrapolated the same trend for the next twenty years, which would leave Fine Gael with only 12.8 per cent of the vote by 2022. 'These graphs do not present a pretty picture,' the report said, but it presented a third graph to provide some grounds for hope. This showed the party's share of the vote declining in the 1970s and rising in the early 1980s. 'This shows what can be achieved and that is why a new and dynamic strategy is needed for 21st century Fine Gael.' To drive home the point, the report went on:

> Every year long established institutions and so on disappear without trace. Whatever happened to the Irish Press group with its three strong titles and thousands of readers? Why should a political party be any different? … The truth is that whilst Ireland has changed beyond recognition over the last generation, Fine Gael has stood still.

The report asked why the party's great rival, Fianna Fáil, was so successful. 'Fianna Fáil is essentially a pragmatic, populist party and, by definition is perpetually renewing itself.' It concluded that Fine Gael's way forward was to play to its strengths while also playing to theirs. 'It lies in combining the best facets of Fianna Fáil populism with a rejuvenated expression of the great ideals which Fine Gael stands for.' This it described as the 'progressive centre'.

The report set out a series of recommendations designed to make the party a far more professional organisation at a structural level. It also advocated an expanded voter research programme with an emphasis on focus groups to understand the concerns of the electorate and guide a professional communications strategy. The role of the party leader was identified as critical to recovery. 'A lousy party can succeed with a brilliant leader – the opposite does not work.'[10]

Flannery in his introduction suggested that adopting the report would transform the party, and he suggested that the goal should be nothing less than winning sixty seats at the next election. It seemed a far-fetched ambition in the gloom of 2002, but it had one important thing going for it: Kenny's unremitting energy and optimism.

He needed every ounce of that optimism in his first two years as leader. In Dáil exchanges he rarely laid a glove on the Taoiseach, Bertie Ahern, and was regularly outperformed by Pat Rabbitte, who had replaced Ruairí Quinn as Labour leader. That drew unfavourable comparisons in the media, but Kenny had concluded early on that his Dáil performance was not going to make too much of a difference one way or another. Instead he put his focus on visiting every constituency on multiple occasions to meet the voters and build party morale in the process. It took nerve to ignore the shenanigans in Leinster House for the less glamorous trek around the country but he stuck with it, even when an *Irish Times* opinion poll in May 2003 put Fine Gael on 20 per cent, two points behind Labour. Even worse, Kenny's satisfaction rating was only 26 per cent, compared with 49 per cent for Pat Rabbitte and 41 per cent for Bertie Ahern[11]

One important decision that Kenny took early on was to face up to the financial problems that had beset Fine Gael for more than a decade. Immediately on taking the leadership he reversed Noonan's ban on corporate donations, and he implemented a recommendation in the Flannery report to hire a full-time fund-raiser. The person appointed to this role was the formidable Anne Strain, a party activist who had formerly worked for the Alzheimer Society. She revitalised the party members' draw so that it brought in €1 million a year and instituted an annual €120-a-head presidential dinner, something Fianna Fáil had been doing for years, which not only raised funds but served as a morale-boosting annual social occasion for the party.

Following other recommendations in the Flannery report, Gerry Naughten was appointed to the position of political director in the leader's office, Ciarán Conlon was made communications director, and Andrew McDowell became economic adviser to Kenny. Flannery worked closely with them in a voluntary capacity and in a relatively short space of time a more professional and dynamic approach began to develop.

In his early years as leader Kenny was driven around the country by a lifelong friend and party activist, Liam Coady, who took on the role of his driver but was much more than that: a trusted confidant who could be relied on to keep morale up during difficult times. The two men had lively political discussions on their journeys. Coady was well known in Leinster House for his gentle humour and his fierce loyalty to his leader. His premature death of a heart attack at the age of sixty-four in August 2010 was a shocking blow for Kenny.

Although the seeds of success were being sown, the public perception of Fine Gael remained that of a party deep in crisis. Journalists queued up to write Fine Gael's obituary, and RTÉ commissioned a three-part series on the internal conflict and rivalries that had beset it for more than a decade. When it was broadcast in 2004 'Family at War' painted an unflinching picture of the party since the FitzGerald era, with many former leading figures giving blunt assessments of what had gone wrong.

Inside the party, however, the time for self-analysis was over. As Kenny crisscrossed the country meeting activists, councillors and local constituency officers he emphasised the need to begin selecting candidates to contest the next local elections, which were due in June 2004, in tandem with the European elections. Flannery had emphasised that the local elections were the critically important ones for the future, even if the European contest was going to be the primary media preoccupation. He pointed out that the foundation for FitzGerald's revival of the party had been the 1979 local elections, when a whole crop of new councillors provided the talent for the Dáil breakthrough in the 1980s.

Flannery and Curran painstakingly interviewed every potential Fine Gael council candidate in the country. The appointment of five full-time regional organisers was an important help in the process of identifying potential candidates. Getting them in place for the Euro elections was also vital, as the party's performance in that contest would provide the head-lines that could make or break morale. Kenny approached Jim Higgins, his defeated rival and colleague from Mayo, to ask him to be the candidate in Connacht-Ulster. Simon Coveney emerged as the candidate in Munster, and Gay Mitchell was prevailed on to run in Dublin. The sitting Leinster MEP Avril Doyle was joined on the ticket for the new three-seat East constituency by the farming journalist Mairéad McGuinness. It took a lot of persuasion to get her to run, as she was also being courted by the PDs, and her decision to opt for Fine Gael was a morale boost in itself. 'Ambitious people had to be persuaded that there was a future in standing for Fine Gael,' Phil Hogan recalls.[12]

Phil Hogan was the national director of elections and he believed the two high-profile women candidates in Leinster could confound the odds and win a seat each. That was fine in theory but it meant that the two candidates were soon at each other's throats. Doyle was furious because she had to contend with a big-name running-mate in a constituency that had been reduced from four seats to three. Soon the newspapers were captivated by the 'Avril versus Mairéad' stories and, as John Downing commented, it was a colour writer's dream. Stories with such headlines as 'Designer handbags at 100 paces' and 'Political catfight' grabbed more attention than worthy reports about disagreements over EU issues. 'For Kenny and his backroom team it was simple: friction meant publicity and publicity meant votes,' Downing wrote. 'But keeping a lid on a furiously boiling pot was easier said than done.'[13]

The pot boiled over occasionally as the two women fought each other the length and breadth of the province. The outcome, though, was that Fine Gael won two seats in Leinster and one each in the other three constituencies, giving the party five out of the thirteen European

Parliament seats, as against four for Fianna Fáil. It was the first time Fine Gael had ever managed to win more seats than the old enemy in any kind of national electoral contest.

The results in the local elections were not quite as dramatic but were probably even more important in the long run. Fine Gael gained 16 council seats, to win a total of 293, only 11 behind Fianna Fáil. Crucially, a raft of young ambitious councillors who would make their name in the years ahead were elected. They included Leo Varadkar, Lucinda Creighton, Kieran O'Donnell and Michael D'Arcy. A mere two years after its general election disaster Fine Gael was back in business as a serious contender for government.

Another plus was Kenny's decision to sidestep a presidential election in 2004. He concluded early in the year that it would not make political sense for Fine Gael to run a candidate against the popular Mary McAleese, who had indicated her desire for a second term. Kenny was acutely aware of how Alan Dukes's mishandling of the presidential election campaign of 1990 had undermined his leadership and he was determined not to make the same mistake. Some party activists were critical of his decision not to run a candidate, and it also provided more ammunition for his media critics, but Kenny was adamant that there was nothing in it for Fine Gael and he announced in the summer that he was endorsing McAleese for a second term.

Another example of Kenny's decisiveness was his decision in April 2004 to sack the young Waterford TD John Deasy, the party's Justice spokesman, from the front bench after he smoked in the Dáil bar, defying the recently introduced ban on smoking in pubs and restaurants. It was a difficult decision for Kenny, who had been a good friend of Deasy's father, Austin, and by doing it he made a political enemy for life.[14]

Boosted by the local and European election results, Kenny and his close advisers decided to get the best international advice on electoral strategy. Hogan and Kennelly went as observers to the Democratic Party convention in Philadelphia in 2004 with the specific intention of sounding out the Washington political consultants Greenberg Quinlan Rosner, who had helped Bill Clinton win two presidential elections. A deal was concluded and GQR provided critical election planning advice to Fine Gael for more than a decade, sending a team to Ireland to analyse and interpret focus group and polling research and advise on messaging. The contribution of the Americans was not widely known but it proved vital to the party's electoral prospects.

The outcome of the local and European elections prompted a belief in Fine Gael and the Labour Party that the government could be vulnerable if a clear alternative was put before the electorate. In early September Kenny and Rabbitte met in Mullingar, ostensibly to discuss a pact between the two parties on Westmeath County Council; in fact they used it as a launching-pad to announce that they would 'do whatever it takes' to agree a joint platform to put before the people at the next election. They didn't specify any policy details, but the 'Mullingar Accord', as it came to be known, locked the two parties together in an alliance to oust the Fianna Fáil-PD government.[15]

Contests that could not be avoided were two by-elections in early 2005. One was to fill a vacancy in Meath created by the appointment of John Bruton as EU ambassador to the United States; the other was in Kildare North to replace the Minister for Finance, Charlie McCreevy, who had been appointed Ireland's new European Commissioner. Fine Gael comfortably held the seat in Meath with a strong showing by Shane McEntee, and while the party didn't win in Kildare the performance was respectable.

McCreevy's departure and his replacement by Brian Cowen heralded a more relaxed approach to the public finances by Bertie Ahern's government, which would have devastating consequences for the economy in the long term.

A political bombshell was dropped in the autumn of 2006 when Colm Keena of the *Irish Times* disclosed that the Mahon Tribunal on planning corruption had uncovered an unexplained payment of between €50,000 and €100,000 to Bertie Ahern.[16] While the revelation generated a political and media storm it had little or no impact on public opinion. After first challenging the report, Ahern did a long interview on RTÉ's Six One News with Bryan Dobson. In a typically humble and effective performance he explained that the money was a 'dig out' from a number of friends at the time of his separation from his wife. There were a number of contradictions in his story, particularly in relation to a payment for speaking at a dinner in Manchester organised by a bus company owner, Michael Wall. Yet, to the astonishment of the political world, support for Ahern and Fianna Fáil actually increased in the wake of the disclosures.

Fine Gael's efforts to capitalise on the mounting evidence of low standards in high places proved futile. At the party's presidential dinner in the Burlington Hotel on 14 October, Phil Hogan attempted to stir up enthusiasm by saying that a new prize of a dinner for twenty-five had been added to the members' draw. 'But you must be good pals with the people in the room, deal only in cash and have no bank account,' he said, to general hilarity. Kenny tried to put the focus on the prospect of an alternative government by referring to Mayo's defeat in the all-Ireland final a few weeks earlier, saying: 'But the next Mayo team that will take the field, Pat Rabbitte and myself, will not lie down.'[17] He got a standing ovation from the party faithful, but it was an uphill battle to convince the public that Fine Gael could lead a credible alternative government.

The party's Finance spokesman, Richard Bruton, had been warning about two important threats to the sustainability of the Celtic Tiger. One was the benchmarking deal which provided significant increases in pay for public servants without any serious evidence that public-service pay was lower than equivalent pay in the private sector; the other, even more important issue was the increasing dependence of the economy on a construction boom fuelled by ever-increasing bank lending. Bruton argued in the Dáil day in and day out that this simply couldn't last, but his warnings were widely ignored. There was little public appetite for the argument that the boom was unsustainable, so instead Fine Gael focused its attacks on the shortcomings in public services, particularly health.

When the election finally came in 2007 Ahern asked the President to dissolve the Dáil in a bizarre fashion. He went to Áras an Uachtaráin shortly after 7 a.m. on Sunday 29 April, as the President was due to fly out to the United States later the same day. Probably more to the point, the Mahon Tribunal was due to make an opening statement about his finances the following day. That statement was postponed once the election was called. Nonetheless, Ahern's personal finances were a major issue for the opposition and the media in the opening weeks of the campaign. The PDs debated pulling out of government but baulked at the last moment, demanding instead that Ahern make a statement about his finances, which he duly did.

Kenny launched his campaign amid great fanfare, predicting that Fine Gael would get 29 per cent of the vote. He claimed the ten years of Fianna Fáil-Progressive Democrat broken promises was over. 'It's time for a government that keeps its word and delivers the public services that people need and deserve. That's why I am offering a "Contract for a Better Ireland". That's why I am putting my own neck on the line to show how serious I am about delivering it.'[18] The gimmick of a contract with the people to provide better public services was lifted from the US Republican Party's successful congressional campaign in 1994, adapted to Irish conditions by the American political consultants GQR, with commitments on more hospital beds, free GP visits for children under five and 2,000 more gardaí. The director of elections was Phil Hogan, who knew every constituency backwards, while GQR advised on focus group research and the election messaging.

To reinforce the message, on the day the election was called two of the party's young Dublin candidates, Paschal Donohoe and Lucinda Creighton, led a group of supporters to Government Buildings, where they unfurled a banner with a giant P45 form, sacking Ahern and his government. The main thrust of the Fine Gael campaign was on the shortcomings of the health service and on questioning the source of Ahern's personal finances. While early warning signs were beginning to emerge that the Celtic Tiger economy was heading for trouble, all the parties competed with each other to offer tax cuts and more spending to an electorate that didn't want to hear that the good times might be coming to an end.

Kenny set off on a tour of the country, doing what he was good at: meeting people, shaking hands, kissing babies and making rousing speeches. He was photographed again and again punching the air as he ran from one event to the next, apparently inexhaustible. There was an air of confidence about the Fine Gael campaign that inspired party workers to believe that big inroads were possible into the fifty-seat lead held by Fianna Fáil. By contrast, the Fianna Fáil campaign was on the back foot in the early stages as journalists demanded answers, and failed to get them, from Ahern about the source of the money he had accumulated during his time as Minister for Finance. Ahern, with a little help from his friends Ian Paisley, Tony Blair and Bill Clinton, managed to successfully shift the focus from the grubby details of his personal finances to his role as an international statesman. He travelled to Belfast for a photocall with Paisley and Martin McGuinness to mark the restoration of power-sharing in Northern Ireland; a few days later he followed this by welcoming Paisley to the site of the Battle of the Boyne in Co. Louth. Best of all, he addressed the joint Houses of Parliament in London at the invitation of Blair. To cap it all, the Fianna Fáil party-political broadcast contained tributes to Ahern from Clinton, Blair and the former chairperson of the peace talks, George Mitchell.

Then, in the final week, Fianna Fáil launched a strong counter-attack, spearheaded by Brian Cowen, which cast doubt on Fine Gael's capacity to manage the economy. That was ironic in the light of what was to come but was effective in May 2007 as people began to worry that the boom might be under threat.

A sinister development was the emergence of a dirty tricks campaign designed to damage Kenny and Flannery. 'Fianna Fáil was clinging to power and it was willing to throw whatever mud was necessary to discredit it opponents,' was the verdict of the journalist Kevin Rafter. Allegations of financial impropriety against Flannery during his management of Rehab were quickly shown to be baseless. A laughable but salacious rumour designed to damage Kenny was touted to journalists. 'Having consulted with Kenny the Fine Gael team decided not to engage with the subject – no comment would be provided – and considerable work was required to convince some newspapers that not only was the rumour totally untrue but that publication of a denial would play into the hands of those who were orchestrating what increasingly looked like an organised smear campaign.'[19]

The televised leaders' debate on 17 May came, in retrospect, to be regarded as the turning-point in the campaign. Kenny looked calm and did reasonably well for the first half of the debate, but over the hour and a half Ahern was able to call on his experience of office to convey an air of authority on most of the major issues. 'On the night Ahern came across as the more competent, the more informed, the more controlled,' was the assessment of the MRBI pollster Damian Loscher. 'Kenny scored points with his composure and enthusiasm but did not succeed in convincing voters he had all the answers.'[20]

The final campaign poll, published four days before the election, showed a decisive swing to Fianna Fáil and a drop in support for both Fine Gael and the Labour Party. Suddenly, after all the optimism and hype, it dawned on people in Fine Gael that the prospect of power was slipping from their grasp. Kenny and his team battled on to the end and came within touching distance of victory but just fell short. With 27 per cent of the vote the party won 51 seats, a gain of 20, which was no mean achievement, but Labour remained stuck on 20 while the Greens got six and Sinn Féin won four. Fianna Fáil, with 78 seats, was in pole position to return to office.

Some people in Fine Gael did not immediately give up on the prospect of power and there were suggestions of overtures to the Green Party about sounding out the prospect of Sinn Féin's support for an alternative government. The Green Party leader, Trevor Sargent, claimed two years later that Kenny had asked him to establish whether Sinn Féin would vote for him as Taoiseach. This was furiously denied by Kenny, who said, 'Can you imagine anything so ludicrous as the leader of a party asking the leader of another party to contact the leader of another party?'[21] Whatever happened, nothing came of it. The Green Party chose to make a coalition deal with Fianna Fáil, and Bertie Ahern was Taoiseach for the third time in a row.

There was deep disappointment in Fine Gael that, although the party had come so far since the desperate days of 2002, it had fallen just a bit short. Although not apparent at the time, it was an extremely lucky escape. The economy was about to crash in spectacular fashion, and if ever there was an election to lose, the 2007 one was it. Of course Kenny didn't know that but his natural optimism quickly reasserted itself. On the day that Bertie Ahern was elected Taoiseach, Kenny told Lise Hand of the *Irish Independent*: 'There's 100 weeks to the local elections and we're already working on that. We are going after specific issues and we'll be ready. Anyway, anything could happen with this government.'[22]

One of the things Fine Gael had going for it in the wake of the 2007 general election was a much stronger parliamentary party. Party stalwarts such as Alan Shatter, Charlie Flanagan and Brian Hayes who had lost their seats in 2002 were back in the Dáil, and so were a crop of talented new TDs, including Leo Varadkar, Lucinda Creighton, James Reilly and Catherine Byrne. The party was in far better shape than it had been for a long time; but it was still in opposition.

It did not take long for things to look up for Fine Gael as Ahern found himself mired in the Mahon Tribunal's investigations into his personal finances. More importantly, the bill for the profligacy of the Celtic Tiger years was about to come in. A year after his three-in-a-row election victory, Ahern was forced to step down as Fianna Fáil leader and Taoiseach in May 2008 because of the embarrassing revelations at the tribunal. He was replaced by Brian Cowen just as the warning signs of the impending financial crash could no longer be missed. Cowen suffered an immediate setback a month later with the defeat of the referendum on the EU Lisbon Treaty, and from then onwards it was downhill all the way for him and his government.

Shortly after the referendum defeat it became clear that the public finances were heading for trouble in 2008 with a sharp decline in tax revenue. On top of that an unprecedented banking crisis began to unfold, leaving the new Minister for Finance, Brian Lenihan, appointed in May 2008, facing a truly appalling vista. Lenihan joked shortly after taking up his appointment that he had the 'misfortune' to become Minister for Finance just as the building boom came to 'a shuddering end'.[23] The media criticised him for an alleged gaffe, but he never spoke a truer word.

His efforts to deal with the collapse that followed the boom of the Celtic Tiger years saw the government's popularity plummet. Tough budget decisions, the blanket bank guarantee and the subsequent bailout, the establishment of the National Asset Management Agency and a precipitous slide in tax revenue combined to make the government the most unpopular in the history of the state.

Fine Gael began to gain ground and even passed out Fianna Fáil for the first time in an *Irish Times* opinion poll in November 2008. With 34 per cent support, as against 27 per cent for the main government party, a transformation of Irish politics was on the cards. However, there was one worrying note in the poll. In satisfaction ratings Kenny had fallen behind the new Labour leader, Eamon Gilmore, and he was barely ahead of Cowen. That became an even bigger worry with the first poll of 2009, which showed Fine Gael holding on to its status as the biggest party, with 32 per cent, but there was a massive surge for Labour, which was now on 24 per cent, two points ahead of Fianna Fáil. What was really notable was that Gilmore was now the most popular party leader, with a 44 per cent satisfaction rating, far ahead of Kenny on 30 per cent.[24]

With the local and European elections looming in May there was no time for distraction by polls. As in 2004, the party hierarchy had put a huge effort into finding new local election candidates and selecting the strongest team for the European contest. The local elections were an unqualified success. For the first time ever, Fine Gael won more council seats than Fianna Fáil, with a total of 340 around the country and a bevy of potential Dáil candidates among them. The European Parliament election also went well, although the number of seats had been reduced by one to 12. Fine Gael dropped a seat because of this, but it was still the biggest party, with four seats.

The headline-grabbing story of the day was the victory of George Lee, the prominent RTÉ economics correspondent, who stood as Fine Gael candidate in the Dublin South by-election caused by the death of Séamus Brennan. Lee had been persuaded by Frank Flannery and Tom Curran that he could make a contribution to sorting out the financial crisis by becoming involved in national politics. His electoral performance was stunning: he won 27,768 first-preference votes, which was more than 50 per cent of the total poll. To put the performance in context, it was almost twice the share that Fine Gael's three candidates had obtained between them in the general election two years earlier.

An *Irish Independent* headline the following Monday illustrated just how far Fine Gael had come under Enda Kenny and just how much the media view of him had remained the same. 'Why Taoiseach Enda Kenny doesn't sound so funny,' read the grudging headline describing his latest electoral success.[25]

As the financial crisis deepened and the Fianna Fáil government's ratings sank to record low levels over the following twelve months it should have been plain sailing for Fine Gael; but all the party's old failings came back to haunt it. TDs became jittery as Flannery and Hogan imposed strong new running-mates in a number of constituencies as part of a strategy aimed at winning seventy seats. Opinion polls showed Fine Gael doing well but with Labour breathing down its neck and Kenny trailing far behind Gilmore in popularity.

Gilmore had become the strongest critic of the government in the Dáil, going so far as accusing Brian Cowen of 'economic treason'. At its annual conference in the autumn of 2009 Labour started a campaign with the slogan 'Gilmore for Taoiseach', and a number of Fine Gael TDs began to panic that they were seeing a rerun of 1992, when Dick Spring eclipsed John Bruton and Fine Gael was left isolated. Gilmore's role in forcing John O'Donoghue to step down as Ceann Comhairle following disclosures about expensive foreign trips fuelled that fear.

Kenny made an effort to recover ground in October 2009 with a speech to the Fine Gael presidential dinner in which he called for sweeping reform of political institutions, including a reduction in the number of TDs, pay cuts for ministers and the abolition of the Seanad. The proposals came like a bolt from the blue to the senators at the function, including the leader of the Seanad, Frances Fitzgerald. A number of them expressed their disquiet in public and pointed out that Kenny had made proposals for reforming the Seanad only six months before. Privately a number of them said his speech was designed as a distraction from another opinion poll showing Labour closing in on Fine Gael which was published in the Sunday papers that weekend.[26]

Things became worse for Kenny in early 2010 with the shock decision of George Lee to resign his Dáil seat and return to RTÉ. He said he was disillusioned by the fact that he had no input into Fine Gael policy and had been 'frozen out' by the party's Finance spokesman, Richard Bruton. It had become apparent in Leinster House that Lee, who had been a star turn on the RTÉ news for more than a decade, was having difficulty adapting to life as an opposition backbencher, but his decision to abandon politics only eight months after his extraordinary by-election victory was a serious blow to Fine Gael. The move led to furious speculation that a leadership heave was on the way.[27]

It was not long in coming, and the catalyst, as in the Bruton era, was a poor opinion poll in the *Irish Times*. It showed Fine Gael down four points to 28 per cent and Fianna Fáil down to 17 per cent; but the startling news was that Labour, up eight points to 32 per cent, was now the most popular party in the state, for the first time in its history. To make matters worse, Kenny's satisfaction rating had plunged to a measly 24 per cent, while Gilmore was far ahead on 46 per cent.[28]

Kenny was made aware of the poll findings during a parliamentary party meeting and proceeded to read them out to the stunned TDs and senators, who greeted the news with a deathly silence.[29] The poll was the first item on the RTÉ television news at 9 p.m. and on the *Prime Time* programme that followed. The party's deputy leader, Richard Bruton, who was appearing to speak about the financial crisis, was asked about Kenny's leadership. 'I'm just as much in the dock in terms of Fine Gael's failings,' he conceded, but he declined to express confidence in his party leader. This was a decisive change in Bruton's attitude. For the previous year or more he had been encouraged by a group of TDs, most notably Brian Hayes, Billy Timmins and Lucinda Creighton, to lead a revolt against Kenny. Bruton resisted their blandishments, not simply because he genuinely liked and respected Kenny but because he thought a split was the last thing the party needed when it was on the verge of power.

In the fraught atmosphere following the poll it quickly became clear that there was going to be a heave one way or another and if Bruton wouldn't lead it somebody else would. One TD recalled: 'I began to get calls from constituents saying "What is wrong with Fine Gael," or "When are you going to get rid of Kenny".[30] Ironically, on the day before the poll was published Kenny had put down a motion of no confidence in the Taoiseach, Brian Cowen, which was due to be debated in the Dáil the following Tuesday and Wednesday. That quickly became irrelevant, as Fine Gael TDs and senators were preoccupied with the plot to remove Kenny. There were conflicting signals from some TDs. Leo Varadkar initially declared that the party would not change its leader on the strength of one poll, but he then remained silent before emerging as a rebel a few days later. The plotters were convinced they had a majority of the parliamentary party on their side, and they gave extensive media briefings over the weekend, making no bones about their plan to remove the leader the following week.

As these briefings were going on, Kenny and Bruton had a number of phone conversations, beginning on Saturday 12 June. Kenny tried to convince Bruton not to instigate a leadership heave and asked him for a public declaration of confidence. Bruton demurred, and they agreed to talk the following day. Kenny drove from Castlebar on the Sunday morning and met his deputy leader in head office, but Bruton again refused to express confidence in his leader and suggested instead that Kenny should stand down to avert a crisis in the party.

The following morning the *Irish Independent* had a banner headline, 'Bruton tells Kenny: I have lost confidence in you', over a report by its political editor, Fionnán Sheahan, on the leadership crisis.[31] The two men had another fruitless conversation that morning, but in the afternoon Kenny rang Bruton and sacked him as deputy leader. He then rang the chairman of the parliamentary party, Pádraic McCormack, in Galway to say he wanted to table a motion of confidence in himself.

McCormack called a meeting of the parliamentary party for the following Thursday. Kenny issued a statement saying he had sacked the deputy leader, describing the move as 'very regrettable and very disappointing'.[32] Bruton, now in open revolt, declared himself confident that he had enough support in the parliamentary party to defeat Kenny. 'I believe he does not have the capacity to deal with the difficult problems the country faces,' he said.[33]

Although it soon became clear that at least half the front bench was against him, Kenny still had some powerful weapons in his armoury. Phil Hogan, with whom there had been some coolness because of his failure to bring in a running-mate in Kilkenny in 2007, had rallied to his leader immediately and had been canvassing support and calculating the numbers over the weekend. Nobody better knew the entire membership of the parliamentary party and the best way to influence each of them. Kenny's other principal defender was the chief whip, Paul Kehoe from Wexford. As the anti-Kenny faction took the media spotlight, Hogan and Kehoe began working on the backbenchers and the senators to drum up support. In all there were seventy members of the parliamentary party – fifty-one TDs, fifteen senators and four MEPs – and they all had an equal vote.

There was huge publicity surrounding a supposedly secret meeting of the senior rebels in the Green Isle Hotel on the morning of Tuesday 15 June on their way to Leinster House for the weekly front-bench meeting. Bruton, Hayes, Varadkar, Timmins, Mitchell, Creed, Naughten and Fergus O'Dowd were in the hotel, and they were joined on speakerphone by Coveney and Olwyn Enright. The plan was that they would all speak at the front-bench meeting and present Kenny with an ultimatum: either he resigned or the majority of his front bench would. The rebels were absolutely confident that there was no way he could survive the loss of virtually the entire officer corps of the party.

However, they seriously underestimated their man. When the front-bench meeting began the plan was that each of the rebels would tell Kenny why he was no longer fit to lead. Instead, as soon as Mark Kennelly had read the minutes of the previous meeting Kenny launched into a speech giving the rebels a tongue-lashing. 'I have never seen Enda so angry as he was at that meeting,' said one of those present. He accused his opponents of treachery by going to the newspapers to outline their concerns instead of coming directly to him. He finished by saying he was standing down the entire front bench and would be picking a new one the following week. If any of them wanted to speak to him in private they could do so in his office, and he then adjourned the meeting and walked out.

The rebels were furious, and Creed and a number of others called on Kenny to stay, but he brushed past them and marched down the corridor to his own office. Timmins ran after him, and a short, furious argument ensued in Kenny's office. The other rebels stayed in the room for about twenty minutes in amazement before adjourning to Olwyn Enright's office to consider their tactics.

What appeared to be particularly galling to Kenny was that Timmins, Naughten, Enright and Creed were children of TDs he had been personally close to as a young man. He found their involvement in the conspiracy much harder to forgive than that of people such as Varadkar and Coveney, with whom he never had close personal ties.

Eventually the shocked rebels marched out onto the plinth in Leinster House and posed before the assembled media. The spokesman for the group, Denis Naughten, said they had hoped that Kenny would stand down, as a contest would be extremely damaging for the party. Asked if it was not the wrong time to move against the leader, he replied: 'There is no wrong time to make the right decision.'[34] The rebels put on a brave face but they had clearly been stunned by the turn of events. Miriam Lord summed it up.

> Downed by their own presumption the Green Isle Nine were left reeling. The received wisdom had it that Baby Bruton only had to say the word and Inda would be toast. But it didn't happen that way. When their quarry had the temerity to fight back Richard's rebels nearly died of shock. That wasn't in the game plan.[35]

Chairman Pádraic McCormack observed some years later: 'It was very naive of those members of the front bench to expose the exploits of the pro-Bruton group as it gave Kenny and his backers forewarning and time to plot another course of action.'[36]

The rebels were thrown into further confusion by suspicions that they had a spy in their camp. This probably arose from a bit of eavesdropping by one of Kenny's supporters, who overheard Timmins in conversation with Varadkar saying, 'Leo, you will have to go on air to counteract Hogan.' Later in the Dáil chamber Hogan approached Timmins and said, 'I hear you are going to get Leo to counteract me.' This led the rebels to suspect each other of leaking and diverted their attention from canvassing support. Some of them blamed Coveney as the leaker, much to his consternation. 'I know Coveney took this very badly,' wrote McCormack. 'I often met him at his office which was adjacent to mine on the second floor. He was very upset all day Tuesday. The result of this incident meant the Bruton backers were now arguing among themselves.'[37]

In one of the most bizarre political scenes anybody could remember, Kenny addressed the Dáil that same evening on a motion of no confidence in Brian Cowen. He was flanked by his new interim deputy leader, James Reilly, while his former deputy leader of eight years, Richard Bruton, sat on the back benches along with his sacked colleagues. 'It was extraordinary that Kenny was speaking on a motion of no confidence in the Taoiseach while at the same time he had to table a motion of confidence in himself to try and save his own leadership,' the party chairman observed.[38]

The next day, however, there was another dramatic twist, which seemed to turn the tide back against Kenny. Twenty-four hours before the critical leadership vote the Limerick TD Kieran O'Donnell, who had been promoted only the day before to replace Bruton as the party's acting Finance spokesman, announced that he was voting against Kenny. As if that was not bad enough, the party Justice spokesman, Charlie Flanagan, who had stayed aloof from the plot, went to Kenny's office to tell him he could not vote confidence in him. Kenny calmly responded by telling Flanagan he was making a big mistake as he (Kenny) was going to win. The defection of two high-profile frontbenchers the day before the vote created a media sensation, but Kenny remained confident.

At this stage Hogan was in overdrive, canvassing almost every member of the parliamentary party, using inducements or threats, whichever he felt was more appropriate to the individual case. One of his arguments to backbenchers and senators was to ask if they were going to let the 'posh boys', such as Bruton, Coveney and Varadkar, who had attended private schools, dictate to the ordinary Fine Gael politicians who was or was not fit to be leader. It was a crude argument but it got some support. The plotters found it hard to believe that the party's senators would not come out against Kenny as a bloc, given his pledge to abolish the second house. In fact the opposite happened, largely thanks to Hogan's closeness with senators such as Paddy Burke, Paul Coghlan and Jerry Buttimer, whom he persuaded to back their leader.

At the height of the campaign Varadkar went on television to announce that if Kenny stood down he would still have a future in the front ranks for Fine Gael, possibly as Minister for Foreign Affairs. This had the effect of 'consolidating support for Kenny from backbenchers who resented the newer upstarts on the front bench,' according to McCormack. Another, less dramatic but probably more telling television appearance was made by the Kenny loyalist Jimmy Deenihan of Kerry. Asked how the party could recover from the loss of two Finance spokesmen in forty-eight hours, Deenihan said it would be no problem, as they had an ideal replacement in Michael Noonan.

This was a significant intervention, because Noonan had become a pivotal figure. Over the preceding year or so he had frequently joined the discontented front-bench members, such as Creighton, Creed, Deasy and Varadkar, for chats in the Dáil members' bar. While Noonan didn't openly encourage revolt, the rebels believed they had his support, but now he was suddenly being touted by Deenihan as Kenny's saviour. What nobody knew was that at an early stage in the heave he had a long conversation with Kenny, who was confident of his support.[39]

Noonan avoided any comment on the rift in the party, saying that as a former leader it would be inappropriate for him to get involved. 'I know how I'm voting,' he informed inquiring journalists. 'I'm just not telling anyone.'[40] One way or another the heave provided him with an opportunity to revive his political career. If Bruton won he would almost certainly be back on the front bench, while the clear signal from Deenihan was that if Kenny won he would be back as Finance spokesman and in pole position to be the next Minister for Finance.

Kenny did not personally canvass support but was kept in close touch with how things were going by Hogan and Kehoe. At no stage did they think there was any real prospect of their leader losing. The evening before the vote Phil Hogan led more than twenty members of the parliamentary party onto the plinth in Leinster House in a public display of support for Kenny. 'We want to make sure there is a decisive majority to strengthen his position,' said the bullish Hogan. His breezy confidence began to shake morale in the Bruton camp. There was also word from the Kenny camp that if he was ousted there would be a contest for the leadership. This would have to take place under new rules, which involved the entire party membership and the councillors in the process and would take at least a month, if not two. The prospect of a divisive, long-drawn-out leadership election at a time when the government was on the ropes was a nightmare scenario for the party.

At the crucial meeting on 17 June, which lasted for a little over three hours, forty-six members of the parliamentary party spoke. Kenny wound up the debate with a twenty-minute speech in which he trenchantly defended his record and attacked some of the speakers who had criticised his leadership style. Varadkar was among those singled out for special mention. His supporters loved it, but there was some shock in the Bruton camp at his vehemence. 'Some thought he went too far,' McCormack observed, but with his political life at stake Kenny went for broke.[41]

After that the TDs, senators and MEPs cast their votes in a booth at the back of the room. McCormack and the secretary of the parliamentary party, Senator Paschal Donohoe, counted the ballot papers. When that was done McCormack announced the result. The vote of confidence in Kenny had been carried, but in accordance with an agreement at the beginning of the meeting no figures were disclosed.

When McCormack went out onto the plinth there was a roar of 'Up Mayo!' from a crowd of Kenny supporters who had travelled up to give moral support to their leader. They were quickly shushed by Fine

Gael officials concerned that they would feed the media narrative of a party run by a 'country and western' wing. They needn't have worried, as Kenny's resilience and fighting spirit had impressed most observers, and it was his opponents who came in for ridicule. 'It's the defeat of the cappuccino generation by the men who eat their dinner in the middle of the day,' wrote Miriam Lord approvingly, quoting one long-serving TD. 'Kenny's response to adversity may or may not improve his public image but it has certainly demonstrated that he has the qualities necessary to serve as Taoiseach,' was the assessment of one commentator.[42]

When the exuberance of his supporters died down Kenny came out onto the plinth, flanked by Hogan and Kehoe. Declaring himself thrilled and relieved, he said, 'For me this is the end of the tensions that were building up. We move on from here, a united party.' Bruton, putting a brave face on it, came out and shook hands with Kenny in front of the photographers. 'The issue has been resolved. I think Enda has demonstrated his resilience,' he remarked. 'There will be no vindictiveness,' Kenny maintained.[43]

That commitment was honoured, up to a point, when he announced his new front bench two weeks later. Noonan returned to the national stage as spokesman on Finance as Kenny shrewdly put past slights behind him and decided that Noonan was the best person for the job. He also showed both magnanimity and wisdom by appointing his challenger to a senior economic post as Enterprise spokesman. Kenny didn't hold a grudge against Bruton for the heave, believing he had been forced into it by hot-headed younger colleagues. Other leading rebels, Coveney, O'Dowd, Flanagan and Varadkar, were also appointed.

However, Naughten, Timmins, Creed, Enright, Hayes and Olivia Mitchell were dropped. James Reilly was confirmed as the new deputy leader, while such prominent Kenny supporters as Hogan and Deenihan were back in senior roles. Alan Shatter, who had clashed with Kenny in the past, was rewarded for his loyalty on this occasion by being given Justice.

When the Dáil returned in the autumn, attention was no longer on Fine Gael but on the steadily worsening financial crisis, which threatened to wreck the economy as the government began working on a four-year recovery plan in conjunction with the European Commission.[44] The Commissioner for Economic and Monetary Affairs, Olli Rehn, visited Dublin in November 2010 to try to soften up public opinion and the opposition to accept the necessity for the plan. By that stage, though, events were spinning out of control. The international money markets lost confidence in the ability of the Irish state to repay the enormous sums being swallowed up by the banking bailout. Strong pressure was applied by the European Central Bank on the government to accept a bailout from the European institutions and the International Monetary Fund.

The government's handling of the episode destroyed whatever remaining credibility it had. Negotiations on the terms of a bailout began even as ministers protested that media reports on the issue were 'fiction'. On top of the ignominy involved in the loss of sovereignty from entering the EU-IMF programme the government had to contend with opposition taunts that it had lied to the public. It was a political and economic shambles, and the Green Party had had enough. On 22 November the party leader, John Gormley, announced that they would withdraw from government once the budget and the Finance Bill had been passed.

That objective was achieved, but the government's days were numbered. Cowen survived a leadership challenge from Micheál Martin early in the new year but he resigned as party leader shortly afterwards and called a general election for 22 February. He remained on as Taoiseach while Martin replaced him as party leader.

For Enda Kenny and Fine Gael the general election of February 2011 could not have come at a better moment. The scale of the financial crash, the national humiliation represented by the EU-IMF bailout and the shambolic disintegration of the Fianna Fáil-Green Party government over the previous few months left the main opposition party in a position of strength beyond the wildest dreams of its supporters. The only question was whether it would be able to seize the opportunity fully or whether others might seize the prize from its grasp.

Labour was also geared up to take advantage of Fianna Fáil's weakness, as were Sinn Féin, smaller left-wing parties and a raft of independents. 'We are feasting over the carcass of Fianna Fáil,' remarked Brian Hayes in the middle of the campaign. 'This isn't an election between us and Fianna Fáil. It is between Fine Gael and Labour.'[45]

A party strategist recalls the mood in Fine Gael at the start of the campaign. 'Fianna Fáil was crumbling before our eyes and Labour was our main competitor. The issue was whether the voters would opt for Labour, which had effectively articulated the public anger over the previous two years, or for Fine Gael, which was offering a path out of the morass.'

This time around, in contrast to so many previous occasions in its history, Fine Gael was fully prepared and eager for the fray. The director of elections, Phil Hogan, chief election strategist, Frank Flannery, general secretary, Tom Curran, and volunteer election specialist Mark Mortell had prepared a detailed campaign strategy that left nothing to chance, either in regard to the party programme or the selection of candidates. The American consultants GQR had analysed the focus group research conducted by the polling company Amárach and devised a detailed plan for how the party's election message should be delivered.

Fine Gael kicked off its formal campaign with a five-point plan that promised voters a path to economic recovery, even if it was vague on the details. The tactic worked like a dream and Enda Kenny became the star of the election campaign as he stuck to the five-point plan and refused to be drawn into detailed arguments about future economic policy. He was dubbed the 'Val Doonican of Irish politics' because he was suddenly a popular and respected national figure after thirty-five years in the business. He set off once again on a marathon tour of the country, doing what he did best: meeting voters in towns and villages in every constituency and promising that his party's blueprint for economic recovery was going to work.

Kenny had the confidence to dictate the timing of the television debates, which were his perceived weakness. He refused to take part in a debate on TV3, saying bluntly, 'I will not participate in any programme that Vincent Browne has anything to do with.'[46] Relations between the two had never been good, but a few months earlier Browne had pushed things to the limit by saying on TV3 that Kenny should be sent to a darkened room with a bottle of whiskey and a revolver. He later apologised for the insult, but Kenny flatly refused to have anything to do with his election debate. The decision generated a lot of negative media comment but had no impact on public opinion.

Kenny willingly agreed to participate in the first three-way debate in Irish on TG4 with Eamon Gilmore and Micheál Martin and then in a five-way debate involving the smaller parties before the final three-way debate in English on RTÉ. Debating had always been his weak point, but he performed competently in all of them, to the relief of his supporters.

The Labour campaign didn't catch fire to the same extent. While Gilmore had articulated the anger of voters over the previous two years, Labour was not as convincing about charting a way out of the mess. Gilmore also made an error early on that raised questions about his political judgement. He maintained at a press conference that the election was about whether the country's budget would be decided by the European Central Bank in Frankfurt or by the democratically elected government of the Irish people. 'It's Frankfurt's way or Labour's way,' Gilmore declared. He went on to describe the chairman of the ECB, Jean-Claude Trichet, as 'a mere civil servant'.[47]

Miriam Lord commented that Fine Gael tapped in to the public mood for policies and direction, and the fact that its five-point plan was delivered with 'brain-deadening monotony' didn't matter. 'Enda Kenny plugged it relentlessly, saying it would give "light, clarity and direction to what will be a difficult journey to a better future ahead". And the people bought it. In time, they bought into Enda Kenny too.'[48] In a clever ploy, Hogan called on Fianna Fáil supporters to lend Fine Gael their vote just for this election to ensure that there would be a competent government in place.

At the beginning of the campaign there was a widespread assumption that when it was all over the old firm of Fine Gael and Labour would be back in coalition. However, as the campaign drew to a close the polls indicated that the impossible dream was on the cards: Fine Gael had a chance of winning an overall majority as Fianna Fáil voters responded to Hogan's appeal.

In the event the surge to Fine Gael was halted in the final days of the campaign by a strong counter-attack from Labour. In a national campaign with the slogan 'Every little hurts' (a parody of the Tesco advertising slogan 'Every little helps') Labour described a series of actions that it claimed Fine Gael would implement to cope with the financial crisis if it won an overall majority. These included water charges, increases in VAT and DIRT and a euro extra on a bottle of wine. The campaign was successful in halting the swing to Fine Gael, but in the long run it became a millstone around Labour's neck, as the government in which it was a partner implemented virtually all the cuts it had promised to prevent Fine Gael introducing.

Even though it lost momentum in the final days of the campaign, Fine Gael won 36 per cent of the vote and 76 seats in the 166-member Dáil. The outcome was far better than the party strategists had dared to hope at the beginning of the campaign, when a target of 60 seats was set, purposely on the low side. For the first time since 1927 it was the biggest party in the Dáil. The director of elections, Phil Hogan, masterminded a daring strategy that eked out a massive seat bonus and brought the party to within touching distance of an overall majority. With 76 seats Fine Gael had not only passed out Fianna Fáil, which came back with a paltry 20, but was more than twice the size of Labour, which also had a record election, winning 36 seats with 19 per cent of the vote. The icing on the cake as far as Fine Gael was concerned was winning four out of five seats in Kenny's own constituency of Mayo. In all the years of Fianna Fáil dominance it had never pulled off four out of five in any constituency, despite repeated attempts to do so.

Fine Gael celebrated its historic victory with a party in the Burlington Hotel on the night of Saturday 26 February as the final counts were coming in. The joy of party supporters was unbounded when Kenny arrived from Co. Mayo. There was hardly a dry eye in the hall when he began a short speech by saying that he had just received a phone call from the 91-year-old former Taoiseach Liam Cosgrave, who had said to him, 'I am an old man now but you have made me proud.'[49] Becoming the largest party in the Dáil was something nobody in Fine Gael had ever in their wildest dreams believed would happen and, for a night at least, made up for all the years of defeat and derision.

The scale of the electoral change that took place in February 2011 was truly astonishing. One of Ireland's leading political scientists, Peter Mair, later pointed out that the contest was not only one of the most volatile in Irish political history but was one of the most volatile elections in Europe since 1945. 'In fact, the Irish election emerges as the third most volatile in western Europe since 1945, being surpassed only by Italy in 1994, when the Christian Democrats and Socialists collapsed and Berlusconi's Forza Italia first came to power; and by the Netherlands in 2002, when Pim Fortuyn led the first Dutch populist revolt,' he wrote.[50]

What made the Irish result unique was that it did not involve a new party storming onto the scene, as happened in Italy and the Netherlands, but showed the electorate turning back to a party that last enjoyed dominance almost eighty years earlier.

It took some time for the scale of the changes to sink in. Fianna Fáil lost an astonishing 59 seats while Fine Gael gained 25 and the Labour Party gained 16. The Green Party lost all six seats while Sinn Féin gained 10 and independents 14. After decades in which little changed in the relative positions of the major parties, 2011 marked a shift to a more volatile series of elections.

14

ENDA KENNY IN GOVERNMENT

'Just as Collins was undeterred by the dire financial straits in which Ireland found itself in the 1920s, the government I lead is equally determined.'

— ENDA KENNY, SPEAKING AT THE ANNUAL BEALNABLATH
COMMEMORATION, 19 AUGUST 2012.

Enda Kenny and Fine Gael did not have a lot of time to enjoy their stunning election triumph. The new Dáil was scheduled to meet ten days later, and rapid decisions had to be made about the formation of a government. With seventy-six seats, Fine Gael had the option of attempting to form a minority government with the support of independents, but such an approach was never seriously considered. The dire state of the public finances convinced Kenny and his senior colleagues that the only option was to do a deal with Labour to provide a strong government that would be able to take the tough decisions required by the terms of the country's bailout. There was some resistance in Labour to going into government in such circumstances, but Eamon Gilmore and his leading frontbenchers were convinced that they should join a coalition to protect the interests of the most vulnerable in society from whatever cuts were coming down the line.

There was also some serious haggling over ministerial positions in the talks between the two parties. Kenny offered Labour five cabinet posts, but Gilmore wanted six. Labour also sought Finance, as had happened in the last coalition between the two parties, but Fine Gael insisted on holding the post this time. Both sides compromised in the end. The Department of Finance was divided, with Fine Gael taking responsibility for the revenue side and Labour for public expenditure. Labour had to settle for five cabinet ministers but got the right to appoint the Attorney General, which meant the party would have six seats at the cabinet table. The deal was ratified by both parliamentary parties on Sunday 6 March, a little over a week after the election, and Kenny and Gilmore posed for photographers in Herbert Park that afternoon.

When the 31st Dáil met on 10 March a jubilant Enda Kenny was elected Taoiseach, just nine months after surviving a leadership heave. The nomination was made by the youngest member of the Dáil, the 25-year-old Wicklow TD Simon Harris. When he got to his feet on 9 March 2011 he captured the emotion of the day, telling those present in the chamber and watching the coverage on television:

> Today is a moment in this country's history where we set about realising the hopes, dreams and aspirations of our people. Today, the period of mourning is over for Ireland. Today, we hang out our brightest colours and together, under Deputy Kenny's leadership, we move forward yet again as a nation. It is with pride, honour and delight that I propose to Dáil Éireann the election of Deputy Kenny as the next Taoiseach of this country.[1]

For those steeped in the Fine Gael tradition, Harris's speech carried a special message. 'Tear up your mourning and hang out your brightest colours' was a line from a letter written by George Bernard Shaw to the sister of Michael Collins on the day after Bealnablath. By invoking this phrase Harris was linking Kenny to the special place occupied by Collins in the party's pantheon of heroes. But it was also a warning that the task facing the new Taoiseach was of a similar magnitude: nothing less than saving the state from ruin.

In a reversal of fortune, W.T. Cosgrave had handed over the reins of government to Éamon de Valera on the same date, almost eighty years earlier. The change of power in 1932 was the beginning of Fianna Fáil's dominance. But with an overwhelming majority in 2011 the Fine Gael-Labour coalition comfortably elected Kenny Taoiseach by 117 votes to 27. 'It's the party's greatest day' was the consensus among Fine Gael supporters who thronged Leinster House for the occasion. Over the lifetime of the 31st Dáil, however, the Fine Gael-Labour coalition suffered defections and became embroiled in various controversies, while the party system became more competitive and the certainties of Irish politics seemed destined to disappear.[2]

Kenny's choices for his cabinet included Michael Noonan as Minister for Finance. It was a remarkable comeback for the party's former leader, and over the next few years he disproved Enoch Powell's assertion that 'all political careers end in failure' by leading the country out of the bailout and back to strong economic growth. Kenny also gave three of the leading rebels from the previous June important positions. Bruton got Jobs and Innovation, Coveney was given Agriculture and Marine, while Varadkar got Transport, Tourism and Sport.

Kenny's principal defenders were also rewarded. Hogan was given Environment, Shatter was given Justice, Deenihan was given Arts and Heritage and Paul Kehoe was appointed chief whip. Dr James Reilly was made deputy leader and Minister for Health. Frances Fitzgerald was the only Fine Gael woman to be appointed to the cabinet, and she was given responsibility for Children and Youth Affairs. The Labour ministers were Gilmore as Tánaiste and Minister for Foreign Affairs, Brendan Howlin in Public Expenditure, Joan Burton in Social Protection, Ruairí Quinn in Education and Pat Rabbitte in Communications, Energy and Natural Resources.

There was considerable criticism of the fact that there were only two women cabinet ministers out of fifteen, although the appointment of Máire Whelan as Attorney General meant there was another woman at the table. Kenny and Gilmore tried to make amends by appointing a number of women junior ministers. Among them was Lucinda Creighton, one of Kenny's most outspoken critics in opposition, who was given the critical post of Minister of State for European Affairs – a role in which she excelled.

Advocating the Shannon electrification scheme in the Dáil only two years after independence, Patrick McGilligan, Cumann na nGaedheal Minister for Industry and Commerce, said that without economic freedom political freedom meant very little.[3] With the collapse of the Irish economy from late 2007 his words had renewed meaning. On 21 November 2010 the Fianna Fáil-Green Party government requested financial assistance from the European Commission, European Central Bank and International Monetary Fund. The arrival of the Troika at the end of the month was marked with 'IMF out' scrawled on walls, while the *Irish Times* quoted W.B. Yeats and asked, 'Was it for this?' that the men of 1916 died.[4] Fianna Fáil and the Green Party stood accused of giving away Ireland's sovereignty.

This was the economic reality that Fine Gael and Labour inherited in 2011. The ferocity of the financial whirlwind meant there was no escaping the need for stringent control of the public finances. Fine Gael was better prepared for this than Labour, but the scale of the inevitable cuts in public spending was a shock to the leadership of both parties. Kenny confided to associates that within a year he expected there would be tens of thousands of people on the streets baying for his blood. 'Welcome to my world,' was the comment of the outgoing Minister for Finance, Brian Lenihan.[5]

The day after he was elected Taoiseach, Kenny was thrust into a European power play, the outcome of which was critical for the future of the Irish economy. He travelled to his first European Council meeting in Brussels to argue for a reduction in the interest rate the country was paying for the €67 billion bailout, knowing that some of the big EU states saw this as an opportunity to get rid of Ireland's low 12½ per cent corporate tax regime. The day before, the German Chancellor, Angela Merkel, had told her MPs at a closed-door meeting in Berlin that she would back a lower interest rate for Ireland only if Kenny agreed to a common corporate tax base for the euro region.

Arriving at the meeting, Kenny, who knew Merkel well from EPP gatherings over the previous ten years, kissed the smiling Chancellor on both cheeks, but their exchanges behind closed doors were frosty as she pressed the Taoiseach to agree to changes in the Irish corporate tax regime. If Merkel was cool the French president, Nicolas Sarkozy, was hotly intemperate in his exchanges with Kenny, at times verging on the abusive. 'It was an ambush; an inexcusable attempt to take advantage of the Taoiseach's inexperience and bully him into a massive concession,' said an official who attended the Council meeting. Kenny was not intimidated and stood his ground, saying he could not compromise on a fundamental aspect of Ireland's tax strategy, as it would be critical in the country's economic recovery.

Late on the second night of the meeting the president of the European Council, Herman Van Rompuy, called Kenny up to his office and presented him with a new draft of the presidency's conclusions, containing a paragraph that committed him to accepting changes in Ireland's corporate tax regime. Von Rumpuy adopted a conciliatory tone, telling Kenny that he had finessed the wording so that Ireland would be able to wriggle out of the commitment at a future date. He urged him to accept it so that the French and Germans would agree to the cut in the interest rate. Kenny still refused to budge, saying that he could not go home from his first Council meeting having conceded something that would be so damaging to his country. At this point Sarkozy and Merkel came into the room.

> They stood there waiting for the Taoiseach's answer. Von Rompuy looked up and said, 'He won't sign.' Merkel remarked that in that case Ireland would not get the interest rate reduction which had been agreed for Greece, and the two of them walked out of the room.[6]

Some of the Irish officials were dubious about taking such a hard line and felt that Kenny should have accepted an 'empty formula', in the great tradition of Irish politics, but he was having none of it.

At 2 a.m., not long after the meeting had ended, the Taoiseach gave a briefing to Irish journalists. 'It wasn't possible to reach a deal for Ireland this evening,' he calmly told them, although he did concede that there had been 'a good vigorous debate'. The media rightly declined to buy that version of events. Arthur Beesley wrote in the *Irish Times*: 'For new Taoiseach Enda Kenny it was a case of being thrown in at the deep end of European politics to face bruising head on encounters with Dr Merkel and French president Nicolas Sarkozy on a matter of huge strategic interest to Ireland. Greece accepted the offer but the terms were not on for Ireland as Mr Kenny rightly held the line.'[7]

The former government press secretary Feargal Purcell recalls the episode as a defining moment for Enda Kenny as Taoiseach. 'He was put under extreme pressure just days after taking office. Some of the Irish officials were for yielding but he just wouldn't contemplate it. It was the single most important decision he faced in office and was a huge moment for the government and Fine Gael.'[8] In time Ireland got a number of interest rate reductions as a reward for complying with the bailout terms, while Greece failed to implement the terms and lurched from one crisis to the next. But all that was in the future. Kenny had made his entrance on the international stage, and while he did not win any friends he established himself as a political leader to be reckoned with. Before the end of the year Merkel was praising Kenny for setting an 'outstanding example' of how to deal with the financial crisis, while Sarkozy declared that Ireland was already 'almost out of the crisis'.[9]

From Brussels he flew to Washington for the annual St Patrick's Day festivities in the White House and was back to his amiable breezy self as he sought to convince American business that Ireland was on the road to recovery. 'Enda Kenny's optimism was a vital ingredient in Ireland's recovery,' Brendan Halligan later remarked. 'People were going through a really tough time, but he lifted our spirits and convinced us that if we pulled together recovery was possible. The importance of that cannot be overstated.'[10]

The scale of the task that confronted Kenny and his government was truly staggering. The banks were ruined, unemployment was soaring and the rating agency Standard and Poor's reduced the Irish debt to junk status. While in Washington in June for the annual meeting of the International Monetary Fund, Noonan suggested that Ireland wanted senior bondholders for the broken Anglo Irish Bank to accept that they would not get all their money back. The European Central Bank immediately vetoed any such move. Leo Varadkar, who in opposition had been an advocate of burning bank bondholders, revealed some time later that the European Central Bank had warned that 'a financial bomb would go off in Dublin' if the bondholders were not repaid. Noonan was chastened by the experience, and any ambitions of 'burning' senior bondholders were abandoned, although some junior bondholders in the banks did take a cut.[11]

From the moment it entered office, the path forward had already been set for the coalition. The 2011 budget had been passed before the general election and was now coming into effect. Although framed by their predecessors, voters would associate the coalition partners with the terms.

The 2012 budget, unveiled in December 2011, was the first overseen by the new Minister for Finance. Michael Noonan was keen to prove that the government was committed to reducing the deficit, but his inclination to overshoot the target was resisted by Labour. Eventually a target of €3.8 billion was agreed. Of that, €2.2 billion would have to take the form of spending cuts, with €1.6 billion achieved through additional taxes. Two Labour TDs voted against the measures: Tommy Broughan, who had lost the party whip the previous week, and a very recent by-election winner, Patrick Nulty.

By the time the coalition came to power, with quarterly targets that could not be missed and a succession of severe budgets, there was a general perception that the Troika dictated policy. It was relatively flexible on methods, however, and officials attempted to work, when possible, within existing frameworks. Where it had reached an agreement with Brian Cowen's government to reduce the minimum wage, for example, it consented to reversing that decision when the coalition came to power, because Labour was opposed.[12] Nonetheless the public's perception of how the Troika worked was useful to the new government and was a convenient shield against criticism. As one Central Bank official commented, 'the Troika is used by the government to get things done.'[13] This included the sale of state assets.

While many of the measures taken by the government in the process of implementing the bailout terms generated controversy and protests, opinion polls showed strong support for the role of the Troika. A referendum on the EU Fiscal Treaty, which set down strict criteria for the supervision of national budgets in the future, was passed by a majority of 60 per cent in July 2012. There was considerable nervousness in the government at having to hold the referendum, but the outcome indicated that a clear majority of Irish voters were happy that the EU had taken such a decisive role in the Irish economy.

From the beginning Kenny was adamant that tackling unemployment was the priority of his government. When he took office, unemployment was 14.5 per cent of the work force, and it peaked the following February at 15.1 per cent, or over 400,000. In November 2011 Kenny, Gilmore and Richard Bruton announced a plan for jobs that included a wide range of ambitious targets and actions with time limits for each item. Monthly meetings were co-ordinated by the Department of the Taoiseach to ensure that the deadlines were met. Over the following four years the plan was more successful than anybody in the government had dared to hope, with unemployment falling to a little over 8 per cent in 2016 and less than 5 per cent by 2019.[14]

Judged with the benefit of hindsight, the actions taken by the new government in its first year to implement the bailout programme put the country on the road to a strong recovery, but at the time every decision was hard-fought and controversial. It was not long before the pressure began to tell on Fine Gael.

The party suffered a defection only four months after taking office when Denis Naughten of Roscommon-South Leitrim – who had entered national politics after winning his father's vacant Seanad seat in a by-election in 1997 – lost the whip when he voted against the government on 7 July. He opposed the plan to replace Roscommon A&E with an urgent-care unit and an out-of-hours GP service. The decision had led to a furious row, as the Minister for Health, James Reilly, had promised in opposition that the A&E service would be protected. A week before the vote a page appeared on Facebook calling for Naughten and Frank Feighan, the party's other TD in the constituency, to resign. The first post, from 1 July, read: 'Elected on the lies they fed us, it's now time to stand DOWN and be counted! They are OUR representatives after all.'[15]

Both Naughten and Feighan had previously criticised the plan, and while a visibly stressed Naughten honoured his pledge to oppose any such move, Feighan subsequently explained on Newstalk's *Breakfast Show* that a shortage of junior doctors and other events had superseded the promises he had made in February.[16] Naughten lost the whip and was expelled from the parliamentary party, never to return.

There were plenty more difficult decisions to come, and losing a TD at this early stage in the life of the government, despite its overwhelming majority, was worrying. As it turned out, Naughten was only the first in a string of party TDs to go overboard during the lifetime of the government. It was no coincidence that most of them, most notably Lucinda Creighton, had been inveterate opponents of Kenny in the 2010 heave.

A less pressing problem was a group of newly elected TDs dubbed the 'five a side' by Miriam Lord, as they regularly played indoor soccer together. They began agitating for a more aggressive defence of Fine Gael-style policies in the coalition with Labour. Their behaviour began to annoy Kenny, who regarded them as impertinent and had no hesitation in telling them so. The leading members of the group – Eoghan Murphy (Dublin Bay South), Seán Kyne (Galway West), Pat Deering (Carlow-Kilkenny) and Brendan Griffin (Kerry) – were closely associated with the ambitious Leo Varadkar.

A more serious immediate difficulty for the government was the efforts of Minister for the Environment, Phil Hogan, to implement the Troika's demand for the introduction of a property tax. All the parties in the Dáil had made this a political football since the abolition of rates by Fianna Fáil in 1977, but the issue now had to be faced. As a first step, Hogan introduced a household charge of €100, to be paid by all home-owners in 2012. There were protests, backed by a variety of left-wing groups, urging non-compliance, but after a shaky start the majority of households paid the charge that year.

The important second step was a move the following year to a local property tax based on house valuation. Crucially, collection was moved in 2013 from the Department of the Environment to the Revenue Commissioners, and there was a high level of compliance. Hogan also had the task of implementing a long-postponed inspection scheme for septic tanks, which caused more controversy.

His real problem, though, lay with the introduction of a national system of water charges. Like property tax, this had been a hot potato for a long time, and all parties had played politics by opposing such charges while in opposition. In the 1990s Labour had scuppered a plan to install water meters in new houses, for fear they would be accused of facilitating charges. Now, however, it was part of the bailout programme, and Hogan set up Irish Water to introduce a national system of metered charging for water. This became the lightning rod for all the pent-up resentment at the implementation of austerity. A political campaign, initiated by the Trotskyist left and joined by Sinn Féin, became a real problem for the government. Protests and disruption of the metering work became a feature of political life.

Leaving aside the struggling economy, the Fine Gael-Labour coalition had an otherwise dream start in positive public relations opportunities. Accepting the invitation of President Mary McAleese, Queen Elizabeth II became the first British monarch to visit the state. The last royal visit was that of King George V in 1911, before independence. Having greeted her with his wife, Fionnuala, at Government Buildings on 17 May, Kenny later described the Queen as 'awesome'.[17] The normalisation of British-Irish relations was best symbolised during the state dinner at Dublin Castle when the Queen began her speech in Irish. Beside her, President McAleese could not hide her surprise and delight. When she mouthed 'wow' she seemed to be expressing the reactions of many who had tuned in for the televised coverage. Journalists in Britain and Ireland reported the conciliatory message of the visit, often playing down the voices of protest by emphasising the marginality and minority status of such groups.[18]

No sooner had the royal visit ended than the charismatic American president Barack Obama arrived. He delighted reporters and local people alike as he visited his ancestral village of Moneygall. He received a huge cheer from the crowd that came to hear him in College Green, Dublin, when he concluded his speech with the phrase, 'Is féidir linn,' the Irish translation of his slogan 'Yes, we can.' May proved a busy and expensive month for the government, but the positive coverage that these high-profile international visitors brought was priceless. If only temporarily, the country experienced a lift.

May also brought a period of mourning for the Fine Gael family as the party said goodbye to one of its greats. Garret FitzGerald, former leader and Taoiseach, died following a short illness on 19 May at the age of eighty-five. His passing during the Queen's visit was poignant. As Paul McElhinney noted in *Magill*, 'the Queen's visit was, in so many ways, the crowning glory of all Garret had striven to achieve in his lifetime in the field of Anglo-Irish relations.'[19] 'Gentleman', 'Statesman' and 'Servant' all trended on Twitter as people paid tribute.[20] When his coffin, draped in the Tricolour, left the Church of the Sacred Heart in Donnybrook on 22 May it was greeted by spontaneous applause, a gesture repeated by those who lined the funeral route to Shanganagh cemetery.

Through his extensive writings and the publication of his hefty auto-biography, FitzGerald had essentially written his own place in history. Such was the regard for the former leader that criticisms of him were not welcomed, as Leo Varadkar discovered in 2010 when he disparaged FitzGerald's record on the economy as Taoiseach.[21] A more caustic, though arguably accurate, view was expressed by Eamon Sweeney in the *Irish Independent,* that 'Garret FitzGerald is unique in Irish public life in that he is judged not by his achievements, but by his intentions.'[22]

As the party mourned the loss of FitzGerald, Enda Kenny demon-strated his capacity for statesmanship when he delivered his most significant speech up to then. The Cloyne Report, examining how alle-gations of the sexual abuse of children in the diocese were handled by church and state, was published on 13 July 2011. Kenny responded in the Dáil a week later. Acknowledging that he is a practising Catholic, he took a stern line. 'Today, that Church needs to be a penitent Church', he said, 'a church truly and deeply penitent for the horrors it perpetrated, hid and denied.'[23] Colm O'Gorman, a survivor of clerical sexual abuse and campaigner, tweeted, 'I cannot find the words to express how moved I am by [the] Taoiseach's speech on #Cloyne today. This has been a long, hard road.'[24]

Kenny's performance was formidable, though some critics dismissed the speech as a polemic rather than a contribution to debate. But, as Noel Whelan observed, to do so was to miss the point of what Kenny was doing. He was making a clear statement of attitude: that the government would be adopting a new and less deferential attitude towards the Vatican.[25] It was a stance he would repeat when his government prepared to introduce new measures that allowed for abortion.

Meanwhile preparations were being made for the presidential election, due later that year. Fine Gael has an appalling record when it comes to presidential elections, but with confidence at its highest level ever after the February general election, it was decided to contest the October presidential election. With John Bruton, the preferred choice, ruling himself out, Pat Cox, Avril Doyle, Seán Kelly and Mairéad McGuinness – all experienced politicians in the European Parliament – were mentioned. Gay Mitchell later expressed his interest in standing.

What followed was a democratic process, whereby an electorate of about seven hundred delegates, made up of councillors, the parliamentary party and the National Executive, voted at a special convention on 9 July to select their candidate from among Cox, McGuinness and Mitchell. Cox was eliminated after the first count, leaving Mitchell ahead of McGuinness. Although the exact figures were not released, it was reported that Mitchell won by 55 per cent of the vote, compared with McGuinness's 45 per cent.[26] He had aimed his campaign for the nomination at the grass roots, and his strategy paid off.

Mitchell had an impeccable political record. He represented Dublin South-Central from 1981 until 2004, when he was elected MEP for Dublin. He was Lord Mayor of Dublin from 1992 to 1993 and served as Minister of State for European Affairs between 1994 and 1997. Jimmy

Deenihan, who had proposed McGuinness, said afterwards, 'He won it fair and square,'[27] but Mitchell was not the leadership's preferred choice. When the result was announced, Kenny was seen to slump and could barely contain his disappointment.[28] Pat Cox had been his choice.

What followed, played out in front of the media, set the tone for the canvass. Both leader and candidate took shots at one another in their comments to the press, with the result that the tension between the two men featured heavily in the subsequent reporting. It hardly inspired confidence. Kenny rarely appeared on the canvass, and it was reported that Mitchell had not wanted to be seen with him at events such as the Ploughing Championships, in case it alienated Fianna Fáil voters.[29] The distance between Mitchell and his party leader destroyed any potential the MEP had.

The field for the presidential election was vastly expanded, and, while Fianna Fáil decided not to contest the election, seven candidates in total appeared on the ballot paper. Despite investing the most money, Gay Mitchell made little impact on the polls – a consequence of the type of campaign he ran. Aside from the organisation of the canvass and the noticeable absence of Enda Kenny, the Mitchell campaign concentrated too much on the Sinn Féin candidate.

Seeing the election as an opportunity to make further inroads into politics in the Republic, Sinn Féin had nominated Martin McGuinness. His past as an IRA commander inevitably followed his campaign, and Fine Gael repeatedly homed in on this controversial history. Alan Shatter was the first minister to comment, saying in an RTÉ interview that he did not believe McGuinness was an 'appropriate person' to be president, while Phil Hogan later referred to the Sinn Féin candidate as a terrorist.[30] Invoking a well-worn Fine Gael mantra, Mitchell spoke of how he had spent his life defending the state and was not about to surrender it to people who would change it from the inside.[31] McGuinness branded such interventions 'pathetic'.[32]

It was later reported that Fine Gael had gambled on this strategy in the belief that the election would be a straight choice between Mitchell and McGuinness.[33] The argument can be made that when candidates attack each other, raising doubts about views or qualifications, both voters and the democratic process benefit, and the 2011 election was certainly notable for the extent of negativity and close scrutiny of the candidates.[34] But Fine Gael's obsession with McGuinness's past in the IRA proved to be a turn-off. Such negative campaigning resulted in a steady loss of support for Mitchell, and when asked about this trend in the polls in one of the televised debates he actually shouted at the moderator.[35]

Mitchell achieved a mere 6.4 per cent of the national vote, which put him behind Austin Currie's disappointing 17 per cent in 1990 and gave the party its lowest vote ever in a presidential election. Despite his vote being highly partisan, he was unable to mobilise a great deal of Fine Gael support.[36] In the post-election analysis some party members apportioned blame to Enda Kenny for not offering direction on the candidate selection process. An unnamed TD was quoted as having said, 'If he had called the turnips [backbenchers] in, he could have influenced it.' Mitchell was not without blame either, and a senior campaign source described him as having been 'difficult from every perspective'.[37] Mitchell's poor performance was an embarrassment for Fine Gael, although the party could at least console itself with the belief that the result was not the product of a protest vote against the government.

Fine Gael's coalition partner was riding high. Not only had Labour's presidential candidate, Michael D. Higgins, been elected with a first-preference share of 43 per cent but the party had also gained a seat at the by-election held on the same day. The death of the Fianna Fáil deputy Brian Lenihan had created a vacancy in the constituency of Dublin West, and Patrick Nulty became the first government candidate in twenty-nine years to win a by-election. Fine Gael ran Eithne Loftus, but she made little impact, receiving only 5,263 first preferences. The director of elections, Brian Hayes, played down the dismal result, deeming it to be a local contest that did not foreshadow a decline in support for the party. It was a reasonable assumption. Nulty may have made history, but were voters really endorsing Labour, over Fine Gael, in government?

Nulty had been opposed to Labour joining the coalition, and speaking after his election he said he would be a 'principled, constructive voice' in the party. Even more tellingly, he declared that the seat he had just won belonged to the people of Dublin West, and not to any one person or party.[38] It was a noble sentiment, but he had the air of someone who would operate as an independent, and this may have been influential in his decisive victory. Within six weeks of being elected he lost the whip when he voted against the budget. He later resigned as a TD over a social media scandal, and his vacant seat was won by the Socialist Party at a by-election in May 2014 – an early indicator of how the hard left in opposition became a welcome alternative for those critical of Labour in government.

As 2011 gave way to a new year there was little to lift the mood of a country experiencing austerity. The 1st of January brought with it new measures announced in the 2012 budget, such as an increase of 2 per cent in VAT on most consumer goods, a reduction in child benefit for the third and subsequent child, and an increase in university registration fees for students. Pay cuts, taxes and job losses dominated the front pages of the daily newspapers in January, and the Minister for Finance, Michael Noonan, caused outrage when he suggested that young people, who were emigrating in their thousands, were doing so because many 'simply want to get off a small island'.[39] Such out-of-touch social commentary foreshadowed a bizarre and ill-considered plan by Fine Gael to mark the party's first year in government.

Reverse-engineering the publicity stunt in which Fine Gael presented the Fianna Fáil-PD coalition with a P45 because of 'broken promises' in 2007, the party intended to show voters exactly what they had done for the country. According to the press notice for an event to be held on 8 March, TDs and senators would gather in Merrion Square, holding coloured stars that represented significant Fine Gael achievements in government. At a meeting of the parliamentary party on the eve of the event John Deasy questioned the concept. Kenny later attempted to distance himself from it, claiming that he only learned about it on the morning of 8 March, and he then cancelled it. His version of events does not quite align with the time frame, as he would have been present at the meeting on 7 March when Deasy raised the issue.[40]

Enda Kenny and Eamon Gilmore had shown a united front by giving a joint press conference to mark their first year in office. But this additional event gave the appearance of one-upmanship, with one senior Labour source likening the stars to medals that Fine Gael was awarding itself. The planned event was described as 'inappropriate' and 'misguided'.[41] To make matters worse, it was only when the political correspondent David McCullagh mentioned the event on RTÉ's Six One News that Labour even became aware of it.[42] Had the event gone ahead it would have been a public relations disaster, and even though it was ultimately cancelled it left many people wondering how sensitive Fine Gael really was to the grim reality facing many citizens.

In addition to the traditional St Patrick's Day visit, Kenny made several trips to America during February and March. When he rang the famous opening bell on Wall Street he shared the platform with a group of prominent Irish and American business leaders. The photo opportunity ended up being controversial because Denis O'Brien, who had been heavily criticised the previous year in the Moriarty Tribunal, was among those present. But the photograph also reinforced the purpose of Kenny's repeated trips to America. Each event he attended provided access to important business leaders. As Kenny explained on one of his visits, 'We have to use every opportunity to reach out across the globe to give the message that Ireland is open for business and investment.'[43] It was a message repeated to Xi Jinping, vice-president of China, who was accompanied by 150 business executives when he made Ireland the only European stop on his world tour in February. The hope was that Chinese companies would follow the American lead and make Ireland the home of their European head offices.[44]

By the time the 76th Fine Gael ard-fheis got under way on 30 March 2012, despite the positive coverage abroad, the strain of overseeing austerity at home was apparent. Inside the Dublin Convention Centre delegates enjoyed gathering as a party of government for the first time in sixteen years. Such was the turnout for Enda Kenny's speech on Saturday evening that an overflow room was needed to supplement the 2,000-seat auditorium. But outside the venue a crowd of about six thousand gathered on the second day to protest against the household charge, the deadline for payment of which fell on that date.

The optics were unfortunate. The glass front of the five-storey building on Spencer Dock facilitated the narrative that, as one woman present in the street said, 'they're up there in their lovely convention centre looking down and they don't care about the real people down here.'[45] Those inside were asked to stay back from the windows, and the blinds were drawn, an act that further enraged the protesters. 'Pulling the blinds', mocked one Twitter user, was 'just like the scene in *Oliver* where the kids look through the windows at the fat cats seated at the trough.'[46] Alan Shatter had not helped matters by earlier advising that the protesters should 'get a life'.[47] Amidst the heightened atmosphere, with arriving delegates heckled and, in some cases, spat at or knocked to the ground, gardaí were needed to create a security cordon.

The protest was the latest in a string of such gatherings. There had been protests outside Leinster House against Hogan's proposed septic tank charges in January and against austerity measures in February. A few days before the ard-fheis, on 24 March, thousands of people packed into the National Stadium to show their opposition to the household charge.

But a windy Sunday in August provided Fine Gael with an opportunity to deliver a positive message. Kenny became the first serving Taoiseach to deliver the annual address at Bealnablath since W.T. Cosgrave unveiled the roadside monument to Michael Collins in 1924. The 90th anniversary of Collins's death was the perfect occasion for Enda Kenny to position his government as saviours of the state. Invoking Collins and those who built the Free State after independence, he told an audience of about four thousand that his government had 'retrieved and reinstated' the values of the state's founders.[48] The ghost of Collins was used to add legitimacy to the policies that the government was pursuing. As his audience heard, Collins was a pragmatist who did not shy away from making difficult decisions. This was typical Fine Gael rhetoric: it was a party always ready, the claim went, to take a stand in defence of the state, no matter the cost in popularity.

Unrest continued as 2012 progressed, with thousands of farmers descending on Dublin in October and students protesting against austerity in Cork in November. The Minister for Health, James Reilly, survived a motion of no confidence, tabled by Fianna Fáil and Sinn Féin after further cuts to the health service. Ministers became accustomed to being heckled. This was now part of the pattern of government life, and by the summer of 2013 Enda Kenny reported that he had received letters written in blood that called him a murderer.[49] The correspondence came as the government prepared to legislate for abortion – a major test of the government's third year in office.

The *Irish Times* had reported on 14 November 2012 that a woman 'denied a termination' had died in University Hospital, Galway, on 28 October. Savita Halappanavar had presented with lower back pain, but it transpired that she was suffering a miscarriage. Her husband maintains that repeated requests for an abortion were denied. She later died from septicaemia. News of her death motivated a candlelight vigil outside Leinster House that attracted three thousand people; as a reminder of the outpouring of sympathy and anger that had occurred, the surrounding paths were coated in wax the following morning.

The Halappanavar case was a complicated one, but the headline for most people was the remark by the hospital's midwife manager, Ann Maria Burke, that 'Ireland is a Catholic country.' This was widely repeated, followed by expressions of disgust and disbelief. People turned to social media to share their outrage. 'A woman dies because of a 1861 law and religion – Ireland in 2012. Disgraceful,' one tweet read.[50]

Pro-life groups grew concerned that the immense response to Savita's death would be harnessed into a campaign that would overturn the country's abortion laws. The ultra-conservative senator Rónán Mullen lamented that 'some people are seeking to use this tragedy as an argument for legislating for the Supreme Court decision in X,' while David Quinn of the Iona Institute, a Catholic think tank, tweeted that 'Legislating for X which had to do with suicidal intent would have done nothing whatever to help #Savita. Why are they being linked?'[51] But the government was already grappling with the law.

A landmark ruling by the European Court of Human Rights on 16 December 2010 had found that that the absence of access to abortion where a woman's life is at risk violated article 8 of the European Convention on Human Rights. The judgement came in the last days of the Fianna Fáil government, ensuring that abortion would feature as an element of the 2011 election campaign and that whatever government took power would finally have to tackle the issue. Politicians were naturally wary of engaging with the subject. Although society's attitude towards women's reproductive and sexual autonomy had gradually evolved since the eighth amendment, the 1983 referendum had cast a long shadow. The bitterly divisive debate that surrounded that amendment – once described as the second partitioning of Ireland – shaped the willingness, or otherwise, of various political parties to engage with the issue of abortion.[52]

Youth Defence, an organisation opposed to the legalisation of abortion, had written to all political parties and independents during the 2011 election and received a response from Enda Kenny, on behalf of the party, that categorically stated Fine Gael's opposition to the legalisation of abortion.[53] This position would prove problematic for some of its TDs when the Dáil came to consider new legislation.

What became the Protection of Life During Pregnancy Bill had its roots in the expert group on abortion, which was appointed in January 2012 by the new coalition. Its long-awaited and much-delayed report was finally published on 27 November, and while it did not make recommendations it did offer four options for dealing with the ECHR ruling, which included implementing the judgement without recourse to legislation or amending legislation to regulate access to lawful termination of pregnancy in accordance with the X Case, the requirements of the European Convention on Human Rights and the ECHR judgement.[54]

'Didn't I warn you,' David Quinn asked from his weekly column, 'that voting for Labour would be voting for abortion?'[55] The potential fallout for Fine Gael was immediately apparent, with the *Irish Independent* dramatically reporting, 'Fine Gael is tearing itself apart over abortion law' and following up the next day with 'Kenny faces revolt as TDs hit out at abortion law rush'.[56] Lucinda Creighton, Dublin South-East TD and Minister of State for European Affairs, was the most vocal. Speaking on RTÉ's *Today with Pat Kenny*, she said she was not convinced that there was no choice but to legislate.[57]

Agreement was reached at the final cabinet meeting of 2012 that the government would legislate by the summer of 2013, and after a marathon cabinet meeting on 30 April it was agreed to put the proposed legislation before the Oireachtas. During the six-hour session, ministers went through the draft line by line.[58] The Galway West TD Brian Walsh became the first Fine Gael deputy to confirm that he would not vote for the legislation, telling the *Connacht Sentinel* that the proposal was a 'stepping stone to abortion on demand'.[59]

Members of the parliamentary party had the opportunity to voice concerns and criticisms when they gathered the day after the cabinet had given its approval. John O'Mahony, Anthony Lawlor and Michael Mullins were said to have been very emotional, with Senator Mullins having to step out of the room to compose himself. Senators Paul Bradford and Fidelma Healy-Eames expressed their discomfort, while John Paul Phelan is reported to have 'demolished' the argument for the risk of suicide as grounds for abortion. Peter Mathews, Terence Flanagan and Lucinda Creighton also expressed opposition. The party was reported to be 'closely split' on the subject.[60]

This was an important test of Enda Kenny's leadership, and how he handled the challenge would be crucial for the success of the proposed legislation. Considered a pro-life, conservative politician, he was in a position to bring like-minded colleagues with him if he followed the right strategy. Mindful of the critics in his own party and of the conservative elements among Fine Gael voters, it is no accident that he drew on the language used by the pro-life lobby to emphasise the limits of the legislation. He often spoke of how the proposed bill would not provide for 'abortion on demand', a very particular expression used almost exclusively by those who oppose the procedure.[61] He also emphasised that the government would not go beyond the decision resulting from the X Case.[62]

The accusation in the Dáil by the independent TD Clare Daly – one of the leading figures in the campaign to liberalise abortion laws – that the terms of the bill were 'so restrictive' that most women would continue to make the journey to Britain, arguably aided Kenny's efforts to steady his party.[63]

But there were limits to the extent to which Kenny would placate critics. Despite being a practising Catholic, he demonstrated a separation of church and state in his handling of the hierarchy's response to the proposed legislation. In the Dáil he declared: 'My book is the Constitution ... That's the people's book and we live in a republic and I have a duty and responsibility, as head of government, to legislate in respect of what the people's wishes are.' Following his stringent criticisms after the Cloyne Report, this was a significant statement. It contrasted greatly with the Fine Gael Taoiseach John A. Costello, who had said in 1951, 'I, as a Catholic, obey my Church authorities,' and it also spoke to the transformation of the state.[64]

The Protection of Life During Pregnancy Bill was approved by the Dáil in the early hours of 11 July 2013. In the end five Fine Gael TDs voted against the legislation, the junior minister Lucinda Creighton being the most high-profile, but not unexpected, member of the party to defy the whip. Speaking afterwards, she maintained that the legislation was a breach of Fine Gael's election commitment on abortion.[65] Terence Flanagan, Peter Mathews, Billy Timmins and Brian Walsh also lost the whip. But other deputies who had previously expressed concerns fell into line.

Creighton went on to found Renua in March 2015. A centre-right party, it provided a new political home also for Timmins and Flanagan. Despite the initial buzz around it, the party never really got off the ground and it struggled to find candidates for the 2016 general election.

The new legislation was problematic, and its shortcomings were exposed little more than a year later. The difficulty posed by the ambiguity of the legislation was shown by the case of a teenage girl pregnant as the result of rape in her home country who was given asylum in 2014, and subsequently in the case of a brain-dead pregnant woman that appeared before the High Court the same year. The UN Committee on Economic, Social and Cultural Rights urged that new, straightforward legislation be drafted.[66]

Earlier in the year the McAleese Report was published. Martin McAleese had chaired a committee, established in July 2011, to explore state involvement with ten named Magdalene institutions, covering the period 1922–96. The report has since attracted criticism from the advocacy group Justice for Magdalenes, the UN Committee Against Torture, and some academics. While a full exploration is beyond the remit of this chapter, it is worth noting that criticisms have been based on both the methodology adopted and the resulting findings.

Nonetheless the report resulted in an important state apology, delivered by Kenny in the Dáil on 19 February 2013. Addressing those survivors who had gathered in the visitors' gallery, he spoke of a 'national shame' and, acknowledging the role of the state in their ordeal, unreservedly apologised for the hurt that was done to women in such institutions. He also explained that a redress scheme would be established. As he concluded his speech it was evident that Kenny was struggling with the emotion of the occasion. Though he was widely lauded for his speech, the redress scheme later came under scrutiny. In November 2017 the Ombudsman, Peter Tyndall, found that the manner in which the scheme was administered by the Department of Justice constituted maladministration, and his report, *Opportunity Lost*, made the damning observation that 'a scheme intended to bring healing and reconciliation has, for some, served instead to cause further distress'.[67]

As the year drew to a close there was some good news as Ireland became the first EU country to leave the bailout process. The Troika had made their final visit at the beginning of November, and although critical of the slow pace of reform to the banking sector, health system and legal profession, their departure provided some confidence on the international markets. That the country would not be seeking additional funding was also seized upon by the president of the European Commission, José Manuel Barroso, as evidence that the euro zone could stage a full recovery.[68] The 2015 budget, presented in October 2014, was mildly expansionary, although this was a calculated gamble, as the government could not sustain any further austerity budgets. It paid off, and the economy's performance improved.[69]

The year 2014 brought new woes for the government when the Minister for Justice and Defence, Alan Shatter, became embroiled in a succession of controversies in the early months of 2014. Shatter was widely regarded as a reforming and innovative minister, but he was dragged into the raft of controversies surrounding the whistleblower Sergeant Maurice McCabe, and he became a target for the opposition parties and the media. In May 2014 a series of events led, in Shatter's words, to 'a category five hurricane which destroyed my reputation and laid the foundations for ending my over 30 years of active involvement in Irish politics'.[70]

As far as most people were concerned, it was business as usual when Shatter took routine questions in the Dáil as Minister for Defence shortly after 2:30 p.m. on 7 May; yet two hours later the Taoiseach announced in the chamber that he had received the minister's resignation. In his memoir, *Frenzy and Betrayal*, Shatter describes the incredible sequence of allegations, events and falsehoods that that led to his forced resignation. It reads like a Kafkaesque nightmare.

Shatter felt that at an early stage in the controversy that he was stabbed in the back by Leo Varadkar, whom he described as 'a Fine Gael cabinet colleague orchestrating or engaging in extensive briefing to bolster his reputation and image and deliberately damage mine'.[71] He was also deeply critical of Kenny, who he felt sacrificed him on the basis of a deeply flawed report by the barrister Seán Guerin. Over the following five years almost all the claims and allegations that forced Shatter's resignation from office were discredited or shown to be false by judicial inquiries and decisions handed down by the Court of Criminal Appeal and the Supreme Court. However, in May 2014, as the country moved towards the local and European elections, the political fallout for Fine Gael was negative.

The European elections resulted in Fine Gael retaining its four seats but, more significantly, the party lost a whopping 105 seats in the local elections, and it ended up with only 235 councillors. The hard-won gains of five years earlier were lost, and the party was back to its traditional role of playing second fiddle to Fianna Fáil, which gained 49 seats to end up with 267. 'We anticipated a wallop,' one senior party figure admitted, 'and it was worse than we expected.'[72] Ominously, Fianna Fáil edged ahead of Fine Gael in the popular vote, with 25.5 per cent to 24 per cent. Not a lot of attention was paid to that at the time, as opinion polls continued to put Fine Gael ahead of its old rival, but the writing was on the wall, if anybody in the party cared to read it.

The outcome of the elections prompted big changes in government personnel. There had already been a change in the cabinet with the departure of Shatter in May. He was replaced in Justice by Frances Fitzgerald, while Charlie Flanagan took over her position as Minister for Children's Affairs. Now Phil Hogan, the other minister at the centre of the other major controversy in the first half of 2014, also departed national politics. Hogan sought from Kenny, and was given, the post of European Commissioner. He proved to be a highly successful Agriculture Commissioner and established himself as a serious political figure in Brussels, but the water charges continued to haunt the government. Labour responded to the very poor election results by switching leaders: Eamon Gilmore resigned and was replaced by Joan Burton.

As 2015 approached, preparations were being made for two referendums. Voters would be asked to consider amending the Constitution to allow for marriage irrespective of the sex of the couple and to reduce the age of candidates for the office of president of Ireland from thirty-five to twenty-one. The latter received far less coverage, and was rejected, but the referendum on marriage equality captured the attention of the country. The coalition's programme for government had included a promise to convene a constitutional convention within twelve months that would, among other things, consider same-sex marriage. Both parties had strongly supported the Fianna Fáil-Green government's civil partnership legislation in 2010. The convention eventually assembled for its first meeting in December 2012, with monthly meetings thereafter.

Marriage equality was discussed at the April 2013 meeting. Jerry Buttimer, a Fine Gael TD for Cork South-Central and one of three LGBT members of the Oireachtas at the time, was among the delegates. As the authors of *Ireland Says Yes* have documented, the debates that later shaped the referendum campaign were well rehearsed at the convention.[73] Ultimately, the convention called for legal changes that would provide for equal status for same-sex couples and their families, and, accepting the recommendations, the government announced that a referendum would be held in 2015. It has been suggested that the coalition purposely referred the marriage question to the constitutional convention, rather than simply announcing a referendum. Doing so created the impression that the people, as represented by the members of the convention, had had their say and that they had indicated that they were in favour of the measure.[74]

Kenny was a gradual convert to the case for marriage equality and sought to evade questions from journalists on the issue during his early period in government. However, in response to pressure from the Tánaiste, Eamon Gilmore, who had declared it to be 'the civil rights issue of our time', and growing public pressure, his views on the subject evolved. The 'coming out' of a Fine Gael TD as a gay man had a decisive influence in persuading him to support marriage equality.[75]

The referendum campaign is beyond the scope of this chapter, and the Yes campaign in particular has been well documented elsewhere.[76] One of the defining moments was Leo Varadkar's appearance on Miriam O'Callaghan's programme on RTÉ Radio 1 in early 2015. 'I am a gay man. It's not a secret, but not something that everyone would necessarily know,' the then Minister for Health told listeners. He had decided to speak publicly about this aspect of his identity for the first time before the referendum because he did not want to be accused of having a 'hidden agenda'.[77] Later Simon Coveney's embracing of Varadkar as he arrived at Dublin Castle for the declaration provided one of many touching moments in the coverage of the results.

All parties in the Dáil backed the referendum. Innumerable Twitter users updated their profile pictures to include the 'Yes to Equality 2015' ribbon, while #HometoVote trended as Irish people abroad streamed back to have their say (raising questions about the state of the electoral register!). An iconic same-sex marriage mural by the artist Joe Caslin appeared overnight in Dublin city centre the month before the vote.

There was a clear sense of momentum behind the Yes campaign. With 62 per cent of voters in favour, the referendum passed on 22 May 2015, making Ireland the first country to approve same-sex marriage by popular vote. With the exception of Roscommon-South Leitrim, every constituency in the country voted in favour of the measure.

Varadkar likened the result of the referendum to a 'social revolution'.[78] Caught up in the emotions of the day, this was possibly an overstatement. Nonetheless there was a sense that a shift had occurred. When Cardinal Pietro Parolin, the Vatican Secretary of State, deemed the outcome a 'defeat for humanity', his comments had the appearance of belonging to a past age.[79] The Marriage Act came into effect on 16 November 2015, and the following day Richard Dowlin and Cormac Gollogly became the first same-sex couple to marry. Feargal Purcell believes that in his approach to marriage equality, abortion and the Cloyne Report Kenny performed a crucially important task for Fine Gael by moving it to a more liberal position that helped the party redefine itself for the modern age. 'In Fine Gael the divisions have always been on social rather than fiscal issues. Enda was seen as coming from the more conservative rural wing of the party but precisely because of that he managed to shift it without causing a serious split.'[80]

In an attempt to give the government a new image before the next general election, Kenny announced a reshuffle in July in which Paschal Donohoe and Heather Humphreys were promoted to the cabinet, a number of senior ministers moved around, and Jimmy Deenihan dropped down to the junior ranks. There were even bigger changes on the Labour side, with three new cabinet ministers: Jan O'Sullivan, Alex White and Alan Kelly.[81]

Kenny clearly hoped that the departure of Shatter and Hogan and the new faces in the cabinet would prompt a recovery in support for Fine Gael. For a time that appeared to be the case. An *Irish Times* poll in November 2015 had Fine Gael back up to 30 per cent, from a low point of 19 per cent the previous December, and Kenny was back ahead of

Micheál Martin as the most popular party leader.[82] When the poll results were published senior Fine Gael people were angry that Kenny had not taken the initiative and gone to the country for a November election.

Although Kenny had been strongly of the view in early October that it was the right time to call an election, he had not been able to get Labour to agree to the timing. Kenny had never developed the same rapport with Burton as he had with Gilmore, and relations between them grew increasingly strained during 2015. It became public knowledge in early October that he was contemplating a November election, but this provoked a furious reaction from Burton and Labour. After a few days of fevered media speculation about an election Kenny announced that he had no intention of calling it in 2015. With that he forfeited any prospect of surprise, and all began to gear up for a February contest.[83]

To make matters worse, election preparations were marred by a legal action taken against Fine Gael by one of its own TDs, John Perry from Sligo. In March 2012 Perry was appointed Minister of State for Small Business, but, following a Commercial Court judgement against him in September 2013, he was dropped in the 2014 reshuffle. At a chaotic constituency selection convention in October 2015, Perry failed to win a nomination. He immediately launched a High Court challenge against the party, claiming the convention had been rigged. After general secretary Tom Curran gave evidence on the fifth day of the case, Fine Gael backed down, paid the costs of the action and added Perry to the ticket.

On the morning of 3 February 2016 Kenny announced, firstly to the Dáil and then to the rest of the country via Twitter, that he would be advising the President to dissolve the 31st Dáil. During the life of the Dáil two new parties, Renua and the Social Democrats, had been formed, while Sinn Féin had experienced a revival in fortunes at the 2011 election. The growth and assertiveness of the left in opposition proved attractive to those disenchanted with Labour's role in an austerity government. As Labour was accused of betraying the working class, Fine Gael faced into the 2016 election comfortably ahead of the other parties in the opinion polls.[84] Enda Kenny appeared on course to become the first Fine Gael Taoiseach of two successive governments.

In his short video on Twitter announcing the election Kenny said that when he became Taoiseach five years earlier 'Ireland was on the verge of collapse.' Having made 'real progress', he appealed to the electorate to 'continue on the path to recovery with Fine Gael'. The alternative was that 'those who wrecked our country in the past or those who would wreck it in the future'. The expression 'keep the recovery going' was used multiple times, and a call to action – 'Let's keep the recovery going' – became the theme of the Fine Gael campaign.[85] The Troika was gone and there were signs of progress, so it seemed an obvious slogan. In England the Conservative Party had successfully campaigned on the theme of 'chaos v. stability', and senior Fine Gael staff members travelled to London to learn more.[86]

Ultimately, though, the party misjudged the mood of the electorate. The ambivalence felt by voters towards the slogan was summed up in comments reported in the *Financial Times*. Paddy Flannery, a community activist in a deprived area of Limerick, was quoted as saying about economic recovery: 'I can see it. But I can't feel it. It will be a while yet before people [here do].'[87] Critics claimed that the recovery was too Dublin-centred. Whether accurate or not, this was the perception for many, rendering Fine Gael's slogan ineffective.

In general, Fine Gael did not have a great campaign, and it was accompanied by poor performances by Kenny. At the opening press conference, which has been described as a 'confused and clumsily managed affair', Kenny appeared unprepared and lacking in knowledge on the party's fiscal policies. Telling journalists that 'I'm not going to get into economic jargon here, because the vast majority of people don't understand', he left himself open to accusations from opponents that he was the one who did not understand.[88]

Then, on the last weekend, he made a terrible gaffe. At a party rally in his native Castlebar he lashed out at those who were constantly bemoaning the lack of economic activity in Co. Mayo. 'These people are All-Ireland champions when it comes to whingeing,' he told his stunned supporters.[89] The comment made headlines in the national media in the final days of the campaign, and social media were awash with angry responses. Fine

Gael tried to play down the clanger, claiming that the Taoiseach was talking about rival politicians and not voters themselves. Kenny repeated this explanation on RTÉ's Six One News two days later when he joined Bryan Dobson to offer his 'full apologies to the people of Castlebar'.[90]

The outcome of the election was deeply disappointing. Fine Gael had expected that, in spite of the tough decisions taken in government, the party would win about 30 per cent of the vote and hold on to at least 60 seats. Instead the vote plunged by more than ten points, to 25.5 per cent. The party lost 26 seats and was lucky not to lose more. With 50 seats, it was back to where it had been in 2007. Labour plummeted from 19 per cent of the vote in 2011 to a mere 6.6 per cent, and the proportional drop in seats was even greater, from 37 to 7.

Dublin was the highlight for Fine Gael, with the party pulling off well-worked doubles in Dublin Bay South and Dún Laoghaire as well as remarkable victories in tough three-seat constituencies such as Dublin Central and Dublin North-West. But Munster was the weak spot, and the party vote throughout the country was a few percentage points short of expectations. Party strategists calculated that with a vote of 1½ per cent more it could actually have made it to its pre-election target of 60 seats.

Despite the steep drop in votes and seats Fine Gael retained its newly found position as the biggest party in the state, if by a whisker. After its record-breaking performance in 2011 it achieved a not-so-enviable record in 2016: this time it was to end up as the biggest party in the Dáil on the smallest share of the vote in the state's electoral history.

Kenny and his ministers were left scratching their heads about why the election had gone so badly wrong. In government, Fine Gael had presided over an economic recovery that was remarkable by any standards. When Kenny took over as Taoiseach in 2011 the country was in a deep economic depression, unemployment was spiralling upwards and the harsh measures required by the bailout threatened to unleash social unrest. By the time the 2016 general election came around, Ireland had exited the bailout, economic growth was the fastest in the EU and, most importantly, unemployment had more than halved. If Kenny and his government had expected thanks for this turnaround, they were left sorely disappointed.

15

LEO VARADKAR TAKES OVER

'I stand here, leader of my country, flawed and human, but judged by my political actions, and not by my sexual orientation, my skin tone, gender or religious beliefs.'

– LEO VARADKAR, SPEAKING IN AMERICA DURING THE ANNUAL ST PATRICK'S DAY VISIT, 14 MARCH 2019.

There was shock in Fine Gael at the outcome of the 2016 general election. The result was far worse than anybody had anticipated, even in the final stages of the campaign, when it was clear that something was wrong. The Fianna Fáil recovery was as much of a surprise as the Fine Gael slump, and there were now only six seats between the parties, compared with 56 in 2011. In the days following the election it was not at all clear how a government would be formed, or who would lead it.

It was in this dire situation that Enda Kenny's political skill and sheer willpower dragged a victory of sorts from the jaws of defeat. In many ways the election disaster was his responsibility: he got the timing wrong and the message wrong, and he compounded the party's problems with his ill-judged comment about whingers on the last weekend of the campaign.

Instead of brooding on his mistakes he set out to ensure that he remained Taoiseach and his party remained in power. 'Enda was really determined,' Charlie Flanagan recalled. 'He showed the kind of steel he had in him during the heave in 2010. His resilience was what kept him and Fine Gael in government.'[1]

Kenny's initial strategy was to see if he could garner enough support among the smaller parties and independents to put him in a position to lead the new government. For a time it appeared that Micheál Martin might be in a better position to pull this off. He had been the star of the election campaign, and his message of fairness had resonated with the electorate in a way that Fine Gael's emphasis on keeping the recovery going had not. While he was still six seats behind Fine Gael, many of the independents appeared at first more inclined to back him than Kenny.

That message was reinforced when Shane Ross and his Independent Alliance TDs met Kenny on the Friday after the election for a preliminary discussion on the formation of a government. Immediately after the meeting Ross wrote in a column for the *Sunday Independent*, 'Sometime in the middle of the exchanges an awful truth dawned. We were possibly in dialogue with a political corpse.'[2] Ross's contempt for their leader shocked Fine Gael ministers, who now began to have serious doubts about whether any deal with independents was feasible, and it fuelled media speculation that Kenny was finished.

When the 32nd Dáil met for the first time on 10 March, Kenny, as in 2011, was proposed for Taoiseach by the youngest TD in his party. This time it was the newly elected Noel Rock who proclaimed: 'I am proud this Taoiseach has always put the country first and confident he always will put the country first ... I will stand with him today and always.' Unlike 2011, though, Kenny was not elected Taoiseach at the first attempt, winning only 57 votes, with 94 against. Labour's seven TDs voted for him, but the party made it clear that once its debt of honour had been repaid it would not be supporting him in subsequent votes. Kenny's only consolation was that Micheál Martin was defeated by the even bigger margin of 108 votes to 43.

Kenny then travelled to Áras an Uachtaráin and formally resigned his post, although he would remain in office until the Dáil could decide on a replacement. It was a grim situation, but he maintained a sunny optimism which transmitted itself to his cabinet colleagues. 'He was adamant that he would bring us back into government, and he did have the advantage that he was in possession of the Taoiseach's office and was not going to give it up unless he was forced out,' says Flanagan, who was still Minister for Foreign Affairs at that stage.[3]

A few days later Kenny headed off to the United States for the annual St Patrick's Day meeting with the President, Barack Obama, in the White House and Congressional leaders on Capitol Hill. Vice-President Joe Biden reportedly sympathised with the Taoiseach on the election outcome and remarked that if he had been running for office in the United States he would have got 80 per cent of the vote, given his out-standing record in government.[4]

In the weeks that followed, Kenny and Martin engaged in a desper-ate race to see who could line up more of the independents, who were split into three loose groups. The Independent Alliance, headed by Ross, had six TDs, the Rural Alliance, whose spokesman was Denis Naughten, had five, while some of the remaining twelve were also interested in the formation of a government.

When the Dáil voted a second time on selecting a Taoiseach on 6 April, Kenny's level of support dropped to 51, with Michael Lowry the only non-Fine Gael TD to support him. That evening Kenny made a dramatic move to break the deadlock. Having first got the approval of his cabinet colleagues, he met Micheál Martin and offered a historic deal to bury the long-standing rivalry between Fine Gael and Fianna Fáil and establish a partnership government. A central element of the offer was that the post of Taoiseach would rotate between the two of them during the lifetime of the government. Martin was taken aback by the move, but although he was unenthusiastic he undertook to consult his colleagues.

The two parliamentary parties met the following day to consider the offer but, as Martin had anticipated, there was strong opposition to it at the Fianna Fáil meeting.[5]

During a short and frosty meeting on 7 April, Martin formally rejected Kenny's offer, saying that Fianna Fáil stood by its election campaign commitment not to enter government with Fine Gael. He said the main reason was that if the two big parties came together they would create an opening for Sinn Féin to lead the opposition and become a potential alternative government.

Kenny was furious that what he regarded as a historic move to end Civil War politics has been rejected with such little consideration by Fianna Fáil. 'I believe that this decision is a serious mistake and one which was driven by narrow party interests rather than the national interest,' he said in a statement. Martin was equally testy, questioning the integrity of Kenny's approach and saying that relations between them left a lot to be desired. He added that Fianna Fáil would be prepared to facilitate the formation of a Fine Gael minority government but said ominously that he would try to form one if Kenny could not get the numbers.[6]

In spite of the public acrimony it triggered private contacts between the two parties to see if a compromise was possible. Leo Varadkar got in touch with Fianna Fáil's Justice spokesman, Jim O'Callaghan, and the two met in O'Callaghan's house the following Saturday, where they were joined by Kenny's economic adviser, Andrew McDowell, and Martin's chief adviser, Deirdre Gillane. Both sides accepted that a coalition was a non-starter and they began to explore how a minority government could work instead. It was tacitly accepted by the Fianna Fáil side that Fine Gael was in a stronger position to put it together and they agreed that talks should get under way to see if a confidence and supply arrangement could be worked out.

Formal negotiations between the two parties began on 11 April, with Varadkar and Simon Coveney joined on the Fine Gael negotiating team by Frances Fitzgerald, Paschal Donohoe and Simon Harris. Michael McGrath and Jim O'Callaghan headed the Fianna Fáil delegation, with the talks starting in the Sycamore Room in Government Buildings and moving to Trinity College for some sessions.

Before the next meeting of the Dáil on 14 April, Martin made one final effort to see if he could build more support from independents, but he failed to persuade any of them to vote for him. Instead it was Kenny who slightly increased his advantage, with Katherine Zappone, who had been appointed a senator at Labour's request in 2011, getting off the fence with impeccable timing. She agreed to back Kenny on receiving an assurance that the issue of repealing the eighth amendment to the Constitution, which dealt with abortion, would be referred to a Citizens' Assembly. Kenny's support inched up to 52, while Martin remained stuck on 43.

Following this, the talks between the Fine Gael and Fianna Fáil negotiating teams got serious. While there were seven more meetings of the Dáil in late April and early May, things moved inexorably towards a deal, but it was not achieved without some rancour, and both parties came close to pulling out of the talks at different stages. One particular point of difficulty was the demand by Fianna Fáil for an end to water charges. This had been a hugely contentious issue for the Fine Gael-Labour government, but despite all the problems, by the spring of 2016 a majority of households were paying the charge. Fine Gael was deeply reluctant to abandon such an important project just when it was beginning to work. However, Jim O'Callaghan was insistent, and eventually Fine Gael conceded that it was a price that would have to be paid if it wanted to stay in office.

The talks between Fine Gael and Fianna Fáil ended on 29 April with an agreement on the shape of a minority government that would last a minimum of three years. It committed Fianna Fáil to backing three budgets and to abstaining on votes of confidence or cabinet reshuffles. Fianna Fáil received a commitment that any extra resources that became available would be spent in a ratio of 2:1 on improving public services rather than cutting taxes. The main opposition party also reserved the right to oppose day-to-day legislation and to support private members' time motions. In terms of Dáil numbers Fianna Fáil insisted that Fine Gael would have to build enough support from independents to have a secure majority on major votes on which Fianna Fáil would agree to abstain. It meant that the minimum number of Dáil votes Fine Gael required to lead a new government was 57.[7]

Seeing the writing on the wall, Shane Ross decided that Kenny was not a political corpse after all, and he led five of the Independent Alliance TDs into a deal to join the minority government. Denis Naughten was the only member of the Rural Alliance to formally join up, although another Clare TD, Michael Harty, was prepared to vote for Kenny as Taoiseach.

With Katherine Zappone and Michael Lowry already on board, it brought the number up to 59 – two more than the minimum requirement.

On 6 May, seventy days after the general election, Enda Kenny was elected Taoiseach for a second term, by a margin of 59 votes to 49 in the 158-member Dáil. Five years earlier he had been elected by the biggest majority in the history of the state. This time around he was elected Taoiseach by the lowest number of TDs ever, and his survival in office was in the hands of his party's traditional foe – Fianna Fáil. Still, as the journalist Gavan Reilly wrote, 'It was the election nobody won yet Enda Kenny still managed to come out on top.'[8] He was the first leader since W.T. Cosgrave to lead his party back to office for a second successive term.

There was some irony in the fact that his election was made possible only by the appointment to the cabinet of three of his staunchest critics: Denis Naughten, who had led the revolt against him in 2010 and then left the party in a rancorous break-up a year later; Shane Ross, who had insulted him in print and in the Dáil at every opportunity; and Katherine Zappone, who had repaid her appointment to the Seanad in 2011 by regularly voting against his government. Ross was given Transport, Tourism and Sport, Denis Naughten was appointed to Communications, Climate Action and Environment, while Katherine Zappone was given responsibility for Children and Youth Affairs.

With three cabinet positions going to independents, Kenny had room for eleven Fine Gael ministers. He appointed Frances Fitzgerald as Tánaiste and Minister for Justice and left Michael Noonan in Finance and Charlie Flanagan in Foreign Affairs, but he moved a number of other ministers and promoted new ones. There were big promotions for Paschal Donohoe, who got Public Expenditure, Simon Harris, who was appointed to Health, and Michael Creed, who got Agriculture.

The Dún Laoghaire TD Mary Mitchell O'Connor was the surprise promotion to Enterprise and Employment, while Heather Humphreys retained Arts and Heritage. There were moves for Simon Coveney, who was given responsibility for Housing, Leo Varadkar moved to Social Protection, and Richard Bruton got Education. Regina Doherty was appointed chief whip. In all, more than half Fine Gael's fifty TDs were rewarded with senior or junior ministerial positions, while six of the seven independents involved in government held ministerial office.

Having survived in office against the odds, it seemed as if Kenny was invincible and that Fine Gael might, after all, be able to take advantage of the rapidly growing economy to establish itself as a party of power rather than the semi-permanent occupant of the opposition benches. It was not long, though, before things began to go wrong.

On 23 June, less than two months after Kenny took office, the British people voted to leave the European Union. The decision threatened to have devastating consequences for Ireland, and it became the immediate priority of the government, dominating all other issues. There were some calls for the appointment of a special Brexit minister to follow the UK example, but Kenny was adamant that the Taoiseach and his department would take the lead in determining the Irish position in the complex negotiations that were to be so important over the following three years.

Kenny's initial approach to protecting Ireland's interests was to co-operate with the British to try to ensure the smoothest possible exit from the EU that would do the least damage to both countries. However, when it soon became apparent that the British government was intent on leaving the single market and the customs union there was a dramatic change in the Irish approach. Kenny took a much more assertive line with the UK and set out on a concerted diplomatic campaign around the EU to win support for the Irish position that there could be no return to a hard border on the island of Ireland. That campaign was so successful that the EU negotiating team, led by Michel Barnier, made it one of the three conditions for entering formal talks with the UK. That decision was ratified by the European Council in May 2017. The scale of the Irish diplomatic achievement stunned the British and won admiration from the rest of Europe.

Instead of being able to bask in the glory of his international triumph, Kenny discovered the truth of Albert Reynolds's rueful observation that in politics it is often the little things that trip you up. He had given a hostage to fortune in the summer of 2015 by announcing that he would not remain as Fine Gael leader beyond 2020. He felt it necessary to say he would not lead the party into a third general election after his chief whip, Paul Kehoe, inadvertently said he would do just that. Kenny's focus was on becoming the first Fine Gael leader to win two elections in a row, and he never had any intention of leading the party into a third, but in the face of the immediate media clamour that followed Kehoe's faux pas he felt the need to clarify the position. Some of his closest advisers felt it would be a fatal mistake to put any time limit on his leadership, as it would inevitably start the succession race, but Kenny felt he had no choice. Speaking in his native Co. Mayo, he declared, 'I have no intention of staying beyond the remit of the next government to be Taoiseach.'[9]

That declaration triggered a surreptitious succession race, which gained impetus after the 2016 election. Leo Varadkar had never made a secret of his ambition to become party leader and as a minister had made a habit of cultivating backbenchers to build a support base in the parliamentary party. While he was not a natural socialiser, like Kenny, he made sure that TDs had open access to his ministerial office to air their concerns, whether about national policy or purely local issues.

Fiach Kelly observed in the *Irish Times* that during his time in the cabinet Varadkar had built a ministerial machine around him to respond to the political needs of backbenchers and councillors. His special adviser Brian Murphy, who had served as chairman of Young Fine Gael and come up through the ranks of the party, co-ordinated the effort. He was widely known as the man who asked the question on RTÉ's *Questions and Answers* that led to the downfall of Brian Lenihan during the 1990 presidential election. Another adviser, John Carroll, acted as liaison with the parliamentary party, looking after local concerns of TDs and senators. The Dublin Bay South TD Eoghan Murphy acted as point man for Varadkar and co-ordinated the activities of the awkward squad, the likes of Michael D'Arcy, John Paul Phelan, Pat Deering, Brendan Griffin and Jim Daly, telling them when to voice criticism of Kenny and when to ease off. After the 2016 election they made no secret of their hostility to Kenny and began to agitate for a change of leader even before the minority government was formed.[10]

Although Varadkar was one of the leading Fine Gael negotiators in the aftermath of the 2016 election, he was privately critical of the way Kenny had conducted the election campaign. The journalists Niall O'Connor and Philip Ryan recount an episode in the middle of the negotiations when Varadkar called over to Murphy's apartment for discussion of the leadership over a few beers before going to a rugby match in the Aviva Stadium.

> Varadkar had clearly given a lot of thought to the matter and listed the reasons he believed he was the man for the job. He said the election campaign was the catalyst for his decision. Kenny's handling of the campaign had been a mess from day one, Leo said, before explaining the strategies he would have deployed if he had been leader.[11]

Although Kenny's assured handling of the Brexit issue in the autumn of 2016 bought him some time, a series of events in February 2017 put his continued leadership at the centre of political debate. A complicated series of events connected with the continuing saga of the Garda whistleblower Sergeant Maurice McCabe and the handling of a claim of impropriety about McCabe by the child family agency Tusla was the catalyst for the final phase of Kenny's leadership. The Taoiseach came into the picture because he told the Dáil he had consulted the Minister for Children, Katherine Zappone, before she met the McCabe family to discuss Tusla's handling of the issue. Zappone stated publicly that Kenny had not spoken to her about the matter, and the issue developed into a full-blown controversy in which the Taoiseach had to apologise to the Dáil. 'I might say mea culpa … I'm guilty here of not giving accurate information.'[12]

The Dublin North-West TD Noel Rock, who seven months earlier had proposed Kenny for Taoiseach and declared his undying loyalty to him, was the first out of the traps, demanding that he set a time limit for his departure. That sparked a frenzy of speculation among Fine Gael TDs about Kenny's future, spooked by the prospect of a general election. Fiach Kelly wrote in the *Irish Times*:

TDs saw the tensions sparked by the Maurice McCabe controversy and feared Fianna Fáil could run to the country. Fine Gael would be fighting an election at best in the throes of a leadership contest or, at worst, with Kenny at the helm. The mood has shifted decisively in the party – from the Cabinet to the backbenches, and even among Kenny loyalists. Backbenchers who just weeks ago saw no rush in changing leadership are now revising their views.[13]

A few days later Varadkar stepped up the pressure on Kenny by breaking cover to tell journalists that the Taoiseach needed to be clear about his intentions. 'The current situation is distracting and destabilising for the government, the party and the country,' he said.[14] That sparked fevered speculation about an immediate leadership challenge, but the pressure on Kenny was eased by an intervention from Simon Coveney, widely regarded as Varadkar's likely rival for the succession. Coveney said there needed to be a cooling-off period of a few months while Kenny travelled to the United States for the annual St Patrick's Day events and prepared for the European Council at the end of April, which would make vital decisions about the EU approach to Brexit.[15]

Varadkar and his supporters backed off when Kenny addressed a meeting of the Fine Gael parliamentary party, at which he gave a broad hint that he would be gone by the summer. That lowered the political temperature, with a consensus in the party that he should be given the time and space to choose the moment of departure.

Kenny was in a relaxed mood on the evening of 16 May when he launched *Nealon's Guide to the 32nd Dáil and 25th Seanad*, edited by Tim Ryan. After the launch he adjourned to Smyth's pub in Haddington Road with some of his oldest friends, including Maurice Manning, for a few convivial pints. The following day he announced to the Fine Gael parliamentary party that he was standing down as leader. The party had two weeks to elect a new leader; but the race between Leo Varadkar and Simon Coveney was over before it began.

Varadkar had an unspectacular start to politics. As a twenty-year-old medical student he contested the 1999 local election for Mulhuddart and achieved only 380 votes. Having diverted his energies into canvassing, he also failed his exams that year at Trinity. Interviewed by Annette O'Donnell of RTÉ before the election, the party's youngest candidate spoke of how doctors can help patients but that 'the Minister for Health can really change things'.[16] It was this outlook that had brought him into politics.

Varadkar was an active member of Young Fine Gael, serving as PRO and reforming the branch in Trinity, along with Lucinda Creighton. He used the party's youth wing to network and increase his profile. As a student he also earned a place on the prestigious Washington Ireland Program for Service and Leadership. But his first election ended in failure.

When Senator Sheila Terry had to vacate her seat for Castleknock on Fingal County Council after the dual mandate was brought to an end in 2003 Varadkar was co-opted in her place and also became the Council's Leas-Chathaoirleach. Eight months later, with a first-preference count of 4,894, which was almost double the quota, he retained the seat at the 2004 local elections. Banishing his 1999 position as the party's third lowest performing candidate, Varadkar had received the highest vote in the country of any party. With such a strong performance, he was tipped as a future TD.[17]

Born in Dublin in January 1979, Varadkar does not come from a political family, although he describes his father as being politically interested. The dinner table in the family home was the scene of many discussions between father and son. 'We would be discussing Mikhail Gorbachev and the Ayatollah Khomeini's war in Iran, Iraq, Charlie Haughey, and whatever else was happening in the news.'[18] Ashok Varadkar, a native of India, met his wife, the Irish-born nurse Miriam Howell, when they were both working in the medical sector in England. Having tried living in India for a spell, they moved to Ireland in the 1970s. Medicine runs in the family. Varadkar's older sister, Sophia, is a doctor and his younger sister, Sonia, is a midwife. Having begun his studies in law, he graduated from Trinity's School of Medicine in 2003 and subsequently qualified as a GP in 2010.

When Varadkar really emerged onto the national political scene he divided opinion but nonetheless fascinated people. The correct pronunciation of his name alone was the subject of chatter. But the young politician also knew how to grab attention. Nestlé Lion bars emblazoned with 'Vote No. 1 Leo the Lion' were passed out to the voters of his Dublin West constituency for the 2007 general election. He was the second candidate elected in the closely contested three-seat constituency. Kenny subsequently promoted him to the front bench and gave him the prominent Enterprise, Trade and Employment portfolio.

For many, Varadkar appeared cocky and a bit too sure of himself. A blog entry on his web site in which he wrote 'I really can't wait to get the keys to one of those government jets' raised more than a few eyebrows. It was a joking comment, made in the context of experiencing bowel problems on a long-haul flight after volunteering in Mongolia. It also betrayed his ambition, although he made no secret of this. Speaking after his election to the Dáil, the first-time TD explained, 'I'm certainly ambitious. I'm not going to be sitting around the Dáil bar for the next five years.'[19]

Behind the scenes he was extremely hard-working and brimming with ideas. Paul O'Brien, a member of Kenny's backroom staff, recalled arriving to work several mornings to find Varadkar already waiting at his office door to discuss the latest policy proposals on which he had been working. 'He was an ideas factory in opposition.'[20] His politics were firmly on the right wing, and he appealed to the party's more traditional voters, but he has become more socially liberal. His own evolution mirrors or, perhaps more accurately, is part of the changes that Fine Gael has undergone.

It was in the period before the marriage referendum, as discussed in the previous chapter, that he spoke about his sexuality on Miriam O'Callaghan's radio show. When asked why he had chosen to share that element of his identity, he responded, 'Well, in part personal reasons, because I'm sort of comfortable to talk about it now, wasn't always but I have been in the last couple years, it's not a big deal for me any more.'[21] With the benefit of hindsight, this timeline seems to coincide with Varadkar becoming more relaxed and jovial.

The transformation of his personality should also be seen in the wider political context. With a reputation for straight talking, he was prone to getting himself into trouble. Not long after taking a seat in the Dáil for the first time he annoyed the normally unflappable Bertie Ahern. His exchange of words with the then Taoiseach, in which he said that history would judge Ahern to be both devious and cunning, was well publicised, and Ahern called on Fine Gael to 'rein in the coarse interventions'.[22] Two months later Varadkar asked the then Minister for Justice, Brian Lenihan, if prisoners could be charged for the cost of their time in jail. The party distanced itself from such right-wing thinking, with its Justice spokesman, Charlie Flanagan, suggesting that it was a personal view.[23] By 2011 he had largely, though not entirely, reined in the outbursts. This political maturity was a necessary part of preparing for future leadership.

Varadkar seemed uncomfortable around people at times. Philip Ryan's and Niall O'Connor's biography of him is full of stories from childhood onwards about being shy and socially awkward. As a politician Varadkar certainly isn't the type of person who works a room in the way that Enda Kenny did. But he has developed a quiet sense of humour and has demonstrated a willingness to poke fun at himself, evidenced at times in his Twitter feed, which has won many over. During the Covid-19 quarantine he shared a picture of two Easter eggs, intended for his nephews, on his Instagram account and ran a poll asking if he should eat them himself.

The leadership contest to succeed Enda Kenny happened on a scale never previously seen and was more structured than ever. Past competitions tended to be largely quiet affairs, with some media interviews. Signing a code of conduct agreed by the party's Executive Council, Varadkar and Coveney embarked on a sixteen-day campaign, which included designated regional hustings. In Dublin, Carlow, Galway and Cork the two men participated in debates that were streamed on the Fine Gael Facebook page. Varadkar's performance in these head-to-heads was not particularly outstanding, but before the campaign ever began he had already covered enough ground in the parliamentary party to secure his position. The day after Kenny resigned, a succession of ministers and TDs had declared their support for Varadkar in a carefully orchestrated series of announcements that had been planned for some time. It became clear within twenty-four hours that Varadkar had the committed support of more than 50 of the 73-member parliamentary party.

Amidst their visions for Fine Gael, familiar themes emerged, particularly from Coveney, who anchored his ideas in the party's past. Declan Costello's Just Society proposal of 1964–65 has offered a useful slogan for Fine Gael politicians, who, in the decades since, generally use it as shorthand to imply or demonstrate a commitment to social justice. Coveney employed the term frequently, and writing in the *Sunday Business Post* he urged support for his leadership bid so that Fine Gael could be 'a party that builds on the history, tradition and timeless aspirations of the Just Society and seek[s] to unite, rather than divide, society so that everyone can make a contribution and lead a fulfilling life'.[24] This was rhetoric. Beyond the title, the idea that the document's aspirations are 'timeless' is dubious. The content was highly specific to the 1960s. By invoking Costello's legacy Coveney was attempting to set himself apart from Varadkar. It was, according to Coveney's presentation, those committed to social justice versus those who 'got up early' (an expression closely associated with Varadkar). Such contributions, as well as his references to the Garret FitzGerald era, were clearly intended to win grass-roots support. Arguably, Coveney also had an eye on the long game by talking in terms appealing to the public. But his campaign had had a slow start, and, as Varadkar's biographers have noted, he was outmanoeuvred at every turn by a man who was obsessed with becoming Taoiseach.[25]

The parliamentary party gathered in Dublin on 2 June to vote, while polling stations around the country had been open to all others with a vote between 29 May and 1 June. The ballots were then taken to a national count centre for sorting on 2 June. The votes cast by the seventy-three members of the parliamentary party accounted for 65 per cent of the total vote; almost 21,000 party members, who had held their membership for at least two years, accounted for 25 per cent; and 235 local representatives made up the remaining 10 per cent of the vote. Coveney easily won the popular vote of the membership, but the overwhelming majority of ministers and TDs backed Varadkar, on the grounds that he was the candidate most likely to save their seats and lead them back to power for a third successive term.

When the declaration came, Varadkar was hoisted on the shoulders of his supporters. Returned to the ground, he embraced his parents and then his partner, Matthew Barrett. The fact that he had been expected to win did not detract from the emotion of that moment. Varadkar later recalled that receiving a hug from his father had been a 'weird experience; I can count on the one hand the amount of times that happened.'[26]

Exactly ten years after taking a seat in the Dáil for the first time, Leo Varadkar was elected Taoiseach on 14 June 2017. At thirty-eight, he was the youngest politician to hold the office. He also became one of a small group of openly gay prime ministers in Europe, which included Xavier Bettel in Luxembourg and Ana Brnabić in Serbia, elected a few days after him. Recalling both Michael Collins and Arthur Griffith in the Dáil after his election, Varadkar, like Fine Gael leaders before him, positioned himself as heir to an important legacy. This was reaffirmed the following month in an interview with the American news magazine *Time*. Readers learned that he had a copy of the first sovereign bond issued to the Irish Free State ready to be hung on the wall in his new office. The bond was there, he explained to the journalist Jennifer Duggan, as a daily reminder that 'no matter what happens even the revolutionaries had to go to the bond market in order to sustain the Free State'.[27]

Though a modern, forward-looking Taoiseach who tasked his government with building 'an Ireland, a republic of opportunity', history would also have an important place in his government, as we will see later in this chapter.[28] It is notable that he appointed a historian, Professor Patrick Geoghegan of Trinity College, to his staff as speech-writer and researcher.

The change of leadership brought with it departures and new arrivals in the Taoiseach's backroom staff. Varadkar's was a new administration, and the majority of those who had worked under Enda Kenny left with their former leader. However, the new Taoiseach wanted a degree of continuity, and so Angela Flanagan continued as a special adviser and Feargal Purcell remained on as government press secretary for a few months.[29] Sarah Meade, who had previously been media adviser to Heather Humphreys, and Clare Mungovan, formerly adviser to the minister of state Paul Kehoe, both joined the team. His trusted confidant Brian Murphy was appointed chief of staff.

Varadkar's new cabinet was also a mix of continuity and change. One of the notable features was the prominence of younger politicians in leading positions. Simon Coveney moved from Housing to Foreign Affairs, with responsibility for Brexit; his handling of the latter greatly enhanced his profile. Eoghan Murphy, Varadkar's campaign manager, was rewarded for his support and replaced Coveney in Housing. Also rewarded was Paschal Donohoe, who stayed in the Department of Public Expenditure and Reform but also took on Finance.

Resisting pressure to remove him, Varadkar kept Simon Harris in Health. Harris's inclusion is interesting. He was the only senior minister, apart obviously from Coveney, who had not supported Varadkar's leadership bid. The two men had something of a strained relationship, although it is reported to have since improved.[30]

Though achieving something of a generational shift among those who would be most prominent, the gender aspect of the new cabinet was somewhat lacking. Arguably this was more noticeable than ever because of the comparisons with Trudeau and Macron, who had both achieved gender balance in their cabinets. Speculation that the position of Tánaiste would pass from Frances Fitzgerald to Coveney proved unfounded. Varadkar was loyal to Fitzgerald, but his decision to retain her as his deputy could also be seen as an attempt at balancing the leadership of the government. Joining her at the cabinet table was Regina Doherty in Employment and Social Protection and Mary Mitchell O'Connor, who was made a super-junior minister. This was a demotion and a blow to the Dún Laoghaire TD. Following Frances Fitzgerald's resignation (discussed later in this chapter), Josepha Madigan joined the cabinet as Minister for Culture, Heritage and the Gaeltacht in November 2017.

Among ministers of state, Marcella Corcoran Kennedy went to the back benches, while Helen McEntee moved from Mental Health and Older People to become Minister of State for EU Affairs in the Department of the Taoiseach. Another young politician, McEntee played a very visible role in the Irish response to Brexit, further adding to the youthful image of Varadkar's government.

Like Kenny in 2011, Varadkar's term began with an important visit, although the arrival of the Canadian Prime Minister, Justin Trudeau, attracted less attention than that of Queen Elizabeth or President Obama. It did, however, afford a photo opportunity that seemed to sum up politics at that time. The pair were photographed enjoying an evening jog in the Phoenix Park. Though the top positions in Britain and America were held by older politicians, Varadkar became Taoiseach at a time when international politics appeared to be defined by youth, and there was a moment when the media's gaze seemed to fix on this wave of young leaders. Emmanuel Macron was elected President of France a month before Varadkar became Taoiseach. Vivienne Walt captured the reasons for the interest when she observed of the two men in a feature '40 under 40' in the American business magazine *Fortune*, 'strikingly young, they have shattered not only the age floor, but the hidebound rules and assumptions to which previous generations have clung for decades.'[31]

Over the following two years the state also hosted the Duke and Duchess of Sussex, Pope Francis, and the American Vice-President, Mike Pence. Varadkar's partner Matthew Barrett made appearances during all of these visits. Varadkar made use of such occasions to deliver pointed speeches that also highlighted the transformations Irish society had undergone. Speaking in St Patrick's Hall in Dublin Castle during the visit of Pope Francis, the Taoiseach did not shy away from the dark history of the Catholic Church in Ireland, making reference to the Magdalene Laundries and clerical sex abuse scandals. The conclusion of his speech built on the message previously heralded by Enda Kenny about the position of the church. He spoke of how he hoped that church and state could build a new relationship, 'one in which religion is no longer at the centre of our society, but in which it still has an important place'.[32]

With a record of opposition to LGBT rights and dogged by accusations that he is a supporter of conversion therapy, Pence's visit in September 2019 was watched with interest. Judd Deere, the deputy White House press secretary at the time, subsequently attempted to present a lunch at which Matthew Barrett was also present as evidence that Pence was not 'anti-gay' – a claim that was widely ridiculed.[33] Earlier that year Varadkar had made a pointed comment to the assembled media following a St Patrick's Day breakfast at the Vice-President's residence.

> I lived in a country where if I'd tried to be myself at the time, it would have ended up breaking laws. But today, that is all changed. I stand here, leader of my country, flawed and human, but judged by my political actions, and not by my sexual orientation, my skin tone, gender or religious beliefs.[34]

Becoming Taoiseach in the middle of 2017 meant that Varadkar's time in power would coincide with Britain's withdrawal from the European Union. Addressing the Dáil on the day that he became Taoiseach, he confirmed that Ireland would be at the 'heart of Europe'.[35] Brexit is a complex subject, and the Irish relationship to Britain's withdrawal contains enough material for a book of its own, as Tony Connelly's excellent *Brexit and Ireland* demonstrates. This chapter does not allow the space for more than a brief look at Fine Gael's position.

Varadkar took a hard line from the outset and was adamant that the border question was one for Britain to solve. As he put, 'if [the British] want to put forward smart solutions, technological solutions for borders of the future and all of that, that's up to them.' This attitude angered the DUP, with a furious Nigel Dodds threatening to use his party's influence over the British government to prevent any border in the Irish Sea. As far as the DUP was concerned, a sea-based border was a nationalist attempt to cut Northern Ireland off from the rest of the United Kingdom.[36]

Theresa May confirmed on 8 December 2017 that, on the basis of the first phase of talks, there would be no hard border in Ireland. As the months ticked by, the border remained a permanent companion to the discussions, and in June 2018 Brussels warned that serious differences remained. On 15 January 2019 the House of Commons rejected by a staggering margin the withdrawal agreement that Theresa May had negotiated. British isolation was highlighted in April when the German

Chancellor, Angela Merkel, flew to Dublin to meet Varadkar. This was the moment that David Davis, formerly Secretary of State for Exiting the European Union, had been waiting for: that Merkel would tell the Irish government that the border would have to be sacrificed. But, as Fintan O'Toole observed, 'She understood the border question more deeply, and had much more emotional investment in it, than the government that is actually responsible for it … ever had.' Merkel had, after all, lived behind the Iron Curtain.[37]

An embattled Theresa May finally announced on 24 May that she would be standing down as leader of the Conservative Party, and in the contest that followed, Boris Johnson was elected her successor. This change of personality had some benefits for Ireland, as Johnson and Varadkar appeared to work well together. As one member of the Taoiseach's backroom staff put it, 'there probably wouldn't have been a deal without the personal connection between Boris Johnson and Leo Varadkar. They hit it off and were able to go back and forth to each other confidentially, which helped.'[38] Of particular significance was their meeting in October 2019. Having demanded major changes to the Brexit deal and been rebuffed in August, Johnson was faced with the reality that Europe would not abandon the backstop. When he met Varadkar in Cheshire that October the two leaders spent an hour and a half talking alone before issuing a joint statement about their 'detailed' and 'constructive' discussion, saying that they could 'see a pathway to a possible deal'.[39] As we will see in the next chapter, Fine Gael gave prominence to that deal in the 2020 election.

Despite the convivial relationship between the two men, Varadkar did not hold back from criticisms. In January 2020, before Britain's leaving the EU, he blamed British ignorance of Ireland for the Brexit impasse.[40]

The Covid-19 pandemic complicated the British transition period and the country's scope for negotiating a trade deal with the EU before the year-end deadline. Nonetheless the Johnson government has maintained that it will not be seeking any form of extension. At the time of writing (May 2020) Simon Coveney warned of a 'very difficult crisis' that could result in no trade deal in the autumn.[41] Clare Foges in the *Times* commented that a no-deal Brexit would previously have been 'deeply unwise' for Britain but that in the light of the pandemic it would now be 'unhinged'.[42] The implications for Ireland would be considerable.

Although Brexit has dominated European politics, the 2020 exit poll would reveal that it mattered little to Irish voters. Brexit was essentially an abstract idea, and though there were implications for the border and for the diaspora in Britain, for the majority of people in Ireland it was happening in another country. More significantly, as we will see later in this chapter, more pressing issues, such as housing and health, which had far greater and more immediate relevance to voters' everyday lives, inevitably took precedence. Brexit was Fine Gael's equivalent of Cumann na nGaedheal's achievements in the area of what was then called external affairs. Such things as membership of the League of Nations, the Balfour Declaration and the Statute of Westminster were all important for the new state's status but they were too removed to have any impact on the ordinary voter.

Only months after becoming Taoiseach, Varadkar faced a crisis that threatened to bring down his government. The events played out over the course of a week, culminating in the resignation of his Tánaiste. Interest in the McCabe whistleblower controversy, discussed earlier in this chapter, was revived after parliamentary questions from Alan Kelly of Labour brought to light an email from May 2015. The Minister for Justice, Frances Fitzgerald, had been informed at that time of allegations that a legal team, on behalf of the Garda Síochána, had attempted to undermine Sergeant McCabe's testimony to the O'Higgins Commission. The date contradicted her claim that she only became aware of the aggressive strategy he was subjected to a year later, in May 2016. She maintained that she did not recall receiving the email. The email was subsequently published in edited form on 21 November, and the following day Varadkar instructed department officials to conduct a review of other relevant correspondence with the Department of Justice.

A report by the *Irish Times* on 23 November that the department had actually unearthed the email two weeks earlier was raised in the Dáil during leader's questions by Jim O'Callaghan of Fianna Fáil, who described the timeline as 'mind-boggling'. He also accused Fitzgerald of seeking to undermine legitimate concerns about what the state had known and of denying the seriousness of the issues raised by the opposition. Four times, in various forms, Fitzgerald responded on the occasion that there had been no effort by her to suppress the May 2015 email.[43]

At that point both Sinn Féin and Fianna Fáil threatened to table a motion of no confidence in the minister. The confidence and supply deal would have been brought to an end if Fianna Fáil went ahead with such a motion, causing the government to collapse. Efforts by Varadkar on 24, 25 and 26 November to head off such action by meeting Micheál Martin were unsuccessful. Varadkar's overtures had included an apology from Fitzgerald and an offer to break up the Department of Justice as part of an overhaul of its workings, but while Martin was receptive to the latter he wanted Fitzgerald removed from her post.[44]

New documents uncovered during the search that Varadkar had ordered and that were released after 6 p.m. on Monday 27 November seriously undermined the Tánaiste. The latest set of emails revealed that Fitzgerald had 'noted' the May 2015 email and that she had also received further briefings, including advice on how to respond to the media. At 9:49 that evening Fitzgerald tweeted that, as Minister for Justice, she could not have interfered in the O'Higgins Commission and in a follow-up tweet commented that the Disclosures Tribunal would 'objectively judge the appropriateness' of her conduct.[45]

The following day the *Irish Examiner* was reporting on the front page that 'Ministers desert Fitzgerald as pressure rises'.[46] The cabinet met that morning, and, amid mounting pressure and to avoid a snap election, Fitzgerald announced her intention to resign. Varadkar had been clear in his support for his colleague throughout the crisis and accepted her resignation with reluctance. Later she would be vindicated by the third interim report of the Disclosures Tribunal, otherwise known as the Charleton Report, which found that she acted appropriately at all times. Speaking afterwards, Micheál Martin expressed regret over what had happened to Fitzgerald but refused to apologise, making it clear that the Dáil had lost confidence in her because of withheld information.[47]

Varadkar had first crossed political paths with Fitzgerald when he was a teenager and he spent a week in her Leinster House office on transition year work experience.[48] Over the years a friendship developed and endured. He expressed his anger about her treatment over the whistleblower affair on more than one occasion, describing it as 'bang out of order'.[49] He is said to have been 'personally delighted' that she was exonerated by the Charleton Report and by her election to the European Parliament in July 2019.[50]

On becoming leader of Fine Gael, Varadkar announced that a referendum on the eighth amendment would be held within a year. There had been a growing grass-roots campaign to repeal it, and following the marriage referendum there was an immediate sense that the momentum for change could be harnessed and translated into support for another campaign. Amidst the celebrations the question of 'what next?' first appeared on social media and soon made its way into the national press. The eighth amendment was immediately identified, and the minister of state Kathleen Lynch was quoted as saying that, following the success of the marriage referendum, repeal should be 'do-able'.[51]

On 29 January 2018 the cabinet gave formal approval to holding a referendum. When the Minister for Health, Simon Harris, announced in the Dáil that it would be put before voters later in the year he appeared to place the explanation in the context of the 'what next?' line of thinking. 'Every now and then an issue comes before us,' he began, 'which challenges us to think about what kind of a country we want to be and what kind of a society we are.'[52] What was most noticeable about the campaign that followed was the strength of women's voices and their growing determination to repeal legislation that had made such an impact on their lives. As the author Tara Flynn had put it at the annual March for Choice gathering in September 2015, Irish women who wanted access to abortion were not on the fringes of society, they were society.[53]

That was the striking thing about Harris's speech in the Dáil. He spoke about women not as abstract or shadowy figures but as actual people, in a way that was lacking in presentations of the issue by previous governments. They were not 'faceless women', he said, rather 'they are our friends, neighbours, sisters, cousins, mothers, aunts, and wives.' The need for politics to recognise the distinct identity and needs of women was a point that feminist and women's groups had been making for decades. Although not dealing with abortion specifically, publications such as *Chains or Change* by the Irish Women's Liberation Movement in the 1970s had revealed just how 'faceless' women were in society.

Fine Gael took what could be described as an unneutral-neutral position in the campaign. Varadkar informed the parliamentary party that Fine Gael would not take an official stance, leaving TDs free to campaign as they saw fit. However, Josepha Madigan was made campaign co-ordinator of a group within the party that favoured a Yes vote. Having only been in the cabinet for four months at that point, it was a big undertaking. Her remit was to work in tandem with Together for Yes, an umbrella group made up of more than seventy organisations, groups and communities representing a cross-section of civil society. Though Madigan has always maintained that she is a politician who happens to be a woman, she recalled that it was hard not to feel acutely female in this campaign. Her motivation echoes the aforementioned women's groups.

> As the first female lawyer at cabinet (solicitor/barrister) and only the 19th female Cabinet Minister since the foundation of the state, I felt an enhanced sense of duty in terms of representing all those women whose voices never got heard over many centuries in Ireland. Our voices, both individually and collectively, were silenced on many issues.[54]

Varadkar's instruction that TDs were free to campaign on either side was a wise one, born of the fact that there was a difference of opinion in the party (as there was also in Fianna Fáil). In the 1980s, when the eighth amendment was first inserted in the Constitution, Garret FitzGerald had asked members of the parliamentary party to refrain from any interventions, but he was ignored. Oliver Flanagan, Tom O'Donnell, Michael Joe Cosgrave and Alice Glenn all campaigned extensively, and often outside their own constituencies. Defying the leader only deepened divisions in the party at that time. In 2018 there were a number of deputies and senators who were either completely opposed to or uneasy about repealing the eighth amendment, although few came out publicly in support of the No campaign. It has been suggested that Varadkar learned from the fallout over the 2013 legislation (see Chapter 14) and knew that a top-down approach could result in further resignations. In addition to allowing a free vote he also reassured members of the parliamentary party that the position they took would not affect promotion prospects. 'There were audible sighs of relief.'[55] The campaign was less divisive for party morale than had previously been the case. From Madigan's point of view, 'we respected each other's views and they [colleagues on the No side] knew I had a job to do and it wasn't an easy one.' She was never lobbied by her No colleagues.[56]

The referendum was held on 25 May 2018. The exit poll indicated that it would be carried by a strong majority, confirmed the following day as ballot boxes were opened to reveal that 66.4 per cent had voted Yes. With the exception of Co. Donegal, the country had endorsed repealing the eighth amendment. For Varadkar personally this was a success. His first major challenge as party leader and Taoiseach was an issue that most politicians had been deftly avoiding for years. Although the referendum was arguably inevitable, that it was brought to the voters by a Fine Gael government also indicated that the party was not reliant on a partner of the left to embrace social change. It showed how much the party had changed.

The arrival of 2018 had brought regular front-page news stories about overcrowding in hospitals. The scandal of patients, particularly the elderly, left on trolleys was not a temporary one. The annual figures from the Irish Nurses' and Midwives' Organisation that showed overcrowding in 2018 to be the worst on record were surpassed by the 2019 figures, with University Hospital, Limerick, being the worst affected. Simon Harris was heavily criticised.

The government was also dealing with another health scandal, one that stretched back several years. Cervical Check, the national cancer screening scheme, was launched in September 2008. Vicky Phelan is now a household name as a result of the failure of the system. She was told in 2011 that her routine smear test had come back normal, but an audit of tests for educational and training purposes by Cervical Check in 2014 found that this was incorrect. Mrs Phelan herself was only informed in 2017, and by then she was terminally ill. She subsequently sued the American laboratory that was subcontracted by Cervical Check and was awarded €2½ million by the High Court in April 2018. There were 208 women wrongly diagnosed; 162 of them had not been informed of the revised results and, of those, seventeen had died.

Controversy followed the Minister for Health into 2019. Aside from the continued overcrowding crisis, the cost of building the National Children's Hospital was spiralling. Sinn Féin had tabled a motion of no confidence in Harris on 20 February but, with Fianna Fáil abstaining, it was defeated by 58 votes to 53.

The Department of Health is something of a poisoned chalice for politicians. The young TD seemed to age and looked visibly strained as his time as minister wore on. In February and again in April 2019 protesters from the 'Fingal Battalion Direct Action Group' acted on their slogan of #BringItToTheirDoors and gathered outside Harris's home in Greystones. Politicians across the political divide were critical of this invasion of his privacy, particularly as his wife and three-week-old daughter were in the house on the first occasion. Responding to such criticisms, the administrators of the group's Facebook page posted, 'Simon Harris is not invincible because he now has a family, what about all the families that Simon and his party have affected.'[57] Although most comments on the page support the group's actions, one comment on that particular post captured the broader mood. 'Not in the name of nurses #notinmyname,' it read. Other ministers and Fine Gael politicians were subjected to similar protests over the course of 2019.

The motion of no confidence in Harris was the third that Varadkar's government had survived. The other two were tabled in relation to the Minister for Housing, Eoghan Murphy. The first came in September 2018. Earlier in the year two men who had been sleeping rough in different parts of the country had died from hypothermia within forty-eight hours of each other. The shocking headlines were not isolated, and other homeless deaths exposed the inadequacies of the country's housing system. Introducing the motion, Eoin Ó Broin, Sinn Féin's spokesperson on housing, presented a stark picture of Murphy's fifteen months in the department.

> Homelessness has increased by 25 per cent, child homelessness has increased by 34 per cent, pensioner homelessness has increased by 40 per cent, rents have increased by 7 per cent and house prices by 6 per cent, delivery of social housing remains glacial, not a single affordable home has been delivered by any central government scheme, private sector output in the main is overpriced and unaffordable, and vacant housing stock remains higher than the norm in other comparable countries.[58]

Murphy survived on that occasion by 59 votes to 49, while Fianna Fáil abstained, in line with the confidence and supply deal. Anger grew, and in May 2019 thousands gathered in Dublin for the 'Raise the Roof' rally to protest against the housing crisis and homelessness. In an effort to tackle the shortage Murphy had floated the notion of 'co-living'. This was widely ridiculed, and the *Irish Times* columnist Una Mullally accused the minister of being tone deaf.[59] Murphy took to Twitter to defend his proposal.

> CoLiving is one option as part of bringing greater choice into the housing market. Works in other cities across the world. We wouldn't judge concept of houses on one planning app. & should not do that here. Politicians trying to restrict choice for younger generations is wrong.[60]

The idea failed to gain traction. By October the homelessness figures had exceeded 10,000 for eight consecutive months. A year after surviving Sinn Féin's motion of no confidence, Murphy was heading towards another, this time tabled by the Social Democrats. Thirty-five abstentions saved the government from political embarrassment that December. The motion was narrowly lost, by 56 votes to 53, and it was obvious that the government was nearing the end of its life.

The housing and homelessness crisis, together with health, dominated domestic politics and later became the big issues on doorsteps during the 2020 general election. Indeed the exit poll showed that these were the most important issues when people decided how to vote. Having done quite poorly at the local and European elections in 2019, Sinn Féin refocused its message, emphasising the positive steps the party would take to deal with the housing crisis and to address the problems in the health service.[61] Mobilising on these issues (as we will see in the next chapter) really paid dividends for Mary Lou McDonald's party.

Under Varadkar's leadership, Fine Gael took time to reflect on its past, but not on those elements that typically excite the party faithful. The declaration of the republic in 1948 has not been an event routinely marked by the party, nor has it received the same level of interest that is applied to remembering Michael Collins. Readers will recall from Chapter 3 that the decision to remove Ireland from the Commonwealth and to make the country a republic was not welcomed by elements within and supporters of the party. During the 2011 presidential election Gay Mitchell had said that rejoining the Commonwealth was something that should be discussed, a view echoed by Senator Frank Feighan in 2016, while as recently as 2018 Senator Neale Richmond tweeted that rejoining would be 'good for increasing levels of reconciliation on this island; for expanding Ireland's global network; providing new trade opportunities; allowing access to [the] world's second largest games.'[62] But, according to Varadkar, Ireland returning to the Commonwealth was not something that was on the agenda.[63]

Varadkar has shown greater interest in commemorating the birth of the republic than any of his predecessors. As Patrick Geoghegan explained,

> This is part of what Leo Varadkar promised to do when he became leader, to reconnect Fine Gael to its history, what the party had done and should be proud of having done. The members are connected to the Michael Collins part of its history, have an

awareness of the Just Society period and the ambitions of the Garret FitzGerald era of reform. But so much of party history is underappreciated.[64]

In April 2018, at Varadkar's request, Geoghegan organised a gathering of the parliamentary party and National Executive to reflect on the republic and to discuss what a more formal commemoration might look like. That June, Varadkar also delivered the address at the annual John A. Costello Commemoration in Dean's Grange Cemetery, where he spoke of his desire to mark the 75th anniversary of the republic in 2024. The following April, on the occasion of the 70th anniversary, the Department of the Taoiseach worked with the Royal Irish Academy to organise a public event at which Varadkar gave the opening remarks. There, he described the Republic of Ireland Act as a testament to the vision of the inter-party government and the revolutionary generation. A video about the declaration of the republic, to be shared with the party's members in 2020, had also been planned, but it was disrupted by the Covid-19 crisis.

During the questions-and-answers portion of the event at the RIA one strand of the Fine Gael view was represented by a member of the audience, Murt O'Sullivan. A long-time member of the grass roots, he shared his view that withdrawing from the Commonwealth was a mistake. But Varadkar clearly sees 1948–9 as a key moment in Fine Gael's history. His eagerness to commemorate the event can be interpreted in different ways. By the time he became Taoiseach the decade of centenaries was in its fifth year. According to Geoghegan, commemorating the republic was seen as something separate.[65] But although the creation of the republic has clearly not reached its one-hundredth anniversary, marking it is certainly in the spirit of the programme of commemoration that began in 2012. And it affords Fine Gael the opportunity to emphasise the leading role that the party played at crucial moments in the country's evolution.

Remembering the republic also allows Fine Gael to stake its claim to republicanism. When Mercier Press published Kevin Boland's book *Fine Gael: British or Irish?* in 1984, the provocative choice of title spoke to a long tradition that saw Fine Gael's critics position the party in relation to Britain. Dismissively labelled as West-British or pro-Commonwealth, Fine Gael's declaration of the republic undermined such accusations, but they resurfaced periodically. When Jeffrey Donaldson of the DUP spoke at the Fine Gael annual conference in March 2019 and suggested that Ireland rejoin the Commonwealth his speech was met with applause. This was interpreted by critics as evidence of Fine Gael's leanings. Discussion boards were rife with the type of language traditionally used to slur the party, as illustrated by one contributor to Reddit who suggested, 'Neale Richmond, although a nice fella, is a straight up west Brit, and I suspect he's not the only one.'[66]

With the growth of Sinn Féin was Varadkar attempting to wrestle back the meaning of republicanism from its associations with a particular movement? Geoghegan admitted, 'I think that was definitely a factor,' but he added, 'with Brexit such a dominant issue no one was doubting FG's nationalist credentials.'[67] Yet, as the Donaldson episode showed, there were plenty willing to question Fine Gael's intentions. Speaking after the 2020 election, Varadkar was keen to remind voters that Fine Gael was the party that founded the republic while describing Sinn Féin as having a 'fake history'.[68] This was the classic Fine Gael trope.

Jeffrey Donaldson had been invited to the party's conference in Wexford to participate in a panel discussion about north-south relations. Such relationship-building exercises were essential because of the political impasse that had paralysed Stormont. His attendance at the conference afforded Simon Coveney a further opportunity to speak to him. As Minister for Foreign Affairs, Coveney had already begun work with the then Northern Ireland secretary, Karen Bradley, to discuss the return of devolution, and he would play a central role in restoring power-sharing after a three-year deadlock.

When Coveney and Bradley first met at the beginning of 2018 it had been just over a year since Martin McGuinness of Sinn Féin had resigned as Deputy First Minister in protest over the 'cash for ash' scandal, bringing an end to almost ten years of devolved government. Briefly put, the First Minister, Arlene Foster, had introduced the Renewable Heat Incentive, a 'green energy' scheme, in November 2012 as part of Northern Ireland's strategy to meet renewable-energy targets in her then capacity as Minister for Enterprise, Trade and Investment. However, the scheme did not actually offer any incentives to be efficient, and instead businesses were paid higher subsidies for the more heat they generated. The scandal caused a crisis of confidence in the North's political institutions.

By failing to step aside or to show any contrition when this was exposed, Foster essentially forced Sinn Féin to act in January 2017, and the climate in which devolved government was toppled would make it difficult to restore Stormont, even when both leaderships were willing to compromise to do so.[69] The Assembly elections in March reduced the DUP's ten-seat lead over Sinn Féin to just one, and the subsequent talks for re-entering government failed. The initial three-week time limit for agreeing a basis for government was repeatedly extended, so that by July the parties were into their fourth set of talks. By then it was marching season, and discussions were parked.

Divided on issues such as the Irish language, same-sex marriage and abortion, the assembly remained closed for business but was haunted by the spectre of Brexit. The political landscape had been gradually shifting since 2012. A new generation of Tory politicians, and some in the British Labour Party, seemed comfortable with disregarding the principles that underpinned the Belfast Agreement, perhaps even willing to abandon it altogether. What Brexit would mean for Northern Ireland in a climate when the credibility of British commitments to the state were questionable was worrying.[70] Having a functioning Assembly was hugely important. There were moments when it looked as if a breakthrough in the impasse might come – when Varadkar and May both travelled to Stormont in February 2018, for example – but they never amounted to anything substantial.

It took the tragic and senseless death of Lyra McKee to really concentrate minds. The 29-year-old journalist was murdered by the New IRA as she observed rioting in the Creggan estate in Derry in April 2019. The following month Coveney and Bradley led renewed, intensified talks with the Stormont parties, but it was not until January 2020 that anything tangible was achieved. In the meantime Boris Johnson had replaced Theresa May, and Karen Bradley, undone by her own ignorance of the Northern Ireland state, was sacked. A week of intensive talks finally produced wide-ranging proposals on 9 January that included an office of identity and cultural expression, a reduction in the powers of the petition of concern, which had been used to block same-sex marriage, and a package of measures to create more robust and sustainable institutions.

It had been a long road, and in a tweet thanking his team in the Department of Foreign Affairs, Coveney joked, 'Hopefully their families haven't changed the locks when they get home tonight.'[71]

Leo Varadkar was on top of the world in October 2019. The much-feared no-deal Brexit, with the consequent re-emergence of a hard border in Ireland, had been avoided, thanks to his walk in the Wirral with Boris Johnson. His ratings in the opinion polls, and those of his government, soared. When Johnson moved within days to capitalise on the breakthrough by calling a general election in the UK, some of Varadkar's ministers urged him to do the same. Instead he hesitated and then backed away from a snap election. It was a disastrous decision for Fine Gael and arguably for the country as well.

THE END OF CIVIL WAR POLITICS?

'In the middle of this extraordinary pandemic and crisis in the country, you're trying to put together a government with, of all people, Fianna Fáil. Historically, it's extraordinary to see yourself and Micheál Martin holding hands, if you'll excuse the expression.'

'We haven't done that yet – and we can't do that any more either!'

– RYAN TUBRIDY AND LEO VARADKAR,
THE LATE LATE SHOW, 1 MAY 2020.

Leo Varadkar demonstrated genuine leadership qualities in his handling of Brexit. Right through 2019 he stuck rigidly to the line that there could be no change to the Irish backstop, which formed a central part of the UK withdrawal agreement.

Boris Johnson flew to Dublin to meet Varadkar on 9 September. It was the first meeting between the two and, as noted in the previous chapter, the two men struck up a personal rapport.[1] On the way back to London, on board a small Royal Air Force plane with his closest advisers, Johnson was in a buoyant mood, full of bravado. 'We're going to get a deal,' he declared to his aides, pacing up and down the aisle, throwing his arms out wide and pushing out his chest, according to journalist Tom McTague, citing senior official sources.[2]

Varadkar also got an immediate sense that a deal might be possible.

> The personal dynamic I had with Boris Johnson was very different to that with Theresa May. She's a very good woman. We never had a row or anything, but every time I met her or spoke to her she stuck to script. So we never managed to have the meeting where the deal gets done, where you have that conversation without officials where you can say, 'If I were to say this, what would you do?' Unfortunately we never were able to have that meeting with Theresa even though I did try it on occasion.[3]

The Taoiseach and Prime Minister met again on 24 September at the UN, and Varadkar was hopeful. He recalled, 'I managed to build that relationship with Boris in our meetings and phone conversations and just exchanging text messages. His kind of red line was that he needed to perform a "backstopectomy", as he put it. I'm not sure if that was for my benefit as a doctor, but he kept saying he had to have a backstopectomy.'[4]

By early October, though, with no sign of the EU backing down, Johnson was in a tight corner. British business was aghast at the consequences of a sudden crash out of the EU single market, for which no preparations had been made. On the Irish side there was serious worry that the backstop, designed to prevent a hard border on the island, might actually create the very thing it was designed to avoid. Johnson had a fraught phone call with Angela Merkel on 8 October. The Chancellor told the Prime Minister that the backstop was fundamental to the EU position and would not be abandoned. Immediately after that call Johnson phoned Varadkar, and the two men spoke for 45 minutes and agreed to meet two days later in a final effort to find a compromise.[5]

The Taoiseach suggested that the meeting should take place near Liverpool, a city with close Irish associations. The media were only informed the night before and were not given the location, which turned out to be Thornton Manor in the Wirral. A team of high-powered officials from both sides accompanied the two leaders, but they met on their own for an hour and a half. During their discussions Johnson made a major concession. He let go of the insistence that any customs checks between Ireland and the UK would have to be on the island of Ireland, accepting instead that there would be a trade border between the two countries in the Irish Sea. For his part, Varadkar made an important concession by agreeing that any deal would have to be reviewed by the Northern Ireland Assembly in 2022. The agreement transformed the doom-laden atmosphere.[6]

'Leading up to that meeting in the Wirral I think part of the dynamic was that Boris was keen to get a deal and then have an election, and I was coming to the point where the election was coming up in Ireland as well. And then there was the deadline of Brexit itself,' Varadkar observed.

> I think all that helped to set the environment, under which we could come to a compromise. Because in the Wirral it was just the two of us in the room. And we called in the officials afterwards to give them a rough outline of what we'd agreed. Although obviously I didn't go into that meeting, not having apprised John Callinan [the top Irish official on Brexit] as to where this was likely to end up and where we might be able to move to. By that stage Boris had convinced us that he definitely wanted a deal, although some people were still questioning that. For me the backstop was not totemic. It was the outcome that mattered. We came up with what effectively turned out to be a front stop.[7]

The compromise was immediately accepted by Michel Barnier and the EU negotiating team and was ratified by the European Council in Brussels a week later. The backstop was replaced by the Irish protocol, which would put the trade border with the UK down the middle of the Irish Sea. From an Irish point of view the deal ensured that there would be no hard border. From the British standpoint the hated backstop, which would have kept the UK closely aligned to the single market, was gone.

Varadkar never doubted that the new formula would be acceptable to Barnier and the EU, but he hoped that it might also be acceptable to the Democratic Unionist Party.

> At that point in the Wirral we thought that might be possible, because ultimately the decision was being left with the people of Northern Ireland. We hoped that we would get the DUP to come on board, but ultimately we didn't. And of course that was up to the Prime Minister, not me. The DUP were not going to be told by an Irish Taoiseach what to think, and you have to respect that. It was unfortunate, but Boris was faced with the same choice as Theresa May, whether he was willing to stand up to the DUP to get a deal with Europe, and he did.[8]

When they refused to play ball, Johnson abandoned the DUP. One observer noted that officials in both London and Dublin were clear that if the talks had been left in the hands of technocratic negotiators, a deal would not have been reached. 'This was an agreement made by Johnson and Varadkar themselves, built on risk and face-to-face diplomacy.'[9]

The outcome was generally greeted in Ireland as a triumph for Varadkar. He showed an ability to grasp a sensible compromise that involved a serious concession to the British but delivered the fundamental Irish goal. When Johnson got the deal through the House of Commons and called a general election there was fevered speculation that Varadkar might do the same.

The Minister for Finance, Paschal Donohoe, had delivered the final budget of the confidence and supply arrangement with Fianna Fáil in early October. It was not the pre-election splurge so many had expected but rather a prudent measure that aimed at a significant budget surplus in 2020 to cope with the inevitable fall-out from Brexit. Time would quickly prove the importance of that approach with the economic dislocation resulting from Covid-19. With the confidence and supply agreement at an end and the prospect of a hard border caused by Brexit gone, there was an overwhelming argument in favour of going to the country. Young ministers, such as Simon Harris and Eoghan Murphy, were in favour, but the Fianna Fáil leader warned against an election until the Brexit process was finally settled.

Faced with conflicting advice, Varadkar announced on 30 October that there would not be an election in 2019, and instead he expressed a preference for May 2020. It was reported that Varadkar had told his cabinet he was Taoiseach first and Fine Gael leader second and 'that while an election now may be the best time for the party it might not be for the country.'[10]

With the benefit of hindsight, Varadkar regrets not having gone in November, but he does not accept that it inevitably would have been a better result. 'I always thought we'd get more than 35 seats. Some days I thought it might only be forty-something, but we did much poorer in the election than that. So, if I could go back again I probably would have risked it in November. But I'm not so naïve as to think the same dynamics might not have played out.' He recalls that Bertie Ahern once advised him that he should try and have a summer election, as the good weather and better mood helps the incumbent by a few points. The other bit of advice from Ahern was to ignore opinion polls, because it is impossible to judge whether public opinion will reset for or against you once the election is called.

Varadkar found himself in the worst of both worlds. When he did not call a November election the opposition quickly moved to close off his favoured option of May 2020. He was increasingly vulnerable, because his minority government lost another vote in the Dáil with the resignation of the Cork TD Dara Murphy to take up a position with the EPP in Brussels. This turned out to be far worse than the simple loss of a TD. Murphy had been working for the EPP for more than a year but had continued to sign in to Leinster House on his way to and from Brussels and was receiving a Dáil salary and expenses. When details of this emerged in November it dominated the headlines and damaged the government's image. When combined with the negative publicity generated by 'swing-gate', resulting from Maria Bailey's compensation claim for falling off a swing at a Dublin hotel, and the ill-judged comments of Wexford Fine

Gael by election candidate Verona Murphy about immigration, the party's image was dented.

The opposition kept a relentless focus on the failures of the government, particularly in the areas of housing and health. By this stage it was widely accepted that the Minister for Housing, Eoghan Murphy, was out of his depth in a portfolio that required a level of commitment and political skill he simply did not possess. In early December he survived a motion of no confidence by just three votes, and the focus then moved to the Minister for Health, Simon Harris, who was being lined up as the next target for the opposition in the New Year.

As there was no guarantee that the minister would survive a vote of confidence, Varadkar had little choice but to seek a dissolution of the Dáil on 14 January, with an election to be held on 8 February. Fine Gael was always going to face an uphill battle to retain power after nine continuous years in office, but it made things worse by appearing unprepared for the fray. The election slogan 'A future to look forward to' was deeply uninspiring.

Fine Gael's failure to begin the campaign with a coherent message was compounded by a tragic event. Under the watchful gaze of an Eoghan Murphy election poster, a homeless man was left with life-altering injuries during a tent-clearing operation on the banks of the Grand Canal in Dublin the day the election was called. The appalling incident captured the headlines and set the tone for a campaign that was dominated by an unrelenting focus on housing and health, the government's weak spots. The proposed extension of the state pension qualifying age to 67 was also a big – and controversial – issue in the campaign.

Charlie Flanagan's planned event in January to commemorate those who died in the service of the Royal Irish Constabulary and the Dublin Metropolitan Police during the War of Independence resurfaced. Both groups had recruited from Irish men, of Catholic and Protestant faith, and, although there were pockets of tension, they were generally well respected until the period before the First World War. But, as the historian Brian Hanley explained, 'Ultimately, their role was to defend the State and that meant defending the British state in Ireland.'[11]

Flanagan's proposal illustrated the perils of commemoration, and a debate exploded in the media, while the hashtag #blackandtans trended on Twitter. Though Varadkar had insisted that Ireland should be 'mature enough as a State to acknowledge all aspects of our past', the decision was taken to cancel the event.[12] But the damage had already been done. While, as the journalist Ronan McGreevy noted, the impact of the controversy on the election was difficult to gauge, it certainly surfaced on the doorsteps.[13]

Achievements in the areas of the economy and Brexit barely featured in the election campaign. Paschal Donohoe, the party's director of elections, concedes that the Fine Gael message was drowned out from the start.

> We were never able to successfully overcome the critique of how was it that we were able to fix profound economic difficulties and not make similar progress on the challenges that we had like housing and health. And then in the opening days of the campaign we had the terrible incident of the poor homeless man in the tent getting injured by the City Council vehicle. It was followed by a sequence of awful crimes in the first week of the campaign so it was a very difficult backdrop.

He recalls, 'The polling that we were doing at that point [the start of the campaign] indicated that that gap [between Fianna Fáil and Fine Gael] was real and we were facing into an exceptionally poor result.'[14]

The first *Irish Times* poll a week into the campaign reinforced the bad news. Fine Gael was down six points to 23 per cent, while Varadkar's satisfaction rating had dropped 16 points to 35 per cent, and the government was down by a similar margin. Fianna Fáil was stuck on 25 per cent; but the ominous development was that Sinn Féin was up seven points to 21 per cent.[15] A *Sunday Times* poll had reinforced the conventional wisdom that Fianna Fáil was on course to be the biggest party and would probably lead the next government, but now it was clear that a three-way race to be the biggest party was under way. Pat Leahy observed in the *Irish Times*:

In Fine Gael headquarters the difficult start and the flaccid poll ratings were not unexpected. Party chiefs knew that they would be trailing Fianna Fáil; they never imagined they would soon be trailing Sinn Féin too. Don't worry, they told the troops, this is what we expected. There's no need for panic. But they were wrong. There was every need for panic. But Fine Gael didn't realise that until it was too late.[16]

The poll findings on issues were also deeply dispiriting for Fine Gael. Forty per cent of people said health was the most important issue in deciding how they would vote, followed by 32 per cent who said it was housing. Only 8 per cent were influenced by the economy and a paltry 3 per cent by Brexit. Although he knew from an early stage that the situation looked hopeless, Varadkar held his nerve and performed reasonably well. In his tour of the country he finally began to look comfortable chatting with voters, and he performed well in the television debates. However, the strategy of attacking Fianna Fáil as the party's main rival allowed Sinn Féin free rein to capitalise on the mood for change that had clearly gripped the electorate.

The final *Irish Times* poll of the campaign, on 3 February, confirmed that Fine Gael was in serious trouble. The party was down another three points, to 20 per cent. It was behind Fianna Fáil on 23 per cent; but the real shock was that Sinn Féin had surged into first place with 25 per cent. Trailing in third place with less than a week to go was a desperate position for the government party which had been riding high just three months earlier.[17]

Donohoe's assessment of the situation finds some positives in it. 'What we were successful in doing was to eliminate the large gap between ourselves and Fianna Fáil,' he remarked. 'In the last week of the campaign we went back to basics. We focused back on the economy, the success with jobs and the risk of Brexit. Even though it wasn't a message that chimed in with the population as a whole, it was successful in shoring up a base of Fine Gael voters. And I believe what we did for the last week and a half of the campaign averted an even more difficult electoral result.'[18]

There were many reasons for the collapse in Fine Gael support, but one of them was the way the party inexplicably surrendered the war on social media to Sinn Féin. Back in 2011 the party had placed a big focus on social media, launching a 'Twolicy [i.e. Twitter policy] to Get Ireland Working' on Twitter and even bringing in experts from the US to advise on the strategy.[19] In 2020, with social media now a far more important ingredient of public discourse, Fine Gael devoted few resources and little attention to it, and as a result younger voters were bombarded with Sinn Féin messaging. A study by two academics, Jane Suiter and Kirsty Park, found that Sinn Féin vastly outperformed its rivals with an 'anti-elite populist narrative' on social media. During the campaign Sinn Féin had 567,020 'interactions' or responses, compared with 55,152 for Fine Gael.[20]

Varadkar believes that the poor election performance cannot be put down to any particular thing.

> It was a confluence of events. We hoped that our good record on the economy and on Brexit and international affairs would stand to us, but it didn't particularly. All the way from June through to January events chipped away and undermined support in us and damaged our credibility. There was the dynamic that emerged during the election where people who wanted a change of government gravitated towards Sinn Féin rather than Fianna Fáil.[21]

The mood for change swept everything before it to an extent nobody anticipated. The traditional party system had been in a state of collapse since 2011 and was now broken as Sinn Féin won a record number of seats, finishing in first place in terms of votes and second in terms of seats. The party's brand seemed unstoppable. With the benefit of hindsight, it is clear that the party could have won more than thirty-seven seats if it had run a greater number of candidates; but they had been cautious after disappointing local elections in 2019. Since then, Sinn Féin had repackaged its message. The party refocused on being a party of government, and Mary Lou McDonald repeatedly spoke of being part of a future coalition.

The established parties had an awful election as voters responded to the message of 'Vote left, transfer left'. The concept began organically with the hashtags #voteleft and #transferleft being used on Twitter by party supporters. Not surprisingly, the left did well in Dublin and other urban areas, but it also organised very effectively to win seats in some rural constituencies. In Donegal, Sinn Féin enjoyed a success that was unprecedented for any party of the left.[22] This mobilisation of support did not translate into votes for Labour, however, and Brendan Howlin's party had its worst election ever. Only one first-time TD, Duncan Smith in Dublin Fingal, was elected.

In spite of everything, Varadkar looked remarkably relaxed on the day of the count, probably because he knew that it could have been much worse.

> Some of the polls in the closing days had us sub-20 per cent, and they weren't totally off. Our sense, whether we're right or not, is that we did pull back some support in the last week. Some of that was down to the debates, and some of that was down to the fact that we kind of changed our strategy to try to firm up what was left of our base rather than seeking a wider appeal, which is what I had certainly sought to do as Taoiseach.

Another factor accounting for his relaxed demeanour was the *Irish Times* exit poll the night before, which put Fine Gael neck and neck with Fianna Fáil and Sinn Féin. 'We almost thought we had pulled it out of the bag that night. I was sitting on the couch at home watching the numbers come in and I thought the chances are we'll do a bit better than we had been expecting but it didn't work out.'[23]

By the time he arrived at his count centre Varadkar appeared to have taken a decision to go into opposition, leaving Sinn Féin to initiate talks on the formation of a government. Interviewed on arrival, he confirmed that he would not be entering discussions with Sinn Féin in any circumstances. 'I meant what I said ... I can't eat my words. Maybe other people can, but I can't.' As tallies confirmed that he had comfortably retained his seat, he and his partner, Matt, snacked on popcorn while making light-hearted conversation with those around them. He seemed a man unburdened. He insists that had Fianna Fáil decided to talk to Sinn Féin and form a government he would have happily accepted it as the outcome of the election and gone to the opposition benches with gusto. 'That was the scenario that was appearing that day, and I think 80 or 90 per cent of us, including me, were up for that. But it was really the decision of Micheál Martin not to go down that road that presented us with the dilemma of participating in a coalition with Fianna Fáil or somehow being the cause of an election, in which we would then have to tell the country that we did not want to be in government with anyone. That would not have been a very credible position.'[24] 'Dilemma' is, perhaps, a stretch. As we will see, Varadkar said on the occasion of his own election as party leader that he would not rule out coalition with Fianna Fáil.

Was Varadkar also thinking the same way that W.T. Cosgrave had almost ninety years earlier? Sinn Féin in government was an unknown quantity in the republic – just as de Valera's Fianna Fáil had been in 1932. When the change of power occurred after that election Cosgrave had accepted it, mostly because he was a committed democrat but also because he, and his Cumann na nGaedheal colleagues, believed Fianna Fáil to be incapable of governing successfully. As we know, Fianna Fáil ended up dominating the political scene. But for a brief moment there was the possibility that an untested party would fail, and voters would welcome Cumann na nGaedheal back to power. In opposition, Sinn Féin had the luxury of making promises and talking about alternative ways of doing things. The reality of being in government would either confirm the party's abilities or expose shortcomings in its policies, and presumably Varadkar was banking on the latter.

With counting completed in all the constituencies, Fine Gael ended up with thirty-five seats, a loss of twelve. Not only was the party back in 2002 territory but, for the first time in its history, it was in third place. Varadkar's own performance in Dublin West was somewhat disappointing. He was the first serving Taoiseach not to top the poll, and he was also the first Taoiseach since Garret FitzGerald in 1987 not to bring in his running-mate. However, in the competitive constituency that is Dublin West the party has not been able to add a second seat since Jim Mitchell and Austin Currie were both elected in 1989.

A cabinet minister, Regina Doherty, two ministers of state, Catherine Byrne and Mary Mitchell O'Connor and two TDs, Marcella Corcoran-Kennedy and Kate O'Connell, were among the high-profile Fine Gael losses. It was a bad election in general for women in the traditional three parties. Altogether only thirty-six of the 160 TDs elected were women, an increase of one, leaving Ireland 99th in the world for female representation at that time.[25] Only six of Fine Gael's thirty-five elected deputies were women. They included a newcomer, Jennifer Carroll MacNeill, a recently elected councillor and former legal adviser to Fine Gael, who had been a late addition to the ticket in Dún Laoghaire after 'swing-gate'. Although the circumstances leading to her addition were unusual, Fine Gael, like Fianna Fáil, used the 'add on' route to increase its number of women candidates and to meet the minimum requirement of the gender quota. Forty-four per cent of women candidates were added after selection conventions, compared with only eighteen per cent of men.[26]

When it came to the Seanad election, no Fine Gael women were elected. Catherine Noone, who had been a key figure in the Yes campaign during the abortion referendum, was another high-profile casualty for the party. She had damaged her prospects when she made an off-the-cuff remark on the campaign trail about Varadkar being autistic and 'on the spectrum'.[27] Although he accepted her apology, there was considerable backlash over her ill-judged comments. Under the agreement reached by the coalition partners, Varadkar was able to nominate four senators as part of the new Taoiseach Micheál Martin's appointments to the Seanad. He used this as an opportunity to address the absence of women Fine Gael senators, selecting the former minister Regina Doherty, his running-mate, Emer Currie, and councillors Aisling Dolan and Mary Seery Kearney.

The efforts at forming a government that followed the election had the makings of a political thriller, full of twists and unexpected turns, with a global health crisis playing an important role in the drama. The

Sinn Féin narrative was clear: the public had voted for a change that did not include the establishment parties, and so both parties should step aside to facilitate that change.

Led by Pearse Doherty, Sinn Féin's negotiating team initially sought to form a coalition with the parties of the left. From early on, its own history was under the spotlight. Foreign observers were quick to caption their reporting on the election results with reference to Sinn Féin's connection to paramilitarism. The *New York Times* went with 'Party with old IRA ties soars in Irish election', while the *Economist* framed one column 'From balaclavas to ballots'.[28] Sinn Féin could not escape its history, and it seemed as if some of its members did not want to. When Dessie Ellis and his supporters learned that he was on course to hold his seat in Dublin North-West they marked the news with a rendition of 'Come Out, Ye Black and Tans'. Then a video surfaced of David Cullinane, the party's TD for Waterford, shouting 'Up the 'RA' at a gathering of his supporters. Sinn Féin teams in count centres around the country were easily identifiable thanks to the presence of the Tricolour, a cause of anger to those in other parties that do not accept the right of any one party to the national flag. The implications of such behaviour were satirised by *Waterford Whispers News*, which reported a fictional chastising by McDonald of her new team: 'I hope you're proud of yourselves now, there's some lovely middle class people who voted for us and now they're shitting themselves.'[29]

When Mary Lou McDonald announced a series of public rallies to promote the case for her party in government, Varadkar's response was unrestrained. 'I think these rallies are designed to be the next phase in Sinn Féin's campaign of intimation and bullying. We saw that online and now we are seeing it in their rallies, and I wouldn't be surprised if the next step is that they take it to the streets. It just shows you, again, that they are not a normal party; this is a party that has a casual relationship with democracy.'[30] Micheál Martin shared that view, saying at the inaugural meeting of the new Dáil, 'We do not believe that Sinn Féin operates to the same democratic standards held by every other party in this House.'[31] The reactions to the proposed rallies proved unwarranted.

It quickly became apparent that the numbers for a left government simply did not exist, raising questions about who else Sinn Féin might work with. Martin had repeatedly said during the election that he would not participate in such a coalition, and he stuck to that position, despite some internal pressure to reverse his stance. Varadkar later claimed he never doubted him.

> As somebody who had been speaking on [and] off to him for a couple of years, I know he has a deep dislike and distrust of Sinn Féin which goes back to his time as Foreign Affairs minister. I remember him saying to me that if Sinn Féin got into coalition with Fianna Fáil they would approach it in such a way that they'd be looking to collapse at a time of political advantage in order to get the upper hand.[32]

When the 33rd Dáil met for the first time on 20 February, Varadkar, Martin, McDonald and Eamon Ryan of the Green Party were in turn proposed for Taoiseach. Reflecting the inconclusive results of the general election, the question was declared lost by a sizeable margin each time. Leaving Leinster House about 9 p.m., Varadkar travelled to Áras an Uachtaráin, where he tendered his resignation. With the Dáil having failed to elect a new Taoiseach, Varadkar and his cabinet would remain in office until a new government was formed.

According to Paschal Donohoe, there was an inevitable period of reflection within Fine Gael after the election.

> We began with the view: Look, we haven't done well here, the best thing for us to do is go into opposition. But what began to happen then is the party began to realise that there wasn't a clear route of going into opposition. Once the party made a decision that we were not going to do supply and confidence again, and Micheál Martin made a decision that Fianna Fáil was not going to go into government with Sinn Féin, it began to become very clear to a number of people within the party that a very likely outcome

was going to be a grand coalition. Obviously the process took a gigantic amount of time. And there were times along the way when it looked to us if it wasn't going to happen.[33]

For some in Fine Gael and Fianna Fáil the idea of coalition was abhorrent, but the reality was that senior figures in both parties had been making soundings for some time and that they were open to exploring the possibility. Brian Hayes spoke of a Fine Gael–Fianna Fáil grand coalition in 2017. Having been the party's director of elections the previous year, his comments were interpreted as a scoping exercise.[34] Martin subsequently said that he had not 'ruled anything in or out' after the next election.[35] By not rejecting outright the notion of coalition with Fine Gael, Martin's comments represented a shift from his refusal of a partnership government, including a rotating Taoiseach and a ministerial split in the cabinet, which Enda Kenny had offered after the 2016 election. Later, though, he ruled out a coalition with Fine Gael after the 2020 election, although Varadkar remained open to the prospect.[36] When elected as Fine Gael leader he had confirmed that he could not 'honestly' rule out such an arrangement.[37]

The stage was set, and while the prospect of Sinn Féin in government seemed to provide a motivation to the two traditional rivals, it was ultimately the outbreak of the coronavirus pandemic in the country that focused minds. Writing to members of the parliamentary party on 10 March, Varadkar noted that Sinn Féin and Fianna Fáil had had more than a month to form a government and that his intention had been that Fine Gael would go into opposition. But Covid-19 constituted a 'dramatic change in context'.[38]

While Dáil candidates campaigned in the 2020 election, a worrying situation was unfolding on the other side of the world. A 61-year-old man had died in China as a result of a new type of coronavirus on 11 January. As the virus spread, the World Health Organization declared a global health emergency on 30 January. These developments were covered by the Irish media, but for the majority of the population there was a sense that this was a crisis developing somewhere else. Varadkar recalls that a party member approached him and Mairéad McGuinness during an election rally in Cavan to say she was very worried about the virus in China. 'I said to her, "I'm a bit worried about it too, you know we're way overdue for a pandemic", but I never really thought it was going to happen.'[39]

But then the news came on 1 March of a confirmed case in Ireland. When the WHO declared a pandemic on 11 March, Varadkar responded decisively, his actions shaped by the advice of the National Public Health Emergency Team, which was set up to advise on the best response. As a member of Varadkar's backroom staff pointed out, being a medical doctor helped him.[40]

'The first time I really realised how serious this would be was the first cabinet subcommittee meeting,' Varadkar recalled. 'It must have been in early March and we got the presentation from Tony Holohan with the epidemiological models. We were told that if 20 per cent of the country was infected we'd be facing 60,000 deaths. I remember saying to the subcommittee, it might be an achievement to get out of this with 20,000 deaths. We did actually think it was going to be far worse than it turned out.'

On the advice of NPHET, the government took its time about cancelling the annual St Patrick's Festival, but compared with some other European countries it was quick to act in crucial areas. The first phase of a national quarantine was announced while Varadkar was on a visit to Washington on the morning of 12 March: schools, colleges and creches were closed; travel restrictions were introduced; working from home, where possible, was advised; and a ban was imposed on large gatherings. Pubs and hotel bars were subsequently asked to suspend service. As time wore on, in an effort to flatten the curve, the range of restrictions was expanded.

Varadkar's televised address to the nation on St Patrick's Day was a defining moment early on. 'In years to come let them say of us: when things were at their worst we were at our best,' he said, patiently explaining why the quarantine was necessary. 'To all those living in the shadow of what is to come – we are with you,' he concluded. [41] In that moment, the speech struck an immediate chord with the majority of the public, and there was an overwhelmingly positive response to the quarantine measures. At the time, Varadkar was not sure how the public would react.

> Thinking the way I think as a politician, I wondered if the speech was any good, because I was not really saying anything, not announcing anything, as the shut-down had already been announced. But, for whatever reason, it connected with the moment. Maybe it was because it was St Patrick's Day. We did enter one of the moments that don't happen a lot in politics: that kind of wartime feeling where everybody was behind the government, behind the country, and wanted us to succeed. That's rare. We experienced that to a certain extent on Brexit, where people felt Ireland was under threat and they wanted the government to succeed. This was like that but on a much bigger level. I kind of wish it was like that all the time. I wonder what we might have been able to achieve in other areas if it was.[42]

The speech was widely noted abroad, where the reception was coloured by the incoherent responses from Boris Johnson and Donald Trump. Cody Keenan, Barack Obama's chief writer, took to Twitter to praise the speech, which he predicted 'will be remembered'. 'Reassuring, empathetic, directly addresses young people, the world, and fear itself. Brings everyone into the front lines', was Keenan's assessment.[43]

Although his St Patrick's Day address could be the defining speech of his career, some elements of Varadkar's other speeches drew criticism, particularly his penchant for referring to lines from films. Having already quoted from *The Lord of the Rings*, Sean Astin, an actor in that film, bet Varadkar '50 quid' that he could not fit the film *Mean Girls* into his next speech. Varadkar subsequently spoke, to a mixed reaction, of how 'some have asked whether there's a limit to what we can achieve. My answer is that limit does not exist' – a line delivered in the film.[44]

Nonetheless, support for the government remained high. Donohoe believes that one of the things that helped was that the government was able to respond economically with such power. 'We showed during the

Covid crisis the value of having regained our credit-worthiness so that we were able to do whatever it took to protect the livelihoods of our people.' He recalled being told by officials immediately after the pandemic hit that hundreds of thousands of people would be coming into unemployment offices by the weekend, and the system simply would not be able to cope. 'And that led to the pandemic unemployment payments. We brought that in at around €200 but we realised that it wasn't going to be enough, and we increased it to €350. These are the kind of decisions that a decade ago just couldn't have been contemplated. The money just wasn't there. This time around we were able to do those things. And I think that made a big difference to the stability of our country.'[45]

It was against this backdrop that Fianna Fáil and Fine Gael prepared to enter talks. Beginning in the last week in March, the two parties exchanged detailed policy papers as a starting-point for the discussions. 'The pandemic was definitely an accelerator,' says Varadkar. 'After the election we were resigned to opposition and extremely reluctant to enter into coalition talks. But around those days when the pandemic became a reality I and others in the party took the view that we needed to dive in now and try to come to an agreement with Fianna Fáil. Because we just couldn't leave the country without a government in those circumstances.' At that stage he had no reason to believe that the pandemic would actually improve the government's standing. 'I didn't assume that and wasn't thinking that. I was more inclined to think this was going to be a catastrophe for the country and not a political opportunity. It's kind of weird that you actually sometimes make your best decisions when you're not thinking at all about what the political implications might be.'[46]

With a combined total of seventy-two seats, Fine Gael and Fianna Fáil were eight short of the number required for a majority in the Dáil. A third group, whether in the form of some of the independents or one of the smaller parties, would be needed. But at that stage the Green Party took the position that the negotiations should be stopped and that a national government to tackle the Covid crisis be formed instead.[47]

Fine Gael and Fianna Fáil rejected any arrangement that would include Sinn Féin. Instead they continued to talk to each other. Eventually, on 15 April, they published a joint framework document designed as the basis for talks with other parties on the formation of government . This document was widely criticised for woolly commitments to increased government spending while simultaneously ruling out tax increases or spending cuts. 'I know that that document was criticised by many people, but it did have a very specific role. That was to be able to demonstrate to the Green Party that we were willing to sit down and try to put together a very different type of government,' Donohoe explained.[48] According to Varadkar, the framework document also provoked some serious opposition within Fine Gael, on the grounds that it was too left-wing. 'Some people felt that we almost apologised for our time in government, whereas I thought showing a bit of humility wasn't a bad thing and demonstrated that we'd heard what the electorate had to say.'[49]

The framework document achieved the desired objective of prompting a rethink by the Green Party. Both Varadkar and Donohoe believe that a government without the Greens would simply not have been feasible. 'Fianna Fáil were up for arrangements that we weren't up for,' says Varadkar.

> We would have considered Labour plus independents. It would have been a smaller number, so the ones we really wanted were the Greens. Having experienced minority government for four years, I really felt it had to be a majority government this time. I didn't want a confidence and supply, and I also felt that with the Greens the new government might have more democratic legitimacy. The three parties together won more than 50 per cent of the vote. I also felt the Greens would inject genuine change and would challenge us on policy, challenge us intellectually in a way that Fianna Fáil would less, because they are so similar to us.

He says that in the negotiations the policy gap between Fine Gael and Fianna Fáil was not wide. 'So in many ways the negotiations were between Fine Gael and the Greens. Fianna Fáil were very keen to make the government happen; both Fine Gael and the Greens were reluctant.

We had to demonstrate to our supporters that we had our stamp on the programme for government. The fact that it took so long was probably a good thing, because it gave us time to get to know each other a bit. And not just tease out what people's different policies are but to actually understand how they came to that policy in the first place, which is important. We know what is behind the Green thinking and behind their policies, so that helps.'[50]

Donohoe also says it would have been impossible to present the country with the option of a Fianna Fáil–Fine Gael minority government, or even one with the involvement of independents. 'I certainly couldn't have supported either of those options, and there was no appetite for that happening. If they were the only options I would have been recommending another election, because my view was that you needed a multi-party government with a majority, which is thankfully where we've ended up.'[51]

As the negotiations continued in the background, the government continued its work to deal with the health crisis. There were light-hearted moments found on social media. A reassurance came from Harris's Twitter account that the Easter bunny would still come, while Varadkar's answered a video from a seven-year-old girl to confirm that the Tooth Fairy, immune to the virus, would visit her. The girl's mother responded to the Taoiseach that the tweet had 'meant the world' to her daughter and that he had earned 'superhero status' in her house as a result.[52]

When the *Irish Times* reported on 5 April that Varadkar had rejoined the medical register in March there were some who questioned his motivation. However, no press statements were issued, and no official photographs of him at work. Details of the specifics of the one afternoon spent in service each week were not generally disclosed. However, Eddie Hoare, a Fine Gael councillor for Galway City, offered a glimpse of the Taoiseach at work when he shared two photographs of Varadkar helping with community testing in Blanchardstown.[53] Hoare had spotted the photographs on the Blanchardstown Traveller Development Group's Facebook page. Believing they 'captured the mood of solidarity across all communities', he saved them to tweet from his own account.[54] Scrolling through the responses to the tweet, there is obvious scepticism from some about the photos. Others echoed the wider praise that Varadkar was receiving. The Hollywood actor Matt Damon even joined that broader chorus of praise, describing the Taoiseach as a 'badass' for returning to medical work.[55] In one of the more bizarre sub-plots of the health emergency, Damon, who had been filming in Ireland, had decided to stay for the quarantine, and he and his family were happily 'adopted' by local people in the Dublin suburb of Dalkey.

Not everything went smoothly. A poorly judged comment by the Taoiseach about the wage subsidy scheme drew the ire of Una Mullally in the *Irish Times*. Referring during a press briefing to the weekly €350 payment, Varadkar suggested that the rate might be an incentive to lower-paid workers to request that their employer lay them off. For Mullally, this was evidence that Varadkar's mask had slipped, as he seemingly deviated from the caring demeanour to which viewers of his addresses had become accustomed. Her own article attracted criticism, and three letters to the newspaper from different parts of the country the following day questioned what was perceived as a quickness to ascribe additional meaning to his suggestion.[56]

The announcement that schools and creches would close from 15 March immediately raised questions about child-care arrangements, particularly for health workers and those in essential services – employees who did not have the option of working from home. As the weeks ticked by, the problem was regularly acknowledged, and there were various references to plans being considered. Eventually, on 6 May, the Minister for Children, Katherine Zappone, announced a scheme that would commit the state to subsidising child-care workers minding children of health staff in their own home. The scheme was immediately beset with problems, and the government ended up announcing on 14 May that the plan was being scrapped.

A further controversy, which underlined the gendered nature of the impact that the crisis had, emerged after it was discovered that women due to return to work from maternity leave were not provided for under the wage subsidy scheme. The National Women's Council of Ireland, SIPTU and the ICTU jointly wrote to Paschal Donohoe on 23 April to raise their concerns, and the issue was subsequently referred to the Irish Human Rights and Equality Commission. The government eventually announced on 29 May that changes, backdated to 26 March, had been made to cover those returning from maternity or adoptive leave.

History is likely to judge the government's approach to care homes as one of the greatest stains on its record on handling Covid. The spread of the virus through such facilities raised serious questions about preparedness and response measures. By May there had been 900 deaths, a figure that accounted for more than half of all deaths attributed to the virus in Ireland.[57] Tadhg Daly, CEO of Nursing Homes Ireland, was adamant that the crisis that occurred was not inevitable.[58] A future review is likely to make for uncomfortable reading.

The initial strategy for containing the virus was made possible by the good will shown throughout the country, but over time there were signs of citizens becoming frustrated with the indefinite suspension of normality. That sense of frustration manifested itself in some of the responses to Varadkar's appearance on *The Late Late Show* on Friday 1 May. He joined Ryan Tubridy to discuss the timetable for the potential easing of restrictions, announced earlier that evening. When questioned about certain elements, the Taoiseach produced a sheet of paper from his pocket. Some viewers felt that this reliance on the printed plan suggested a lack of knowledge, while others considered it unreasonable to expect him to recall the specifics of a road map only just announced. Compared with Boris Johnson's rambling and vague announcement a week later about the easing of restrictions in Britain, Varadkar's readiness to refer to a specified plan was reassuring.

As the interview drew to a close the Taoiseach was also asked about the continuing talks on forming a government. Referring to how extraordinary it was to see Fine Gael and Fianna Fáil negotiating, given the historical divide, Tubridy spoke of the two leaders figuratively holding hands. In a momentary break from the seriousness, a grin broke across Varadkar's face as he quipped that such activity was no longer permitted. By that stage, the efforts to form a government had become, in the words of Paul Cunningham of RTÉ, an 'excruciating political marathon'.[59]

Varadkar was clearly making overtures to the Green Party during his conversation with Tubridy, telling the host that his party was 'very keen' to meet the 7 per cent target for annual reductions in carbon emissions.[60] The previous week Eamon Ryan had written to the two parties setting out seventeen issues arising from the joint framework document that the Green Party felt needed to be addressed 'as a matter of urgency' before they could participate in any negotiations.[61] At the top of the list was the request for a commitment to an average annual reduction in greenhouse gas emissions of at least 7 per cent. Among the party's other demands was the replacement of direct provision with a non-profit system; a guarantee of the exclusive allocation of public land for public and social housing; and a rebalancing of spending on transport infrastructure so that at least 20 per cent would be in the area of cycling and walking.

The target for reducing carbon emissions was a sticking-point. When Ryan had informal talks with Fianna Fáil and Fine Gael, the two parties had stopped short of committing themselves to the 7 per cent target. The Greens began to pull back. But Varadkar's comments appear to have had the desired effect, and the Green Party formally entered discussions the Monday after the television programme. This was an important development, as the scope for a third coalition partner was narrowing. The Social Democrats confirmed in a two-page letter on 13 May that they would not be participating in talks, while the Labour Party announced two days later that it would not be taking part either. Neither had really been expected to join the negotiations.

The pandemic was Varadkar's redemption. At one point, in a survey conducted by Lucid Talk market research, he was the most popular leader in Northern Ireland, before Boris Johnson, Arlene Foster, Michelle O'Neill and Robin Swann.[62] An astonishing opinion poll in the *Irish Times* in June recorded a satisfaction rating of 72 per cent for the government and 75 per cent for Varadkar, a staggering jump of 51 and 45 points, respectively, since the poll taken just days before the February general election.[63]

Then an unexpected move by four Green Party councillors from Cork threatened to derail the negotiations. They wrote to the deputy leader, Catherine Martin, urging her to challenge Ryan for the leadership, which she confirmed on 6 June that she would do, urging that any hustings be delayed until after the government negotiations had concluded. One Fine Gael party member neatly summed up the implications on Twitter: 'I have a Fine Gael vote in the formation of government. How am I going to make an informed decision if I do not know who the leader of the Green Party will be in coalition?'[64]

As the three parties moved closer towards agreement, Eamon Ryan found himself embroiled in a controversy that laid bare the internal divisions in the Green Party. The killing of George Floyd by a white policeman in Minneapolis on 25 May sparked protests throughout the United States, and the Black Lives Matter movement drove an international conversation about racism. Ryan addressed the Dáil about the need to ensure that 'policing, as it evolves, will be blind to colour, ethnicity, post code or where someone comes from'.[65] It was a speech that condemned discrimination against people of colour, Travellers and members of other minorities. In an effort to illustrate what some members of the Irish community have had to deal with, he quoted the experience of Seán Gallen, as reported in the newspapers. By retelling the name that Gallen had found himself called, Ryan unwittingly entered the full 'n-word' into the Dáil record.

The incident further exposed the divisions within the Green Party. Tensions were so heightened that any misstep – even one by someone who usually campaigns for equality – was seized upon to show Ryan as someone unfit for leadership. As the journalist John Downing observed, the Greens were suffering a full-blown heave in the midst of negotiating an agreement for government.[66] Regardless of who wins the contest to lead the party, the in-fighting and manoeuvring that has occurred is ominous of future divisions.

Agreement was finally reached on the draft programme for government on 15 June, and the final act of the drama got under way on Friday 26 June. The three parties spent the afternoon sorting and counting postal ballots. Fine Gael was the first to make a declaration. Shortly after 4 p.m. Fiona O'Connor, chairperson of the Executive Council and returning officer, announced that there had been a 95 per cent turnout, and 80 per cent of the 674 votes cast were in favour. Requiring only a simple majority of 50 per cent plus one, Fine Gael, as expected, endorsed the programme for government.

The party uses an electoral college system, made up of constituency delegates, a council of local representatives, the Executive Council and the parliamentary party. All four component parts endorsed the programme, with the strongest response coming from the parliamentary party, of which 90 per cent voted in favour. The margin was much narrower when it came to local representatives, with 57 per cent in favour and 43 per cent opposed.

Later that evening journalists and photographers began gathering just before 7:30 p.m. for the Fianna Fáil announcement. Not long afterwards it was announced that, with a turnout of 77 per cent, or 11,071 votes, 74 per cent of the party's members voted in favour of the programme for government.

All eyes then turned to the Green Party. Doubts about whether the party would reach the required two-thirds majority had been expressed throughout the day, but Ossian Smyth, the party's TD for Dún Laoghaire, sent rumours flying when he tweeted a smiley face at 7:17 p.m. 'White smoke?!' quipped the political geographer Claire McGing in response.[67]

'Historic' was the word of the day when the Dáil convened on Saturday 27 June. The fact that it met in the Convention Centre, and not Leinster House, was in itself historic. That Covid had necessitated the change of venue was acknowledged by the Ceann Comhairle, Seán Ó Fearghail, who remarked that 'this is certainly a very effective demonstration of social distancing' as he took his seat.

By 93 votes to 63, with three abstentions, the Dáil agreed to nominate Micheál Martin for appointment by the President to be Taoiseach. He had been supported by Fianna Fáil, Fine Gael and the Green Party, as well as nine independents. Speaking in favour of Martin's nomination, Varadkar referred to the historic nature of the event. 'I believe Civil War politics ended a long time ago in our country', he told those gathered, 'but, today, Civil War politics ends in our parliament'. The formation of the government was historic for Fine Gael for other reasons, too. As Varadkar pointed out, the party was about to embark on a third consecutive term – something that had never been achieved before by Fine Gael. Indeed two consecutive terms in office had eluded them until 2016. But despite this record, there is also the inescapable fact that the party's share of seats has been steadily declining.

In a moment of humility, Varadkar presented this return to government as 'a second chance, an opportunity to get right some of the things we did not get right in the years gone by'.[68] A similar sentiment was shared on Twitter later that day by Simon Harris.[69]

Clearly tired of the Sinn Féin narrative, Varadkar also launched a stinging rebuke of the recurring use of 'change'.

> We all know what change means for Sinn Féin. For Sinn Féin, change means Sinn Féin ministers in ministerial offices and Sinn Féin ministers in the back seats of ministerial cars. They are willing to go into power with Fianna Fáil. They are willing to go into power with Fine Gael. They are probably willing to get into power with both Fianna Fáil and Fine Gael. That is what change means to Sinn Féin.

The disgust in his voice was clear as he concluded with the observation, 'What a load of spin and nonsense.'

After the vote, Micheál Martin delivered a gracious speech in which he acknowledged the work of the outgoing government in managing the Covid crisis. He too addressed Sinn Féin, albeit in a more veiled way. Referring to the first Dáil, he placed the formation of his government in the country's long democratic tradition.

By that evening, after 140 days, the composition of the new government was known. Martin was Taoiseach and Varadkar his Tánaiste, as well as Minister for Enterprise, Trade and Employment. Paschal Donohoe remained in Finance and Simon Coveney as Minister for Foreign Affairs but with the addition of Defence, while Simon Harris moved to the newly created Department of Higher Education, Innovation and Research. Helen McEntee was promoted to Justice, and Heather

Humphreys was appointed Minister for Social Protection, Community and Rural Developments, and the Islands. Hildegarde Naughton became Minister of State with the right to attend government meetings.

With departments divided among the three coalition partners, disappointments were inevitable. Eight high-profile Fine Gael ministers lost their place in the government. The most prominent was Richard Bruton, who had served under four Fine Gael Taoisigh. Michael Creed, Charlie Flanagan, Paul Kehoe, Joe McHugh, Josepha Madigan, Eoghan Murphy and Michael Ring also departed.

Photographs of the new government receiving their seals of office served as a reminder of the pandemic. Rather than visiting Áras an Uachtaráin, the new ministers assembled for a socially distanced ceremony in Dublin Castle. Afterwards the government held its first meeting, at which they formally adopted the programme for government.

Varadkar was happy that the programme contains a number of the party's central principles.

> The economic and fiscal strategy is very Fine Gael. We will borrow until the economy recovers and we are back to jobs growth, when we will try and bring the deficit down again. What's there on tax is quite significant. It will be index-linked, and more and more people won't fall into higher tax net just by virtue of earning more or getting pay increases. I think it's good on issues like Europe and free trade, where we thought there might be difficulties getting the Greens to accept things like Pesco and free-trade agreements.

He also pointed to a strong focus on home ownership.

> The Greens brought good stuff to the table on issues like the cost of rental, tenants' rights and social housing but we still believe that most people in Ireland want to own their own home and we still think that's a good thing.[70]

Although it took 140 days to form a government, Paschal Donohoe is of the view that the very lengthy process actually augurs well for the future. 'Because even though we did take a lot of time, and that was criticised by many, it did mean that two things happened. The first thing is we thrashed out a lot of things. And the second thing is we all got to know each other. The foundation for resolving difficulties is that people know each other and have built up a level of trust. I feel that we have made a decent start on that.'[71]

The origin story of Fianna Fáil and Fine Gael is based in the Civil War that sundered the unity of the old Sinn Féin party almost a century ago. The two have dominated Irish politics, in opposition to each other, in the decades since, but they have been moving closer to each other for some time. There was the Tallaght strategy in 1987 and more recently the confidence and supply deal. And when Varadkar became leader of Fine Gael he was clear that a coalition with Fianna Fáil was not something he would rule out. As historic as the election of a Fianna Fáil–Fine Gael (and Green Party) government was, the drama of Civil War politics had been in its last act for quite a while. The new relationship between Fine Gael and Fianna Fáil was illustrated by the decision of the incoming Taoiseach Micheál Martin to retain the portrait of Michael Collins in his new office, alongside one of his party's founder, Éamon de Valera.[72]

Many people observing the creation of the new government will have wondered what the party system might look like in the future. At the time of writing, Paschal Donohoe, who achieved the honour of being elected chairperson of the Euro group of Finance Ministers in July, was adamant that a merger between the two Civil War parties is not at all likely for the foreseeable future.

What I think is more likely is that there will be more structured cooperation between the two big political parties of the centre. The grand coalition like this might continue a lot further into the future or you might see the repetition of a supply and confidence arrangement. There are some people who would view the end of Civil War politics as the death knell for the centre of Irish politics. There are other people like me who believe that the new relationship between Fine Gael and Fianna Fáil might be a great opportunity for the Irish political centre. I believe very firmly that the political centre across the sweep of history has served our country well.

According to him, whatever happens, Fine Gael can face the future with confidence.

If you look at the generation that we have now, we are the political children of Enda Kenny, because he used the early tenure of his leadership to completely change and rebuild the party and bring all these young people along and we are here now. We are all Enda's political children.[73]

Varadkar is due to return to the Taoiseach's office in December 2022. The timing pleases him. 'What will happen shortly after the hundredth anniversary of the founding of the state is that there will be a handover of the Taoiseach's office from Fianna Fáil to Fine Gael. There is a kind of poetry in that.' He thinks that in time he will look back with a degree of satisfaction at the fact that he was the party leader who brought Fine Gael into coalition with Fianna Fáil and ended Civil War politics. As to the future, he expects that Ireland will move to a much more northern European style of politics, with lots of different types of coalitions.

It will be a lot more like Dutch or Belgian politics or politics in some of the Nordic countries. In any given election any one of three or four parties can come first, second, third or fourth. And that is going to mean all sorts of different coalition arrangements.[74]

In this new, volatile political environment, he believes that Fine Gael needs to guard against a serious party emerging on its right, either a PD-style liberal market party or a socially conservative one.

What we need to do in the party over the next couple of years is to talk to each other and define what our identity is. I often hear this question about how to preserve our identity in coalition, but if our identity was simply not being Fianna Fáil that has gone a long time ago. The public have moved on from that. Our identity has to be what we are about. We are the party of enterprise and reward, we are the party of equality of opportunity. That has to be our identity, a positive identity.[75]

ENDNOTES

Introduction

1   White, *Kevin O'Higgins*, p. 83–4.
2   RTÉ News, 12 February 2020.
3   *Irish Times*, 24 February 2010.
4   Quoted in Meehan, *A Just Society for Ireland? 1964–1987*, p. 105.
5   'Fine Gael: A Family at War', episode 1 (2004).
6   *Dáil Debates*, volume 994, number 3 (27 June 2020).

Chapter 1

1   The main secondary sources used for this chapter are Collins, *The Cosgrave Legacy*, Meehan, *The Cosgrave Party*, and Mel Farrell, *Party Politics in a New Democracy*.
2   *Dáil Debates*, vol. 3, 19 December 1921.
3   Kenny, *The Enigma of Arthur Griffith*.
4   Dolan and Murphy, *Michael Collins*.
5   Valiulis, *Portrait of a Revolutionary*, p. 172.
6   Collins, *The Cosgrave Legacy*, p. 33–4.
7   Curran, *The Birth of the Irish Free State*, p. 251.
8   *Irish Times*, 9 September 1922.
9   Collins, *The Cosgrave Legacy*, p. 65.
10 Curran, *The Birth of the Irish Free State*, p. 267.
11 Collins, *The Cosgrave Legacy*, p. 38.
12 O'Sullivan, *The Irish Free State and Its Senate*, p. 208.
13 Farrell, *Party Politics in a New Democracy*, p. 73.
14 Dorothy Macardle, *The Irish Republic*, p. 780.
15 Meehan, *The Cosgrave Party*, p. 9.
16 Farrell, *Party Politics*, p. 74.
17 Meehan, *The Cosgrave Party*, p. 8–9.
18 Meehan, *The Cosgrave Party*, p. 46.
19 Collins, *The Cosgrave Legacy*, p. 43.
20 Farrell, *Party Politics*, p. 76.
21 Meehan, *The Cosgrave Party*, p. 50.
22 Farrell, *Party Politics*, p. 202.
23 Meehan, *The Cosgrave Party*, p. 39.
24 Meehan, *The Cosgrave Party*, p. 61–8.
25 Sean O'Casey, *Autobiographies*, vol. 2 p. 132.
26 Collins, *The Cosgrave Legacy*, p. 50.
27 Collins, *The Cosgrave Legacy*, p. 51.
28 Meehan, *The Cosgrave Party*, p. 142.
29 Meehan, *The Cosgrave Party*, p. 200.
30 Collins, *The Cosgrave Legacy*, p. 52.
31 Laffan, *Judging W.T. Cosgrave*, p. 262–4.
32 Collins, *The Cosgrave Legacy*, p. 53–4.
33 Collins, *The Cosgrave Legacy*, p. 54.
34 Lee, *Ireland, 1912–1985*, p. 174.
35 Ryan, *Unique Dictator*, p. 240.

Chapter 2

1   For a detailed discussion of O'Duffy's childhood, influences and development, see the early chapters in McGarry, *Eoin O'Duffy*.

2   Barry Egan to Liam Burke, 25 May 1932 (Egan Papers, U404/3, Cork County and City Archives).

3   Manning, *James Dillon*, p. 61.

4   Minutes of the Standing Committee of the National Farmers' and Ratepayers' League, 22 September 1932 (Cumann na nGaedheal papers, P39/Min/6, UCD Archives).

5   Jason Knirck, '"A Regime of Squandermania": The Irish Farmers' Party, Agriculture and Democracy, 1922–27' in Farrell et al., *A Formative Decade*, p. 179.

6   *Westmeath Examiner*, 7 January 1 933.

7   Manning, *The Blueshirts*, p. 53.

8   Report by Eoin O'Duffy, 27 July 1931 (Department of the Taoiseach, S5864B, National Archives).

9   Reported by the *Anglo-Celt*, 16 September 1933.

10 Michael Tierney to Frank MacDermot, 27 November 1934 (MacDermot Papers, 1065/4/4, National Archives).

11 McGarry, *Eoin O'Duffy*, p. v.

12 Dolan and Murphy, *Michael Collins*, p. 34–5.

13 Cronin et al., *The GAA*, p. 306–7.

14 McGarry, *Eoin O'Duffy*, p. 12–14.

15 For a discussion of O'Duffy's rise to prominence within republican circles, see chapters 2–4 of McGarry, *Eoin O'Duffy*.

16 *Kilkenny People*, 9 September 1933.

17 Quoted in the *Irish Independent*, 9 September 1933.

18 Mel Farrell, 'Cumann na nGaedheal: A new "National Party"?', in Farrell et al., *A Formative Decade*, p. 37.

19 Marie Coleman, 'John Dillon Nugent', *Dictionary of Irish Biography*.

20 In his foreword to Brian Maye's history of the party John Bruton wrote that 'Fine Gael carried forward the tradition of constitutional nationalism going back through Redmond and [Isaac] Butt to Daniel O'Connell': Maye, *Fine Gael*, p. v.

21 Quoted in the *Anglo-Celt*, 9 November 1933.

22 *Dáil Debates*, vol. 50, col. 1659, 15 February 1934.

23 *Dáil Debates*, vol. 60, col. 557, 12 February 1936.

24 For an excellent discussion of this topic see Mike Cronin, 'The Blueshirt movement, 1932–35: Ireland's fascists?' *Journal of Contemporary History*, 30, 2 (1995), p. 311–32. The following paragraph draws on this article.

25 Mike Cronin, 'The socio-economic background and membership of the Blueshirt movement, 1932–5', *Irish Historical Studies*, 29, 11 (1994), p. 234.

26 *Dáil Debates*, vol. 50, no. 15, 28 February 1934.

27 *Dáil Debates*, vol. 50, no. 15, 28 February 1934.

28 For a more detailed discussion of the social life attached to the Blueshirt movement see Mike Cronin, 'Blueshirts, sports and socials', *History Ireland*, 3, 2 (Autumn, 1944).

29 Ferriter, *The Transformation of Ireland*, p. 360.

30 Quoted in Cronin, 'Blueshirts, sports and socials'.

31 Maye, *Fine Gael*, p. 39.

32 McGarry, *Eoin O'Duffy*.

33 Cronin, *The Blueshirts and Irish Politics*, p. 24.

34 Quoted in E.M. Hogan, 'James Hogan: A Biographical Sketch', in Ó Corráin, *James Hogan*, p. 14.

35 James Hogan to Michael Tierney [1933?] (Tierney Papers, LA30/363, UCD Archives).

36 Manning, *The Blueshirts*, p. 134.

37 McGarry, *Eoin O'Duffy*.

38 James Dillon to Frank MacDermot, 17 October 1934 (MacDermot Papers, 1065/2/6, National Archives).

39 Dolan, *Commemorating the Irish Civil War*, p. 69.

Chapter 3

1 Quoted in McCullagh, *A Makeshift Majority*, p. 7.

2 For more on the life of Clann na Poblachta see Rafter, *The Clann*, and MacDermot, *Clann na Poblachta*.

3 A photograph of this protest is reproduced in Meehan, *The Cosgrave Party*, p. 227.

4 Quoted in McCullagh, *The Reluctant Taoiseach*, p. 161.

5 McCullagh, *The Reluctant Taoiseach*, p. 163.

6 Rafter, *The Clann*, p. 100.

7 Quoted in McCullagh, *The Reluctant Taoiseach*, p. 168.

8 McCullagh, *A Makeshift Majority*, p. 66–8.

9 Fanning, *The Irish Department of Finance*, p. 456–8.

10 Daly, *Sixties Ireland*, p. 39.

11 Finola Kennedy, 'Public expenditure in Ireland on housing in the post-war period', *Economic and Social Review* (http://www.tara.tcd.ie/bitstream/handle/2262/68929/v3n31972_2.pdf).

12 McCullagh, *A Makeshift Majority*, p. 150–51.

13 Quoted in Manning, *James Dillon*, p. 251.

14 Daly, *Sixties Ireland*, p. 21.

15 Maye, *Fine Gael*, p. 84.

16 Manning, *James Dillon*, p. 251–2.

17 Quoted in Manning, *James Dillon*, p. 242.

18 For a fuller discussion of the events surrounding the declaration of the Republic see Chapter 8 of McCullagh, *The Reluctant Taoiseach*.

19 Quoted in Gallagher, *Political Parties in the Republic of Ireland*, p. 48.

20 FitzGerald, *All in a Life*, p. 45.

21 *Dáil Debates*, 24 November 1948.

22 *Dáil Debates*, 24 November 1948.

23 *Irish Times*, 18 April 1949.

24 Kennedy, *Division and Consensus*, p. 111–12.

25 Mansergh, *The Unresolved Question*, p. 315.

26   See Stephen Kelly, 'A policy of futility: Eamon de Valera's anti-partition campaign, 1948–1951', *Études Irlandaises*, 36, 2 (2011), p. 1–12.

27   McCullagh, *A Makeshift Majority*, p. 134.

28   *Dáil Debates*, vol. 112, no. 5, 20 July 1948.

29   Noël Browne, *Against the Tide* (Dublin, 1987 edn), p. 124.

30   *Dáil Debates*, vol. 100, 3 April 1946.

31   *Dáil Debates*, vol. 105, 1 May 1947.

32   McCullagh, *A Makeshift Majority*, p. 224.

33   McKee, 'Church-state relations and the development of Irish health policy', p. 194.

34   McCullagh, *A Makeshift Majority*, p. 214.

35   Conroy, 'From the fifties to the nineties', pp. 34–35.

36   Browne, *Against the Tide*, p. 140.

37   Garvin, *Preventing the Future*, p. 258.

Chapter 4

1   The principal source for this chapter was McCullagh, *The Reluctant Taoiseach*. Other important books on the period are O'Higgins, *A Double Life*; Garvin, *Preventing the Future*; McCarthy, *Planning Ireland's Future*; and Lindsay, *Memories*. Prof. Frank Barry's paper on the origins of export tax relief, 'Foreign Investment and the Politics of Export Profits Tax Relief in 1956', is another important source.

2   McCarthy, *Planning Ireland's Future*, p. 25.

3   O'Higgins, *A Double Life*, p. 156.

4   McCullagh, *The Reluctant Taoiseach*, p. 266–7.

5   McCullagh, *The Reluctant Taoiseach*, p. 281.

6   McCarthy, *Planning Ireland's Future*, p. 24.

7   *Dictionary of Irish Biography*.

8   McCullagh, *The Reluctant Taoiseach*, p. 285.

9   O'Higgins, *A Double Life*, p. 186.

10   Interview with James Dooge, March 1996.

11   Lindsay, *Memories*, p. 168.

12   McCullagh, *The Reluctant Taoiseach*, p. 289.

13   O'Higgins, *A Double Life*, p. 156.

14   O'Higgins, *A Double Life*, p. 163.

15   McCullagh, *The Reluctant Taoiseach*, p. 291.

16   McCullagh, *The Reluctant Taoiseach*, p. 296.

17   McCullagh, *The Reluctant Taoiseach*, p. 293.

18   Barry, 'Foreign Investment and the Politics of Export Profits Tax Relief in 1956'.

19   McCarthy, *Planning Ireland's Future*, p. 42.

20   McCullagh, *The Reluctant Taoiseach*, p. 298.

21   Lindsay, *Memories*, p. 167.

22   McCullagh, *The Reluctant Taoiseach*, p. 351.

23   McCullagh, *The Reluctant Taoiseach*, p. 351–5.

24   McCullagh, *The Reluctant Taoiseach*, p. 356.

25   Chambers, *T.K. Whitaker*, p. 28.

26 Garvin, *Preventing the Future,* p. 233.

27 *Documents on Irish Foreign Policy,* vol. X, p. 686, 695.

28 *Documents on Irish Foreign Policy,* vol. X, p. 668–9.

29 McCullagh, *The Reluctant Taoiseach,* p. 361.

30 McCarthy, *Planning Ireland's Future,* p. 35.

31 Lindsay, *Memories,* p. 171–2.

32 McCarthy, *Planning Ireland's Future,* p. 43.

Chapter 5

1 TheJournal.ie, 6 June 2011; *Irish Times,* 8 June 2011.

2 O'Higgins, *A Double Life,* p. 188.

3 Manning, *James Dillon,* p. 329.

4 Jackson, *Home Rule,* p. 21.

5 Manning, *James Dillon,* p. 46–68.

6 Quoted in Manning, *James Dillon,* p. 48.

7 Manning, *James Dillon,* p. 327.

8 Manning, *James Dillon,* p. 327.

9 *Fine Gael Digest,* 8, 1 (February 1958).

10 Marsh and Gallagher, *Days of Blue Loyalty,* p. 51, 57.

11 Circular from Richard Mulcahy to all front bench members, 30 October 1957 (Mac Eoin Papers, P151/804, UCD Archives).

12 Evans, *Seán Lemass,* p. 160.

13 Niamh Puirséil, 'Political and party competition in post-war Ireland', in Girvin and Murphy, *The Lemass Era,* p. 19.

14 Quoted in Manning, *James Dillon,* p. 330.

15 Minutes of the Fine Gael parliamentary party, 6 March 1963.

16 Minutes of the Fine Gael parliamentary party, 26 February 1964.

17 Ard-fheis speech, 5 February 1958 (Costello Papers, P190/315, UCD Archives).

18 Minutes of the Fine Gael parliamentary party, 9 July 1958.

19 John A. Costello to James Dillon, 13 January 1960 (Costello Papers, P190/340, UCD Archives).

20 Manning, *James Dillon,* p. 346.

21 *Irish Times,* 21 February 1964.

22 Quoted in Halligan (ed.), *The Brendan Corish Seminar Proceedings,* p. 13.

23 This is discussed in greater detail in Chapter 2 of Meehan, *A Just Society for Ireland?*

24 Marsh and Gallagher, *Days of Blue Loyalty,* p. 26.

25 *One to One* interview, RTÉ, first broadcast 14 September 2009.

26 McCullagh, *The Reluctant Taoiseach,* p. 296.

27 Minutes of the Fine Gael parliamentary party, 26 May 1964.

28 *Irish Times,* 20 May 1964.

29 *Irish Times,* 20 May 1964.

30 Meeting of the parliamentary party, 20 May 1964 (Fine Gael minute books).

31 FitzGerald, *All in a Life,* p. 77.

32 *Kerryman,* 23 May 1964.

33 Meehan, *A Just Society for Ireland?* p. 38.

34 For a fuller discussion of the content of 'Towards a Just Society' see Meehan, *A Just Society for Ireland?* p. 42–51.

35 Quoted in Meehan, *A Just Society for Ireland?* p. 52.

36 Fianna Fáil handbill, 1965 election (Fine Gael Election Papers, P39/GE/141, UCD Archives).

37 *Irish Times*, 20 March 1965.

38 Notes for National Council Meeting, 4 May 1965 (Fine Gael Election Papers, P39/GE/125, UCD Archives).

39 Quoted in Meehan, *A Just Society for Ireland?* p. 54.

40 J.H. Whyte, 'Reconciliation, rights and protests, 1963–8', in Hill, *A New History of Ireland: Vol. 7*, p. 314.

Chapter 6

1 Interview with James Dooge, April 1996.

2 Quoted in Meehan, *A Just Society for Ireland?* p. 66.

3 T.F. O'Higgins, *A Double Life*, p. 191.

4 Interview with James Dooge, April 1996.

5 *Irish Times*, 30 April 1965.

6 Collins, *The Cosgrave Legacy*, p. 88.

7 *Irish Times*, 23 April 1965.

8 Interview with Dick Burke, March 1996.

9 FitzGerald, *All in a Life*, p. 7.

10 O'Higgins, *A Double Life*, p. 206.

11 Böll, *Irish Journal*, p. 114.

12 FitzGerald, *All in a Life*, p. 76–7.

13 Interview with James Dooge, April 1996.

14 Quoted in Meehan, *A Just Society for Ireland?*, p. 67.

15 *Irish Times*, 7 October 1961.

16 Interview with Brendan Halligan, April 1996.

17 Lindsay, *Memories*, p. 190.

18 Interview with John Bruton, April 1996.

19 Collins, *The Cosgrave Legacy*, p. 94.

20 FitzGerald, *All in a Life*, p. 78.

21 Ursula Halligan, unpublished MA thesis, UCD.

22 *Irish Times*, 26 May 1969.

23 FitzGerald, *All in a Life*, p. 92.

24 Interview with Dick Burke, March 1996.

25 Interview with Brendan Halligan, October 2019.

26 Interview with Brendan Halligan, October 2019.

27 Collins, *The Cosgrave Legacy*, p. 103, 109.

28 Ned Murphy, in conversation with Stephen Collins, 1980s.

29 Interview with James Dooge, April 1996.

30 Interview with Brendan Halligan, April 1996.

31 Interview with Dick Burke, March 1996.

32 Interview with Richie Ryan, February 1996.

33 FitzGerald, *All in a Life*, p. 105–6.

34 FitzGerald, *All in a Life*, p. 109.

35 *Irish Times*, 30 November 1972.

36 O'Higgins, *A Double Life*, p. 244, 248.

37 Halligan, thesis.

38 FitzGerald, *All in a Life*, p. 109.

Chapter 7

1 Collins, *The Cosgrave Legacy*, p. 126.

2 *Irish Times*, 8 February 1973.

3 *Irish Times*, 12 February 1973.

4 *Irish Press*, 25 February 1973.

5 *Irish Press*, 21 February 1973.

6   Interview with Brendan Halligan, April 1996.

7   Collins, *The Cosgrave Legacy,* p. 137.

8   Interview with Richie Ryan, February 1996.

9   FitzGerald, *All in a Life,* p. 113.

10   FitzGerald, *All in a Life,* p. 113.

11   Collins, *The Cosgrave Legacy,* p. 139.

12   Collins, *The Cosgrave Legacy,* p. 140.

13   Halligan, thesis.

14   Halligan, thesis.

15   *Irish Times,* 10 April 1973.

16   Halligan, thesis.

17   Collins, *The Cosgrave Legacy,* p. 157.

18   Interview with Richie Ryan, February 1996.

19   Interview with Richie Ryan, February 1996.

20   Interview with Richie Ryan, February 1996.

21   Interview with Richie Ryan, February 1996.

22   FitzGerald, *All in a Life,* p. 309.

23   Interview with Conor Cruise O'Brien, April 1996.

24   FitzGerald, *All in a Life,* p. 309.

25   Interview with Peter Barry.

26   Interview with Conor Cruise-O'Brien, April 1996.

27   Collins, *The Irish Times Nealon's Guide to the 30th Dáil and 23rd Seanad,* p. 169.

28   FitzGerald, *All in a Life,* p. 196.

29   Halligan, thesis.

30   Faulkner, *Memoirs of a Statesman,* p. 21.

31   FitzGerald, *All in a Life,* p. 211.

32   Halligan, thesis.

33   FitzGerald, *All in a Life,* p. 279, 281.

34   Interview with James Dooge, March 1996.

35   *Irish Times,* 19 October 1976.

36   FitzGerald, *All in a Life,* p. 317.

37   Interview with Brendan Halligan, April 1996.

38   Collins, *The Cosgrave Legacy,* p. 191.

39   FitzGerald, *All in a Life,* p. 315.

40   Collins, *The Cosgrave Legacy,* p. 194.

41   Interview with Richie Ryan, February 1996.

42   Interview with James Dooge, March 1996.

43   *Irish Times,* 2 June 1977.

44   Collins, *The Cosgrave Legacy,* p. 199.

45   Interview with Conor Cruise-O'Brien.

46   Collins, *The Cosgrave Legacy,* p. 200.

47   Collins, *The Cosgrave Legacy,* p. 201.

Chapter 8

1   Collins, *The Cosgrave Legacy,* p. 200–204.

2   FitzGerald, *All in a Life,* p. 322.

3   Collins, *The Cosgrave Legacy,* p. 203.

4   FitzGerald, *All in a Life,* p. 25.

5   O'Leary, *Party Animals,* p. 93.

6   FitzGerald, *Towards a New Ireland,* p. 179.

7   *Irish Times,* 28 June 1971.

8   Collins, *The Cosgrave Legacy,* p. 204.

9   Quoted in Meehan, *A Just Society for Ireland?,* p. 177–9.

10   Quoted in Meehan, *A Just Society for Ireland?*, p. 20.

11   John Bruton, 'Young Fine Gaelers' in Barbara Sweetman FitzGerald, *The Widest Circle: Remembering Michael Sweetman* (Dublin, 2011), p. 49.

12   FitzGerald, *All in a Life*, p. 326–7.

13   Interview with Peter Prendergast, 13 December 2019.

14   Interview with Kieran Calnan, 31 March 2020.

15   Interview with Peter Prendergast, 13 December 2019.

16   *Irish Times*, 6 February 1978.

17   Interview with Peter Prendergast, 13 December 2019.

18   *Financial Times*, 22 December 2019.

19   O'Byrnes, *Hiding Behind a Face*, p. 77.

20   Interview with Peter Prendergast, 13 December 2019.

21   FitzGerald, *All in a Life*, p. 339.

22   Dwyer, *Charles Haughey*, p. 34.

23   Collins, *The Power Game*, p. 45–6.

24   FitzGerald, *All in a Life*, p. 342–3.

25   Interview with Peter Prendergast, 13 December 2019.

26   Collins, *The Haughey File*, p. 47.

27   Interview with Peter Prendergast, 13 December 2019.

28   FitzGerald, *All in a Life*, p. 355.

29   O'Byrnes, *Hiding Behind a Face*, p. 67.

30   Interview with Peter Prendergast, 13 December 2019.

31   *Irish Independent*, 25 May 1981.

32   FitzGerald, *All in a Life*, p. 357.

33   Collins, *The Power Game*, p. 138.

34   O'Byrnes, *Hiding Behind a Face*, p. 100.

35   FitzGerald, *All in a Life*, p. 360.

36   *Irish Times*, 29 June 1981.

37   FitzGerald, *All in a Life*, p. 362, 363.

38   O'Byrnes, *Hiding Behind a Face*, p. 110.

39   O'Byrnes, *Hiding Behind a Face*, p. 108.

Chapter 9

1   FitzGerald, *All in a Life*, p. 361.

2   Desmond, *Finally and in Conclusion*, p. 199.

3   O'Byrnes, *Hiding Behind a Face*, p. 114.

4   FitzGerald, *All in a Life*, p. 367.

5   O'Byrnes, *Hiding Behind a Face*, p. 116.

6   Ronan Fanning in Lynch and Mennan, *Essays in Memory of Alexis Fitzgerald*, p. 14.

7   FitzGerald, *All in a Life*, p. 374.

8   FitzGerald, *All in a Life*, p. 376.

9   *Irish Times*, 30 September 1981.

10   FitzGerald, *All in a Life*, p. 378.

11   *Irish Times*, 10 October 1981.

12   FitzGerald, *All in a Life*, p. 380.

13   O'Byrnes, *Hiding Behind a Face*, p. 126.

14   Interview with Peter Prendergast, 13 December 2019.

15   FitzGerald, *All in a Life*, p. 397.

16   O'Byrnes, *Hiding Behind a Face*, p. 134.

17   FitzGerald, *All in a Life*, p. 398.

18   O'Byrnes, *Hiding Behind a Face*, p. 137.

19   *Irish Times*, 5 February 1982.

20   O'Byrnes, *Hiding Behind a Face*, p. 146.

21   FitzGerald, *All in a Life*, p. 407.

22   Walsh, *The Globalist*, p. 53.

23 FitzGerald, *All in a Life*, p. 419.

24 Finlay, *Snakes and Ladders*, p. 2.

25 FitzGerald, *All in a Life*, p. 421.

26 Meehan, *A Just Society for Ireland?* p. 179; FitzGerald, *All in a Life*, p. 434.

27 Finlay, *Snakes and Ladders*, p. 11.

28 FitzGerald, *All in a Life*, p. 425.

29 Collins, *Spring and the Labour Story*, p. 106, 110.

30 Collins, *The Power Game*, p. 147, 149.

31 Collins, *Spring and the Labour Story*, p. 109.

32 Hussey, *At the Cutting Edge*, p. 60.

33 FitzGerald, *All in a Life*, p. 440.

34 FitzGerald, *All in a Life*, p. 444.

35 Collins, *Spring and the Labour Story*, p. 120.

36 Collins, *Spring and the Labour Story*, p. 126.

37 Hussey, *At the Cutting Edge*, p. 114.

38 FitzGerald, *All in a Life*, p. 613.

39 Interview with Peter Prendergast, 13 December 2019; Walsh, *The Globalist*, p. 77.

40 FitzGerald, *All in a Life*, p. 614.

41 FitzGerald, *All in a Life*, p. 462, 575.

42 FitzGerald, *All in a Life*, p. 630.

43 Collins, *Breaking the Mould*, p. 56.

44 Hussey, *At the Cutting Edge*, p. 200–202.

45 FitzGerald, *All in a Life*, p. 639.

46 Hussey, *At the Cutting Edge*, p. 251.

Chapter 10

1 'Fine Gael: A Family at War', episode 1.

2 Hussey, *At the Cutting Edge*, p. 235.

3 *Irish Examiner,* 12 and 16 March 1987.

4 FitzGerald, *All in a Life*, p. 647.

5 Interview with Alan Dukes, June 2009.

6 *Sunday Independent,* 22 March 1987.

7 Hussey, *At the Cutting Edge*, p. 8.

8 *Evening Herald,* 21 March 1987.

9 Interview with Alan Dukes, June 2009.

10 RTÉ news report, 21 March 1987 (RTÉ Archives, https://www.rte.ie/archives/collections/news/21242760-alan-dukes-new-leader-fine-gael/, accessed 21 February 2019).

11 RTÉ news report, 22 March 1987 (RTÉ Archives, https://www.rte.ie/archives/collections/news/21242761-alan-dukes-fine-gael-leader/, accessed 21 February 2019).

12 *Evening Herald,* 21 March 1987.

13 RTÉ news report, 14 March 1987 (RTÉ Archives, https://www.rte.ie/archives/collections/news/21242684-alan-dukes-on-fg-leadership/, accessed 21 February 2019).

14 'Fine Gael: A Family at War', episode 1.

15 Gallagher and Marsh, *Days of Blue Loyalty*, p. 32.

16 Brian Farrell and David M. Farrell, 'The general election of 1987', in Penniman and Farrell, *Ireland at the Polls, 1981, 1982 and 1987*, p. 241.

17 *Dáil Debates,* 31 March 1987.

18 *Irish Times,* 25 June 1987.

19 Peter White, memo to Dukes, in possession of Peter White.

20 Interview with Peter White, February 2020.

21 *Irish Times*, 3 September 1987.

22 'Taoiseach: 1982–1994,' episode 5.

23 Murphy, *Electoral Competition in Ireland Since 1987*, p. 34.

24 Interview with Peter White, February 2020.

25 *Irish Times*, 21 April 1988.

26 *Sunday Tribune*, 20 August 1988.

27 Collins, *Breaking the Mould*, p. 92–3.

28 Nealon, *26th Dáil and Seanad*, p. 156.

29 Collins, *Breaking the Mould*, p. 92–3.

30 *Irish Examiner*, 29 June 1989.

31 'Fine Gael: A Family at War', episode 2.

32 Collins, *Spring and the Labour Story*, p. 172.

33 'Haughey', episode 3.

34 Eoin O'Malley and Matthew Kerby, 'Chronicle of a death foretold? Understanding the Decline of Fine Gael', *Irish Political Studies*, 19, 1 (2004), p. 41.

35 *Dáil Debates*, 31 May 1990.

36 *Sunday Tribune*, 3 June 1990.

37 *Irish Times*, 1 June 1990.

38 *Dáil Debates*, vol. 399, 1 June 1990.

39 O'Reilly, *Candidate*, p. 16.

40 *Irish Press*, 16 January 1990.

41 O'Reilly, *Candidate*, p. 18.

42 Quoted in O'Reilly, *Candidate*, p. 19.

43 'Fine Gael: A Family at War', episode 2.

44 *Sunday Independent*, 27 May 1990; *Irish Press*, 4 August 1990; *Irish Independent*, 10 August 1990.

45 *Kerryman*, 13 July 1990.

46 Currie, *All Hell Will Break Loose*, p. 400.

47 *Irish Press*, 19 September 1990.

48 Currie, *All Hell Will Break Loose*, p. 378.

49 *Belfast Telegraph*, 4 December 1968.

50 Quoted in O'Reilly, *Candidate*, p. 15.

51 'Fine Gael: A Family at War', episode 2.

52 O'Reilly, *Candidate*, p. 27.

53 Currie, *All Hell Will Break Loose*, p. 401.

54 *Irish Independent*, 9 November 1990.

55 'Haughey', episode 3.

56 *Irish Independent*, 9 November 1990.

57 *Sunday Independent*, 11 November 1990.

58 'Fine Gael: A Family at War', episode 2.

59 Currie, *All Hell Will Break Loose*, p. 407.

60 *Evening Herald*, 10 November 1990.

61 O'Leary, *Politicians and Other Animals*, p. 57.

62 Quoted in Ciara Meehan, *A Just Society for Ireland?*, p. 195.

63 O'Leary, *Politicians and Other Animals*, p. 22.

Chapter 11

1 *Irish Times*, 21 November 1990.

2 Hussey, *At the Cutting Edge*, p. 8–9.

3 Interview with Ivan Doherty, 9 April 2020.

4 *Irish Times*, 27 May 1991.

5 *Irish Times*, 27 May 1991.

6 Interview with John Bruton, 18 March 2020.

7 Collins, *Breaking the Mould*, p. 134.

8   *Sunday Press,* 8 March 1992.
9   Collins, *Spring and the Labour Story,* p. 189.
10   Collins, *Spring and the Labour Story,* p. 189–190.
11   Murphy, *Electoral Competition in Ireland Since 1987,* p. 58.
12   Collins, *Spring and the Labour Story,* p. 198.
13   Interview with Ivan Doherty.
14   Collins, *Spring and the Labour Story,* p. 198–9.
15   Collins, *Spring and the Labour Story,* p. 194.
16   Murphy, *Electoral Competition in Ireland Since 1987,* p. 58.
17   Murphy, *Electoral Competition in Ireland Since 1987,* p. 160.
18   Yates, *Full On,* p. 130.
19   Yates, *Full On,* p. 133.
20   Interview with John Bruton, 18 March 2020.
21   Interview with Peter White, 9 February 1993.
22   *Irish Times,* 7 February 1994.
23   *Sunday Press,* 13 February 1994.
24   Interview with Ivan Doherty.
25   Yates, *Full On,* p. 139.
26   *Irish Times,* 16 February 1994.
27   McCormack, *The Rocky Road to the Dáil,* p. 200.
28   *Irish Times,* 5 December 1994.
29   *Sunday Independent,* 26 April 2020.
30   Finlay, *Snakes and Ladders,* p. 270.
31   *Irish Times,* 27 April 1994.
32   Whelan and Masterson, *Bertie Ahern,* p. 139.
33   Interview with Ivan Doherty.
34   *Irish Times,* 10 December 1994.
35   Yates, *Full On,* p. 141.
36   Interview with Ivan Doherty.
37   Interview with Ivan Doherty.
38   Finlay, *Snakes and Ladders,* p. 277.
39   Interview with John Bruton, 18 March 2020.
40   Interview with John Bruton, 18 March 2020.
41   Finlay, *Snakes and Ladders,* p. 278.
42   Paddy Teahon speaking at conference in RIA, 2018.
43   Finlay, *Snakes and Ladders,* p. 279.
44   Interview with John Bruton, 18 March 2020.
45   Interview with John Bruton, 18 March 2020.
46   Brian Girvin, in Marsh and Mitchell, *How Ireland Voted, 1997,* p. 23.
47   Yates, *Full On,* p. 153.
48   Interview with Phil Hogan, December 2019.
49   Murphy, *Electoral Competition in Ireland Since 1987,* p. 74.
50   Finlay, *Snakes and Ladders,* p. 298.
51   *Irish Times,* 2 December 1996.
52   Interview with John Bruton, 18 March 2020.
53   Interview with John Bruton, 18 March 2020.
54   Interview with John Bruton, 18 March 2020.
55   *Irish Echo,* 21 November 2000.
56   Yates, *Full On,* p. 194.
57   *Irish Times,* 1 February 2001.

Chapter 12
1   'Fine Gael: A Family at War', episode 3.
2   *Limerick Leader,* 10 February 2001.
3   *Irish Times,* 20 May 2002.
4   Byrne, *Political Corruption in Ireland,* p. 161.
5   *Irish Independent,* 10 February 2001.

6   *Irish Examiner,* 10 February 2001.

7   *Irish Independent,* 16 February 2001.

8   *Irish Independent,* 16 February 2001; *Irish Examiner,* 16 February 2001.

9   Quoted in Rafter, *Road to Power,* p. 48.

10   *Kerryman,* 16 February 2001.

11   *Irish Times,* 28 February 2001.

12   *Irish Independent,* 5 March 2001.

13   *Irish Independent,* 7 March 2001.

14   *Sunday Independent,* 18 March 2001.

15   *Irish Independent,* 7 March 2001.

16   *Evening Herald,* 6 March 2001.

17   *Irish Independent,* 16 May 2001.

18   'Fine Gael: A Family at War', episode 3.

19   *Irish Examiner,* 2 July 2001.

20   *Irish Times,* 10 February 2001.

21   *Irish Times,* 10 February 2001; *Fortnight,* February 2001.

22   *Irish Examiner,* 6 February 2002.

23   *Irish Times,* 7 February 2002.

24   'Fine Gael: A Family at War', episode 3.

25   Irishhealth.com, 6 February 2002.

26   *Irish Independent,* 6 February 2002.

27   *Irish Times,* 29 January 2002.

28   *Irish Examiner,* 20 February 2002.

29   *Sunday Independent,* 10 March 2002.

30   Gail McElroy and Michael Marsh, 'Why the opinion polls got it wrong in 2002' in Gallagher et al., *How Ireland Voted, 2002,* p. 161.

31   Quinn, *Straight Left,* p. 398.

32   'Fine Gael: A Family at War', episode 3.

33   *Irish Independent,* 25 April 2002.

34   *Irish Times,* 22 January 2002.

35   Ahern, *Bertie Ahern,* p. 257; Quinn, *Straight Left,* p. 397.

36   Stephen Collins, 'Campaign strategies', in Gallagher et al., *How Ireland Voted, 2002,* p. 29.

37   'Fine Gael: A Family at War', episode 3.

38   *Irish Independent,* 1 May 2002.

39   *Limerick Leader,* 29 April 2002.

40   *Irish Examiner,* 1 May 2002.

41   *Irish Independent,* 8 May 2002.

42   Interview with Jim Glennon, 30 March 2020.

43   *Evening Herald,* 18 May 2002.

44   Interview with Jim Glennon, 30 March 2020.

45   *Evening Herald,* 18 May 2002.

46   *Irish Times,* 1 May 2004.

47   *Dáil Debates,* vol. 623, 4 July 2006.

48   *Irish Examiner,* 11 January 2012.

49   *Evening Herald,* 30 June 2012.

50   'Fine Gael leader resigns', RTÉ Archives (https://www.rte.ie/archives/exhibitions/688-elections/701-general-election-2002/139407-fine-gael-leader-resigns/).

51   Fiona Buckley, 'Women and politics in Ireland: The road to sex quotas', *Irish Political Studies,* 28, 3 (2013), p. 346, 347.

52   'Fine Gael leader resigns', RTÉ Archives (https://www.rte.ie/archives/exhibitions/688-elections/701-general-election-2002/139407-fine-gael-leader-resigns/).

53   *Evening Herald,* 1 June 2010.

54   *Irish Examiner,* 14 June 2017.

Chapter 13

1   McCormack, *The Rocky Road to the Dáil*, p. 241–2.
2   John Downing, *Enda Kenny*, p. 232.
3   *Irish Times*, 7 February 2001.
4   Downing, *Enda Kenny*, p. 212.
5   *Sunday Independent*, 7 September 2002.
6   Downing, *Enda Kenny*, p. 236.
7   Downing, *Enda Kenny*, p. 242.
8   Downing, *Enda Kenny*, p. 241.
9   *Sunday Tribune*, 17 November 2002.
10 *21st Century Fine Gael*.
11 *Irish Times*, 19 May 2003.
12 Interview with Phil Hogan, December 2019.
13 Downing, *Enda Kenny*, p. 247.
14 *Irish Times*, 2 April 2004.
15 *Irish Times*, 7 September 2004.
16 *Irish Times*, September 2006.
17 Downing, *Enda Kenny*, p. 259.
18 *Irish Times*, 30 April 2007.
19 Rafter, *Road to Power*, p. 232–3.
20 *Irish Times*, 21 May 2007.
21 *Irish Independent*, 4 June 2009.
22 *Irish Independent*, 15 June 2007.
23 *Irish Examiner*, 21 June 2008.
24 *Irish Times*, 13 February 2009.
25 Downing, *Enda Kenny*, p. 268.
26 *Irish Times*, 19 October 2009.
27 Downing, *Enda Kenny*, p. 273.
28 *Irish Times*, 12 June 2010.
29 McCormack, *The Rocky Road to the Dáil*, p. 300.
30 McCormack, *The Rocky Road to the Dáil*, p. 300.
31 *Irish Independent*, 14 June 2010.
32 McCormack, *The Rocky Road to the Dáil*, p. 280.
33 McCormack, *The Rocky Road to the Dáil*, p. 281.
34 *Irish Independent*, 16 June 2010.
35 *Irish Times*, 16 June 2010.
36 McCormack, *The Rocky Road to the Dáil*, p. 283.
37 McCormack, *The Rocky Road to the Dáil*, p. 285.
38 McCormack, *The Rocky Road to the Dáil*, p. 287.
39 Rafter, *Road to Power*, p. 293–4.
40 *Irish Times*, 17 June 2010.
41 McCormack, *The Rocky Road to the Dáil*, p. 292.
42 *Irish Times*, 18 June 2010.
43 McCormack, *The Rocky Road to the Dáil*, p. 294.
44 *Irish Independent*, 4 October 2010.
45 Nealon, *Ted Nealon's Guide to the 21st Dáil and Seanad*, p. 8.
46 *Irish Times*, 4 February 2011.
47 *Irish Times*, 4 February 2011.
48 Nealon, *Ted Nealon's Guide to the 21st Dáil and Seanad*, p. 11.
49 Downing, *Enda Kenny*, p. 285.
50 Peter Mair, 'The election in context' in *How Ireland Voted*, 2011, p. 287.

Chapter 14

1   *Dáil Debates*, vol. 728, no. 1 (9 March 2011).
2   Gary Murphy, 'The background to the election', in Gallagher and Marsh (eds.), *How Ireland Voted, 2016*, p. 3.
3   *Dáil Debates*, vol. 9, no. 27 (19 December 1924).
4   *Irish Times*, 18 November 2010.
5   Comment to Stephen Collins.
6   Comment to Stephen Collins.
7   *Irish Times*, 14 March 2011.

8   Interview with Feargal Purcell,
     24 April 2020.

9   *Irish Times,* 17 November 2011.

10   Interview with Brendan Halligan,
     March 2020.

11   *Irish Times,* 22 June 2011.

12   Emmanuelle Schön-Quinlivan,
     'The Troika in Ireland', p. 11.

13   Quoted in Schön-Quinlivan,
     'The Troika in Ireland', p. 14.

14   CSO unemployment statistics.

15   See 'Call for Denis Naughten and
     Frank Feighan to resign as
     promised' (https://www.facebook.
     com/pg/Frank.Feighan.is.a.Traitor/
     about).

16   TheJournal.ie, 7 July 2011.

17   TheJournal.ie, 20 March 2012.

18   Dekavalla and Rafter, 'The
     construction of a "historical
     moment"', p. 237.

19   *Magill,* 22 June 2011.

20   TheJournal.ie, 19 May 2011.

21   *Dáil Debates,* vol. 705, 23 March
     2010.

22   *Irish Independent,* 28 May 2010.

23   *Dáil Debates,* vol. 739, no. 3,
     20 July 2011.

24   Colm O'Gorman, tweet, 20 July
     2011 (https://twitter.com/
     Colmogorman/status/
     93754209798848512).

25   *Irish Times,* 23 July 2011.

26   *Sunday Independent,* 10 July 2011.

27   *Irish Times,* 9 July 2011.

28   *Sunday Independent,* 10 July 2011.

29   *Irish Independent,* 31 October
     2011.

30   *Irish Independent,* 23 September
     2011; *Irish Examiner,* 2 October
     2011.

31   *Irish Times,* 24 September 2011.

32   TheJournal.ie, 11 October 2011.

33   *Irish Independent,* 31 October
     2011.

34   See Gerr, *In Defense of Negativity*;
     O'Malley, 'Explaining the 2011
     Irish presidential election', p. 653.

35   O'Malley, 'Explaining the 2011
     Irish presidential election', p. 643.

36   O'Malley, 'Explaining the 2011
     Irish presidential election', p. 653.

37   *Irish Independent,* 31 October
     2011.

38   *Irish Independent,* 29 October
     2011.

39   *Irish Examiner,* 20 January 2012.

40   *Irish Independent,* 9 March 2012.

41   *Irish Examiner,* 8 March 2012.

42   *Irish Independent,* 9 March 2012.

43   *Irish Independent,* 15 February
     2012.

44   *Evening Herald,* 21 February 2012.

45   *Irish Examiner,* 2 April 2012.

46   Paul Anthony, tweet, 31 March
     2012 (https://twitter.com/
     Dub_Snapper/status/
     186087076394049536).

47   *Irish Examiner,* 31 March 2012.

48   Enda Kenny, speech, 19 August
     2012 (https://merrionstreet.ie/
     en/news-room/speeches/speech-
     by-an-taoiseach-to-commemorate-
     the-90th-anniversary-of-the-
     death-of-michael-collins-at-beal-
     na-mblath.html).

49   *Irish Times,* 13 June 2013.

50   Liz Carolan, tweet, 16 November
     2012 (https://twitter.com/
     LizCarolan/status/
     269434431331266560).

51   *Irish Independent,* 15 November 2012; David Quinn, tweet, 17 November 2012 (https://twitter.com/DavQuinn/status/269874060576559106).

52   See the title of Tom Hesketh, *The Second Partitioning of Ireland? The Abortion Referendum of 1983* (Dublin, 1990).

53   The full response can be found here: https://thelifeinstitute.net/youth-defence/election-2011-political-responses (accessed 10 April 2020).

54   Report of the Expert Group on the Judgement in A, B and C v. Ireland (November 2012), p. 44–52.

55   *Irish Independent,* 30 November 2012.

56   *Irish Independent,* 27 and 28 November 2012.

57   RTÉ Archives, 'Divisions within Fine Gael on abortion report' (https://www.rte.ie/news/2012/1129/355774-divisions-within-fg-on-abortion-report).

58   *Irish Independent,* 1 May 2013.

59   *Connacht Sentinel,* 30 April 2013.

60   *Irish Independent,* 2 May 2013.

61   See, for example, *Evening Herald,* 27 November 2012; *Irish Independent,* 3, 9 January, 2 May 2013.

62   *Irish Independent,* 2 May 2013.

63   *Dáil Debates,* vol. 801, no. 3, 1 May 2013.

64   *Dáil Debates,* vol, 125, no. 5, 12 April 1951.

65   *Irish Times,* 11 July 2013.

66   *Irish Times,* 22 June 2015.

67   Office of the Ombudsman, *Opportunity Lost,* p. 5, 9.

68   *Guardian,* 13 December 2013.

69   Pat Leahy, 'Campaign strategies: How the campaign was won and lost', in Gallagher and Marsh (eds.), *How Ireland Voted, 2016,* p. 77.

70   Shatter, *Frenzy and Betrayal,* p. 2.

71   Shatter, *Frenzy and Betrayal,* p. 231.

72   Quoted in Pat Leahy, 'Campaign strategies: How the campaign was won and lost', in Gallagher and Marsh (eds.), *How Ireland Voted, 2016,* p. 76.

73   Healy et al., *Ireland Says Yes,* p. 3.

74   Brian Tobin, writing in the *Irish Times,* 17 November 2015.

75   Interview with Feargal Purcell.

76   See, for example, Healy, *Crossing the Threshold;* Healy et al., *Ireland Says Yes;* Tiernan, *The History of Marriage Equality in Ireland.*

77   *Irish Times,* 18 January 2015.

78   *Irish Times,* 23 May 2015.

79   *Irish Times,* 30 May 2015.

80   Interview with Feargal Purcell.

81   *Irish Times,* 11 July 2014.

82   *Irish Times,* 21 November 2015.

83   *Irish Times,* 8/10 October 2015.

84   Gary Murphy, 'The background to the election', in Gallagher and Marsh (eds.), *How Ireland Voted, 2016,* p. 6.

85   Enda Kenny, tweet, 3 February 2016 (https://twitter.com/EndaKennyTD/status/694822324692844544).

86 Pat Leahy, 'Campaign strategies: How the campaign was won and lost ', in Gallagher and Marsh (eds.), *How Ireland Voted, 2016*, p. 78.

87 *Financial Times*, 25 February 2016.

88 Pat Leahy, 'Campaign strategies: How the campaign was won and lost', in Gallagher and Marsh (eds.), *How Ireland Voted, 2016*, p. 90.

89 *Sunday Independent*, 21 February 2016.

90 TheJournal.ie, 22 February 2016.

Chapter 15

1 Interview with Charlie Flanagan, May 2020.

2 *Sunday Independent*, 4 March 2016.

3 Interview with Charlie Flanagan, May 2020.

4 *Irish Independent*, 18 March.

5 *Irish Times*, 8 April 2016.

6 *Irish Times*, 9 April 2016.

7 Reilly, *Enda the Road*, p. 16–17.

8 Reilly, *Enda the Road*, p. 24.

9 *Irish Times*, 9 August 2015.

10 *Irish Times*, 3 June 2017.

11 *Irish Independent*, 2 September 2018.

12 *Dáil Debates*, vol. 938 (14 February 2017).

13 *Irish Times*, 14 February 2017.

14 *Sunday Independent*, 19 February 2017.

15 *Irish Times*, 20 February 2017.

16 RTÉ Archives, 'What attracted Leo Varadkar to Fine Gael?' (https://www.rte.ie/archives/2017/0530/879015-leo-varadkar-and-young-fine-gael/).

17 *Irish Examiner*, 14 June 2004; *Irish Independent*, 15 June 2004.

18 Quoted in Ryan and O'Connor, *Leo Varadkar*, p. 22.

19 *Irish Independent*, 26 May 2007.

20 Exchange with Paul O'Brien, 15 May 2020.

21 Transcript of interview, *Irish Independent*, 18 January 2015.

22 *Irish Independent*, 1 October 2007.

23 *Irish Independent*, 15 December 2007.

24 *Sunday Business Post*, 28 May 2017.

25 Ryan and O'Connor, *Leo Varadkar*, p. 1.

26 Ryan and O'Connor, *Leo Varadkar*, p. 23.

27 *Time*, 13 July 2017.

28 *Dáil Debates*, vol. 953, no. 4 (14 January 2017).

29 Email exchange with Patrick Geoghegan, 4 May 2020.

30 Ryan and O'Connor, *Leo Varadkar*, p. 279.

31 *Fortune*, 17 August 2017.

32 Leo Varadkar, speech, 25 August 2018 (https://www.gov.ie/en/speech/d9f784-speech-of-an-taoiseach-leo-varadkar-on-the-occasion-of-the-visit-of-/).

33 *Washington Post*, 3 September 2019.

34 *Washington Post*, 14 March 2019.

35 *Dáil Debates*, vol. 953, no. 4 (14 January 2017).

36 Connelly, *Brexit and Ireland*, p. 334.

37 O'Toole, *Heroic Failure*, postscript.

38 Email exchange with Patrick Geoghegan, 4 May 2020.

39 *Guardian*, 10 October 2019.

40 *Irish Times*, 27 January 2020.

41   *Irish Times,* 8 May 2020.

42   *Times,* 11 May 2020.

43   *Dáil Debates,* vol. 962, no. 2 (23 November 2017).

44   *Irish Examiner,* 27 November 2017.

45   Frances Fitzgerald, tweet, 27 November 2017 (https://twitter.com/FitzgeraldFrncs/status/935264271897948160).

46   *Irish Examiner,* 28 November 2017.

47   *Irish Examiner,* 15 October 2018.

48   Ryan and O'Connor, *Leo Varadkar,* p. 20.

49   *Irish Examiner,* 15 October 2018.

50   Email exchange with Patrick Geoghegan, 4 May 2020.

51   *Irish Times,* 25 May 2015.

52   *Dáil Debates,* vol. 963, no. 6 (17 January 2018).

53   *Irish Independent,* 26 September 2015.

54   Email exchange with Josepha Madigan, 11 May 2020.

55   Email exchange with Patrick Geoghegan, 4 May 2020.

56   Email exchange with Josepha Madigan, 11 May 2020.

57   Fingal Battalion Direct Action Group, Facebook post, 10 February 2019 (https://www.facebook.com/FINGALBATTALIONphotos/a.1252007958286538/13443959957 14400/).

58   *Dáil Debates,* vol. 972, no. 4 (25 September 2018).

59   *Irish Times,* 20 May 2019.

60   Eoghan Murphy, tweet (https://twitter.com/MurphyEoghan/status/1130862331355979781).

61   *Irish Times,* 9 February 2020.

62   *Irish Examiner,* 12 October 2011; *Irish Times,* 21 June

2016; Neale Richmond, tweet, 28 December 2018 (https://twitter.com/nealerichmond/status/1078764570578219009).

63   TheJournal.ie, 24 March 2019.

64   Email exchange with Patrick Geoghegan, 4 May 2020.

65   Email exchange with Patrick Geoghegan, 4 May 2020.

66   'Applause at FG national conference for Jeffrey Donaldson suggesting that Ireland rejoins the Commonwealth', Reddit, 23 March 2019 (https://www.reddit.com/r/ireland/comments/b4p3p4/applause_at_fg_national_conference_for_jeffrey/ej88wgc, accessed 4 May 2020).

67   Email exchange with Patrick Geoghegan, 4 May 2020.

68   RTÉ News, 12 February 2020.

69   McBride, *Burned,* p. 257.

70   Coakley and Todd, *Negotiating a Settlement in Northern Ireland,* p. 554.

71   Simon Coveney, tweet, 10 January 2020 (https://twitter.com/simoncoveney/status/1215700778062700544).

Chapter 16

1   *Irish Times,* 11 September 2019.

2   *Atlantic,* 31 October 2019.

3   Interview with Leo Varadkar, 9 July 2020.

4   Interview with Leo Varadkar, 9 July 2020.

5   *Irish Times,* 9 October 2019.

6   *Irish Times,* 9 October 2019.

7   Interview with Leo Varadkar, 9 July 2020.

8   Interview with Leo Varadkar, 9 July 2020.

9   *Atlantic,* 31 October 2019.

10   *Irish Times,* 31 October 2019.

11   'The RIC Commemoration Controversy', *History Now,* 25 February 2020.

12   *Irish Independent,* 7 January 2020.

13   *Irish Times,* 13 February 2020.

14   Interview with Paschal Donohoe, 3 July 2020.

15   *Irish Times,* 21 January 2020.

16   *Irish Times,* 8 February 2020.

17   *Irish Times,* 3 February 2020.

18   Interview Paschal Donohoe, 3 July 2020.

19   For further information about Fine Gael's social media strategy see Sean Farrell, Ciara Meehan, Gary Murphy and Kevin Rafter, 'Assessing the Irish general election of 2011: A Roundtable', *New Hibernia Review,* 15, 3 (2011), p. 44–49.

20   Kirsty Park and Jane Suiter, 'Media and the election' in *How Ireland Voted, 2020* (Basingstoke, forthcoming).

21   Interview with Leo Varadkar, 9 July 2020

22   Michael Marsh, 'Has there really been a swing to the left and what is the left?' (https://www.rte.ie/news/election-2020/2020/0210/1114416-election-analysis/).

23   Interview with Leo Varadkar, 9 July 2020.

24   Interview with Leo Varadkar, 9 July 2020.

25   *Irish Times,* 4 March 2020.

26   Fiona Buckley and Yvonne Gallagher, 'The 2020 general election: A gender analysis', *Irish Political Studies* (2020), p. 6.

27   *Irish Examiner,* 28 January 2020.

28   *New York Times,* 9 February 2020; *Economist,* 5 March 2020.

29   *Waterford Whispers News,* 11 February 2020.

30   *Irish Examiner,* 24 February 2020.

31   *Dáil Debates,* vol. 992, no. 1 (20 February 2020).

32   Interview with Leo Varadkar, 9 July 2020.

33   Interview with Paschal Donohoe, 3 July 2020.

34   *Irish Examiner,* 22 July 2017.

35   *Irish Examiner,* 31 July 2017.

36   *Irish Times,* 23 January 2020.

37   *Irish Examiner,* 3 June 2017.

38   *Herald,* 11 March 2020.

39   Interview with Leo Varadkar, 9 July 2020.

40   Email exchange with Patrick Geoghegan, 4 May 2020.

41   Department of the Taoiseach web site, 17 March 2020.

42   Interview with Leo Varadkar, 9 July 2020.

43   Cody Keenan tweet, 17 March 2020 (https://twitter.com/codykeenan/status/1240028242846900224).

44   TheJournal.ie, 19 June 2020.

45   Interview with Paschal Donohoe, 3 July 2020.

46   Interview with Leo Varadkar, 9 July 2020.

47   *Irish Examiner,* 25 March 2020.

48   Interview with Paschal Donohoe, 3 July 2020.

49   Interview with Leo Varadkar, 9 July 2020.

50   Interview with Leo Varadkar, 9 July 2020.

51   Interview with Paschal Donohoe, 3 July 2020.

52   Simon Harris tweet, 7 April 2020 (https://twitter.com/SimonHarrisTD/status/1247422521701523456); Leo Varadkar tweet, 20 March 2020 (https://twitter.com/LeoVaradkar/status/1240991235625582598); Olivia Duff tweet, 21 March 2020 (https://twitter.com/olivia_duff/status/1241309678342221828).

53   Eddie Hoare tweet, 27 April 2020 (https://twitter.com/EddieHoareFG/status/1254891713832857605).

54   Exchange with Eddie Hoare, 16 May 2020.

55   *Guardian*, 14 May 2020.

56   *Irish Times*, 6 and 7 April 2020.

57   'Two months: How covid-19 hit Ireland's nursing homes', RTÉ, 31 May 2020 (https://www.rte.ie/news/primetime/2020/0528/1143221-how-covid-19-hit-irelands-nursing-homes/).

58   TheJournal.ie, 23 April 2020.

59   RTÉ 9 o'clock news, 3 May 2020.

60   'The Late Late Show', 1 May 2020.

61   Green Party response to the Fianna Fáil and Fine Gael Joint Framework Document, 23 April 2020 (https://www.greenparty.ie/green-party-response-to-the-fianna-fail-and-fine-gael-joint-framework-document/).

62   Lucid Talk opinion poll, 23 April 2020.

63   *Irish Times*, 16 June 2020.

64   Geraldine Gregan tweet, 20 May 2020 (https://twitter.com/GreganGeraldine/status/1263190714093047810).

65   *Dáil Debates*, 11 June 2020 (https://www.lucidtalk.co.uk/single-post/2020/04/23/COVID-19-Emergency - NI-Views.)

66   *Irish Independent*, 12 June 2020.

67   Claire McGing tweet, 26 June 2020 (https://twitter.com/Claire_McGing/status/1276581111938846722).

68   *Dáil Debates*, vol. 994, no. 3 (27 June 2020).

69   Simon Harris tweet, 27 June 2020 (https://twitter.com/SimonHarrisTD/status/1276942680879218688).

70   Interview with Leo Varadkar, 9 July 2020.

71   Interview with Paschal Donohoe, 3 July 2020.

72   *Irish Times*, 28 June 2020.

73   Interview with Paschal Donohoe, 3 July 2020.

74   Interview with Leo Varadkar, 9 July 2020.

75   Interview with Leo Varadkar, 9 July 2020.

BIBLIOGRAPHY

Ahern, Bertie, with Richard Aldous, *Bertie Ahern: The Autobiography* (London, 2009).

Barry, Frank, 'Foreign Investment and the Politics of Export Profits Tax Relief in 1956' (unpublished seminar paper).

Böll, Heinrich, *Irish Journal* (New York, 1971).

Browne, Noël, *Against the Tide* (Dublin, 1987 edn).

Buckley, Fiona and Gallagher, Yvonne, 'The 2020 general election: A gender analysis', *Irish Political Studies* (2020).

Byrne, Elaine A., *Political Corruption in Ireland, 1922–2010: A Crooked Harp?* (Manchester, 2012).

Chambers, Anne, *T.K. Whitaker: Portrait of a Patriot* (London, 2014).

Coakley, John, and Todd, Jennifer, *Negotiating a Settlement in Northern Ireland, 1969–2019* (Oxford, 2020).

Collins, Stephen, *Breaking the Mould: How the PDs Changed Irish Politics* (Dublin, 2005).

Collins, Stephen, *The Cosgrave Legacy* (Dublin, 1996).

Collins, Stephen, *The Haughey File: The Unprecedented Career and Last Years of the Boss* (Dublin, 1992).

Collins, Stephen, *The Irish Times Nealon's Guide to the 30th Dáil and 23rd Seanad* (Dublin, 2007).

Collins, Stephen, *The Power Game: Fianna Fáil since Lemass* (Dublin, 2000).

Collins, Stephen, *Spring and the Labour Story* (Dublin, 1993).

Connelly, Tony, *Brexit and Ireland: The Dangers, the Opportunities, and the Inside Story of the Irish Response* (London, 2018 edn).

Conroy, Pauline, 'From the fifties to the nineties: Social policy comes out of the shadows', *Irish Social Policy in Context* (Dublin, 1999).

Cronin, Mike, 'The Blueshirt movement, 1932–35: Ireland's fascists?' *Journal of Contemporary History*, 30, 2 (1995).

Cronin, Mike, *The Blueshirts and Irish Politics* (Dublin, 1997).

Cronin, Mike, 'Blueshirts, sports and socials', *History Ireland*, 3, 2 (autumn, 1994).

Cronin, Mike, 'The socio-economic background and membership of the Blueshirt movement, 1932–5', *Irish Historical Studies*, 29, 11 (1994).

Cronin, Mike, Duncan, Mark, and Rouse, Paul, *The GAA: County by County* (Cork, 2011).

Curran, Joseph M., *The Birth of the Irish Free State, 1921–1923* (Alabama, 1980).

Currie, Austin, *All Hell Will Break Loose* (Dublin, 2004).

Daly, Mary E., *Sixties Ireland: Reshaping the Economy, State and Society, 1957–1973* (Cambridge, 2016).

Dekavalla, Marina, and Rafter, Kevin, 'The construction of a "historical moment": Queen Elizabeth's 2011 visit to Ireland in British and Irish newspapers', *Journalism*, 17, 2 (2016).

Desmond, Barry, *Finally and in Conclusion: A Political Memoir* (Dublin, 2000).

Dolan, Anne, *Commemorating the Irish Civil War: History and Memory, 1923–2000* (Cambridge, 2006).

Dolan, Anne, and Murphy, William, *Michael Collins: The Man and the Revolution* (Cork, 2018).

Downing, John, *Enda Kenny: The Unlikely Taoiseach* (Dublin, 2012).

Dwyer, T. Ryle, *Charlie: The Political Biography of Charles J. Haughey* (Dublin, 1987)

Evans, Bryce, *Seán Lemass: Democratic Dictator* (Cork, 2011).

Fanning, Ronan, *The Irish Department of Finance, 1922–58* (Dublin, 1978).

Farrell, Brian, *Chairman or Chief? The role of Taoiseach in Irish Government* (Dublin, 1971).

Farrell, Mel, *Party Politics in a New Democracy: The Irish Free State, 1922–37* (Basingstoke, 2017).

Farrell, Mel, Knirck, Jason, and Meehan, Ciara (eds.), *A Formative Decade: Ireland in the 1920s* (Newbridge, 2015).

Farrell, Sean, Meehan, Ciara, Murphy, Gary and Rafter, Kevin, 'Assessing the Irish general election of 2011: A Roundtable', *New Hibernia Review*, 15, 3 (2011).

Faulkner, Brian, *Memoirs of a Statesman* (London, 1978).

Finlay, Fergus, *Snakes and Ladders* (Dublin, 1998).

Ferriter, Diarmaid, *The Transformation of Ireland, 1900–2000* (London, 2005).

Fine Gael, *21st Century Fine Gael: Report of the Strategy Review Group* (Dublin 2002).

FitzGerald, Garret, *All in a Life: An Autobiography* (Dublin, 1992 edn).

FitzGerald, Garret, *Towards a New Ireland* (London 1972).

Gallagher, Michael, *Political Parties in the Republic of Ireland* (Dublin, 1985).

Gallagher, Michael, and Marsh, Michael (eds.), *How Ireland Voted, 2011: The Full Story of Ireland's Earthquake Election* (London, 2011).

Gallagher, Michael, and Marsh, Michael (eds.), *How Ireland Voted, 2016: The Election that Nobody Won* (Basingstoke, 2017).

Gallagher, Michael, Marsh, Michael, and Mitchell, Paul (eds.), *How Ireland Voted, 2002* (Basingstoke, 2003).

Garvin, Tom, *Preventing the Future: Why Was Ireland Poor for So Long?* (Dublin, 2004).

Gerr, John G., *In Defense of Negativity: Attack Ads in Presidential Campaigns* (Chicago, 2006).

Girvin, Brian, and Murphy, Gary (eds.), *The Lemass Era: Politics and Society in the Ireland of Seán Lemass* (Dublin, 2005).

Halligan, Brendan (ed.), *The Brendan Corish Seminar Proceedings* (Dublin, 2006).

Halligan, Ursula, unpublished MA thesis, UCD.

Healy, Gráinne (ed.), *Crossing the Threshold: The Story of the Marriage Equality Movement* (Newbridge, 2017).

Healy, Gráinne, Sheehan, Brian, and Whelan, Noel, *Ireland Says Yes: The Inside Story of How the Vote for Marriage Equality Was Won* (Newbridge, 2016).

Hill, J.R. (ed.), *A New History of Ireland: Vol. 7: Ireland, 1921–84* (Oxford, 2003).

Jackson, Alvin, *Home Rule: An Irish History, 1800–2000* (London, 2004 edn).

Hussey, Gemma, *At the Cutting Edge: Cabinet Diaries, 1982–1987* (Dublin, 1990).

Kelly, Stephen, 'A policy of futility: Eamon de Valera's anti-partition campaign, 1948–1951', *Études Irlandaises*, 36, 2 (2011).

Kennedy, Michael, *Division and Consensus: The Politics of Cross-Border Relations in Ireland, 1925–1969* (Dublin, 2000).

Kenny, Colum, *The Enigma of Arthur Griffith: 'Father of us All'* (Dublin, 2020).

Laffan, Michael, *Judging W.T. Cosgrave: The Foundation of the Irish State* (Dublin, 2014).

Lee, J.J., Ireland, *1912–1985: Politics and Society* (Cambridge, 1989).

Lindsay, Patrick J., *Memories* (Dublin, 1992).

Lynch, Patrick, and Mennan, James (eds.), *Essays in Memory of Alexis Fitzgerald* (Dublin, 1987).

Macardle, Dorothy, *The Irish Republic* (Dublin, 1951).

McBride, Sam, *Burned: The Inside Story of the 'Cash-for-Ash' Scandal and Northern Ireland's Secretive New Elite* (Dublin, 2019).

McCarthy, John, *Planning Ireland's Future: The Legacy of T.K. Whitaker* (Dublin, 1990).

McCormack, Pádraic, *The Rocky Road to the Dáil: Politics from the Inside* (2013).

McCullagh David, *A Makeshift Majority: The First Inter-Party Government, 1948–51* (Dublin, 1998).

McCullagh, David, *The Reluctant Taoiseach: A Biography of John A. Costello* (Dublin, 2010).

MacDermot, Eithne, *Clann na Poblachta* (Cork, 1998).

McGarry, Fearghal, *Eoin O'Duffy: A Self-Made Hero* (Oxford, 2005).

McKee, Eamonn, 'Church-state relations and the development of Irish health policy: The Mother-and-Child Scheme, 1944–53', *Irish Historical Studies*, vol. 25, no. 98 (November 1986).

Manning, Maurice, *The Blueshirts* (Dublin, 2006 edn).

Manning, Maurice, *James Dillon: A Biography* (Dublin, 1999).

Mansergh, Martin, *The Unresolved Question: The Anglo-Irish Settlement and Its Undoing, 1912–72* (London, 1991).

Marsh, Michael, and Gallagher, Michael, *Days of Blue Loyalty: The Politics of Membership of the Fine Gael Party* (Dublin, 2002).

Marsh, Michael, and Mitchell, Paul (eds.), *How Ireland Voted, 1997* (Boulder, Colorado, 1999).

Maye, Brian, *Fine Gael, 1923–1987: A General History with Biographical Sketches of Leading Members* (Dublin, 1993).

Meehan, Ciara, *The Cosgrave Party: A History of Cumann na nGaedheal, 1923–1933* (Dublin, 2010).

Meehan, Ciara, *A Just Society for Ireland? 1964–1987* (Basingstoke, 2013).

Murphy, Gary, *Electoral Competition in Ireland Since 1987: The Politics of Triumph and Despair* (Manchester, 2016).

Nealon, Ted, *26th Dáil and Seanad: Nealon's Guide, 26th Dáil and Seanad Election, '89* (Dublin, 1989).

Nealon, Ted, *Ted Nealon's Guide to the 21st Dáil and* Seanad (Dublin, 1977).

O'Byrnes, Stephen, *Hiding Behind a Face: Fine Gael under FitzGerald* (Dublin, 1986).

O'Casey, Sean, *Autobiographies* (London, 1939–56).

Ó Corráin, Donnchadh (ed.), *James Hogan: Revolutionary, Historian and Political Scientist* (Dublin, 2000).

Office of the Ombudsman, *Opportunity Lost: An Investigation by the Ombudsman into the Administration of the Magdalen Restorative Justice Scheme* (Dublin, 2017).

O'Higgins, T.F., *A Double Life* (Dublin, 1996).

O'Leary, Olivia, *Party Animals* (Dublin, 2006).

O'Leary, Olivia, *Politicians and Other Animals* (Dublin, 2004).

O'Malley, Eoin, 'Explaining the 2011 Irish presidential election: Culture, valence, loyalty or punishment?' *Irish Political Studies*, 27, 4 (2012).

O'Malley, Eoin, and Kerby, Matthew, 'Chronicle of a death foretold? Understanding the decline of Fine Gael', *Irish Political Studies*, 19, 1 (2004).

O'Reilly, Emily, *Candidate: The Truth Behind the Presidential Campaign* (Dublin, 1991).

O'Sullivan, Donal, *The Irish Free State and Its Senate: A Study in Contemporary Politics* (London, 1940).

O'Toole, Fintan, *Heroic Failure: Brexit and the Politics of Pain* (London, 2019).

Park, Kirsty and Suiter, Jane, 'Media and the election' in *How Ireland Voted, 2020* (Basingstoke, forthcoming).

Penniman, Howard R., and Farrell, Brian (eds.), *Ireland at the Polls, 1981, 1982, and 1987: A Study of Four General Elections* (Durham, North Carolina, 1987).

Quinn, Ruairí, *Straight Left: A Journey in Politics* (Dublin, 2005).

Rafter, Kevin, *The Clann: The Story of Clann na Poblachta* (Dublin, 1996).

Rafter, Kevin, *Road to Power: How Fine Gael Made History* (Dublin, 2011).

Reilly, Gavan, *Enda the Road: Nine Days that Toppled a Taoiseach* (Dublin, 2019).

Ryan, Desmond, *Unique Dictator: A Study of Eamon de Valera* (London, 1936).

Ryan, Philip, and O'Connor, Niall, *Leo Varadkar: A Very Modern Taoiseach* (London, 2018).

Schön-Quinlivan, Emmanuelle, 'The Troika in Ireland: An Institutional Analysis of Financial Regulatory Change', unpublished conference paper (2013). (https://www.academia.edu/13070670/The_Troika_in_Ireland_an_institutional_analysis_of_financial_regulatory_change), accessed 7 April 2020.

Shatter, Alan, *Frenzy and Betrayal: The Anatomy of a Political Assassination* (Dublin, 2019).

Tiernan, Sonja, *The History of Marriage Equality in Ireland: A Social Revolution Begins* (Manchester, 2020).

Valiulis, Maryann, *Portrait of a Revolutionary: General Richard Mulcahy and the Founding of the Irish Free State* (Dublin, 1992).

Walsh, John, *The Globalist: Peter Sutherland: His Life and Legacy* (London, 2020).

Whelan, Ken, and Masterson, Eugene, *Bertie Ahern: Taoiseach and Peacemaker* (Dublin, 1998).

White, Terence de Vere, *Kevin O'Higgins* (Dublin, 1986 edn).

Yates, Ivan, *Full On: A Memoir* (Dublin, 2018).

INDEX

McQuaid, Archbishop John Charles, 63
McQuillan, Jack, 87
McTague, Tom, 390
Meade, Sarah, 372–3
Mean Girls, 405
Mellows, Liam, 9–10
Menlo Park Hotel, 302
Merkel, Angela, 332–3, 334, 376, 390
milk, 66, 201
Mills, Michael, 100
Mitchell, Gay, 225, 246, 258, 281, 297,
 302, 306, 340–2, 384
Mitchell, George, 311
Mitchell, Jim, 175, 192, 207, 210, 221,
 228, 239, 240, 243, 244, 246, 247, 250,
 260, 262, 277, 278–9, 281, 288–9, 332,
 400
Mitchell, Olivia, 282, 293, 323
mobile phone licences, 283
Molloy, Bobby, 230, 238
Molloy, Shane, 177
Molony, David, 301
Monaghan, Philip, 13
Moncrieff, Seán, 285
Moore, Phil, 172
Moore Hall, 11
Moran, Micheál, 123–4
Morgan, Dermot, 279
Moriarty Tribunal, 283, 344
Morning Post, 18
Morrison, Danny, 197
Morrissey, Daniel, 50, 83
Mortell, Mark, 324–8
Mother and Child controversy, 47, 49,
 62–3, 64, 65–6
Mulcahy, Richard
 army mutiny (1925), 16, 17
 Commonwealth, 57
 death of Michael Collins, 4
 Emergency Powers Act, 7
 execution of prisoners (1922), 9–10,
 48

Minister for Education, 50, 73
 political reputation, 3
 president of Fine Gael, 47, 95
 unemployment, 13
Mulholland, Joe, 264
Mullally, Una, 383, 409
Mullen, Rónán, 346
Mullingar Accord, 308
Mullins, Michael, 348
Mungovan, Clare, 373
Murphy, Brian, 365, 373
Murphy, Dara, 393
Murphy, Eoghan, 337, 365, 366, 373,
 382–4, 393, 394, 415
Murphy, Gary, 233, 254, 257
Murphy, Ned, 123
Murphy, T.J., 51
Murphy, Verona, 394
Murphy, William, 3
Murray, Sean, 177
Mussolini, Benito, 31, 32, 38, 40

Nally, Dermot, 195
National Asset Management Agency, 314
National Centre Party, x, 28, 29–30, 37,
 94
National Children's Hospital, 382
National Coalition, 136, 138–9
National Farmers' and Ratepayers'
 Association, 29
National Guard, 31–3
National Labour, 46, 51
National League, 20, 37, 93
National Public Health Emergency Team,
 404
National Women's Council of Ireland,
 409–10
NATO, 61
Naughten, Denis, 302, 318, 319, 323, 336,
 337, 360, 362, 363
Naughten, Gerry, 305
Naughton, Hildegarde, 415

O'Connell, Daniel, 40
O'Connell, Hugh, 92
O'Connell, John, 192
O'Connell, Kate, 400
O'Connell, Maurice, 120–1
O'Connell, T.J., 20
O'Connell Street, 2
O'Connor, Fiona, 412–13
O'Connor, Mary Mitchell, 363, 373, 400
O'Connor, Niall, 366, 370
O'Connor, Niamh, 245
O'Connor, Rory, 9–10, 24
O'Dea, Willie, 283, 293
O'Donnell, Annette, 368
O'Donnell, Kieran, 307, 320
O'Donnell, Pa, 74
O'Donnell, Tom, 141, 181, 217, 242, 380
O'Donoghue, John, 274, 315
O'Donoghue, Martin, 205, 211
O'Donovan, John, 72, 84
O'Dowd, Fergus, 318, 323
O'Duffy, Eoin
  background, 27
  banning of National Guard parade, 32
  control of army, 17
  extremism, 42–3
  fascism, x, 34, 39, 41, 43
  leadership of Blueshirts, 28
  local elections (1934), 42
  Michael Collins, 35
  political development, 34–6
  president of Fine Gael, 36, 43, 47
  relations with W.T. Cosgrave, 25–6
  reputation within Fine Gael, 44, 45
O'Farrell, Joan (wife of Garret Fitzgerald),
  170, 172
Offences Against the State Act (1972),
  130–2, 133–4, 136, 140, 150–1, 157
O'Gorman, Colm, 340
O'Hanlon, Fergal, 87
O'Herlihy, Bill, 177
O'Higgins, Brigid Hogan, 173–4

O'Higgins, Dr T.F., 11
O'Higgins, Kevin, ix, 4–5, 10, 14, 16, 17,
  19, 27, 35–6, 62, 75
O'Higgins, Michael, 118, 124, 148
O'Higgins, T.F., 50, 63
O'Higgins, Tom
  Arms Crisis, 124
  deputy leader, 113
  general election (1969), 122
  on James Dillon, 92
  Just Society, 103
  leadership rival to Garret FitzGerald,
    128
  Minister for Health, 68, 73, 75–7, 82
  Offences Against the State Act (1972),
    132, 133
  presidential election (1973), 141, 144
  relations with Cearbhall Ó Dálaigh,
    158
  relations with Liam Cosgrave, 130
  stands for presidency (1966), 114–15
O'Higgins Commission, 377, 378
oil crisis (1973), 144, 145, 146
Oireachtas Committee on Marital
  Breakdown, 217–18
O'Keeffe, Jim, 91, 108, 175, 228, 246,
  260–1, 262
O'Keeffe, Ned, 251
O'Kelly, Fionnuala, 298
O'Kelly, President, 88
O'Kennedy, Michael, 165, 204, 215
O'Leary, Michael, 141, 191, 193, 200, 207,
  218
O'Leary, Olivia, 170, 247
O'Leary, Sean, 188
O'Mahony, John, 348
O'Malley, Des, 130, 205, 217, 230, 238,
  252
O'Neill, Michelle, 411
Opportunity Lost, 350
O'Quigley, Ben, 113
O'Reilly, Eddie, 240–1